# LAMENT

# FOR AN AFRICAN POL

# Lament for an African Pol

*Mongo Beti*

Translated by Richard Bjornson

**3CP**     An Original by Three Continents

©Richard Bjornson 1985

First English Language Edition

Three Continents Press
1346 Connecticut Avenue N.W.
Washington, D.C. 20036

ISBN: 0-89410-304-0
ISBN: 0-89410-305-9 (pbk)
LC No: 84-51443

Original French Language Edition
©Editions des Peuples Noirs, 1979
as *La Ruine Presque Cocasse d'un Polichinelle*
by Mongo Beti (Alexandre Biyidi)

Cover art by Tom Gladden: ©Three Continents Press 1985

# CONTENTS

# CONTENTS

## INTRODUCTION

Mongo Beti's <u>Lament for an African Pol</u> is an important revolutionary statement by one of Africa's great masters of prose fiction. It is a remarkably gripping story that blends comic irony with an epic depiction of recent African history. It also adds new dimensions to the fictional space that Beti has been clearing for himself since he began writing nearly thirty-five years ago. Like William Faulkner or Gabriel García Márquez, he has succeeded in creating an imaginary universe that links all his novels together and lends a sense of unity to his entire work. Drawing upon reminiscences of the world he knew as a child and young man, he fashions them into a self-contained environment that operates according to principles defined by his own ideological engagement. In Beti's case, the primary motivation behind the creation of this imaginary universe has been a persistent desire to reveal the falsity of myths and stereotypes that deny the full humanity of black Africans while sanctioning relations of dominance that allow them to be exploited for the benefit of others.

The consistency of Beti's imaginary universe has often been overlooked, because his career as a writer is clearly divided into two periods of literary productivity, the second of which is characterized by a more markedly political stance. By 1958, he had already published the four novels that would make his reputation, but at that point he abruptly ceased writing. During the next fourteen years, his early novels gradually achieved an almost classic status, being taught in school and university classrooms throughout the continent as well as in Europe and America. Written before the independence of his native Cameroon, they were satirical attacks upon colonialism and its impact in Africa; their tone and content corresponded admirably with a widespread rejection of the entire colonialist enterprise. Yet as Beti's silence persisted, a new set of abuses were emerging in independent Africa, and very few writers were discussing them. It was safe for African writers to castigate their former colonial masters; it was less safe for them to attack corruption, hypocrisy, and injustice in the present. According to Beti, however, the contemporary situation was of utmost concern, and when he began publishing again in 1972, his first book, Pillage of Cameroon, was not a novel but an explosive polemic against the dictatorial government in his own country.

During the next ten years, Beti brought out four new novels, the third of which was Lament for an African Pol. Like his other works from the later period, this story of three revolutionaries and their contribution to the overthrow of an illegitimate regime in the remote forest community of Ekoumdoum differs from his earlier work insofar as it incorporates identifiable historical events into the narrative; in addition, it focuses less on the crises of young men coping with the perversities of colonialism than on the crystallization of a mature opposition to petty African dictators and their foreign supporters. Because Beti views the contemporary situation as a logical outgrowth of colonialism, it is not surprising that the fictional landscape in his later novels is contiguous with the imaginary universe he created in his earlier ones.

During both periods, he wanted to raise the general level of consciousness about Africa by refuting the false stereotypes that demeaned Africans and contributed to their subjugation. As early as 1950 when he first arrived in France, Beti was appalled by the tendency of journalists, anthropologists, and even Africans themselves to accept the idea that black men are primitive, childlike, and exotic, for such an idea implies that they are

viii

destined by their very nature to remain subordinate to the supposedly more civilized Europeans. Convinced that Senghor and other Negritude writers who emphasized the emotive dimensions of black experience were helping to perpetuate the false consciousness behind this image of Africans, he felt the need for a new kind of literature that would analyze the only "truly profound reality" in pre-independence Africa—"colonialism and its crimes." He attacked Camera Laye's highly regarded Black Child (1953), because he thought its preoccupation with traditional native harmonies reinforced European stereotypes and distracted Africans from recognizing the truth about their own enslavement. Although he realized at the time that the primary audience for books by francophone African writers was comprised of middle-class Frenchmen, he believed the novel could serve as a corrective to their false impressions, while contributing to the psychological liberation of the relatively few Africans capable of reading fiction critically.

When he set out to write his own novels, he invariably focused upon individual Africans to demonstrate the debilitating effects of the colonialist presence on their lives. The superb irony with which he depicts the impossible choice between an assimilation of Western values and a resurrection of traditional ones undoubtedly owes something to Voltaire's Candide and Montesquieu's Persian Letters, read while he was still a schoolboy in Cameroon, but it reflects even more the spirit of mockery so often adopted by Africans when commenting in their own languages about the foibles and follies of men. In Beti's hands, this irony both undercuts European claims to racial or cultural superiority and reveals the impracticability of returning to the past. For example, in Mission to Kala (1957), the protagonist is a young schoolboy who has just failed his examination for the French baccalauréat. Entrusted with the task of travelling to his father's village and bringing his uncle's errant wife back to the city, he discovers that neither his superficial mastery of French culture nor the adulterated customs of the village can offer him a viable basis for defining his own identity. He does return to the city and liberate himself from the dominance of a corrupt, Westernized father, and he does renounce the possibility of marriage to a young woman from Kala, but he never finds a viable alternative, even after years spent wandering about the world in an ambiguous, unrequited search for meaning.

At first, Medza had regarded himself as superior to the "bumpkins" of Kala. His head is filled with the formal subject matter of the European school, and the villagers repeatedly pay hommage to his book-learning. Yet the longer he remains in the village, the more he recognizes the irrelevance of his formal knowledge to the solution of real-world problems; in fact, he begins to sense that the physical prowess, grace, practical wisdom, and communal solidarity of the villagers render them more capable of confronting life than he is. However, their lives are far from enviable. The authority of the chief and the elders is grounded in superstition and reinforced by the introduction of a money economy that allowed them to accumulate wealth and power by exploiting certain traditional practices. The people themselves cling to outmoded systems of belief that alienate them from the benefits of modern science and facilitate their sub-jugation by the colonial administration. Medza is therefore confronted by two equally unattractive alternatives. The only real option is a revolutionary alteration of consciousness that would enable Africans simultaneously to enter the contemporary world and regain control over their own destinies. Medza of course lacks the intellectual penetration and strength of will to pursue this option; in fact, only after Beti begins writing again in 1972 does he clearly articulate this alternative in novels like Lament for an African Pol.

There are positive values in Beti's earlier works: a characteristically African openness toward human sexuality and the celebration of life, the friendship that unites Medza with his cousin Zambo during their long years of wandering, the communal solidarity of women who take turns cultivating each other's fields or men who offer to share the fate of camerades arrested for fighting. Such traits contrast with the loneliness, formalism, and acquisitive individualism that Beti associates with European institutions like schools, churches, administrative bureaucracies, and business enterprises. But despite the judgment implicit in this contrast, none of Beti's early novels openly advocate revolutionary change. By simply placing his characters in a web of corrupt socio-cultural relationships and showing how they are victimized by it, he reveals the nature of the web and the ways in which it deforms the African consciousness. He continues to employ this technique in his later novels, but, as in Lament for an African Pol, his critique of the existing situation is now complemented by a greater awareness of historical process and a conviction that his heroes can attain a stable sense of identity by committing themselves to the struggle against tyranny, moral corruption, and false consciousness.

According to Beti, writing is by nature a political act, for writers must either accept or reject existing conditions. Like Mark Twain and Richard Wright, whose novels he received as prizes for academic excellence during his school years in Cameroon, he felt compelled to take a position against injustice; in fact, it was his anger at the sight of injustice that originally triggered his desire to write. At the heart of each early novel there is a strong resistence to the twin evils of colonialism and the illegitimate authority of corrupt chiefs and elders.

The crucial episode in Cruel City (1954) occurs when Banda's cocoa beans are unfairly rejected by a white merchant; in The Poor Christ of Bomba (1956), Father Drumont seeks to change customs he does not understand as he hypocritically profits from wealth created by the unpaid labor of Africans; and in King Lazarus (1958), Chief Essomba has been arbitrarily imposed on the tribe by French colonial authorities for their own administrative convenience—a practice they frequently adopted, even among peoples who initially had no chiefs. Ironically, they then had the audacity to contend that the Africans owed allegiance to this illegitimate ruler on the basis of traditional custom. Similar injustices occur in Lament for an African Pol, where Beti once again satirizes corrupt merchants, an illegitimate chief who indulges his own appetites rather than governing in the common interest, and priests who proclaim Christian charity while exploiting their parishioners and conditioning them to ignore the true nature of their servitude. Because those who benefit from the exercise of power resent any challenge to the moral rectitude of their activities, Beti's critiques of independent Cameroon have proved as unpalatable to the country's African rulers as his portrayals of colonial Cameroom had been to the French authorities. Just as the latter prohibited the sale of his books in their colonies (the Catholic church even placed The Poor Christ of Bomba on the Index!), the post-independence government of Cameroon has not allowed any of his later novels to circulate within the country. Such acts of censorship bear eloquent testimony to the authorities' unwitting acceptance of Beti's statement about the inherently political nature of literature. They would hardly bother to ban a work of fiction unless they felt it posed some danger to their hegemony.

Yet the step from anti-colonialism in the 1950's to opposition in the 1960's and 1970's was not an easy one for writers like Beti. Although social injustice continued to exist and was often exacerbated by the rise of indigenous elites, it seemed somehow dishonorable to attack one's fellow countrymen in the same way that foreign colonizers had been attacked. A number of francophone African writers became government functionaries after independence, but Beti decided to remain in France, withdrawing from politics and devoting himself to the completion of his education (he achieved the coveted "Agrēgation" in classical languages), the teaching of his classes at a Rouen high school, and the raising of his children. He did not lose interest in the Cameroonian political scene, but despite his opposition to the new regime he did not want to openly condemn the nation-building project undertaken by his fellow countrymen.

The reason he broke his silence in 1972 was a dramatic one, but its significance can only be understood within the context of political developments in his native country. Cameroon was the only area in French-administered black Africa to experience an armed struggle for national liberation. This struggle was conducted by the U. P. C. (Union des Populations du Cameroun) and led for over ten years by the legendary Ruben Um Nyobe, who was killed by French expeditionary forces in 1958. In that same year, the French colonial governor engineered the installation of a Moslem Northerner, Ahmadou Ahidjo, as prime minister of the soon-to-be-independent territory; he later became the first president of Cameroon and ruled until late 1982. Because the U. P. C. considered itself the true guarantor of Cameroonian liberty, its leaders regarded Ahidjo as a usurper and continued their struggle after he came to power. He in turn called upon French troops to quell the rebellion and adopted policies that encouraged an influx of French economic aid, technical advisors, and capital investment; some Cameroonians benefitted enormously from this situation, but the vast majority continued to languish in proverty.

Fearing the popular appeal of the U. P. C., Ahidjo ruled in a highly authoritarian manner, tightening censorship controls and holding thousands of political prisoners in concentration camps throughout the county. Because his government controlled the public media, it had the power to rewrite history, elevating him to the status of national hero and virtually eliminating any recognition of the role played by Um Nyobe. When Beti returned to Cameroon for the last time in the late 1950's, he already understood that the French promise of Cameroonian independence was a ploy for maintaining colonialist institutions under a new guise. He was disgusted by the conspicuous luxury of Cameroonian bureaucrats and the stench of poverty in the New Bell section of Douala, the country's largest city. The ebullient energy of the country's young people impressed him, but he was saddened by the realization that most of this energy would be wasted by a morally corrupt government. New power elites were emerging throughout Africa, and he clearly perceived that they were committed to the subjugation of the masses as a means of protecting their own interests—interests that were closely allied with those of the former colonial masters.

Under these circumstances, Beti thought it would

better for him to stay in France and abandon his career as a writer, but in 1971 he was shocked and angered by a newspaper account of recent events in Cameroon. It appeared in the prestigious Le Monde and had been written by a well-known journalist with years of experience in Africa. The specific occasion for the article was a well-publicized show trial in the capital city of Yaounde. Several months previously, the Ahidjo government had captured Ernest Ouandié, the last of the historic U. P. C. leaders, and arrested the extremely popular Catholic bishop Albert Ndongmo. Along with nearly a hundred other defendants, the two men had been accused of treason.

For Beti, Ouandié and Ndongmo were heroes who had opposed a corrupt and oppressive regime, and yet the article in Le Monde viciously attacked them as dangerous criminals. After reading it, Beti asked himself how a supposedly knowledgeable journalist could fail to mention the truly significant issues of official corruption and social injustice in discussing the charges against the two men. And why, he wondered, would one of the world's most respected newspapers publish such a biased account? His obsession with such questions prompted him to compile a dossier on the recent history of Cameroon, using accounts of the Ouandié-Ndongmo trial to illustrate a persistent pattern of distortion in French reporting about dictatorial regimes in the former French colonies of Africa. As he sought an explanation for this pattern, he perceived even more clearly how the new African elites were collaborating with special interests in the former colonizing country to minimize public awareness of oppression in francophone countries. Even liberal journalists were willing to support this effort, he concluded, because they too had a stake in maintaining French linguistic, cultural, and economic dominance throughout the former colonial empire. In essence, they were all involved in promulgating a new kind of false consciousness that was, in Beti's eyes, just as inimical to African self-respect and well-being as the myths and stereotypes of the colonialist era.

When the results of his investigations appeared under the title Pillage of Cameroon, the French government immediately seized it under provisions of a law that prohibited the publication of inflammatory propaganda by foreigners; however, Beti had by then become a French citizen, and his works should have been exempt from the sanctions of this particular statute. Rather than discouraging him, however, the illegal seizure of his book convinced him that his thesis about the illusory, fraudulent independence of Cameroon and other francophone African countries was basically correct; in fact, the incident stimulated him to redouble his efforts to reveal the truth about this situation. Because he knew the French government would not want to make itself look foolish by confiscating works of fiction, he returned to an earlier mode of expression and transformed some of the material he had collected for Pillage of Cameroon into novels.

The first of these was Remember Ruben (1974), and it set the stage for the later Lament in several important ways. On the most obvious level, it tells the story of Mor-Zamba's life up to the point where the narrative of the Lament begins. Since the character of this gentle giant is clearly linked with the mission entrusted to him in the second book, it is useful to know something about his development into a militant opponent of the existing system. He was a naive and homeless orphan when he originally wandered into Ekoumdoum during the late 1930's. Although he did not know it until many years later, he himself was heir to the chieftaincy of the city, because his mother had been the daughter of the last legitimate chief in Ekoumdoum. The French had long ago dethroned the old man and imposed the outsider Mor-Bita (the Bedridden Chimpanzee in Lament for an African Pol) upon the tribe. The only people who befriended the generous-hearted Mor-Zamba were a wise old man and Abena, a quick-witted child about his own age; most of the others avoided him, and when he grew into a strong young man, Mor-Bita delivered him into the hands of the French authorities, who sent him to a forced labor camp at Oyolo (Yaounde). As in Ekoumdoum, where he had unselfishly helped others even when they refused to help him, he sacrificed his own free time at the camp to care for sick and injured prisoners.

After his release, he almost inadvertantly became involved in several anti-colonialist demonstrations, but he was not a committed revolutionary at this time, and when he moved to Fort-Negre (Douala), he had no qualms about working for the corrupt merchant Robert. Living in Kola-Kola (New Bell), he increasingly identified with the independence movement, not because he had a clear understanding of the historical situation, but because he empathized with the sufferings of the people. Even when he singlehandedly saved the popular revolutionary leader Ruben (Um Nyobe) from his French captors, Mor-Zamba's heroic actions were triggered by his anger at the pain he saw being inflicted upon another human being. One might almost say that he is an exemplary Christian who has shed the inessential trappings of the institutionalized church and retained only its more profound significance for the human soul. Compassionate, charitable, and longsuffering, he is the conscience of the revolution.

On another level, Remember Ruben develops several underlying themes which reach their culmination in Lament for an African Pol. For example, Mor-Zamba and Abena have complementary personalities; their relationship echoes that of "doubles" like Banda and Koumé in Cruel City or Medza and Zambo in Mission to Kala. Yet they function in a different way than their predecessors. Whereas all the paired individuals in Beti's earlier fiction moved toward ambiguity, frustration, or failure, Mor-Zamba and Abena are expressions of an integrated revolutionary vision that endows them with hope and a stable sense of identity. The profound difference in their temperaments is illustrated in a conversation they had in Ekoumdoum after the two of them had built Mor-Zamba's house. Contrary to local custom, none of the other young men in the city had helped them. In reply to Abena's diatribe against the shirkers, Mor-Zamba asks, "Why be angry with them? What would life be without its disappointments?" Abena answered, "Something magnificent! A beautiful dream." But Mor-Zamba corrects him, "an illusion you mean.... You are always exaggerating the sadness of life; you are wrong." Mor-Zamba's Christlike resignation and forebearance contrast shaply with Abena's vision of a more perfect world where men actually treat each other as brothers.

Shortly after this episode, Abena comes to the realization that his more perfect world will never be attained without a struggle: people impose their will on others by force, and force is symbolized by the possession of guns. During the colonial period, white men had guns and black men did not; thus, when Abena follows the captive Mor-Zamba to the forced labor camp in Oyolo, he eventually joins the French army to obtain a gun of his own. For almost twenty years he fights in Europe, in Indochina, and in Algeria; by the time he returns to his native land, he has acquired the guns and the skill to combat the oppressive system that had so unjustly imprisoned his friend in a forced labor camp. In this respect, Abena bears some resemblance to the real-life Ouandié, who led a guerilla compaign against the Cameroonian government for more than ten years. A few months before the colony was to achieve independence, Abena once again meets his childhood companion. At this time he reveals Mor-Zamba's true identity to him and commissions him to regain Ekoumdoum, depose the illegitimate Mor-Bita, and help transform their city into a more decent and equitable community. The complementary relationship between the two men has thus come full circle. At the beginning of Remember Ruben, Mor-Zamba's generosity and his victimization impel Abena toward the development of a practical revolutionary ethos; at the end, Abena gives Mor-Zamba a new sense of purpose in life, enabling him to place his enormous strength in the service of the people rather than wasting it in the employment of a greedy merchant like Robert. If the revolution is to be successful, it must draw upon the utopian vision and military tactics of Abena, but it will also need the spirit of forgiveness and charity represented by Mor-Zamba. In the long run, his contribution may perhaps be even more important than that of Abena, for the name Mor-Zamba echoes a central Cameroonian word for the "primal force," suggesting that his strength of character expresses a divinely inspired urge toward an appropriate ordering of the universe.

On a third and final level, Remember Ruben introduces an historical dimension absent from Beti's earlier novels but central to all his later works and particularly to the Lament. The symbolic significance of Mor-Zamba's life and mission are underlined in two different ways: there are allusions to real events and people from recent Cameroonian history, and the dilemma of Ekoumdoum recapitulates in miniature the crisis of many African countries. Oyolo, Fort-Negre, and Kola-Kola are based upon recognizable places in Cameroon, and the book itself pays hommage to the enlightened, egalitarian, socialistic society that the charismatic Ruben Um Nyobe fought so hard to create. In actuality, however, his dreams were shattered when the French succeeded in suppressing the U. P. C. and having Ahidjo (Baba Toura in Beti's later novels) confirmed as the new country's president. The society he brings into being is exploitive, dominated by foreign interests, totalitarian, paranoid, and per-versely acquisitive. Ekoumdoum suffered a similar breakdown of morality when its people accepted the French decision to replace their legitimate chief with Mor-Bita. Because they could no longer believe they controlled their own destiny, their traditional gener-osity and communal spirit were gradually supplanted by individualistic values that seemed to offer the only kinds of rewards still available to them. As Abena observed, the Ekoumdoumians had become "rotten, despised, and hated by [themselves], like lepers staring at their own pus-bloated limbs."

At about the time of Mor-Zamba's initial entry into the city, two other events occurred, and both contributed to an erosion of the traditional value system. Father Van den Rietter established a perma-nent Catholic mission nearby, and French engineers, using forced labor gangs, carved a highway through the forest and past the city. Within the context of Beti's revolutionary analysis, the new church and its school helped condition Africans to accept the false myths that the colonial authorities found so useful in their exploitation of the area, and the road enabled them to maintain a more strict surveillance over their subjects. By the time of independence, however, the road had fallen into a state of chronic disrepair, and the priest had leagued himself with the corrupt Mor-Bita to preserve existing relations of dominance

xviii

in the city. Isolated from the outside world, the majority of the population was held in bondage by the spurious Christianity of Van den Rietter, the local elites' self-serving interpretation of traditional custom, and the increasingly brutal exercise of power by Mor-Bita and his allies. The situation parallels that in Cameroon and many other African countries, and when Mor-Zamba sets out to "assure the triumph of goodness and the punishment of those who do evil" in Ekoumdoum, he embodies the revolutionary hope of a more humane and decent life for people throughout the continent.

Beti's Lament for an African Pol relates the struggle between this hope and the reactionary forces that attempt to stifle it. Like all petty tyrants in post-independence Africa, Mor-Bita needed help to maintain himself in power. It is true that his putative son Zoabekwe (The Bastard) is not restrained by the old man's respect for ancestral taboos against the arbitrarily brutal use of force, but support and inspiration for the oppressive regime in Ekoumdoum comes primarily from the two white clergymen at the local mission. Their role is the same as that of the French technical advisers who remain active in the former colonies. Father Van den Rietter and Brother Nicholas undertake projects that would certainly be regarded as laudable according to the usual standards for aid to developing countries, and yet all their efforts are based on the assumption that Africans are incapable of making decisions by and for themselves. The true motivation behind their presence in Africa is not the altruism or Christian charity they preach from the pulpit of the mission church, but the overweening desire to demonstrate their white superiority by shaping African reality into what they think it should be. While exhorting a group of young men to work on one of his development projects, Van den Rietter himself declares, "I am the potter, and you are the clay."

These words represent a clear acknowledgement of his own basic premise: white men are superior to black men and should be allowed to mold their destinies for them. If he allies himself with The Bedridden Chimpanzee and Zoabekwe, he does it to acquire a semblance of legitimacy for his own plans to gain psychological ascendancy over the Ekoumdoumians. This alliance is of course beneficial to the corrupt African rulers of the city, because it offers them a means to increase their wealth and privilege. For example, it is Brother Nicholas who supervises construction of the Chief's ostentatious palace with its dungeons and torture chambers, and it is Father Van den Rieter who organizes a detail of young men to clear fields for the chief's wives. Thus, even in the era of so-called independance, Mor-Bita is kept on his throne by the very colonialist institutions that had originally brought him to power.

However, the real strength of the two clergymen lies not in their technical knowledge or in their intellectual superiority or even in their local monopoly on firearms, but in their ability to brainwash the people into accepting the racist myth of black dependency. Because Brother Nicholas is in charge of the boat that transports all the city's produce to market and brings back the only consumer goods sold in the area, the two white men retain effective control over the Ekoumdoumian economy. Even more important, they create the impression that Africans need white Europeans to organize their business affairs for them. Similarly, when Father Van den Rietter organizes unpaid labor gangs to build a dock, a soccer stadium, or a cocoa plantation, the implicit message behind his policy is that black Africans are incapable of conceptualizing and carrying out such projects by themselves. Like Father Drumont in The Poor Christ of Bomba, he is convinced that African customs are primitive and should be replaced by European ones. For that reason, he seeks to prohibit traditional dances and games, and he orders the women to cover their breasts and the men to cease drinking palm wine. He even presumes to interpret their traditions for them. In essence, he has conditioned them not to think for themselves. But people who have lost the capacity to make their own decisions and take initiative in their own behalf are no more than slaves, for they have renounced their claim to become what they can be—free and self-respecting individuals with the responsibility for creating their own future. The clergymen, The

Bedridden Chimpanzee and The Bastard all have a vested interest in perpetuating the slave mentality, and it is the greatest obstacle Mor-Zamba will have to overcome, if he hopes to transform Ekoumdoum into a just and equitable society.

The weakness of Van den Rietter's approach is its reliance upon a false picture of reality. White men are not inherently superior, and Africans are not incapable of defining their own goals and priorities. Even when cloaked in the rhetoric of Christian charity, such myths help prevent the emergence of a collective identity that is both genuinely African and viable in the modern world. As a means of undercutting these myths, Beti structures the fictional universe of Lament for an African Pol to reveal the absurd contradictions which they imply. For example, Van den Rietter preaches a religion of love and forgiveness, but whenever Africans question his right to make their decisions for them, he does not hesitate to flaunt his guns and his ability to use them. Upon occasion, he even resorts to the most sadistic forms of torture. In direct contradiction to the teachings of Christ, he imposes his will on others by subjecting them to the threat of violence.

The vulnerability of this position is twofold. As Van den Rietter strives to ignore the disparity between the Christian principles he espouses and the coerciveness of his actions, he must constantly ward off the suspicion that his image of reality might be inaccurate. The resultant tension quite literally drives him mad. At the same time, his increasingly totalitarian stance helps crystallize opposition to the existing system. Thus, his plan to stem the people's restiveness by erecting walls and creating a police-state atmosphere in Ekoumdoum appears to succeed for a relatively long period of time, but because it frustrates human needs rather than satisfying them, it eventually leads to an outburst of revolutionary counter-violence. Indeed, the success of Mor-Zamba's mission will depend upon his ability to exploit these weaknesses in Van den Rietter's system by persuading people to abandon the slave mentality that prevents them from acting in their own interest.

His primary weapon in this campaign is the truth

he represents. In contrast to Van den Rietter, who hoards penicillin for his own use and recommends prayer as the only remedy for children dying in a flu epidemic, Mor-Zamba places himself in jeopardy to share the small stock of antibiotics he has been able to acquire. The contrast between his generous-hearted action and the ineffectual rhetoric of the white priest serves to convert the women of Ekoumdoum to his cause, and they are the ones who initiate the counter-violence that actually topples the corrupt regime. The important role of women in the Lament is surprising in one sense, because most people assume that revolutions will be carried out by men. In retrospect, however, the commitment of the women seems eminently plausible, for they constitute the exploited working class in rural African society. They cultivate the land; they nurture the children; they accept responsibility for the survival of the race. Because most men in the area have no productive employment, they have lost contact with the material conditions of their existence. As a result, they repeatedly adicate the leadership role they might be expected to fill in overthrowing the forces of oppression. Beti's novel thus reflects a remarkably feminist perspective on contemporary African history, clearly illustrating a major tenet of Ruben's ideological legacy: there can be no meaningful revolution in Africa without the equal participation of women.

In fact, all of Beti's later novels draw attention to African women. In Perpetue (1974), the protagonist reconstructs the story of his beautiful, talented sister, who was "sold" for the price of a dowry to an ignorant party functionary, who in turn prostitutes her for his own political advancement. In The Two Mothers of William Ishmael Dzewatama (1982), a major source of interest is the way in which the African and European wives of a French-educated jurist attained a heightened awareness of the corrupt forces that are distorting their lives. The women of Ekoumdoum need this knowledge in order to free themselves from the slave mentality, and Mor-Zamba's presence in the city serves as a catalyst which enables them to acquire it for themselves.

But Mor-Zamba alone could not have sustained the

revolutionary impulse. His very decency prevents him from adopting the decisive, often brutal strategies required in coping with the forces of oppression; furthermore, he lacks the historical perspective to comprehend the crisis of authority in Ekoumdoum within the context of its relationship to events that have occurred at other times and places, yet because he is part of a revolutionary avant-garde, the talents of his two companions conpensate for his deficiencies and illustrate the necessarily collective nature of their enterprise. Jo The Juggler is a convicted forger and former domestic servant for the French colonial administrator Sandrinelli, one of Baba Toura's closest collaborators, and the young schoolboy Evariste has gained experience as a sapak (i.e., a member of one of the politically engaged youth gangs that roamed Kola-Kola, harrassing French colonial troops and local policemen). The streetwise Jo lacks Mor-Zamba's physical strength and inflexibile moral character, but he possesses qualities that his fellow Rubenist lacks--audacity, quick-wittedness and a willingness to deal ruthlessly with his enemies. Yet it is from Evariste that he learns to place his own revolutionary sentiments into a larger historical framework. Like Medza in Mission to Kala, Evariste has studied the European curriculum at school, but unlike Medza, he committed himself to a cause, and that decision enabled him to relate his book-learning to the life conditions of his fellow Africans.

In communicating his knowledge to Jo, he creates the rationale behind his companion's most successful revolutionary gestures. Jo's ruses do not always succeed, but on several occasions he provides the stimulus needed to maintain the impetus of the revolution. For example, when Van den Rietter stalks to the road in front of the women who have rebelled against established authority, he wantonly shoots several flying hawks as a means of reminding people that he still controls the instruments of power in the city; at this moment Jo fetches one of the Rubenists' concealed guns and calmly proceeds to bring down one final hawk with a single shot. His gesture is merely symbolic, but it destroys the myth of the white man's ability to do what black men could not do, and it reasserts the African's right to take historical initiative in his own name.

Recognizing the significance of Jo's action, the crowd of bystanders burst into frenzied celebration; from then on, Van den Rietter no longer has the power to dominate them psychologically. Jo would never have undertaken this feat, if he had not been motivated by a desire to halt, for once, the recurrent enslavement of Blacks by Whites, and he had discovered the history of this enslavement during his talks with Evariste. Similarily, when he seizes the opportunity to speak from Van den Rietter's pulpit, his anti-sermon on white racism and the mythology of black dependency evokes a spark of revolutionary insight among those gathered in the church, but all his information was derived from his conversations with the sapak. The three Rubenist militants obviously have complementary skills, but only by working collectively with the women of the city do they succeed in triggering the struggle to liberate Ekoumdoum.

In harmony with the revolutionary thesis of Lament for an African Pol, Beti had devised a uniquely appropriate narrative technique for transmitting it to his readers. In a 1979 interview, he contended that "as soon as a people has something to say, its novelists will find solutions to the problem of form in an existential fashion; that is to say, as soon as a subject occurs to an author, this subject automatically offers him a specific or original form that he only has to appropriate for himself."

The original form he appropriated for the Lament involves a sophisticated blend of European novelistic conventions and African story-telling techniques. His extraordinarily complex sentence structures, his classical allusions, and the epic sweep of his tale bear testimony to Beti's long years of teaching Latin and Greek in French schools. At the same time, he skillfully introduces characteristic devices of oral narration—proverbs, parables, extended metaphors, tongue-in-cheek references to members of the imagined audience, allusions to legendary figures (e.g., Mor-Zamba is compared to Akomo, the common ancestor of the Ekoumdoum people, signaling his role in the "re-birth" of the community), and rhetorical questions directed

to his listeners as a way of engaging their mental
participation. Some of these devices are vaguely
present in Remember Ruben, but after having written
that book, Beti read Chinua Achebe's Things Fall Apart
and recognized that the liberal use of oral techniques
did not necessarily imply support for a falsely exotic
and primitive image of Africans. Subordinated to his
overall ideological purpose, they could, he saw, lend
dramatic force and credibility to the epic story of
Mor-Zamba, Jo The Juggler, Evariste, and the rebellious women of Ekoumdoum. This insight was a liber-
ating one for Beti, because it enabled him to create
one of the great revolutionary works of contemporary
African fiction in a style admirably suited to its
content.

The "original form" of Lament for an African Pol
also expresses the author's conscious attempt to
foster a sense of communal identity. His fictive
narrator, who always employs the collective "we" in
preference to the individualistic "I," is telling the
story sometime in the mid-1960's, several years after
the revolution had ended the oppressive reign of
Mor-Bita, Zoabekwe, and Van den Rietter. As the
legitimate chief of the tribe at this time, Mor-Zamba
regards himself as the embodiment of the people's will
and works toward the common welfare, rather than
imposing his will arbitrarily on them and abusing his
position to enrich himself. He has established a
cooperative market where everyone can buy consumer
goods cheaply, and he reads incessantly to overcome
his lack of historical consciousness. Jo occasionally
disguises himself to visit Oyolo and reconnoiter the
corrupt socio-political milieu there, but Ekoumdoum
itself has become a democratic, economically self-
sustaining community; it has become what the country
itself could have become, if it had overthrown Baba
Toura and his French technical advisers. Like traditional African storytellers, the narrator creates a
usable past by incorporating memories, second-hand
accounts, and value judgments into a morally and
socially significant tale; he selects or omits details
on the basis of his desire to justify the present
social organization of the city while revealing the
hypocrisy and injustice of the earlier one (and by

extension of all independent African states dominated
by petty dictators and foreign advisors).  At the end
of the novel, this "we" narrator underscores the
communal significance of the story he has just told by
intimating that the Ekoumdoumians are still confronted
with an unanswered question:  Should Zoabekwe be
executed for his crimes against the people of the
city?  Mor-Zamba advocates clemency; Jo and Evariste
demand justice.  The question is important, because
the solution which the people adopt in this case will
set a precedent for the way they conduct their affairs
in the future.  Even more than that, it is a variation
upon the fundamental question underlying Beti's entire
work:  What is an appropriate identity for Africans in
the modern world, and what must they do to become
masters of their own destiny?

Throughout his life, Beti has been concerned with
power, continually asking who exercises it and why
they exercise it as they do.  He has understood that
people can be reduced to servitude by the false myths
of a dominant culture, and he has consistently striven
to discredit these myths; indeed, he is one of very
few pre-independence African writers with the courage
and intellectual honesty to have pointed out the
essential similarity between colonialist myths and
those of independent Africa.  What distinguishes his
later novels from his earlier ones is the presence of
a utopian element, the suggestion that there are
alternatives to oppression, and the belief that he has
found appropriate revolutionary strategies for attain-
ing them.  More than technological progress, Africans
need psychological liberation.  Rather than conceiving
of themselves as the helpless victims or passive
adjuncts of a superior race, they need to forge an
image of themselves as a people capable of taking
historical initiative and benefitting from the fruits
of their own labor.  And this is precisely the attitude Beti is seeking to inculcate in the readers of
his Lament for an African Pol.

Richard Bjornson
The Ohio State University

xxvi

# PART I

The Long March of Two Rubenists
and One Child

# CHAPTER 1

Well, by one of those cruel paradoxes which, in the dawning era, were to prove so abundant that most people would be seriously troubled or even driven to despair, Mor-Zamba and The Juggler, who had done so much to bring about the event, were obliged to leave Fort Negre and its wretched suburb Kola-Kola on the very day Independence was proclaimed. Freedom fighters defeated in their moment of victory, they were abandoning a familiar field, sown with exploits that only their enemies would now be able to harvest, and going out to seek refuge in places as inaccessible as they were insecure.

Neither of the two friends was the sort of man to brood over a lost battle, and the steadfast Mor-Zamba, tempered by endless years of hardship, had good reason to entrust himself to the ever watchful craftiness of Mor-Kinda; new fireworks would doubtless explode elsewhere, far from Kola-Kola, to illuminate the long night that Hurricane-Viet had predicted as one result of Ruben's disappearance.

Even their departure, like the rest of their journey, did not quite take place as they had expected. On the previous evening each of the two friends had carefully made up his bundle, finding a place there for personal effects as well as the guns presented to them by the Rubenist leader. Nonetheless, The Juggler, who delighted in affecting an air of mystery, contrived to prevent his companion from counting the objects in his pack or even ascertaining their exact nature. Yet he did not fail to appropri-

3

ate for himself the privilege of carrying a large box of pharmaceutical supplies which the underground leader had not only promised, but actually delivered at the very time and date they had agreed upon—much to the astonishment of The Juggler who contended that, with the exception of slave owners, he had never seen such discipline and punctuality.

"What organization!" he murmured ecstatically.

Afterwards, though, the former delinquent almost constantly betrayed his dissatisfaction in gestures perceptible only to Mor-Zamba. Thus, the latter was hardly surprised when his friend finally confided in him, but Mor-Zamba had been far from suspecting the incredible project which suddenly sprang forth, like an inflammatory spark, from his friend's eternally incandescent imagination.

"We don't have enough equipment," The Juggler whispered late in the evening. "A little bird told me that we shall never have enough provisions."

"But provisions for what?" asked Mor-Zamba, intrigued.

"Exactly! When you don't know who or what you'll encounter, it's better to have too many provisions than too few."

"Good enough, but so what?"

"I have an idea. It wouldn't have occurred to you, would it, Bumpkin? Early tomorrow morning, I'll go to the June 18 school complex on the plateau as if I were returning submissively to my job as a good little houseboy. I know Sandrinelli; I can handle him. Besides, I have the best of reasons for going. I'll tell him, 'Forgib me, mastah, dat I no come work yestiday, or de day befaw yestiday, an de day befaw dat. . . . Forgib me, mastah, dat I hab de tokens, dat ebbywhere be full of Ruben's bandits. Ah, mastah, dose bastids should done be wipe out, and right away, yes, mastah. . . .' I know him; he'll burst out laughing and slap his thighs, and after having regained his breath, you know, loudly going heehaw, heehaw . . . , like a donkey, he'll tell me, 'Damned race, damned race. . . . And now, finita la comẽdia, back to work!' As for the rest, grandpa, trust me to settle a few scores that have remained outstanding far too long. Trust me! All I ask is that you be ready

4

to clear out as soon as I come back."

Despite the protestations of Mor-Zamba, made uneasy by the recondite plans of a would-be scoundrel, Jo The Juggler's determination won out.

Now then, on the first of January, events took place more or less in the following manner. Mor-Zamba, who had not slept at all well, got up early, perhaps around four o'clock in the morning, even though he didn't have to, so that he could watch in reproachful silence as his friend, who proved equally talkative out of an impish desire to tease, made his preparations and left.

Then, remaining but a single step from his doorway and with the detached curiosity of an outlaw standing sentry by the opening of his cave, Mor-Zamba began to contemplate the waking up of his Kola-Kola. No one who looked at him would have suspected that this giant, the pupil of whose eye quivered from time to time with some unknown and incompletely mastered combative spark, was suffering from a sentimental case of bad conscience; should he or should he not pay his respects to the Lobila family before leaving Kola-Kola, perhaps forever? They had taken him in, and later they had always treated him with generosity. Nearly all its members had become his friends; he had of course developed strong bonds with the older daughters, but he had also become attached to the youngest boys and particularly to the old couple. His sudden disappearance would hurt them as soon as they became aware of it, and this torment—more or less serious as time wore on—would perhaps never leave them in peace. But, on the other hand, what could he tell them? What could he say? What could he explain to them as he was taking his leave? He had only discussed the matter once with The Juggler, who, in his own colorful idiom, had made the following recommendation: "As far as the old folks are concerned, get out of it any way you like, but mama—that's no business of yours."

Perhaps there was a better solution—entrust some errand boy with the commission of announcing his departure, after the fact, to the family. That way he could easily avoid the embarrassment of saying goodbye to people who were dear to him while at the same time

5

ridding himself of his scruples at leaving them for such a long time in a grievous state of anxiety.

How well chance arranges things, Mor-Zamba suddenly mused as his face brightened; he had just seen Evariste, the youngest Lobila, a child whose age the Rubenist, deceived by a premature growth which promised an unusually tall stature, estimated as sixteen or seventeen; in reality, the boy was no more than fourteen. Under his arm, Evariste carried a small, grotesquely shabby suitcase that could only be kept closed with the aid of numerous strings wound tightly around it and holding it together. Encouraged by the vague smile he had just observed in Mor-Zamba's glance and interpreting it as a sign of unconditional good will, the adolescent announced insouciantly, "I'm coming with you!"

"With us . . . ? Where?" asked the astonished Rubenist.

"You're not going to do that to me, Bumpkin! As if I didn't know all your comings and goings and all your plans, come on! When The Juggler was carried off by brawling sapaks who wanted to tear out his guts because he had supposedly testified for his boss Sandrinelli, who came to tell you about it? Perhaps it wasn't me and my younger brother? And how did I know about all that? When the first pictures of Hurricane-Viet were distributed in Kola-Kola. . . ."

"Yes, yes, yes, yes, I understand. But your family?"

"My family? I told them, 'I'm leaving with Mor-Zamba and The Juggler.' And that's it."

"And what did they say to you?"

"They said, 'Have you thought about it?' I answered, 'Yes, I've thought about it.' Then they said, 'In days like these, who can prevent a child from leaving—a child who in any case is almost a man?'"

"They really said that?"

"They really said that. Word of God!"

"Why don't you come along with us then, after all? It's true: you are almost a man. And in a way, you've said goodbye for both of us."

It was seven, maybe eight o'clock. Mor-Zamba called to an itinerant market woman, who was well

6

known in this section of town, and bought several corn
fritters from her. It was the standard breakfast in
Kola-Kola, and the Rubenist shared it equally with the
child. As he ate, he exchanged bits of news with the
market woman, actually a loyal Rubenist who disguised
herself under this flawless cover. The two adults
spoke in a coded language, but Evariste understood
every word they said.

"Is it true that you're leaving us?" the poor
woman asked Mor-Zamba.

"It's true."

"Is it true that you're going to replace Ruben at
the head of his men? Oh, I always knew it would be
you, believe me; who else could it have been? You're
our lion now; your name alone makes the Saringala
shake more than a palm tree in a cyclone. Listen,
it's like Hurricane-Viet, your brother. . . ."

"Don't fool yourself," Mor-Zamba interrupted. "I
am not going to replace Ruben at the head of his men.
. . ."

"Then he isn't dead? Tell me. He isn't dead, is
he? The Sot spread that rumor to demoralize us,
didn't he?"

"Patience, sita, patience. Kola-Kola will soon
have no further doubts on that subject, and neither
will you."

Mor-Zamba had spoken a bit harshly, brusquely,
for the wretched woman's despair had made him impatient while at the same time upsetting him. Without a
doubt, she had placed all her hopes in Ruben's cause,
and she had a hard time holding back her tears as she
left them.

"As for me," the child said immediately, "I tell
them sometimes that Ruben isn't dead, although he was
hit in the middle of the heart with a bullet or that
he was resurrected on the third day after having died
from his wounds."

---

Saringala: an African member of the police or
armed forces, particularly during colonial times

sita: my sister

"In short, you lead the masses around by the nose, just like The Sot."

"You have to understand; people are absolutely incapable of believing that Ruben has actually disappeared for good.  Last year at school, I read a horrible story in my book—a story which took place a long, long time ago, over there, in a European city. Imagine a city which had remained unconquered until that time, and suddenly its inhabitants learn that their army has been wiped out during a battle in the open countryside and that nothing any longer stands between them and the invading enemy.  Listen well, Bumpkin; here is what those people did in such a hopeless situation.  They collected tree trunks, furniture, in short all the wood that they could find in the city.  They hastily erected an immense funeral pyre, do you understand?  They soon lit it, and, to cut the matter short, they threw themselves into it one after the other.  That's the sort of thing which could happen in Kola-Kola, if the people became convinced that Ruben was dead once and for all."

"What was the name of your city?"

"Ah, I don't remember; in any case, it was over there in their part of the world, in Europe."

"And what happened afterwards."

"What happened afterwards?  History doesn't say. It's a war story.  With war stories, you never know what happened afterwards."

"Did you go very far in school?"

"What do you think!  I had barely begun; I was in the first year of high school.  It's true that you lost track of me for a while.  You couldn't help it. But as for me, I was never more than a step away from you so to speak."

"Why did you quit school?  You had a future."

"Wrong.  The technical high school where I was—they had just changed its name, but it was still the same old vocational training school—it never leads anywhere, because it can't create any new jobs. When you leave after your third year, you're no further along than you were before.  It's not like the two regular high schools; there, with a bit of luck and if your father is a friend of The Sot, you can make it to the diploma.  By that time, in any case, you are already someone, you see?"

"But your brother didn't have a diploma, and yet.
. . ."

"You know, that's easy to understand. Jean-Louis
is a Judas. When you agree to play such a role, you
won't be lacking in funds, believe me. As for me,
I'll never sell a single one of my black brothers even
to become king of the whole world."

Their conversation continued for a long time in
this vein. Mor-Zamba always remained near the door or
one of the windows, alternately sitting down and
standing up, so he could keep his eye fixed in the
direction of the white man's city, hoping at every
moment to see Mor-Kinda's abbreviated silhouette
emerge. Outside, in a detached and even sullen Kola-
Kola, the day promised the boredom of an average
Sunday when, in the midst of a general indifference,
several meager groups of listless believers spread out
aimlessly in search of some temple or church to render
a passionless tribute unto the White Man's God.
Mor-Zamba sighed and reflected with some bitterness on
the curious band he was about to create with a failed
guttersnipe and a child who was undoubtedly the most
precocious sapak in the entire nation.

"Don't move from here," he said suddenly to the
young boy, "and don't let anyone enter until I've
brought back Jo The Juggler."

Without a watch and annoyed by the wait, he
vaguely surmised the time, and believing the morning
must be almost over, he decided to dash off in pursuit
of Mor-Kinda. Reaching Gallieni Avenue, he wended his
way toward Fort Negre, passing beside the burned-out
carcass of a Shell station as he penetrated the outskirts of the European city. He met Kola-Kolans going
in the opposite direction, walking in small groups and
sporting the sad faces of orphans barred from the
celebration. They nevertheless greeted him with signs
of friendship and even preened themselves, thinking he
was there to determine whether or not the directives

---

sapak: a member of one of the youth gangs that
proliferated during the period just before independence; these gangs often harrassed representative of
the colonial order.

9

of the People's Progressive Party were being respected. In actuality, the organization's executive committee had exhorted people not only to boycott the independence day ceremonies, but also to wear mourning as a way of emphasizing how the official masquerade was annihilating all hope of the progress and brotherhood which always reverberated in the word "independence" whenever Ruben had used it.

Scrutinizing the main streets and byways of the freshly scrubbed city center while remaining oblivious to the animated activity and unwonted noises that invaded the city, Mor-Zamba cut through parks, trod on the grass, strode across streets, snaked his way through traffic, and leaped over fences and railings; soon he was at the center of Fort Negre, drawn almost in spite of himself toward the June 18 school complex.

All at once, he ran into a procession which, at first glance, struck him as a parade of people decked out in their Sunday best; he had to walk through their ranks as if he were passing them in review. They were Baba Toura's supporters, those whom he and the Governor had invited, with a certain insistence, to celebrate independence or rather, in actuality, to demonstrate their loyalty to the official politics of the authorities.

The wave of people was breaking from the stadium where it had apparently organized itself into rows under the protective guidance of the police, commanded by Commissioner Maestraci, and it was undoubtedly heading toward the parade ground in front of the Governor's Palace, where, as on every solemn public occasion, protocol had determined that the masses would be herded together to hear a formal reading of the official proclamation.

The enormous size of the crowd was undeniable. With the exception of Kola-Kola, all the black sections of town were represented. Their combined populations were certainly far outnumbered by Kola-Kola's three hundred thousand inhabitants; nevertheless, the next day the Governor and Baba Toura declared, not without a semblance of truth, that the African populace had pronounced itself for realism and wisdom, epithets obviously intended to designate the two confederates themselves.

This human tide was content to jabber incessantly rather than intoning triumphal songs; no one frisked about tumultuously or confusedly on the street, and a stately pace was maintained. This frothy-headed wave resembled an incursion of schoolboys, whose restlessness was held in check by the watchful eye of an omnipresent master. The densely packed, toddling line twisted at the passage of a heavy vehicle or the confluence of a tributary column, and with an unspeakably filthy caress, it forced the Rubenist back onto the edge of the sidewalk.

Obliged to look at individuals whom he could barely regard as fellow countrymen, obliged to think about them, to listen to them, and even to enumerate in detail the inanity of varicolored vestments, the stupidity of slogans splashed across banners, and the unwitting mockery in the likenesses of today's hero as they were replicated, and frequently applauded, even in the cloth which covered undulating matronly posteriors, Mor-Zamba began to lose hope of ultimate victory for a people so quick to subordinate themselves to an enthusiasm on command. As he recalled Hurricane-Viet's parting words during the storm, surrounded by darkness: "In ten years"? Twenty? Thirty? Who knows? Our combat will be a long one, a very long one. . . . Everything you see now in Kola-Kola and in the rest of the colony is no more than a puerile beginning. . . . Several years from now, people will smile at the memory of these amateurish preliminaries. . . ."

Lost in his melancholic reverie, Mor-Zamba paid no attention to what would have certainly seemed to him like the distant roll of thunder, except that it was concentrated at a single point and not spread across the horizon, insistent, unduly abrupt, and, in a word, explosive. Nevertheless, a reflex action triggered by the unconscious fear of an eventual storm caused him to hasten his step. He quickly climbed the hill which led to the school plateau, and about fifteen minutes after his encounter with Baba Toura's partisans, he had reached the wall enclosing the June 18 school complex, which he began to reconnoiter cautiously, because he did not know what tasks Sandrinelli, alias The Gaullist, might have assigned

11

to his watchdogs on this historic day.  In advance he
had decided that, whatever happened, he would not
enter the sanctuary of the slave-owning party for fear
he would be treated as an intruder there, a status
that would have guaranteed him a deplorable fate.

Advancing very slowly and affecting an air of
detachment, he reached the main entrance of the establishment, the one facing north, toward the high
school, and remained there motionless for several
seemingly interminable minutes in order to scrutinize
the scattered assortment of buildings fanned by the
long blue fronds of the adjacent palm-trees.
Discovering no sign of life there, he continued his
leisurely stroll as if he were a listless and quite
innocuous idler; he returned the same way he had come,
resolving to climb the slope at the corner of the wall
which he usually overtopped by a full head and
shoulders and then to survey the school complex from
behind it.

Barely had he turned his back on the main
entrance when he was startled by the deafening jangle
of a bicycle bell close on his heels.  Turning around,
he was astonished to see The Juggler perform a virtuoso descent from the flying trapeze of a solid, well-
preserved Raleigh adorned with a blue chain-guard and
fenders painted to match.  No sooner had he regained
his balance with considerable effort than The Juggler,
who deserved his nickname more than ever at this
moment, offered the contraption to his friend,
enjoining him:  "Hurry!  Hurry!"

"Which way?" asked Mor-Zamba as they almost
simultaneously mounted the bicycle—the larger one on
the seat and the other on the frame—and sped down the
sloping road.

"Through the center of town, come on!  It's the
shortest route and in any case the safest.  You still
haven't understood, have you, Bumpkin?  No one is
attending to anything today, and no one is watching
out for anyone else.  For a long time, I've been on
the look out for such a glorious confusion; I have
indeed.  What a wonderful day for anyone who knows how
to profit from these splendid occasions.  First,
there'll be the actual declaration of independence
with The Sot's speech, written by Sandrinelli, and the

governor's speech, written by himself without any help, like a great man, you know.  Sandrinelli was telling it all to his wife just a little while ago. Then there's going to be an enormous military parade, including sons of the fatherland who have just graduated from Saint-Cyr."

"What's that?"

"The <u>toubabs</u>' military school, understand.  Don't you remember Jean-Louis' confession?"

"You see, <u>they</u> teach war in the schools; so what chance do we have of winning against them?"

"Listen to a story I heard in my mother's village; it was told by the old men, who are very important down there and even very much respected. Once upon a time, there were two young men, each of whom wanted to own a canoe.  The first adopted the habit of sitting next to a man of experience, a man who had undertaken to fashion such a craft by carving it out of a large tree trunk; the other, without any previous apprenticeship, attacked the task at hand, being mindful, however, to compare his work to the canoes moored at the edge of the river.  Well, what happened to them?  The apprenticeship of the first dragged on and on, whereas the other had ample time to fail as many times as he needed to learn all by himself how to carve a canoe from the trunk of a tree. Do you get the underlying lesson of my fable?  One apprenticeship is as good as another.  Well then, after the military parade, there'll be dances everywhere in the streets and public places, at the Parliament building, and the Governor's Palace, and how should I know where else?  Then, finally, late in the evening, a fireworks display will illuminate the firmament to salute the appearance of a new star—higher than the Great Bear—Baba Toura, alias The Sot or Massa Bouza. . . ."

"Be careful!  You talk too much.  Have you had anything to drink?"

"My dear Mor-Zamba, from now until they notice

---

toubab:  The African's familiar and somewhat derogatory term for a white man

13

that The Juggler has left never to return, it'll be at least tomorrow noon. But there's still one thing that I don't understand. Sandrinelli seemed to regard this first of January as his own personal triumph. Yet just a few months ago, maybe even a few weeks ago, The Gaullist became furious whenever anyone mentioned the word independence in his presence. What could have happened in the meantime? I don't need Hurricane-Viet to tell me that there is some kind of deal behind it all; it's really fishy. I'll bet they're still screwing over the poor niggers."

As they approached the wealthy commercial section of town, it was more than ever teeming with people; they had descended from the Raleigh and were wheeling its erect form in convoy between them.

"What's that wrapped in blankets on the baggage-carrier?" asked Mor-Zamba.

"I'll explain it to you later. Besides, what's in the two big saddlebags attached on either side of the baggage-carrier is what'll really bowl you over."

"Well, what is it then?"

"But I'm telling you, I'll explain it all to you later." Then, flourishing his left wrist beneath his friend's nose, he went on: "Take a look at this."

"A watch!" grumbled Mor-Zamba. "You're a monster, a madman, a crook, a real jail-bird, an agent provocateur, a curse. You're going to draw a catastrophe down on our heads. I ought to let you go to the devil!"

"Are you finished?" replied Mor-Kinda defiantly when Mor-Zamba had broken off his string of curses. "I can say something then? To start with, we'll need a watch. Hurricane-Viet had one. It's not you who would have noticed that, eh, Bumpkin."

"What damage you must have done up there! If I understand correctly, they left the shop in your hands for the entire day, as if you were a man they could trust."

"Exactly. Hey, listen! Not only did Sandrinelli swallow my line; just try to imagine how he complimented me on my honesty and my courage. Yes, sir, on my honesty, that's right. Everybody wanted to attend the ceremonies. I volunteered to watch the complex all day long and all night too, if only I could make

14

up for a few of my absences in that way. 'But what do you mean!' exclaimed Sandinelli, 'all your absences have already been made up, all of them. Good little fellow, go on.' He had tears in his eyes; seriously, I'm telling you."

"Damned Jo!" said Mor-Zamba, who couldn't prevent himself from laughing. "People ought to call you the diabolical one."

"Well then, you can imagine how I did exactly what I wanted to do, and even more than that. Guess where I was coming from when I met you. You must at least have noticed that I wasn't coming out of the June 18 complex! I had been to the high school. There too, not a living soul. All the students had gone to see the festivities, even them. Despite the Rubenist party directives, they couldn't resist the temptation. I would have thought them more consistent than that. All in all there was only a single watch-man, and he was already as drunk as a Dutchman. As it happened, I had the tail-end of a bottle of Johnny Walker in one of the saddlebags, top quality, an unwitting gift from Sandrinelli. Well then, I go up to the watchman, I make him gulp down a few mouthfuls, and I ask him to let me go into the infirmary; he replies, 'Go ahead, be my guest.' And that's how I was able to carry off the entire medicine chest from the high school; it's there in one of the saddlebags. Beautiful, isn't it?"

"And the bicycle?"

"Spoils of war, exacted from The Gaullist. I don't even remember any more in which film I learned that the Vietnamese patriots didn't use any other means of transportation; we'll see."

In the neighborhood of Avenue Faidherbe, where, about an hour earlier, Mor-Zamba had threaded his way through the procession of Baba Toura's partisans, the two friends suddenly found themselves submerged in a horde of fleeing demonstrators who screamed, stared wildly about, and convulsively distorted their lips as they tried desperately to save themselves. The terror and confusion did not prevent the two Rubenists from learning that a battle was taking place on the very outskirts of the Governor's Palace.

"Let's go," shouted The Juggler as he dragged the

Raleigh in the direction of the Governor's Palace.
"Let's go, old chap; please, let's go. What! Kola-
Kola was worried about another of Bréde's raids, and
it's our own people who are attacking at the very
heart of the slave-owner's sanctuary!   Incredible!
We've got to go see that; it's got Hurricane-Viet's
trademark on it.  Let's go, come on, Bumpkin."

"Out of the question," was all that Mor-Zamba
replied, as his two hands rested quietly on the saddle
of the Raleigh, which he brought to a standstill by
his inertia alone.

In the end, The Juggler became exhausted as a
result of bracing himself, stamping his feet, and
losing his patience.

"It's not true!" jeered Mor-Zamba at that point.
"You must have been bending your elbow with your
boss's Johnny Walker, and that's why you've lost your
good sense.  Since this morning, there's nothing more
for us to do here.  And if the city is catching fire,
we have just enough time to clear out ourselves."

This line of argument seemed to convince The
Juggler at the same time as it calmed him down.  The
fact is that the city suddenly appeared to be filled
with explosions, shooting, fires, and a strange
thundering—which the initiated declared to be the
firing of a cannon.  At the same time, the festivities, which had barely begun, disintegrated rapidly
under the pressure of mass desertions; whole battalions of new citizens, having put away their signs and
slogans, were returning with a furtive haste to their
native shanty-towns.

The two Rubenists returned to Kola-Kola, where
the reigning calm did not appear reassuring to them,
as it presented too much of a contrast with the spasms
that had just rocked the nearby white city.  The
Juggler betrayed very little emotion when he discovered that young Evariste had rallied to their cause
and would henceforth be a member of the expedition.
The trio aroused no curiosity at all in the neighborhood as they loaded their baggage onto the Raleigh, of
which every part was so encumbered that it looked like
a mechanical dromedary—on the handlebars in front, on
the sagging baggage-carrier in the rear, and on a
frame which groaned with bags and bundles.  They began

their journey unobtrusively. It is true that they were in a hurry, but it is also true that they refrained from an overly intense parting glance at what had been the scene of a lengthy existence for all three of them. For instance, the most sensitive member of the group was Mor-Zamba, and he was opportunely absorbed in the futile anguish of trying to imagine what their fate, and above all that of their equipment, might have been, if Jo The Juggler's magic had not conjured this providential bicycle from out of his sleeve.

Despite a sensible division of labor, however, moving the contraption proved to be a considerable task. The colossal Mor-Zamba charged himself with the most important part of the operation; his hands gripping the two ends of the handlebars, he was primarily responsible for holding the contraption upright, while Evariste and The Juggler were above all supposed to push on the ascents, hold back the bicycle on the downgrades, and activate the brakes, which had proved difficult for the helmsman to manipulate.

They were intending to take colonial route number 3, which passed close to the airport, but when they arrived within two or three kilometers of it, their path was suddenly blocked by an incongruous surge of vehicles and pedestrians, whose disarray and confusion slowed their forward progress; white soldiers had erected a road block a little further on, they were told, and all traffic was being turned back.

The two Rubenists and their very young companion decided to detour by way of Saneongo, where one could follow a trail which was part road and part footpath. Well, as soon as they arrived in that scruffy village, after having covered barely ten kilometers, a thunderstorm replete with fleecy whirlwinds obliged them to take refuge in an already crowded bar, where they stood on the porch in front of the Raleigh, which they leaned against the wall and which they seemed instinctively to protect. Then, there was an endless downpour, punctuated by gusts of wind that shook the thatched roof of the unassuming establishment. Much of the afternoon had already passed, and the trio, primed for heroic self-sacrifice, was seriously thinking of defying the bad weather and getting under-

17

way again, because they did not want to content themselves with such a ridiculously short distance on the
first day of their long march. At that very moment, a
man, youthful and carefree beneath his umbrella,
singing as he passed in front of the three travellers,
suddenly recognized Mor-Zamba. "Is that you, my good
fellow?" he said gaily. "What are you doing here?
Listen, come along and bring your friends; we'll have
a drink together."

As the three Rubenists hesitated and cast anxious
glances toward the Raleigh, the man told them they
would have nothing to fear, even if it were loaded
with sacks of gold. The three companions, however,
appeared undecided until the youngest of them eased
the conscience of his elders by offering to serve as
watchman for the Raleigh, because, as for him, he
never drank alcoholic beverages. Now that's a good
attitude for a sapak, mused Mor-Zamba to himself.

Once inside the bar, the newcomer began to speak
in confidence more to the four walls than to the two
Rubenists. In contrast to his friend Mor-Zamba, he
had been lucky in managing to obtain his license
before the situation had deteriorated completely. For
the time being, he was a driver for the owner of a
trucking firm—a reliable boss. Backing up his request with the offer of a large bonus, this Frenchman
had asked him to go out on the road, in spite of
Independence and in spite of the New Year, to pick up
some produce which could not wait. He had left Fort
Negre a little before noon and thus had been in a good
position to witness the events that had taken place
that morning.

According to the truck-driver, two rounds of
mortar fire, no doubt launched by a Rubenist commando
group, had exploded on the parade ground in front of
the Governor's Palace. They had landed in the midst
of the crowd assembled there by Commissioner Maestraci
to lend the desired solemnity to Baba Toura's reading
of the independence proclamation. The people who
suffered were mostly those in the back rows—those
furthest from the balcony where the official guests
were seated. It was in the back rows that the sight
of injured people and blood stains on the concrete had
incited panic and triggered the stampede. Beneath the

18

balcony for guests of honor, on the other hand, the people in the front rows remained oblivious to the danger and continued to listen piously to the unintelligible stammerings of Sandrinelli's protégé. Nevertheless, Baba Toura himself was soon overcome by fear; allowing the pages of his speech to fall on the ground, and stopping his ears with his two hands, he rushed inside the Palace. But the Governor demonstrated an unflinching sang-froid as he thrust out his chest (and his belly) and boomed forth in an icy monotone, taking up the slack with a reading of his own speech; he was a courageous man, a former paratroop officer in the Indochinese Expeditionary Force.

There had also been fighting at other points in the city. Rubenists had seized the airport and still held it at that moment, despite repeated assaults by the white battalions. They had also attacked the H.Q. of the colonial gendarmerie, but the alarm had been sounded before the rebels could reach the passionately covetted arsenal, and a violent hand-to-hand combat culminated several hours later in the annihilation of the Rubenists, young recruits who, though fanatically dedicated, lacked any previous experience. It was their baptism of fire.

"It's a shame you had such bad luck," continued the truck-driver, addressing himself this time directly to Mor-Zamba without, however, lowering his voice. "And now you tell me you're moving to another city? You're probably right: the outlook is rather bad at Fort Negre and particularly at Kola-Kola! You see, we're going to crawl in the mud now, believe me, because the toubabs are going to want revenge, or I don't know them any more. 'So, it's like that you want to get rid of us, eh? Well, we'll see if the dirty niggers can chase us out of Africa!' That's what they're going to say to us now, by God. I'm sure it'll be harder than before. It's like just after the war, if you can remember a bit; things were apparently going quite well for us at that time, people were beginning to lift up their heads, Ruben was speaking out more and more forcefully. And suddenly, whap! We had to get down on our knees and grovel again. What was it exactly that happened? Big mystery. As for me, I understood then that Ruben was going to get

19

himself killed sooner or later. A chap like him,
here, with the toubabs; it's just not possible. You
have two choices:  either the toubabs remain here and
in that case you, my good fellow, better get down on
your knees, or we hold our heads high and the toubabs
have to clear out.  There aren't that many alternatives.  Well, you see, it didn't take long; they got
Ruben's hide.  Yah, it's going to get worse now,
especially in and around the capital.  You're probably
right to leave."

"And what about independence?" objected a
customer's voice in French from a darkness spawned by
the approach of night.

"Well, my brother, what about independence?"
replied the driver, also in French but appearing to
become annoyed.  "Independence, independence, the
screwing over of niggers, do you call that independence?  If you're screwed up, you believe; if you're
not screwed up, you don't believe.  Me, I don't
believe; I'm not a screwed up nigger.  It's the
toubabs themselves who set up their strawman from the
North, their Massa Bouza; fine, he drinks and drinks ,
he does nothing but drink and let the toubabs do
everything they did before; and what do we screwed-up
niggers do?  We just go on believing it's Massa Bouza
who screwed things up, and you, you believe that
anything can be changed like that, my brother?  Listen
well to what I'm going to say, my brother:  with a
screwed-up nigger president, it's a hell of a lot
better for the toubabs, who can do just as they did
before, but as for us Palace-screwing niggers, it's
even worse."

In response to these virile declarations, a
brouhaha of aggressive uncertainty filled the bar, but
the truck-driver, a good-hearted man, did not deign to
notice the success of his remarks, but rather thought
about Evariste, the sapak who had stayed out on the
porch.

"The young boy who's with you must be hungry," he
said feelingly.  "I could give him something to eat,
if you come over to my truck.  Incidentally, which way
are you going?  Why don't I take you along with me?
It has just stopped raining."

Mor-Zamba was quite embarrassed, for he hesitated

to tell the truck-driver the whole truth. The Juggler, who had fewer scruples, glibly explained that, not yet having pinpointed the village where they expected to stay, they had decided to follow colonial route number 3 and to stop whenever the fancy took them.

"An excellent system!" declared the truck driver gaily. "Personally, I have another sixty kilometers to go on colonial
number 3. So I'll take you that far; it's as simple as that."

"It's possible we might not bring you good luck," said Mor-Zamba, "with all those checkpoints, all those policemen. . . ."

"Nonsense! There are no checkpoints today," the truck-driver declared peremptorily. "Moreover, the police sleep at night; you're well aware of that, my good man. Not to mention the fact that there is always a way to handle these matters, what the hell! I'll put you under the tarp and that way you'll have neither rain nor police to fear."

Next to the truck, he fed not only Evariste but also the other two Kola-Kolans, regaling all three of them with bread and sardines. Then, by lowering the tailgate, he helped them hoist up the Raleigh and place it flat on the floorboards of the truck bed. Following his advice, the three passengers sat down with their backs to the cab but close enough to the side corners so they would not lack fresh air once the tarp had been spread over them like a rumpled shroud.

"Don't be jealous, fellows, if I pick up women on the way," apologized the driver. "I don't know why, but with them, good luck is always guaranteed, whereas with the likes of you, oh, la, la . . . !"

At first, the truck went slowly, although that didn't prompt the Rubenists to resume their conversation, because they were too immersed in unwonted feelings of collective entombment, a sudden shadowy darkness, the stealthy passage of gloomy forest shapes packed together as in a solemn and permeable wall, the engine's purring which alternated between a modulated rhythm and a steady monotone, and, as soon as the storm returned, the awesome drumming of rain on the tarp, which wasn't even drawn taut. Seated between his two older companions, Evariste succumbed to fatigue and drowsines, collapsing on Mor-Zamba's forearm where his head swung back and forth at the mercy of the truck's jolting as it proceeded along colonial 3, a dirt road after Saneongo with nothing but gravel to hold it together.

Distended by the mouth of the river like an enormous blister on the exuberant yet ponderous vegetation of the left bank, the capital and all its suburbs formed an immense, grey clearing of which Saneongo marked the East-Southeast border. Once past Saneongo, the perceptive traveler had the impression, even at night in the darkness, of having finally embraced the very soul of the young Republic, as if it were a woman who had remained away far too long, and beyond it, perhaps, that of Africa itself.

Beginning to feel a bit disoriented in the unfamiliar surroundings, The Juggler was the first to speak, unrestrainedly expressing his satisfaction with the unforeseen set of circumstances which had enabled them to cover some seventy kilometers on their first day: as for him, he had always been in a hurry to start working. Mor-Zamba, who was more deliberate and more gloomy as well, objected that they had made a mistake by consciously taking unnecessary risks aboard the truck: Hurricane-Viet would certainly not have commended them.

"Risks, grandpa?" replied The Juggler ironically, "what risks?"

"Well, suppose a patrol of twenty Saringalas stops your truck and decides to examine our papers. What are you going to do? Perhaps you're going to kill twenty of them? And with a single blow at that? Like Tarzan? For, after all, you surely haven't forgotten Hurricane-Viet's commandment: never submit to any verification of your papers. But refusing to be questioned isn't the whole story; more than any-thing else, you've got to avoid putting yourself in a situation that might attract the attention of a Mameluke. That isn't what we're doing right now."

---

Mameluke: slang term for a member of the African gendarmerie

22

"You really don't have to get angry, grandpa. Whatever the situation is, there's always a way out, I know! Trust me and keep a sharp eye on your little Jo The Juggler."

All at once the truck stopped, as it appeared to them, without having slowed down. The driver raised a small corner of the tarp near the front of the truck bed and requested his passengers to get down and follow him. His invitation was so tersely delivered that they were puzzled and possibly a bit apprehensive. When they complied, they discovered that they were in the middle of a village which was already half asleep. The driver led them inside a house where he had been expected: in a large room, there was a table covered with a white tablecloth and set for a single person. Shortly afterwards, a young boy, probably about the age of Evariste, came to complete the table setting. As sometimes still occurred at villages in that part of the country when a family was receiving a city slicker in whom they saw a future son-in-law, the silverware and china were somewhat pretentious. The fact is that, in the rather surprising absence of the other members of the family, the young boy never said a word while serving them a meal which seemed exquisite to the Rubenists, accustomed as they were to more rudimentary fare; the good food even succeeded in arousing Evariste, who until then had still been inclining toward sleep.

Then they returned to the truck, but instead of setting out again, they waited until a very well dressed and——to the best of their ability to judge in the dim yellowish pall of the cab's overhead light—— beautiful young woman came and sat down next to the driver. Several kilometers later he stopped again and, abandoning the young woman in the cab, once more took his friends to eat at a house in the middle of a half-sleeping village. When they left, two young women were sitting side-by-side in the cab to keep the driver company. After a third stop, three young women had crowded into the narrow metal harem. Leaning discretely against the sides of the truck and experiencing decidedly mixed emotions, the Rubenists admired the incomparable skill of a man who could inveigle three equally young, equally beautiful, and no doubt

23

equally ambitious women into living peacefully and
even happily together. Fascinated, they watched him
talk while gesticulating wildly with his right hand
and plying the steering wheel with the other one; he
undoubtedly proved loquacious and even quite funny,
for the three women burst out laughing in concert,
thrusting their lips apart, shaking convulsively,
gasping for breath, tilting back there heads, and
placing a hand over their hearts.

"Now there's an interesting state of affairs.
You yourself shouldn't have missed trying it," said
The Juggler to Mor-Zamba, who remained inexorably
silent. "Well then," resumed the scoundrel, "What do
you think of that profession?"

"Nothing," replied Mor-Zamba calmly.

Once again, the truck stopped, but this time, it
seems, only after gradually slowing down and parking
with great care on the right-hand side of the road.
At about the same instant, the Rubenists heard the
driver climb the railings on the side of the truck,
and in the faint glimmerings of the tiny overhead
light in the cab, they saw him fold back the tarp in
several vigorous, almost violent movements while
humming as if he were the happiest man in the world.

"That's it; get up, my good fellows," he said
animatedly when he had finished extricating his
passengers. "We'll be parting company. You stay on
the colonial, you lucky dogs. I turn off here on this
side road."

But he had extinguished all the lights on his
vehicle, except the overhead light in the cab, and it
was in vain that he pointed with his finger, because
the Rubenists could see nothing in the darkness. As
the three men and the child first tilted up the
Raleigh, still bedecked in the incongruous cargo that
had been stowed all over it, and then gently lifted it
down to the pavement for fear of losing something in
an overly hasty manoeuvre, the driver proceeded, "I
load the truck tomorrow about noon or ten o'clock;
then I return slowly to Fort Negre. That contraption
of yours is a regular baggage wagon. And what about
you, what are you going to do now? I can put you up
for the night. Where I'm going is only a few kilometers from the colonial; you can do whatever you

24

like."

"It would be better for us to walk a bit further,
maybe until daybreak," replied Mor-Zamba. "After
that, we'll see. What usually happens on this road?"

"After this? Oh, nothing, absolutely nothing. I
thought you chose this region, because you knew
something about it."

Having gotten off the truck to take a breath of
fresh air, the three young women joined the men, and
although they took part, albeit sparingly, in the
conversation, the Rubenists could barely make them out
in the inky blackness of the night.

"Are there any short-cuts?" asked Mor-Zamba.

"Of course," the three young women replied almost
in chorus. "And it's a good thing! Otherwise, how
long it would take to reach one's destination on the
white man's road, which is so long! Whereas on the
black man's secret paths, one's journey is soon at an
end. You'll see! You only have to ask the people in
the villages you'll be passing through. But don't go
taking any chances on the short-cuts at night, you'll
get lost."

"As for the rest," concluded the driver, "don't
worry, my good fellows. No ambushes here, and thus no
Mamelukes, no Saringalas; for the moment, it is certainly the most peaceful part of the colony."

With a fondness that was enhanced by an extremely
melodious voice, one of the women teasingly called his
attention to the fact that, with the coming of independence, the colony had just been transformed into a
republic, but he seemed to get angry again, as he had
in the bar at Saneongo, and began speaking with great
volubility, alternating between sarcasm and jest; the
French expression "screwed-up nigger" or its varient
"the screwing of niggers" recurred like a periodic
refrain during his diatribe. "It's incrediable how
long people hold on to their illusions," he concluded
with a kind of simple-minded and almost farcical
lucidity. "Go on, brothers, have a pleasant trip; the
Good Lord is watching over us all."

Mor-Zamba and his companions shook hands in turn
with the driver and the three young women before
plunging determinedly into the unknown. In a short
while, they heard the truck start and move off down

the side road, where it jolted along for some time,
bouncing noisily on its worn-out shock absorbers.

# CHAPTER 2

The three Kola-Kolans were immediately confronted with the first actual trial of their long march—the torment of a forest gloom at night beneath a moonless sky, overcast despite the time of year. At first they had hoped their eyes would soon become accustomed to those abysmal depths, but after a while they knew that that would not occur, not even for Mor-Zamba, who had grown up in the heart of this country. The darkness was so thick that they imagined each step would precipitate them over a cliff or into an assortment of other dangers which they could not exactly picture to themselves but of which the immanence seemed beyond the slightest doubt.

They soon realized they were seeing nothing but the road gliding between twin hedges of palm trees which arched their branches across it and, except at the entrance to a village or a hamlet, plaited an unbroken canopy above their heads; in such cases, emerging from the tunnel, they found themselves under a no less murky dome as they passed between parallel lines of bulky shadows, no doubt the squat, low-roofed houses of the peasants. At that time of night in these villages, no man's voice could ever be heard; nor a woman's, nor even the barking of a dog; always a somber and martial silence reigned, barely interrupted at times by a new-born's uncertain wail, which would be immediately smothered, probably by a mother's breast being stuffed into its mouth. In this mute wasteland, the rasping of several pairs of sandals and the metallic laments of the Raleigh, creaking inter-

mittently beneath its load, reverberated like the din
of a small army.

But once the village or hamlet was behind them
the three travelers were again embraced by the murky
depths, like shipwrecked sailors clutching desperately
to a lifeboat from some other world and surprised at
being able to fill their lungs with fresh air rather
than inhaling ooze and slime with every breath. More
intensely alert, more tense and aggressive than the
first wave of combat troops mounting an assault, they
advanced with an exaggerated deliberation, peering
suspiciously at the countless ambuscades of the night
and groping forward like a trio of blind men, all
dependent on the same unfamiliar staff. If they
brushed against the dense blades of lemon grass
planted on either side of the highway, they jumped
back in the sudden realization that they had narrowly
avoided miring the Raleigh in one of the two drainage
ditches. What difficulties they would have had then
in trying to extricate it! They hurriedly guided the
machine back to what they thought was the center of
the road. In this manner, they zigzagged wildly,
buffetted by whirlwinds of gloomy shapes which, in
reality, never moved at all.

Sometimes, it seemed as if the Raleigh were
suddenly running  away from them, prancing, plunging,
diving ahead. They braced themselves to calm it and
hold it back; together they stiffened, and their
muscles grew taut. They had just been caught off
guard by a very steep downhill grade that had opened
in front of them like an elephant trap. Further on,
however, during the corresponding uphill climb, they
had to push the contraption, planting a stiff leg
behind them, stretching out their arms at full length,
bending their backs, and exhausting the supply of air
in their lungs.

The general state of emergency had not yet been
declared and endlessly renewed, as it would be later,
nor had the authorities imposed curfews anywhere
except in the white sections of the largest urban
areas. Even so, they saw but a single vehicle on the
road that night, a six or seven ton truck according to
Mor-Zamba's estimate, and that had been his line of
business. For a very long time, perhaps fifteen

28

minutes or more, and from a great distance, the forest, the hills, the valleys, everything reverberated with its incessant, plaintive thunderous trumpeting; as it approached, the clamor grew steadily louder until it became truly monstrous, like the battle cry of an elephant herd in a nightmare.

"Maybe it's a convoy of Saringalas," said The Juggler. "We'll have to take cover. If they see us, they'll undoubtedly stop and want to indulge themselves in the verification of our papers, or perhaps something even worse."

As he silently rehearsed the gratuitous atrocities committed by the bullies of Baba Toura The Sot, Mor-Kinda feverishly ransacked one of the eronmous saddle-bags that hung from either side of the baggage-carrier; he soon extracted the desired object, a flashlight, or as they say in Kola-Kola, a "torch." He aimed its white metallic beam toward the ditch on his right, which happened to be the closest at that moment, and, beyond it, toward the row of palm trees planted behind a low embankment.

"Turn that thing off!" commanded Mor-Zamba in an emotion-filled tone of authority. "Turn it off now. Are you mad? We've seen enough. . . ."

It was not without some difficulty that they succeeded in ferrying the unwieldy contraption across the ditch and over the small embankment before hiding it behind a palm tree and taking cover themselves behind another one, from where they kept a watchful eye on the road. They hardly had a moment to wait. Bursting onto the scene like a bolt of lightning, the incredible brilliance of the truck's headlights revealed an extraordinary splendor in the endlessly straight line of a highway stretched tautly at the base of two sheer cliffs of jungle, as if it were a border that plunged into the abyss.

"Look at that," said Mor-Zamba to his two companions with a mixture of admiration and accusation in his voice. "In a place like this, it's child's play for a driver to spot the glow of a cigarette in a smoker's hand and even easier for him to detect the glare of a flashlight. Under certain circumstances, the person carrying the light can even be seen around a bend. If you don't want to be seen on the road, never show any light."

"Don't cry over spilt milk, grandpa. You're right," pleaded The Juggler humbly for once. "But tell me then, how can you do it any other way? Grope along somehow and lose a lot of time? Don't forget that I waited for an emergency; you didn't even suspect that I had a flashlight, did you? And yet there was no lack of opportunity to use it. Do you think they could have picked up our trail?"

The beast hurled forward in a rage along the washboard surface of the highway, but the three Rubenists relaxed as they savored the sound of the engine's roar, which swelled and increased in intensity rather than diminishing—a sign that would have alarmed them. Finally, the thunder was upon them, and its explosive din momentarily deafened them. They hardly had time to take in the characteristic profile of an enormous rig with a canvas tarp drawn tightly over its distended flanks and to conclude that it was a commercial vehicle; it bounded in front of them as if lifted off the ground by a surge of gloomy shapes which immediately unfurled behind it and swelled into a mountain that submerged the travelers once more.

After the course of the highway had been illuminated by the truck's headlights, it remained etched in their memories, so that when they returned to it, they were able to walk for a long time without difficulty.

"Why didn't you tell us you had a flashlight?" Mor-Zamba asked Jo The Juggler in a muffled tone of voice.

"Why should I tell you if we aren't going to use it in any case?" replied Mor-Kinda, muffling his voice as well.

"What do you mean? You yourself just used it," Mor-Zamba pointed out.

"Well, grandpa, you just proved to me—rightfully, I'll admit—how wrong I was. In the end, you see, it's like guns. Do you remember what Hurricane-Viet said about guns? Not to use them unless you can't do it any other way. And even then. . . . In actuality, I'm convinced there's always another way; you're certainly not going to contradict me now, are you, grandpa? Well then, it'll be the same thing with our other scarce but valuable resources. What's your opinion?"

"All the same, you're mixing up two very different things; guns and flashlights have nothing in common. As for guns, we either don't know how to use them very well, or we don't know how to use them at all; therefore, we have to avoid handling them as much as possible. It's only logical."

"And you think we know how to use a flashlight? Seriously? Imagine for a moment that it breaks down, eh? You wouldn't have thought of that, would you, Bumpkin?"

They had to stop talking; after a bend in the road, the highway had carried them into a village, where it glided between the two obligatory lines of dismal shapes which, this time, appeared unexpectedly more solid, more tangible. And even a rooster crowed once, twice, three times. Unaccustomed to the extraordinary acquisition which had adorned his wrist since the previous day, The Juggler had forgotten it, but he now consulted its pale dial by placing it several centimeters from his eyes; at the edge of the village, he announced to his companions, "Four o'clock, my good fellows! The sun will probably be up shortly. What're we going to do then?"

"It's very simple," declared Mor-Zamba with authority, as he regained the bravado of an exile who lives on the outskirts of generally accepted custom. "It's very simple, because our primary problem is to elude all official controls, to avoid attracting the attention of unfriendly individuals, or better yet, to avoid attracting anyone's attention, if possible, especially on the highway. I assume that hasn't changed much in twenty years; thus, even far from the city, you can always run into undesirable characters on the highway. In contrast, you run few risks on the trails, regardless of whether they're large or small; the authorities hardly ever venture back into these parts. At daybreak, we'll make ourselves comfortable at a spot where the road crosses a depression, as it often does, on a bridge which straddles the river. We'll strip to our waists to give the impression that we're bathing; there's no particular time for taking a bath here, and people even prefer to do it early in the morning rather than later in the day. Thus,

31

nobody will notice. In reality, as far as we're concerned, it might even do us some good to dampen our faces and soak our feet in the water; it makes you feel better after walking for such a long time at night. For that matter, travellers can stay as long as they like on the banks of a river without drawing undue attention to themselves. That's what we'll do, at least until someone from here passes by and can give us some information. After that, we'll see."

"Yes indeed," said The Juggler approvingly with a low whistle. "Your scenario holds up; one might almost say you were a seasoned veteran of the war against The Sot, like me, huh!"

Little by little and without their even becoming conscious of it, they began to proceed less tentatively; their stride became firmer at the same time that the whining wings of a partridge taking off, the chirring of a cricket, and an antelope's hasty flight into the bush could be heard—a whole confusion of sounds which from then on reassured them rather than turning the blood in their veins to ice. A very delicate, dull grey film began to coalesce high up there on the surface above their heads and to filter gradually down toward the bottom of the abyss, descending toward them through the spongy tissue of the night, on the edges of which it sculpted extravagant borders that seemed all the more unreal because the travellers' state of mind remained as exalted as it had been when they left the truck driver, although they were now drooping from lack of sleep and moving as if they were in another world.

Then, just as the darkness lifted perceptibly, they heard voices and became aware that they were in a place which corresponded point-for-point with the one Mor-Zamba had described a moment before; it didn't take them long to climb down unto the riverbank, cache the Raleigh in a thicket, and strip to the waist like people preparing to take a bath or just finishing one. But the voices they had heard soon faded away; perhaps it had been peasants taking the road for a short stretch on the way to their fields.

The water which they sprinkled over themselves and in which they soaked their feet was extremely cool, and it did wake them up, giving them new strength and even restoring Jo The Juggler's lively, bantering spirit, for when he went over to the Raleigh, he returned with a bottle of alcohol, from which he poured several large draughts directly into his mouth without disconcerting Mor-Zamba but eliciting a somewhat puzzled glance from Evariste.

"It's strange," remarked The Juggler, as he dried his mouth on the back of his hand, "we have absolutely nothing to eat. Even if you're never completely lacking for food in the sticks, we should have foreseen that we'd get hungry."

"Don't worry about me," declared Evariste, who was taking part in the conversation for the first time. "Last night with the truck driver, I must have eaten enough for a week."

"Bravo!" said Mor-Zamba. "A man—a true man—not only doesn't compain about being hungry; he never even worries about food."

"Quite right!" parried The Juggler mockingly as he brandished his bottle. "Here's the best possible sustenance for a man, a true man."

He drank a few more swallows and proffered the bottle to Mor-Zamba, who refused, claiming that if he drank so early in the morning, he would have a headache for the rest of the day. Evariste also declined the offer by explaining with utter simplicity, as he had the previous evening in the bar at Saneongo, that he never drank.

"What other loot do you have hidden away besides the flashlight and the bottle of alcohol? How long do you expect to keep that secret all to yourself?" asked Mor-Zamba.

"Don't get excited, grandpa," said The Juggler. "You'll find out soon enough, and then, as usual, you'll overreact."

About seven o'clock, when the abundant, fleecy muslin fog began to unravel, they finally saw a man approaching; he was armed with a machete that had been plentifully nicked with use.

"Are you looking for the little short-cut or the big-one?" he replied in answer to their question.

"What's the difference?" The Juggler asked him.

"On the little short-cut." the peasant responded diligently, "the path is very narrow, especially if

33

you're carrying baggage, so narrow that you yourselves occasionally have to cut the trail and with that thing there . . ." He waved his machete toward the Raleigh. "But you reach the white man's road before nightfall, and from one end to the other you stay in the forest. With the big short-cut, it's a completely different story. Although it's impossible to drive cars on it, it is large enough so that even bicycles can roll along comfortably, but not, to be sure, at full speed. You pass through a beautiful countryside, you see large villages filled with hospitable people, and you walk almost all the time in the shade. But you don't return to the white man's road for four or maybe even five days."

"But tell us then, where does the big short-cut start?" asked Jo The Juggler.

"What! Why, it's quite close, over there, a few hundred steps away; people are constantly going in and out. You mean you haven't seen them . . . ?"

"There's no reason to hesitate," Mor-Zamba decided as soon as the officious peasant had departed. "It's the big short-cut for us. Let's get the Raleigh, my good men, and be off."

Almost immediately, they had occasion to experience the hospitality that had been so highly praised by the man with the machete. After less than an hour of walking, they arrived in a village, where they saw an old man seated on the terrace in front of his modest dwelling, not far from other houses, all of which had covered openings and were completely shaded by the leaves of tall, slender banana trees. They headed toward the man, and Mor-Zamba spoke to him in the following manner: "We salute you with great respect, old man. I have walked all night long with my young brothers who are here with me."

Instead of being shocked by their unusual equipage, he received them with a certain playfulness. "And, my children, you would like to make a stop beneath an old man's roof?" he replied, completing the thrust of Mor-Zamba's unfinished request. "Well then, my house is yours; stay as long as you like. A traveler separated from his people is like an orphan; may every house be a new home for him? Thus spoke our ancestors. But the Whites came; we forgot the wisdom of the past and now think of nothing but independence. But what good is independence all by itself?"

"Not much, venerable old man!" replied Jo The Juggler, restraining himself with great difficulty from bursting into laughter and all the while reflecting to himself: "He hardly realizes how well he has described the situation."

The obliging old man raised no objection when the Kola-Kolans desired to bring the Raleigh inside the house; although they had been beyond Sandrinelli's reach for a long time and even beyond that exercised by the ordinary authorities of the Republic, the Rubenists instinctively persisted in maintaining a proper military vigilence.

The child was exhausted, even though he wouldn't have admitted it for anything in the world; he was the first to stretch out on a bamboo bed where he fell instantly into a deep and, in a manner of speaking, implacable sleep. After a spirited but comical resistence, Jo The Juggler was in turn obliged to surrender without the honors of war.

Having remained at the side of his venerable host on the terrace, Mor-Zamba never tired of drawing upon this seasoned old man's fund of knowledge in order to obtain information for himself. This part of the country was about a hundred kilometers from Fort Negre; the travellers had thus made no more than thirty kilometers under cover of the night! It wasn't much, thought Mor-Zamba, but what a victory nevertheless! Evariste and Jo The Juggler had at least matured as a result of pitting themselves against the formidable universe of darkness—its phantasms, its solitude, its despair.

He himself soon had the pleasure of hearing a confirmation of the diagnosis offered by the truck driver at Saneongo: without fully understanding what was at stake in the struggle, the local people were empassioned supporters of independence, but they hadn't really declared their sympathies for Ruben, except by flocking en masse to the rallies he or his lieutenants had organized now and then in a region where inertia produced a complete disregard for even the most ordinary calls to passive resistence. This calm had not, or at least not yet, prompted Baba

35

Toura's regime to change administrative policy in the province; on the village level, it was still being carried out by indigenous chiefs in a hierarchy which had been rather arbitrarily scrambled during the two preceding years of so-called "internal autonomy." As in the past, these poor fellows lacked any real police powers and were thus as impotent as ever; in actual fact, their function remained limited to the collection of the head-tax.

The Juggler was the first to wake up; then, by means of a rude pummeling, he succeeded in snatching Evariste from a profound sleep which, it seemed to him, was consuming the unfortunate child beyond all reasonable limits of propriety, like an aged prostitute throwing herself on an innocent youth (the rogue had a lively and somewhat unorthodox imagination). As Mor-Zamba was still rapt in conversation with the old man near the doorway, the two younger Kola-Kolans remained convinced that they had slept no more than a few hours; their unpracticed ears failed to register the bustling activity which reigned in the village—the shouts of adolescents and young children in the compounds, the sonorous gossiping of women gathered here and there in small groups, the muted clamor which usually accompanies the preparation of a family meal; their inexperience prevented them from suspecting all the changes which sleep had concealed from them. Still seated on their bamboo bed and with drowsy eyes, they therefore had no qualms about voicing their pretensions of departing forthwith.

"Why, that's interesting, fellows," interjected Mor-Zamba without turning toward them. "Nevertheless, my dear Jo, would you be so kind as to consult your watch? Aren't you ever going to get into the habit . . . ?"

"Five o'clock!" grumbled The Juggler with a curse. "Five o'clock, how is it possible? What an idiot I am. I slept all that time, me, Jo The Juggler, the scourge of the Mamelukes, the man who made a fool of Sandrinelli? I slept like a new-born baby."

"My son," the old man told him with a smile of condescension, "there's no reason to be ashamed; nothing tires one more than a long march at night.

36

That being the case, what could be more natural than to restore one's strength with a long sleep?"

"Eh, fellows," added Mor-Zamba, "you might like to take a little piss? Go on behind the house."

More restless, plucky, and determined than judicious—in brief, a true soldier—Jo The Juggler immediately got to his feet, but then, to the amusement of his interlocuters he suddenly began to stump along while twisting his face into a hideous grimace and crying out in pain. He finally reached Mor-Zamba's chair and collapsed in the dust next to it.

"It can't be true!" he said in a panic as he took off his plastic sandals and looked at his swollen feet. "Tell me it isn't true. At Kola-Kola and Fort Negre, I walked just as far, if not further. What the hell happened?"

Evariste couldn't stand up or even remain sitting; he stretched out again on the bamboo bed, renouncing all sense of dignity, and it was there that they had to feed him as if he were a bed-ridden old man. As a matter of fact, their host soon called over a young peasant woman, his daughter-in-law, who lived in the adjacent house, and said to her, "I realize that you only returned a short while ago from your fields, but I know you well enough to assume that your meal is ready."

"It is ready," the peasant woman responded artlessly.

"Then bring it to us."

They had to serve Evariste separately, for he remained lying down as he more or less acrobatically lapped up the native bitter leaves and devoured the steamed maize which accompanied it—a traditional peasant repast in this province. Immediately after that, he fell asleep again.

"My dear Jo," burst out Mor-Zamba in the midst of dinner, "what time do you think we left the truck driver yesterday? I'm asking you a simple question, knowing full well that you never dreamed of looking at the time on your watch."

"Midnight maybe."

"Certainly not," declared Mor-Zamba. "Remember, we left Saneongo about five or six o'clock at the latest, even though a low-hanging sky created the illusion that night was already falling. All right, we had sixty kilometers to go. It's true we stopped a number of times and rested for a while each time. No matter how slowly we might have been travelling, however, it couldn't have taken us more than three hours to cover that distance. Let's say four, if we estimate generously."

"I follow you," said The Juggler. "According to you, we left the truck driver at the very latest about ten o'clock then? Furthermore, I remember it was between eight and nine this morning when we solicited this venerable old man's hospitality. Well then, we must have marched more than ten hours at a stretch? It can't be true."

"Oh, yes it can," said Mor-Zamba. "Maybe we didn't actually march all the time, but remaining on our feet that long was enough to inflict a certain damage on the lower extremities of our persons, wasn't it, old boy?"

"You mean your legs and feet are sore too, as if they were made of jelly?"

"Come on!" exclaimed the old man with a sly smile. "If not, he would be more beast than man."

"That's exactly what I was thinking. And now, Bumpkin, it's between the two of us to see who will be on his feet first."

"That's it, old chap, we'll run the race tomorrow. While we're waiting, this fine old man, this father whom Providence saw fit to place on our path, insists that we spend the night under his roof. Do you accept this offer, Jo?"

"What do you think! Make it twice."

Jo, the seasoned veteran, didn't realize how truly he had spoken. The next day, far from being able to contest a footrace with Mor-Zamba, The Juggler implored that their departure be deferred until he had recovered full use of his feet and legs. For that matter, the child was in even worse shape; shivering in spite of the wood fire that had been kept burning at the foot of his bed, he remained curled up in a ball like a hunting dog, his eyes alternately closed or staring wildly into space.

"What's wrong with him?" asked Jo The Juggler, more annoyed than worried.

"Oh, it's nothing," claimed the old man. "I know, I have more than twenty grandchildren of that age or even younger. It's only overtiredness."

He reassured the two Kola-Kolans, promising to care for the young boy according to traditional practice in that part of the country and declaring that by the end of the day Evariste's symptoms shall have disappeared. All that was necessary would be for the child to remain with him. As for Mor-Zamba and Jo The Juggler, an entire dwelling a few houses away had just been vacated for their exclusive use.

At the end of the day, when everyone had returned from the fields and brought the village completely back to life, people came running from all directions to welcome the two able-bodied strangers, and each of them insisted upon entertaining them that evening in his own home.

"Come to my house," they implored. "Come enjoy for a short while the hospitality of a man, a man of modest means to be sure, but one who knows how to respect the traditions of hospitality inherited from his noble ancestors."

Pressed from all sides, the two Rubenists displayed an embarrassed hesitancy as they explained why they needed to remain within earshot of their incapacitated young brother. Such a show of familial devotion deeply moved their would-be host, who excused himself while cursing the unfortunate situation and preparing, or so it seemed, to beat a retreat.

"But even though circumstances caused your generous desire to miscarry, why not spend this evening here with us?" proposed Jo The Juggler. "When brothers become acquainted, what difference does it make where they meet?"

"Instead of words," the other smiled approvingly, "it is honey which comes forth from your lips."

Actually, the visitors had barely assembled when Jo The Juggler proposed to treat them, and for that reason, he almost immediately sent someone to fetch a supply of local rum from the peasant who, according to the testimony of his guests, had the best reputation for making it. On that occasion, he had flaunted such a thick wad of small bills that Mor-Zamba was shaken, for he was suddenly able to weigh the havoc which the former delinquent had wrought as a way of bidding farewell to the home of Sandrinelli, alais The Gaullist. As night was falling, the Rubenists' house was already overflowing, and the rot-gut of the most renowned distiller in the village was flowing freely; it was, after all, nothing more than the "Blessed-Joseph" which the people of the village had baptized in their own fashion. The peasants from this backward part of the world had apparently made as much progress in this sector as the residents of Fort Negre, if not those of Kola-Kola itself.

In these nonchalant, down-at-the-heel, hedonistic villagers, Mor-Zamba could already recognize the inhabitants of the larger town Ekoumdoum; it seemed to him as if the present gathering offered a portent of the events which undoubtedly awaited him in Abena's native place, which would henceforth perhaps become his own as well. He was gratified by the ease with which Jo The Juggler flourished in the midst of their visitors, as if he had always lived among them.

For the moment, Jo The Juggler contrived to mystify these people, who were so open, so willing to learn, so trusting.

"Where are you going like this?" the peasants asked him.

"To the place where we were born! Isn't it obvious in the happiness that radiates from our faces and in the cheerfulness of our conversation?"

"And what was the long trip from which you are returning?"

"From the city, of course; take a look at our baggage. We went to seek our fortunes in the city, and there you have it; it's a task accomplished. Why grow uselessly old then in a place which has given us all that we asked of it?"

"If all your possessions are there on that bicycle, it is certain that you are rich. All the same," they protested, "can one really say that you made your fortunes in the city?"

"What you see on the bicycle is a joke," admitted Jo The Juggler, who had an answer for everything. "In the city, we acquired fabulous riches: silverwork, china, table linen in quantities you've never seen before, sewing machines, guns, everything you can imagine. We piled it all up in trunks, suitcases, and sacks that were loaded on the backs of a whole pack of porters, for you can't drive cars on the paths leading to our place. Our porters took the usual route, which is shorter. As for us, we wanted to take the round-about way before returning to our town and basking in the triumph they have reserved for us; we wanted to familiarize ourselves once again with the simple life of humble people, who are like our fellow countrymen, in order to appear before them not as arrogant, offen-sive people returning from the city after having become wealthy, but as humble, deferential men who, rather than neglecting custom and tradition, continue to venerate them as much as anyone else."

"Being out in the country has its advantages in spite of everything!" burst out the peasants in unison, feeling flattered and pleasantly surprised; in short, they were absolutely delighted.

Then, constantly encouraged by the approval of his audience, the most eloquent of the peasants continued: "You were down there, far from your family and friends; nothing was lacking—good food, beautiful women, fine clothes, all the amenities of life—and yet you couldn't forget your part of the country. Ah, the countryside! It's because we're attached to the land that we feel we've nothing to regret. Of course we're poor, and we know it; many things, which may be of no consequence to you, would make us extremely happy, if we possessed them. An unperceptive stranger would perhaps even regard us as pitiful. We ourselves sometimes catch ourselves dreaming about other places and distant cities that are overflowing with great wealth, plastered with bank notes, and inhabited by countless sensuous women. But we struggle with our-selves each time and tell ourselves that, all things considered and despite our poverty, it's still better to live in the country."

"How well you have put it, oh, man from whose mouth flows words of great wisdom," exclaimed Jo The Juggler as he parodied the villagers' style and cast of mind. "How well you have stated it, my brother. Yet the most remarkable thing about the time we spent in the city was not the wealth we acquired there. The truth is we're taking a secret back with us."

41

"A secret!" murmured the peasants, leaning forward.

Although Mor-Zamba had frequently observed his companion's steadiness under the influence of alcohol, he himself became a bit uneasy; what might not be expected from the natural fantasy of such a rogue! Wasn't he on the verge of brushing aside their common resolve to abstain from all Rubenist propaganda during their journey—a resolve justified by their desire to avoid detection?

"Yes, yes, we're taking back a secret, and I will reveal it to you," continued Jo The Juggler after having quaffed a supply of rum. "Listen well to the parable my tender, loving mother used to tell while putting me to sleep when I was very small. A man left his native town, and the love of travelling carried him to a country where a magic plum-tree grew: its fruit was so delicious that, once a person had tasted it, he could no longer exist without it, and, be-witched by its spell, he would take up residence in the vicinity of that marvelous tree. This is pre-cisely what our young man did, for the soft flesh of that extraordinary plum soon made him forget his family and friends. Now, they in turn were astonished not to see him return, and to one of their citizens they delegated the mission of bringing him back, but they awaited his return in vain, for he too had been captivated by the fatal plum-tree. Other ambassadors were dispatched, and each time their fate was equally disastrous for the town. One day, however, they designated a man of nearly miraculous strength to be a member of a new delegation. What did he do when he arrived at the place with his brothers and discovered the truth? He pulled up the magic plum tree—its branches drooping with all its fruit and its trunk bristling with all its roots—and, followed by his fellow citizens who had been held captive by it, he carried it in his arms back to his own town. Well then, instead of gradually losing all its sons and daughters, this fortunate town experienced the influx of men from other towns, men who had tasted the wonderful plum and, being unable to live without it, took up residence in its vicinity."

"Are you really carrying back home the secret

42

that people go to the city to find?" they asked.

"That's what I'm beating my brains out trying to tell you."

"Well, what is it then?"

"Ah, no, not that, not that; ask me anything except that. I took an oath not to reveal our secret before returning home. You know what it is to take an oath. I would be struck by lightning, crushed, burned to a crisp, pulverized, shrivelled up, and vaporized by the spirits of my ancestors. No, anything but that."

As he replied with this final retort, The Juggler had crouched down next to a man who held a drum between his legs, waiting for the proper moment to begin playing; the Kola-Kolan undertook, somewhat awkwardly, to pound on the taut membrane with both hands, much to the amusement of his immediate neighbors, one of whom immediately volunteered to initiate him into the rudimentary techniques of the instrument, which soon began to resound in cadence. Not far from them, a man kept time with the rhythm by spasmodically jerking his shoulders, despite the fact that he was still sitting down; then, encouraged by the audience, he got up and essayed a few tentative steps. The pleasure of dancing radiated from his face, almost as if he were entranced. From the shadows, a woman's voice entoned a syncopated comic song. Other men got up and entered the spontaneously formed circle. Among them, Jo The Juggler was not the last to display his ardor; Sandrinelli's former servant actually adapted to his new activities like a fish in water.

When their guests had finally left, Mor-Zamba, who had been waiting for this moment, pounced on the rogue. "If you continue to flaunt your money like you did all evening long," he said, lowering his voice but not without giving vent to all his anger and all his disapproval, "then we won't be travelling the same route together."

"What have we got to lose, eh? Just what have we got to lose? Tell me."

"You've got your money to lose, that's what! That's nothing, eh? You've even got your life to lose."

"Now, that's a new one. My life to lose, get

43

myself killed! By whom, grandpa? By these raga-muffins? Listen, did you take a good look at them? Can you imagine them stealing or killing anyone at all? If it were possible, you'd know it, certainly! Maybe it wasn't you who told me over and over how these backcountry folk allowed themselves to be scandalously plundered by white traders and their accomplices of Robert's ilk? Well then, you know, if they were capable of getting their dander up, they would already have started by eliminating all those pitiful, miserly cheats."

"You're making fun of them. How you must despise them!"

"Listen, you've got it all wrong, Bumpkin. I'm not making fun of them at all. I only wanted to make clear that these clodhoppers are just the same as those in mama's part of the country. Well, that's all there is to it; they're cast from the very same mould. All peasants must be the same, no matter where they're from. Did you see? In the beginning, strangers like us are always infidels. All right, one merely gives the lie to these preconceived notions by making liberal use of 'my tender, loving mother,' 'respect for the spirits of the ancestors,' 'love of customs and tradition,' and the trick is turned. It's good to know that, no? It was enough to remember what I had seen in my mother's village. Ah, yes, above all you can't forget their mania for drums; the drum alone can be worth the friendship of an entire army of peasants. Our party was pretty successful in any case, wasn't it, Bumpkin? You're fortunate to have me, for without me, I don't know what you'd do."

The next day, Mor-Kinda, alias The Juggler, could once again walk more or less normally. Cured by the rest which a two-day layover in the village had made possible, his legs and feet regained nearly all their previous agility.

It was hardly the same for the child, contrary to the promises of the old man who had been caring for him. He remained in bed, curled up like a hunting dog beneath the well-worn blanket that had been tossed over him; despite the wood fire blazing constantly nearby, he continued to shiver as he had the day before. These symptoms had been joined by two addi-

tional ones. While his companions had been cele-
brating with their new friends the previous day,
Evariste had hardly eaten a thing. He also coughed
convulsively and often spit up quantities of phlegm,
or he became delirious and whimpered almost inaudibly.
When they were once again alone, Mor-Zamba confided
his anxieties about Evariste to Jo The Juggler. "When
old peasants promise to cure an ailment quickly, it's
never a serious matter," he declared bitterly. "I
should have remembered that."

The Juggler's only reply was to walk over to the
Raleigh, take down one of the sacks, and conduct his
friend into the most respectable room of the little
house that had been placed at their disposition—the
bedroom usually occupied by the master of the house
and furnished principally with a blanket that covered
a wooden bed, on which the two travellers had con-
scientiously refrained from sleeping. The Juggler
poured the contents of the sack onto the taut blanket.
Then, stricken by a fearful admiration and trembling
with emotion, Mor-Zamba began to examine the well-
stocked medicine chest and the plentiful supplies
which had suddenly been spread out upon the bed; it
seemed to him that there was enough there to cover the
needs of a combat batallion for many weeks.

The Juggler had surpassed himself when he
pillaged the infirmary at the high school. Passing
rapidly over two syringes as well as assorted compresses and bandages, Mor-Zamba's gaze was attracted
to a thermometer in a shiny case and numerous boxes of
antibiotics. He immediately went to take the
patient's temperature and returned, exclaiming, "More
than a hundred and four degrees! We should have
expected it. I believe I know what it is. At the
Governor Leclerc labor camp, it was the standard
ailment, and I've treated a thousand cases of it.
Necessarily. People who had no preparation and were
not accustomed to it were left outside in bad weather.
Without realizing it, that's exactly what we did, and
with a child too. At least the whites always did it
with adults. I'm going to give him penicillin all day
long; it's undoubtedly bronchitis. And these days,
bronchitis is usually treated with antibiotics."

As he leaned once more over the bed to choose

45

what he needed from among the boxes of medicine, he suddenly jumped back, like a peasant whose blood turns to ice in the realization that he had come within a hair's breadth of placing his foot on a nest of vipers. The Juggler had just unwrapped the rest of his booty from the school plateau and placed it on the bed; what had startled Mor-Zamba was the cold glint, like that in the shifty, fatal eye of a reptile, emanating from an old-fashioned, under-and-over shot-gun and a very small chrome-plated hand-gun, which he later recognized as a cavalry musket and a gentleman's revolver. Both guns nestled amidst cardboard boxes of ammunition, as he learned in the course of time.

But there was also a prodigious quantity of khaki shirts with epaulettes (perhaps Sandrinelli's entire stock), not to mention a pair of binoculars, an enormous knife with a safety catch, a portable electric lamp of classic proportions, a tiny lamp which resembled a fountain pen, a pair of outdoorsman's boots that The Juggler called "squishers," and a half-dozen blankets which had served to wrap up all these provisions.

"Put away those guns!" implored Mor-Zamba, who had regained his composure. "Put away those guns, put them away immediately."

"Calm yourself, old man! Calm yourself! I told you that you'd go into a panic when you saw my loot from the school plateau. How emotional you are! Almost like a young girl. And I who took you for a real fighting man. Yes, yes, I'm going to wrap these guns in the same packet as Hurricane-Viet's."

"All right, but do it quickly."

In fact, Mor-Kinda proceded in a leisurely fashion to untie a small square of household linen, revealing several thick wads of bank notes to the view of his friend, whose breathing became more and more irregular as he took cognizance of this diabolical good-for-nothing's latest feat.

"In the name of God, in the name of God," he repeated softly.

"You're lucky to have me, eh, Bumpkin? Otherwise, I'd sure like to know how you'd get along."

"That too, you found it in the school complex?"

"Not at all, it was in our kitty; you know that.

Damned Mor-Zamba! You'll make me die laughing. Where do you expect me to find so much money at one time, if not in a toubab's house? You know, in spite of my brother-in-law's bad inclinations, he was far from being stupid. Just think about this proposition, which he frequently put forth to us: money, real money, is still only to be found in the houses of toubabs. In actual fact, I was the one who taught him this particular truth, and without ever, or, almost ever, having been to school either. Yes, indeed, I picked up the cookies in Sandrinelli's house; it's the strongbox from the school complex."

When Mor-Zamba returned a half-hour later, after he had gone to care for the child, he remained subject to a somber mood which caused him to regard his companion with a fixed and drawn gaze, as if the rogue had committed some indescribable sacrilege before his very eyes.

"Well then, toubib, how are things going?" said Jo The Juggler to tease him lightheartedly.

"As soon as the young one can get up," declared Mor-Zamba, making a strenuous effort to control himself so that his voice would not quaver. "As soon as the young one can get up, are you listening to me? Without waiting another minute, I mean immediately, well, then we'll be on our way. A toubab won't permit anyone to take that sort of thing from him, and in such large quantities, without breaking his neck to recover them and punish the guilty parties. No matter how far you run, my good fellow, from now on Sandrinelli'll always be at your heels, believe me. You don't know these people."

"Oh, yes I do, Bumpkin; oh, yes I do! I can even say that, if there's anyone I know well, or better than well, it's these people. They're like everyone else, old chap, not tireless, noble, far-sighted, and superior as they'd like us to believe, but lazy, mean, stupid, and petty. Sandrinelli will soon have forgotten everything I took from him, simply because he will soon have replaced it, see. It means nothing at all to him, hardly more than a bottle of beer might mean to you. What frightens you the most? The double-barrelled shot-gun? It won't walk away by itself, see. The revolver? It's a toy; it's never killed anyone. Is it the musket then? I've had it for years, you see, and nothing has ever happened to me. Remember the night we surprised the Saringalas as they were torturing Ruben, no doubt with the intention of assassinating him? Yes, yes, yes, you recall that the Mamelukes never found the third musket? Here it is. Admit that it didn't happen yesterday. Now, if you insist that we clear out of here right away, you have only to draw up your orders, grandpa, and they will be executed immediately."

Mor-Zamba quickly readopted the gestures, the words, and all the other successful habits of the irreplaceable replacement male nurse he had been at the Governor Leclerc labor camp, but the pencillin was undoubtedly inadequate as a treatment, and it was slow to produce its affect on the young patient. To the great disappointment of the makeshift doctor, it took five whole days for Evariste not even to get well, but just to regain the force to stand firmly on his legs. That sufficed for Mor-Zamba to drag his two younger companions away from the rustic delights of their first, but oh so memorable, stopover.

They were passing through a rugged area. Constantly the three travellers had to brace themselves to subdue the Raleigh when it bolted down the hills, only to exhaust themselves pushing it uphill again, gasping for breath and dripping with sweat which gleamed in the broiling sun. Yet beneath the foliage in the valleys, it suddenly became quite dark, and they were overcome with an extremely cool, almost glacial, dampness.

Once in a while, they met or overtook other groups of travellers. First, voices could be distinguised among the thousand and one calls of the forest, springing forth here and there like ephemeral tongues of flame. As one came nearer, scattered fragments of conversation could be made out. Then, burning with curiosity to finally see those who could be heard so distinctly, one scrutinized the shadows beneath the underbrush. The fact that their actual appearance kept one waiting for such a long time was like a small mystery which made one uneasy. And suddenly one was face to face with them: they would be crowded together on a fallen tree trunk or a large rock, having taken a casual pause to refresh themselves. Friendly greetings were exchanged with them, and one was often invited to share a modest repast assembled from stocks already beginning to shrivel around the edges or grow rancid. On these occasions, which unfortunately occurred all too seldom, Jo The Juggler never failed to extract suddenly from amidst the baggage on the Raleigh—which served in a sense as his magician's sleeve—a flask of imported alcohol or a bottle of local rum that he had sequestered there, although no one ever knew how or when; he offered each person a measure of it, which he poured parcimoniously into a tiny glass that he always carried with him; in the end, he tilted back his head, gripped the neck of the bottle between his teeth, and gorged himself with alcohol, allowing it to run down his throat before rinsing his mouth leisurely, his cheeks bloated with air as much as with liquor.

It was a densely populated area; the Kola-Kolans passed through so many attractive villages that they had more than enough places from which to choose when deciding where to stay for the night. By diminishing his endurance, Evariste's convalescence increased the time it took them to reach colonial number 3 again; instead of the four or five days predicted by the peasant with the machete, they needed a full week. In reply to the question which Mor-Zamba obsessively posed to them, those who lived along the highway assured them, to Jo The Juggler's great satisfaction, that no unusual traffic had been observed recently.

Each time a heated discussion between Jo The Juggler and Mor-Zamba ensued, one endeavoring to demonstrate the absurdity of the other's fears, while the other, on the contrary, ardently sought to justify them. In addition to his already familiar line of argument, Jo The Juggler contended that Sandrinelli, far from being able to imagine that his former house-boy had joined up with two other lascars, was incapable of guessing which of the six principal routes the thief might have taken out of the capital, assuming that he left Fort Negre at all. Mor-Zamba pictured The Gaullist scouring in turn each of the six highways which rayed out from the capital, just to make certain that no stone remained unturned; with a decent car,

49

there was nothing to it.

"I can see it from here," affirmed The Juggler as he burst out laughing sarcastically. "I can see it very well; Sandrinelli certainly doesn't know which of the six highways we took out of Fort Negre, but he know very well about how far away we must be, let's say a hundred and fifty, maybe two hundred kilometers from the capital. Well then, imagine him covering that distance round-trip every day on each of the highways serving the capital. Can you imagine? Six times two hundred kilometers multiplied by two. Indeed, and driving all that time, who would play nursemaid to Baba Toura The Sot? For our immortal hero needs an experienced person to watch over him; that's not going to change, simply because he was catapulted into the Presidency of the Republic. Come on, Bumpkin, admit that you're not making sense. And you, Evariste, what do you think?"

"Not the slightest doubt, Sandrinelli's finished," the child declared sententiously, ominously.

They then struggled along such narrow footpaths that they really began to despair when they compared their present experience with their previous ones. Pushing the Raleigh had become an excruciating torture for the three of them and especially for the helmsman; advancing single file along these shortcuts was already a hard enough task. After two days, they abandoned this solution, and when there wasn't a wide trail running parallel to the colonial highway, they resigned themselves to continuing their march at night again, even though they had to stop and sleep during the day. Hardened and seasoned by the trials of the journey, Evariste could now easily bear up under this sort of stress.

They had been gone from Kola-Kola for two weeks when they reached Dinkamenguela, the end point of colonial number 3 and two hundred and sixty eight kilometers from Fort Negre. They immediately had the Raleigh examined by a specialist, who assured them that all the principal organs of the machine were in sound health, although he did advise them to change the inner tubes, for if they did that, the bicycle would be capable, he insisted, of covering up to a

50

thousand more kilometers without any further professional care.

They remained at Dinkamenguela for about ten days, time enough for them to evaluate, select, and acquire a large supply of equipment which The Juggler, adopting an air of mystery, claimed to be absolutely necessary. They therefore loaded up with countless khaki shorts; moreover, the former delinquent, acting as leader because he possessed a certain flair for the logistics of war, had each of them acquire two perfectly fitted pairs of outdoorsman's boots, which he called "Squishers" as if he were an authority on the subject.

"What's all this good for?" asked Mor-Zamba occasionally.

"Good for?" replied The Juggler, "why, it's to disguise ourselves with later on, Bumpkin, don't you see?"

Mor-Zamba didn't insist, for he was embarrassed by the need to acknowledge his perplexity in front of The Juggler, who was always so sure of himself.

On a number of occasions, The Juggler took Evariste to the Moslem section of the city; there he obliged the boy to follow his lead by familiarizing himself with their eating and clothing habits as well as with their language and even their religious practices. Each of their visits to that part of town provided him with an opportunity to acquire some new accessory, for which he bartered interminably and with a comical sort of gaiety that was punctuated by shouts and protestations leading to breakdowns in the negotiations but inevitably followed by exaggerated gestures of reconciliation. First, it was a pair of Arab slippers, then a kind of enormous robe with very ample sleeves; The Juggler immediately put it on, and that prompted cries of amazement from the bystanders. Another time, it was a metal utensil intended for use in daily purifying ceremonies and resembling a kettle; that was the day Evariste, convinced that his companion had decided to convert to Islam, began to disdain if not detest him. Still another time, it was a large straw hat which The Juggler would, moreover, wear almost without interruption until the end of their journey. One final time, he had them show him—at what price Evariste never knew—a pair of long, narrow breeches like those worn by the people from the North under their large robes; he also acquired a turban, and for the child, who allowed himself to be outfitted without betraying his reservations, he bought a flowing tunic cut from a coarse, thick linen cloth.

When they set out again from Dinkamenguela, they once more found themselves on a trail so rudimentary that no motorized vehicle had probably ever ventured along it. How far away Fort Negre seemed to them! Now, it was like another world—perhaps an imaginary world.

Jo The Juggler's excessive self-confidence insidiously spread to his two companions, and the three Rubenists were finally unanimous in the conviction that they had forever escaped Sandrinelli and even the Mamelukes of Baba Toura, The Sot. Relaxing their vigilance, they no longer took such pains, each time they stopped, to inquire about the lay of the land they would be covering the next day, about the mood of the local people, about the risk of unpleasant encounters; they simply went forward, plunging stubbornly and almost blindly ahead. This part of the country was not, however, free of pitfalls for our travellers, who were particularly vulnerable, because they failed to realize that they remained at the mercy of some fatal accident. If the peasant villages were in general dreary and peaceful, it was still possible to pass by or even through one of the widely scattered settlements which, even in this remote part of the country, had been variously affected by the fighting which preceded independence. In diverse places and always in the most unexpected fashion, an exceptionally forceful Rubenist personality—a store keeper, a civil servant, or even a clergyman—had singlehandedly created a center of agitation and rebellion during the colonial period; once independence had been proclaimed, the soldiery of Baba Toura had quickly been called in, and they sought to eliminate these hotbeds of opposition by means of extortion and even, frequently, by means of atrocity.

But, as it actually occurred one day, the accident or fateful event could also be lurking in wait for our travellers at the intersection of their path or trail with the main highway. That morning, they entered a cluster of peasant houses arranged in the form of a cross, the longest arm of which was a prolongation of the track they were following, a rustic avenue flanked by the traditional twin rows of low, mud-walled houses. Far ahead of them, the other arm, consisting of the main highway, also stretched out between two lines of low houses. As frequently happened, the square formed by the intersection of the two streets was adorned with the house of an important personage—imposing, covered by a corrugated iron roof, standing erect on a raised terrace, and dominating the corner.

When they arrived at the level of the first houses, the travellers could see from a distance as a very large and undoubtedly strong man in uniform struggled with a procession of women at the square in front of the important personage's house; he appeared to be treating them roughly and was soon shoving them about and even molesting them, before he finally compelled them to leave the red laterite roadway and go into the imposing house with the corrugated iron roof.

Mor-Zamba had the acutest sense of danger, and he was the first to be struck by the coarse behavior of the uniformed man; he immediately warned his two companions and advised them to hide behind a nearby palmtree so they could reconnoiter the distance scene.

# CHAPTER 3

"A serious matter, my friends," Jo The Juggler declared between two low whistles as he focused the binoculars he had just pulled for the first time from one of the saddlebags.

Before long and almost on the heels of their predecessors, whose humiliation had perhaps been hidden from them by a crook in the road, more women entered the square at the intersection; in any case, it was not without apprehension that Jo The Juggler, who perceived even the smallest details of their attire and their bearing, watched them move forward in a merry group, well-proportioned beneath their short, light cotton dresses. Occasionally it seemed to him that these very young women would stop for a moment to flutter about gracefully before setting off again on their meandering way. "Village girls," thought Mor-Kinda, "walking peacefully to a wedding. They're no doubt singing to themselves."

As soon as he had finished making this observa-tion, the gigantic figure of a uniformed man loomed like a nightmare into the field of vision in his glasses; the man was raising a whip in his right hand and pointing the index finger of his left hand toward the important person's house with its corrugated iron roof, doubtlessly enjoining the women to approach and enter. Having suddenly regrouped like a flock of startled birds, they stiffened into positions of probable resistence; overcome with admiration, Jo The Juggler became fully persuaded when he saw several of them, phantom-like in his lens, motion quickly and set

54

off again with determined expressions on their faces as they sought to outflank the colossus. It was then that the orang-outang went wild: he charged into the unfortunate women and sent them flying head-over-heels to scrape and bruise themselves as they rolled in the gravelly soil on the road; he brandished his weapon, undoubtedly a bullwhip, and lashed out left and right.

Smarting with pain, some women writhed in agony; others instinctively brought a hand to the place where they had been struck and began to rub frantically.

"Bastard! Bastard! Bastard!" grumbled the sapak as he clenched his fists.

"And even at that, you're only seeing half of it," Jo The Juggler assured him, flourishing his binoculars. "What would you say, if you had these in your hands! There's a fellow who needs a little lesson; what do you think, my little papa?"

"A lesson, yes!" said the sapak approvingly, "but what lesson?"

"There's always one," Mor-Kinda declared. "Eh, grandpa?"

Overcome by emotion, Mor-Zamba did not even hear himself being called. Three other uniformed men emerged from the important person's house and strode to the giant's rescue; smaller than he, they carried rifles slung over their shoulders, and each brandished a long whip as well. They surrounded the young peasant women and obliged them to leave the roadway by pushing them in front of themselves like a flock of sheep and shepherding them into the house with the corrugated iron roof.

The rest of the village remained strangely silent and deserted, as if its usual inhabitants had fled. A more careful probe of this enigmatically forlorn setting, however, ultimately enabled the three Rubenists to discern a faint murmuring, and they immediately headed toward it by a sort of intuition; that was how they arrived at the doorway of a nearby house, which was filled with a large number of young people. Having clustered around the threshold in such a way that they could not be seen from the outside, they were watching the pulsating violence of the scene as if it were an almost routine affair. In accordance with his own personal tradition, Jo The Juggler at once offered to treat everyone to a drink if they would agree to keep the Raleigh and its load out of sight—a condition that was immediately and unanimously accepted. While the travellers were being invited to take their places alongside their hosts, the contraption was adroitly conjured away into an adjacent low-ceilinged room, the door of which was promptly shut again.

"Now," Jo The Juggler commanded as he settled himself confidently, "bring on the alcohol, and don't worry about the cost; that'll be my concern. Are they Saringalas?"

"Not even that," one of the villagers replied in a disillusioned tone of voice. "They can speak our language, although with a bit of an accent perhaps. These fellows are more from the area around Oyolo."

Mor-Zamba had appropriated the binoculars, a source of alarm to the young villagers, and was taking his turn at scrutinizing the principal actors in the scene unfolding at the intersection.

"In my opinion," he burst out suddenly as he focused the glasses, "they're not real soldiers. I've known this sort of lascar fairly well; they're auxiliaries who before independence served as watchmen in the parks and doormen in the cities. They received no military training, and they were never sent into combat, under any circumstances. They were occasionally put on display here and there to frighten the people, but their guns could only shoot blanks. I'll bet these fellows don't even make a pretence of having ammunition."

"They sometimes wear waistbands that are apparently quite well supplied with bullets," corrected the villagers.

"Cartridge belts!" the young sapak Evariste exclaimed sententiously in French.

"That doesn't mean anything," persisted Mor-Zamba.

"I don't agree!" declared Jo The Juggler. "We have to expect the worst. The Sot and Sandrinelli could be so short of soldiers that they've given some military instruction, however rudimentary, to the doormen of provincial governors' palaces and sent them out to parade in the most remote villages as a means of intimidating the people."

The young villagers confirmed Jo The Juggler's hypothesis in a way: the giant who was organizing these extortions and in whom the sapak Evariste, when he later caught sight of him in the early evening, would discover a certain resemblance to Genghis Khan, passed himself off as a sergeant in command of a patrol comprised by three individuals who had been scouring the highway for the past several months. They claimed to have been detached from a garrison that was about fifty kilometers north of there and had recently been placed under the orders of a black officer who had been promoted on the occasion of independence. What was certain is that the sergeant and his assistants apparently had no other mission than the tormenting of peasants. No excess seemed too barbarous for them.

The leader of the patrol, a real boor, was a monster perpetually between two drunken jags and an insatiable lecher. He knew but a single method of seduction; whenever he set his eye on a passing woman, whether alone, accompanied by her children or even by her husband, he imprisoned her in an important person's house, which had been requisitioned for that purpose, and gorged himself with food and drink while awaiting the night, because he was too superstitious not to defer the grand feast until the fall of darkness.

"Does the garrison often show any other signs of life?" asked Jo The Juggler nervously.

"No," they answered, "but it's there, all right. It can easily be reached by canoe, and the people from our village who have seen it as they passed by on the river would be able to testify that it actually exists."

"That isn't exactly what I meant," corrected Jo The Juggler, "but rather: do they ever send other soldiers to relieve these fellows or simply to inspect them?"

"Never," the villagers replied. "They probably don't have any vehicles at their disposition, or any stocks of gasoline either. It seems that each patrol takes over its territory for an indefinite period. People say that similar garrisons have been placed all along the highway as far as Oyolo, and even further——toward the North."

To the South, the highway, which was none other than Colonial number 13, descended directly toward the cocoa country and passed right through it; however, before that, about thirty or forty kilometers away, it gave ample berth to a catholic mission, where they had just finished building a brick church, a magnificent edifice according to the villagers, certainly the most beautiful one in the entire Republic. They insisted on this point, although they knew no more of the Republic than their own rustic canton.

For the moment, the most beautiful church in the entire Republic was weighing on the young villagers, paradoxically, as a great misfortune. The Father Superior of the mission, a certain Etienne Pichon, was extremely proud of this architectural masterpiece, and he had decided to proceed with the solemn consecration on Sunday in three days; for this unprecedented cere- mony, he had called his flock to arms, and they were scattered over a vast area, extending for dozens of kilometers in all directions. Their presence at the event was an obligation, under penalty of mortal sin. But, in addition to the children who went en masse to the mission school, Father Etienne Pichon's only faithful were women and girls who regularly attended even the most solemn ceremonies; true processionary creatures, they were just now setting out on the roads and paths. Consigned without the slightest protection to the dangers of the journey, these women would make such a glorious prey! What a feast for the sergeant and his men!

These various explanations did not all emerge from the account of a single young villager, but perhaps from all of them——one completed a thought, and another commented on it, while still another provided an illustration of it. Some of the speakers endeav- ored to lend an air of seeming detachment to their contributions, as if to justify in advance their own apathy; their lewd laughter was calculated to draw a stranger's attention to the true nature of the affair, which was after all a minor one, for no one would even dream of declaring war because a few women had been knocked about, would they? Jo The Juggler knew these kinds of people only too well; they were numerous in Kola-Kola, and he had often been at loggerheads with them. It scarcely surprised him that so many youthful and vigorous men could manifest so little concern for their own dignity in provinces so far removed from the capitol and from the white man's imperious pressures—in provinces where the customs and warlike attitudes of the ancestors might well have been better preserved. Only a few of them were incapable of concealing an anger which was, moreover, barely under control. Jo The Juggler immediately bestowed a visible affection upon this elite and set about to stimulate the desire for vengeance he saw smouldering in them, especially when a ratafia had been brought and served and after everyone, with the exception of the sapak, had downed a glassful of it.

"At Fort Negre where we come from," Jo The Juggler declared insidiously, "the Saringalas don't even respect wives and mothers. I who am speaking to you, my friends, I myself witnessed a terrible scene one day. On a bridge which commands the western approach to the city, I see this immense fellow with a rifle slung over his shoulder, a revolver in his left hand, a revolver in his right hand, hobnailed boots, ammunition belt, and everything. His back to the cement parapet, he lies in wait for young peasant women who at that early morning hour, are hurrying to reach the covered market. Suddenly this bastard motions with his hand for a group of little girls to come over, and he asks them—guess what? Well, to lift up their little dresses, and he inspects them carefully, leaning over and even touching them with his enormous gorilla paws. Believe me if you will, but he actually detained each one who had the slightest trace of fuzz. That's what the Saringalas at Fort Negre are like. But you told me these chaps speak our language; they're sons of this region. Well then, they at least respect wives and mothers, don't they?"

"It's easy to see you don't know our devil of a sergeant," a large young man responded at once; having noticed his empassioned gaze at the very beginning, Jo The Juggler was already counting on him. "Above all it's the sergeant we need to talk about; far from reining in his men, he sets the tempo for them. He's a wild animal who won't put up with any opposition or any obstacle standing between him and the satisfaction of his desires. As far as he is concerned, children, wives, and mothers don't exist. In a pinch, he'd even go after the ancestors."

"Admit that those stupid women had it coming," interrupted another, whose obviously phlegmatic temperament was no doubt paired with a fierce determination. "Yes, had it coming! They should have stayed home with their own families. Does it take no more than the first charlatan who comes along and waves the bugaboo of mortal sin to send our women running off, far away from their men and children?"

"Mortal sin? Is that a serious matter?" asked Mor-Zamba, who had never been initiated into the unfathomable mysteries of the Christian Church.

"It's certainly a very serious matter for Father Etienne Pichon," replied Jo The Juggler, restraining himself from bursting out in laughter, "but it's a fine thing for the sergeant, who, having just filled his granary with an abundant harvest (a miraculous harvest!) is now impatiently awaiting the fall of night in order to relish his favorite dish. In his place, my good fellows, how would you add spice to the anticipation of those delightful moments to come?"

Jo The Juggler's face became radiant, like that of a man possessed by a sudden illumination. The young villagers assured him they knew the sergeant well enough to predict with absolute certainty that a highly spiced chicken and rice, washed down with several bottles of Kiravi, would be a preliminary ecstacy for the uniformed man as he awaited the paradise of unbridled sensuousness.

"Would you like to avenge for once at least the honor of your women and make youselves respected, like true men?" Jo The Juggler abruptly asked the young villagers, who were taken aback by his question.

"What can we do against them?" they replied in chorus. "Those people have guns! Are we going to take up our machetes and throw ourselves against a band of armed men? Guns give orders; you know that very well."

"Guns don't always give orders," said Jo The

Juggler pensively as if speaking to himself without the least intention of entering into a discussion with anyone else, a response which merely intensified the curiosity of his host.

"How you can say that?" they asked him.

"Once upon a time," Jo The Juggler began, "there were two young men, two brothers, who had decided to go out into the wide world. Separately and one after the other, they went to consult their mother and father, for they intended to carry with them the viaticum of parental wisdom, the invaluable legacy of the ancestors. They placed before their parents a variety of situations which life was perhaps going to impose upon them. Among other questions, they separately and one after the other posed this one: 'I am in a forest, and I believe that I am alone. Suddenly the most beautiful young woman in the world appears like a radiant image in front of me. Should I reveal my desire to her in a straightforward way? Or should I attempt to seduce her?' This is the reply which the mother made to each of them in turn: 'My son, if you want to achieve domination over others and in particular with regard to the possession of women, you should be tall, handsome, strong, and proud, and you should wait. As far as the youthful radiance you mention is concerned, my son, tell her of your desire in a straightforward way, and wait scornfully for her to throw herself moaning at your feet. Otherwise, what sting of remorse will torment her for the rest of her life!' That is what the mother said. The father, as for him, delivered the following speech in turn to them: 'My son, there is no woman you can not have by deception. Trick her, but do not tame her. Instead of flaunting your desire, try to forget it. Virility and force are the same thing. Deploy them; they either frighten or humble one's partner. As far as the youthful radiance you mention is concerned, lead her into satisfying your desire in a roundabout way so that she arrives there without realizing it. Instead of scaring her away, the surprise of it will carry her off already vanquished.' That is what the father advised. Well then, my good men, what do you think actually happened to the two brothers in real life, the life of toil and suffering and not simply the life of words and fables? As a result of following the paternal maxims, the elder of the two young men always found favor among women, but no woman ever gave herself to the younger one, who had trusted in his mother. If victory over the enemy resembles the radiance of a young woman desired by everyone, isn't it clear that guns symbolize virility and that deception stands for seduction? Remember, we need to lead the beautiful young woman toward our virility without her realizing it, in a roundabout way."

It did Mor-Zamba no good at all to know from experience that alcohol nearly always produced that kind of effect on his companion; he was just as astonished at the fellow's ramblings as were their hosts, the young villagers, and the fascination that Jo The Juggler exercised over everyone present reduced him as much as the others to a passive docility, at least for the moment. Hardly an hour after the Rubenists' entry into the village, the rogue had established himself as general-in-chief and was issuing orders to a fierce-looking, enthusiastic group of young peasants who were executing them with a sense of discipline unusual even among experienced soldiers.

For the traveller, Colonial Highway 13 had two characteristics well known by administrators and other high-ranking authorities, so well known, if fact, that they had become proverbial. Along the other main arteries, white merchants, jealously guarding their monopoly on all commercial activity during the colonial period, had preferred to congregate in non-descript, out-of-the-way villages which were like oases in a vast desert where no monetary transactions ever took place; here, in contrast, well-stocked bazaars and small shops owned by all sorts of people, even Africans, were scattered along the highway like beads on a rosary, lending the countryside a deceptive appearance of prosperity and even progress. People could rather quickly and easily supply themselves there with provisions that were extremely rare and costly elsewhere.

Furthermore, those who lived along this vital route had the humiliating reputation of having allowed themselves to become so docile and even degenerate under several decades of missionary proselytizing that they no longer possessed the ancestral virtues of courage and valor. Their unfitness for the simplest form of rebellion was a commonplace topic in people's conversations, and if some congratulated themselves and rejoiced in this reputation, others lamented it bitterly. The obsequious submission of the local populace had attracted numerous European traders, seduced by the prospect of extorting a quick profit with impunity and in absolute safety; at the present time, they were taking great pains to remain ostentatiously at a distance from the political effervescence of the Indigenous Peoples, no doubt to avoid reprisals by the P.P.P. in case it ever succeeded in creating party cells in the area. For the moment, it was far from doing that.

Jo The Juggler sent out two commando groups, one toward the North and the other in a southerly direction, each one charged with a specific minutely described logistics mission. He was the first to be surprised at the speed of the villagers, who returned well before evening after having covered, at least in one case, up to ten kilometers on foot to reach a particular bazaar. They brought back all the ingredients for a banquet which the participants—guests as well as spectators—would remember longer than even the organizer himself had originally imagined. The preparation of this food was entrusted to the village's most experienced older women, whom Mor-Kinda did not forget to remunerate at the very moment he solicited their help, nourishing in this manner what had originally been a rather uncertain zeal. About seven o'clock, as night was falling, Jo The Juggler's new friends brought him the assurance that everything was ready and that he should feel free to give the signal for battle.

A large delegation, upon which the necessary pomp and solemnity had been conferred by the big city attire so carefully inspected by Mor-Kinda himself and by Mor-Zamba, made its way into the presence of the sergeant, entroned in the midst of his three confederates on the porch of the important person's house and maintaining a ferocious demeanor to which there could be no reply. With a lavish display of bows, salaams, and all the other signs of an exaggerated servility,

63

Jo The Juggler stepped forward to announce that, at the dawn of this new age of freedom, he had been duly authorized to invite a great soldier whose reputation for valor was well known (a true hero of Independence!) as well as his men to a simple meal, prepared with modest means but an ardent patriotism.

It was a respectful homage being offered to courageous soldiers, who were keeping watch with more paternal benevolence than military harshness over the peace and well-being of their honest fellow citizens, by several humble civil servants, who were passing on their way from Fort Negre to their native region with the intention of spending a well-earned six-month vacation after long years of service to the country. For, if the fatherland was a regal mother whose long, slender neck was adorned with many necklaces, didn't one of them, made of pearls, symbolize the army, while the other, less brilliant to be sure, represented the civil service? The delinquent from Kola-Kola, who had spurred his inspiration in his own fashion, continued to speak for a long time with the same eloquence, even though the intended recipient of this tin-soldier oratory had, as soon as he heard the word "meal," substituted an expression of lively interest for the cruel arrogance originally stamped on his broad, stupid face.

The valiant soldiers hardly waited for the speaker to finish before getting up and fraternizing so fervently and demonstrably with the civil servants from Fort Negre that they seemed like shipwrecked sailors separated far too long from their families; it was the occasion for truly moving embraces in a confusion which, however, did not prevent Jo The Juggler from noticing the sergeant momentarily enter the interior of the house, where he heard him giving orders with a firmness bordering on obscenity to individuals whom one could barely discern, but whom Mor-Kinda later during the banquet heard described as the numerous flunkeys of the four uniformed men. Readily put at ease, the sergeant and his men, like true soldiers, nevertheless refused to leave the house where they held the poor women prisoners until guns had been slung over their shoulders, martial-looking ammunition belts with plenty of bullets cinched around their waists, and floppy plastic sandals attached to their feet.

The uniformed men were received in a fairly spacious house not far from the one where the Raleigh, jealously guarded by the sapak, was being stored, and it can certainly be said that they didn't beat around the bush, for no sooner had they arrived than they sat down at the table. A professional trained by white men in the capital at Fort Negre, Jo The Juggler as usual preformed miracles: he bustled about and multiplied his efforts around the uniformed men to such an extent that it might well have been thought they were enveloped by him alone. His ready wit launched a compliment in the direction of each and at will contrived anecdotes, one more ludicrous than the next; he delivered mock tirades at a breathtaking rate and distributed pennyworths of wisdom in extravagantly original parables.

A regular at the most exclusive officers' mess in Fort Negre could hardly have found fault with the table setting, for although limited by the resources of this very poor village, Jo The Juggler had taken great pains over it. He was careful to avoid having the main dishes brought immediately; he began by serving strongly alcoholic drinks as aperitifs. Following his instructions, Mor-Zamba and three young men from the village, the only others seated at the table, pretended to guzzle down the contents of their glasses to wet the appetites of their four guests, who, it must be added, were hardly in need of their example.

When the chicken arrived, its finely cut pieces floating in a bountiful purple sauce of excellent appearance, an infectious warmth spread over the company to the point that Jo The Juggler and the devil of a sergeant, a giant with a bushy moustache, a real Genghis Khan of the crossroads, were seen slapping each other on the back like two men who had known each other intimately since the beginning of time. Sometimes one of them leaned toward the ear of the other, imparting a confidence which was no doubt salacious, because they immediately went into convulsions while stifling their guffaws.

As far as Mor-Kinda was concerned, the sergeant

never drank a sufficient amount, never emptied his glass quickly enough; hardly had Genghis Khan uncocked his elbow and the rogue was chaffing him gently to let him know that his glass was full. He treated the three other cavaliers no differently, and in this he was seconded, albeit halfheartedly, by Mor-Zamba, for whom the ends didn't entirely justify the means.

At this point events turned in a way so characteristic of Jo The Juggler's temperament, so natural in the flow of each person's actions and the spirit of the evening, so crucial for the outcome of their undertaking, and so consonant with calculations later attributed retrospectively to his companion, that none of this diabolic hero's denials could ever dislodge Mor-Zamba's firm conviction that it had been magisterially premeditated. To judge by his extraordinary self-assurance and the virtually delirious enthusiasm with which the incident inspired him, it might be more appropriate to conclude that, far from having prepared it in advance, Jo The Juggler himself accepted it as the miraculous sign of who knows what fortuitously revealed complicity with Divine Providence. After all, Mor-Zamba now realizes that, from the moment of this remarkable occurrence, his companion no longer experienced the least doubt about his own abilities or about the ultimate success of their enterprise. According to him, the former delinquent from Kola-Kola would henceforth act as if the first whim that entered his head, even when it was shrouded in an alcoholic fog, arose out of a mystical knowledge.

Upon entering the house where the banquet was being held, the four cavaliers had relieved themselves of their guns and ammunition belts, which they threw pell-mell into a corner. This lack of discipline and this scant respect for guns should have enabled even an unitiated observer, granted he were sufficiently perceptive, to suspect how far individuals who so readily made themselves comfortable were from having a truly military soul. Well, it suddenly occurred to Jo The Juggler that the extremely cordial atmosphere of the festivities, in conjunction with the spell of the alcohol, had disarmed the uniformed bandits down to their last reserves, if they had ever had them, but he still doubted whether he could expand the limits of this sinister game indefinitely, as he might like to have done. For the past few moments, he had appropriated, as he did so well, the mask of an over-stimulated man who had reached the verge of inebriated ecstacy and for whom the most abominable crimes could no longer elicit but indulgence or even complicity. Mor-Kinda, who had just filled each glass with a strong dose of alcohol and quickly gulped down his own, suddenly rushed toward the corner which had been transformed into an arsenal by the careless abandon of Genghis Khan and his men. Without paying any attention to the soldiers' surprise and like a man who nurtured not the slightest evil intention but was merely at a loss for clever diversions, he grabbed a rifle, placed it on his shoulder, and was shouting orders which he strove to carry out.

Disconcerted for a moment, then amused, and finally delighted by this piece of buffoonery, the four bandits burst out laughing in chorus; they had to hold their sides when Jo The Juggler shouldered the gun, threw out his chest, and began to parade stiff-leggedly in the space allotted him by the frugal assortment of objects in the room. At that moment Mor-Zamba thought the tragic denouement he feared was actually coming to pass: he saw Genhis Khan rise and noisily, cumbersomely, extricate his voluminous personage from the cocoon in which his gluttony had until then miraculously held it ensconced. Hoping to forestall a catastrophe, he too rushed forward, but Genghis Khan had already leaped to the side of Jo The Juggler, whom he did not grab by the nape of the neck, to Mor-Zamba's great surprise, but in front of whom he stood more or less straight and even stiff, his hands on his hips and his heels together, barking in some unknown language what must have been a flood of critical observations on the mediocre military bearing and capacities of his young recruit.

The impromptu farce quickly spilled out into the courtyard where, despite the darkness which had long since fallen, Genghis Khan insisted upon giving his new friend a shooting lesson according to regulations. Poised to act promptly upon the slightest whim of their leader, his confederates had soon improvised a lighted target out of an oil lamp with a rustic, canopy-like shade that they placed several hundred meters away. Then, they appropriated the torches held by a few idle bystanders, emboldened by the unusual commotion to show themselves at last, and reinforcing their efforts with curt gestures and imperious commands, they moved aside the imprudently curious onlookers and laid out a firing range.

From the threshhold where he was standing, Mor-Zamba saw Jo The Juggler and the sergeant stretched out shoulder-to-shoulder in the dust. The instructor opened fire with a long volley, accompanying each shot with a glib expression of satisfaction or chagrin as the case might be, while the clatter, intensified by the nearby forest against which it reverberated as if it were a metal partition, shook the village. When he hit the target, which occurred rather frequently despite his condition, the slender flame danced crazily or, sometimes, went out entirely, at which point his men immediately rushed forward to replace the wick in the lamp.

After Genghis Khan had fired a half-dozen shots, he handed the rifle to his young recruit, stood up, brushed off his chest and thighs, placed his knee on the ground again, leaned over Jo The Juggler who was still lying on his stomach, explained the gun's operation and the best way of sighting it, and braced his head against that of his student in order to take aim at the same time he did. At a respectable distance from the two and their open-air gunnery school, a glowing hedge of torches billowed in the hands of peasants who held them high and stretched their necks to get a better view of this possibly unreal scene.

According to Mor-Zamba, who never afterwards relinquished what he learned that night, the shooting lesson was too providential to be completely accidental. The fact is that, even if Jo The Juggler proved so clumsy that his shots never hit the target (he was too excited perhaps, unless of course he had decided, as he often did, to play the fool for fear of arousing suspicion), he could at least be counted on not to forget these invaluable rudiments in the near future.

At the end of this fantasmagorical shooting practice, or extravagant waste of ammunition as Mor-Kinda reflected to himself, Genghis Khan and his exhausted pupil wanted to regain the scene of their interrupted banquet, but in order to do so, they had to make their way through a crowd which seemed amazingly dense to the Rubenists, who had not forgotten that they had entered an almost deserted village a few hours earlier.

The presence of several hundred witnesses scattered about in the darkness and the slowness with which they dispersed prevented Jo The Juggler from acting with a free hand until well after midnight, obliging him to prolong the militiamen's drinking bout longer than originally planned. He was annoyed by that, particularly when he observed how these savage animals thought it perfectly natural to be treated with extreme deference and even a great deal of affection.

He abruptly decided to precipitate matters. He baited his guests with endless and contradictory entreaties; he simultaneously urged them to drink, eat, listen to his preposterous tirades, recount their feats of martial valor, and air their political convictions, obviously favorable to Baba Toura, whom they, with a touch of pride, called Baba Lush, that is to say Baba The Sot. Badgered in this fashion, Genghis Khan and his men were soon at bay.

Mor-Zamba, who seldom let the young delinquent out of his sight, shuddered as he realized all at once that, during the meticulously orchestrated confusion, Jo The Juggler had never stopped pouring a sauce he served to no one else over the mountains of rice he piled without respite on the militiamen's plates. I'm an idiot, he said to himself. As often happened at Kola-Kola, Jo The Juggler had carefully kept him in the dark about a diabolical scheme, the significance and simplicity of which suddenly dawned on him. As usual, insight occurred too late for him to influence the course of events and set them aright, because he was always preoccupied with forestalling the catastrophe which stalked them constantly in a thousand guises. With a wild-eyed expression on his face, he hastily elbowed his way out of the room, ran to the house where the child was supposed to be keeping watch over the Raleigh, and shook him rudely awake. All that mattered to him was getting underway; afterwards he would even display a mental and physical agility that belied a temperament in which a certain sluggishness seemed to dominate.

"Our friend is up to his old tricks again," he explained to the child, who rubbed his eyes by the light of an oil lamp as he himself extricated the Raleigh from the room—so gloomy, narrow, and low that it seemed like a cave--where it had been hidden. "Some day all that'll come to a bad end, and he'll be caught in his own trap. This time we're going to hit the road immediately without waiting to see him fall victim to his own devices and perhaps falling victim to them ourselves. At heart that fellow's a vicious traitor, a real snake, with a streak of the assassin in him. Stay on the alert while waiting for me; I'll be back in a second."

He went back to Jo The Juggler with the intention of telling him that he and the child had decided to go on ahead; as soon as the rogue had finished his business, he wou. be free to rejoin them on the way. But Mor-Zamba was overwhelmed by the quickening pace of the drama. When he reentered the room, he stopped short at the ominous scene unfolding before his eyes: the four uniformed men (or four armed bandits, as the sapak had called them when he inquired about their fate soon after waking up a few moments earlier) had been overcome by an irresistible drowsiness, their heads swaying uncontrollably back and forth; they were all muttering in such slurred voices that they seemed to be whimpering, their lips pendulous, their half-closed eyelids taut, their lashes quivering in front of rolled-back eyeballs. They were surrounded by a mob of people who, like dogs just before being unleashed upon their prey, were frozen in fierce swaggeringly eager poses. Apparently the spoils as well as the roles had been distributed in advance; each of the young men held his eyes rivetted on a single one of the four bandits, watching intently for the sign to fall upon him and administer an already agreed upon treatment.

"And, fellows, don't forget to begin by freeing the women," Jo The Juggler recommended. "Also, not a word to any of the elders. You don't know anything; you didn't see anything; you were all somewhere else.

For that matter, nothing happened. It's time, fellows, grab him!"

The oil lamp was suddenly extinguished as if the final words of the leader of the conspiracy had blown it out. At the same time, during a brief but violent outburst soon muffled by angry snarls, the armed bandits were immediately knocked to the ground and submerged beneath a wave of relentlessly attacking enemies who swarmed over them like ants on a dying boa.

"Let's get out of here!" Jo The Juggler came over to whisper in the ear of Mor-Zamba, transfixed with a surprise and horror that the former delinquent picked up despite the darkness and confusion.

The three Rubenists reassembled almost at once and, in spite of the night and its lurking dangers, had no difficulty readopting the familiar gestures and states of mind that characterize the situation of those travelling under a curse. Nevertheless, present circumstances formed such a contrast with the recent past that for many long minutes they were overcome by an impression of floundering through a night more muddy and slimy than a swamp. Mor-Zamba and Evariste alone pushed the Raleigh, and still they hadn't complained.

A timid moon appeared; only then did Mor-Zamba and the child notice that Jo The Juggler was hobbling along at some distance from them and struggling beneath a large bundle with several knob-like protuberances. The giant offered to relieve his companion's burden by carrying the package himself, but the other curtly refused, contending that there could be no question of entrusting the bundle to anyone at all until it was packed and tied more securely; then, moreover, a place could perhaps be found for it on the Raleigh. Yet he himself appeared to be more and more uncomfortable, frequently shifting his load from one shoulder to the other. As the day was beginning to break, he pointed out to his friends that, since they had been walking for quite some time, it would be eminently sensible to stop at the first village on their path and spend the day sleeping peacefully there. His companions surmised that, overcome by the weight of a bundle with knobby protuberances cutting

71

into his shoulders and by a fatigue which had been accumulating for a long time, Jo The Juggler was pleading for mercy. That was so unlike him, but it had to happen some time.

"Don't worry, my children, and don't be afraid of anything," declared Jo The Juggler, pursuing out loud a train of thought that had begun inside his own head. "A little bird tells me that it'll take five or six days and perhaps even longer for the garrison to become concerned about their patrol and that it'll undoubtedly take two weeks before they suspect the catastrophe. And how long will it take for them to discover the truth?"

"An eternity, if any such thing exists," conjectured the sapak.

"That's it, my son," said Jo The Juggler approvingly. "Above all, don't worry; I have excellent references."

The first village they encountered after sunrise was a tiny hamlet, a god-forsaken place in the deep forest where no one would ever think of coming to look for unknown but dangerous Rubenists who had succeeded in rousing a whole village of cowards against four of Baba Lush's and Sandrinelli's lions. Without hesitating for a moment, Jo The Juggler led his friends to the house of a peasant, whose large family welcomed them with an air of complicity. Without failing to mention an individual whose name kept resurfacing in the conversation as if he were a mutual friend, Jo The Juggler almost immediately began chatting with them in an extremely familiar fashion. He conducted himself with complete self-assurance and a touch of insolent authority, specifying to the various members of the family what treatment they should accord to each of the the three travellers; he instructed the mother to heat some water for the swollen feet of his uncle—as he called Mor-Zamba—whose advanced age no longer tolerated long journeys on foot; he advised the man to prepare a comfortable bed for the child, who needed to rest for a long time to compensate for an inordinate lack of sleep these last few days; as for himself, he was going to stretch out on a bamboo couch, where, provided no one distrubed his repose, he would consider himself the happiest of men. Having seen that the Raleigh fascinated the children of the house, he asked them to stand guard over it.

They spent the entire day sleeping in the only room of that low-roofed house, surrounded by the angry outburst of occasional family quarrels, the comings and goings of the local populace, the din and smoke occasioned by the usual domestic chores. Twice they were awakened to partake of rude meals prepared by the mother, but both times they went back to bed and fell asleep again.

It had already been dark for several hours, when the three Kola-Kolans arose and got themselves ready to set out again. At about that time, they were joined by four individuals, whose shadowy forms slipped furtively one after the other into the house, like frogs diving into a swamp. Obviously, Jo The Juggler had arranged to meet them, although he hadn't mentioned a word about it to his companions. The newcomers had brought along several gunnysacks, blackened by use, and with slow, cautious movements so as not to awaken the family members, who were stretched out here and there on bamboo cots and seemed to be sleeping soundly, they wrapped up Jo The Juggler's bundle in them.

Then Jo The Juggler gave the signal to start, and the travellers, who were now seven, silently departed from the house, the last of them drawing the narrow weathered door shut after him.

The four newcomers pushed the Raleigh, their task facilitated for them by an unrivalled familiarity with the terrain. Jo The Juggler finally agreed to part with his package, which had lost some of its knobby protuberances in the new wrapping, and he entrusted it to the care of Mor-Zamba.

The former delinquent waited patiently until they reached the first resting place, at a time when the sun was about to rise and the forest was already filled with signs of animals waking up, before he addressed the four young peasants in the following terms: "Well, my good fellows, did you do it up right?"

The four peasants motioned the Kola-Kolans to gather closely around them to share in the secret they had wanted to hear. The young men of the village had immediately stripped off all the clothes of the four soldiers; at the sight of those enormous, totally naked bodies, simultaneously horrible and harmless as the result of an implacable drowsiness, the idea occurred to them to carry the soldiers deep into the forest and remove their virile wands with a machete. Two men well known for their competence and their scrupulous zeal in every line of work were charged with breaking out the files to sharpen several machetes for good measure and with applying all the requisite art and efficiency to discharge the duties of an office that was, to tell the truth, rather unusual in this part of the country. They had applied themselves vigorously to the task at hand, but they seemed unable to finish it within a reasonable length of time, and they bridled whenever anyone tried to hurry them, arguing that, as long as good work was expected of them, it wouldn't be right to oblige them to do a shoddy job; however, they also proved jealous of their prerogatives and refused the assistance offered them from all sides. And time went by. Then someone suddenly pointed out that this kind of execution would result in spilling torrents of blood, just as it did when pigs were castrated. The image of such a possibility at once filled everyone with nausea, and that is why it had been necessary to abandon the idea of clipping off the armed bandits' wands.

Then they had had the idea of drowning them by casting them into the river which passed a few hundred meters behind the village. But when the preparations were already well advanced, someone objected that the bodies of the drowned men would pop to the surface after several days like corks; in that case, how could they know if the corpses of the militiamen would emerge sufficiently far from the village to deflect the garrison's suspicion and prevent it from wreaking its vengeance upon them?

Finally, they had decided to tie the four prisoners to a raft and set them afloat on the river, allowing the current to carry them downstream; that is to say toward the garrison. In the end, that solution carried the day by a unanimous vote. Nevertheless, its realization had entailed so much work that the villagers, who insisted upon accompanying the raft in

74

their canoes to make certain it actually left their part of the country, had not even reached the level of the garrison before they were overtaken by the rising of the sun. They had been obliged to hide their canoes, camouflaging them in the underbrush which lined the banks of the river, and hope they would be able to retrieve them later when all the hubbub had died down. Taking to the paths of the forest like honest hunters, they had returned to the village.

The Rubenists could not believe their ears as they listened to this story.

As such indecisiveness revealed itself so ingenuously, they were increasingly struck dumb with amazement, and they let the young villagers go on speaking as if they were listening to beings from another planet. Evariste, the sapak, was the first to pull himself together and ask with a gloomy petulance, "But, good God! Why not kill them?"

The young villagers remained silent, perhaps mortified at not having thought of such a simple solution: it was still too dark to make out the expressions on their faces. Then Jo The Juggler in turn intervened, "It's true, one could say that you didn't omit a single reason for not inflicting the only punishment those bandits deserve. What the hell! There are the wild animals who have spent months humiliating your mothers, your sisters, your wives—whipping them and taking them almost beneath your very eyes. As for yourselves, it's almost as bad as if they had reduced you to slavery. They commandeered your meagre possessions, they beat you, and they would have massacred you at the least sign of resistance. It was a reign of terror! We deliver those pigs to you, and instead of slitting their throats, as they deserved a thousand times over, what do you do? You mire yourselves in the most ridiculous scruples. You must be little old men left over from the past, for that's the way you drivel on. For example, after having sliced off their wands, who would have obliged you to stay there and watch the gushing torrents of blood?"

"And what do you do about their bellowing?" one of the villagers protested. "Because, you know, when they slit the throat of a pig, I'd just as soon tell you right away that it can be heard for a great distance. I don't know if you've ever tried it."

"Hey, you only have to put a gag in their mouths," Evariste said tersely with the condescension of a very experienced man.

"All right, let's see," began Jo The Juggler again without the slightest trace of anger in his voice. "The art is in its infancy, so to speak. After that, you decide not to send those rogues to the bottom of the river on the pretext that their bodies will soon return to the surface and betray the village to the revenge of their friends; couldn't you have sewn them into gunnysacks and weighted them down with rocks or even some gravel from the right-of-way on Colonial 13? That way you could have been assured that the fish would have had all the time in the world to finish them off. You're not going to try to make us believe that such a trick was beyond your imagination after all, are you? Well, they're going to croak in any case, your fine friends. Do you know why? I never told you how much sleeping powder I stuffed into them. To tell the truth, I don't even know myself. Listen, my good fellows, to the best of my ability to remember, it must have been at least ten or twenty times more than the dose Sandrinelli—a small man but hardly a sparrow—needed to sleep from one o'clock in the morning until eleven or twelve. For in contrast to the good woman, the husband didn't take that junk except on Saturday nights, since he had to be up before seven o'clock on all the other days."

"You mean he was subject to insomnia?" asked the sapak.

"Why, of course!" replied Jo The Juggler. "That bastard didn't sleep at all any more. Obviously he couldn't have had a completely clear conscience, considering all the people he had assassinated, not even counting the poor chaps he had corrupted by involving them in his dirty schemes. Like me, for example. Well then, if, as is quite likely, your rogues remain tied to their raft for two or three days in a row, sleeping, exposed to the sun and everything else, and naked on top of it all, believe me, they're not going to be a pretty sight when they're taken off."

The day had dawned, and after the rest-stop, the Rubenists made their preparations for getting underway again. As far as the young villagers were concerned, their attitude had changed: their voices lacked assurance, and their eyes were averted; they seemed deeply shaken. They now said they wanted to leave their new friends as soon as possible and return to their village so they could forestall the misfortune that had just been predicted for them.

"A curse, a curse," entoned the four villagers sadly and on the verge of tears as they feverishly scratched their forearms.

"What curse?" laughed Jo The Juggler derisively.

"Spilled blood calls down a curse upon the murderer, listen to it," the four young peasants answered him in chorus. "Spilled blood cries out for vengeance during the night until the murderer has been punished. In the darkness you think you're hearing the hooting of an owl; in reality, it's spilled blood calling out for vengeance and bewailing the fate of the victim."

"That's not possible," commented the sapak in a frankly disparaging tone. "Tell me, you people didn't invent that all by yourselves. Who in the world could have told you such nonsense? Could it by any chance have been the aforementioned Father Etienne Pichon, your missionary, the man with the magnificent church? A simple old fellow no doubt, but a shrewd one who knows how to handle country bumpkins by filling them with fear and then leading them about by the nose."

"Just yesterday," continued Jo The Juggler, intensifying the tone of reproach, "you seemed to be indignantly mocking all that humbug about mortal sin."

"Oh, but that's because this isn't the same," exclaimed the peasant all at once, "not at all the same. It's true that no one ever heard or saw mortal sin, but the cry of spilled blood, the owl and his hooting at night—that's no fairy tale. It's something real; all you need is good ears to hear it."

"Liar!" the sapak replied mechanically, tweaking his own ears painfully and turning his head in all directions. "Look, people always told me I had good ears, and yet I don't hear a thing."

Finally, to convince the four peasants to honor the agreements he had until then kept secret, as a means, no doubt, of keeping the other two Kola-Kolans off his back and retaining the privilege of the initiative for himself, Jo The Juggler was obliged to resort to threats, which were regrettable by his own admission and scandalous according to Mor-Zamba who, though having confined himself to a stony silence, was nevertheless thinking about it.

"You're not leaving us before we reach the destination we agreed upon the other night," said Sandrinelli's former servant and confidant abruptly. "You obligated yourselves in advance by the money you accepted. Did I force you to put my money into your pockets, did I? On my side of the bargain, I will pay you the rest of your wages when we arrive. Well then, get going and right away. Otherwise, I don't have to remind you of how many guns I have; you yourselves wrapped them up twice. And what's more, I know how to use them. From now on, you're going to obey me just like you obeyed those armed bandits who raped your women under your own eyes. Charming sight. Except for the difference that I pay you for your services and don't rape your women. And don't try to make us believe you've lost anything in the bargain."

As soon as the second pause after daybreak, Mor-Zamba managed very adroitly for once to inveigle Jo The Juggler discreetly away from the other travellers and confide in the hollow of his ear that, as far as these poor fellows were concerned, the difference was not as great as he imagined. Bitterly, he explained to the rogue that by jeopardizing forever the spiritual tranquility of these unfortunates, he had deprived them of their most precious possession.

"Don't fret, grandpa," the delinquent replied tartly. "The four uniformed bandits of Baba Sot are going to croak just like I said, may God rest their souls (at this point he solemnly raised his large straw hat). But even if they're found alive, there are only two possibilities. The first: they are saved by local peasants, and in that case, believe me, those lascars will never return to their garrison, because a soldier who allows his gun to be plucked from him by the first person who passes by, that's the sort of thing that leads straight to the firing squad. Consequently, the garrison will know nothing; those

78

fellows will have disappeared, period. That's all; neither seen, nor heard from again. These sorts of things happen in all the armies of the world; there's no reason why our armies should be an exception. No one will be disturbed. The second: they're fished out of the river by their fellow soldiers, and in that case, it's true, I foresee the worst for the whole village, including women, children, and old people. But what do you expect? In a war, it's quite necessary that people die; it has always been like that, as Sandrinelli said, and on that occasion he who lied so often was right. The Sot makes war on black men, his brothers, for the benefit of the toubabs, his masters; there have already been thousands of deaths, and there will be many more. You'll have to accustom yourself to that idea in the end, grandpa. You need to realize it all the same! Are you afraid of blood, like the peasants? Do you too hear the voice of the owl at night and the call of spilled blood crying out for vengeance? But, good God, what is it with all of you, raving on like that? Is it true that our people have no aptitude for war? That we are not warriors at all? Could it be that we are only fit to obey, as that scoundrel Sandrinelli insisted? You, Bumpkin, you should be able to respond to that question after all you've been through. Yes or no, are we only fit to obey, are we? Well then, as for me, I don't very much like always being on the loser's side. You can stay here, if that's your idea."

The discussion went no further as Mor-Zamba once again withdrew into silence. On that day and the following ones, the four peasants displayed an obvious lack of enthusiasm, intending to make clear that they had only submitted to the threat of violence and hoped thereby to prick the guilty conscience of their tormenters. One needed to remain constantly at their heels to hurry them on; it was enough to deaden the atmosphere of a company that was still, after all, quite small. Whenever Jo The Juggler himself was not supervising his hostages, he assigned that duty to the sapak, who was far from reluctant to perform it. For three days and three nights, they devoted themselves to a forced march, sleeping little, eating on the run, and stopping only to grant the indispensible respite

of a short nap to the two youngest travellers in the
group, the sapak Evariste and one of the four
peasants.  This pace, which evoked visions of a night-
marish escape, was above all intended to alleviate the
extreme anxiety of Mor-Zamba, who had been hardly
influenced at all by Jo The Juggler's triumphant mood.

"Let's get moving, let's get moving!" shouted Jo
The Juggler at each stopping place when they were
about to leave.  "I'd run, I'd willingly fly, but for
pleasure.  Who's going to track us down here?  Think
about it a bit."

Mor-Zamba objected that the large number of
people sent out after them improved the chances of
their enemies.

At the end of the third day, after the giant had
once more put forth that argument, the delinquent
enigmatically declared, half in jest, half in earnest,
"If you'd like us to move more quickly, grandpa, you
have only to say the word, and your desire will be
immediately fulfilled.  What'll it be?  Yes?  You'd
like us to move more quickly?  All right, we'll move
more quickly."

That night they slept until shortly before dawn,
but at the instigation of Jo The Juggler, they quickly
abandoned the village that had just sheltered them,
only to stop almost as soon as they had left the last
houses behind them.  Mor-Zamba, who was increasingly
losing patience with the incoherence of the delinquent's initatives, didn't have time to express his
annoyance.  Before the giant had set down his load, Jo
The Juggler had already finished paying the four
peasants what was owed them.  Without further ado and
while still mumbling vague expressions of gratitude,
they rushed away.  As soon as they had disappeared
from sight, Jo The Juggler slipped behind a clump of
underbrush, and it was not long before he reappeared,
disguised as some sort of important military personage, for he had donned various accessories stolen from
the June 18 school complex or taken from the four
uniformed bandits.  Attired in hunting boots, khaki
shorts, a shirt-front with epaulettes and breast
pockets, and a militiaman's betassled chechia, he
transfixed Mor-Zamba with astonishment and at the same
time threw the sapak into an uncontrollable fit of

uproarious laughter.

The giant nevertheless suddenly pulled himself together to express his unrelenting opposition, when Jo The Juggler, having just encumbered his rather short figure with a rifle, set about perfecting his aggressive masquerade with a well-filled cartridge belt. The giant went so far as to threaten that he would abandon his friends there, at once, unless the delinquent renounced his capricious intention.

"Come now, grandpa," entreated Jo The Juggler, "What are you afraid might happen to us? You still haven't understood that the right of the strongest is even more rigidly enforced and more feared in this province than in Fort Negre? And who's the strongest? Guess! He who carries a gun, don't you see. And who would know that better than brother Hurricane-Viet?"

"It's all right with me, if you carry a gun, as long as that amuses you," replied Mor-Zamba, "but certainly not cartridges within easy reach of your hand. Out of the question to play with fire. Out of the question. . . ."

The delinquent's pleas, explanations, and even his tears could not alter the position of Mor-Zamba, and the impromptu soldier had to give in, but only to launch a new offensive on another quite unforeseeable front. Among the odds and ends he had pillaged from the June 18 school complex, he had discovered some paper with letterheads from the French Republic and the High Commissioner's office; with a sheet of this paper, he improvised what he called an act of requisition, upon which he affixed the June 18 school complex seal that Sandrinelli had used in his official correspondence. The resulting document made a considerably better show that Jo The Juggler's military disguise, and one might almost say that, upon cursory inspection, its authenticity was unimpeachable, prompting Jo The Juggler, it must be added, to make the following observation, which was quite consistent with a mentality that had been ravaged by cynicism since an early age, when George Mor-Kinda was still but a child: "That scoundrel Sandrinelli never did any more than that, and it always worked. There's no reason why it won't work even better for us."

As they were passing through the first village

which chance placed in their path, Mor-Kinda suddenly abandoned the highway and went up to a house which appeared to be that of an important personage; his two companions followed him. Inside they found what they had been looking for: an older man, his thin torso bare and his loins skillfully wrapped in a cloth with many tortuous folds, was drawing puffs of cottony smoke from a clay pipe. It seemed as if he had spent the night in breathless anticipation of this exquisite moment, like a bedouin lost in the dunes and dreaming of a cool, clear spring. Jo The Juggler placed the act of requisition in front of him and demanded that four men be placed at their disposal immediately to accompany three civil servants on authorized business, while assuring the transmission over the next thirty kilometers of an important official message. Evariste and Mor-Zamba listened attentively, but they could detect no sign of uneasiness in his voice. The miracle occurred; after having beseeched them to sit down, the old man left, undoubtedly to consult with the other elders of the village, and then returned less than an hour later in the company of four be-wildered young men, each carrying a chicken as a present from the village to the travellers.

Afterwards, they always had all the porters they needed, whenever they asked for them.

# CHAPTER 4

They were spectators or actors in many more scenes that were often farcical and occasionally pathetic; such incidents were undoubtedly also reported to us, but they have long since disappeared from the memory of the tribe, because they exercised no perceptible influence upon the travellers' enterprise, neither endangering its outcome, nor hastening the course of its evolution.

All the rest of the way they walked during the day, walked and slept at night; for less clairvoyant travellers, it would have seemed an eternity, but to banish the sufferings of a long journey, there is nothing to compare with the secret rapture of an extraordinary mission, like the one in which our three friends had become engaged.

It seemed as if they had been condemned to walk eternally in circles, plodding along after an illusory respite under the same leafy canopies that always exuded the same icy humidity, returning to cross the same overly shaded valleys, laboriously rowing the same rafts, and periodically discovering themselves in the midst of scaling the same hills beneath a sun whose fierce ardor chiselled away at their necks and shoulders.

It seemed to them that, at intervals varying from several hours to several days, they again found themselves following the same riverbanks—sometimes high above the water, sometimes right next to it—tramping along the same streams and the same languidly splashing rivers. As if swept into a cursed round, they passed through the same villages, requested hospitality from the same people, who greeted them each time with a thousand smiles that were gracious at first, but soon became forced and fearful. Mor-Zamba still recalls the tribulations of that odyssey with the fascination of a man reliving a nightmare, whereas George Mor-Kinda, better know as Jo The Juggler, has not yet freed himself from its fatal spell.

Of all times during the year, the dry season is the one which most resembles a long journey; then too one lives through an interminable succession of days with molten lead skies; deprived of sleep, the nights take on a cadaverous stiffness; a feverish thirst continually wracks the body; holding its tail between its legs, hope prowls about, futilely pursuing a mirage of cool solace. One day, however, a cloud, which no one any longer expected, overspreads the sky without being perceived until an immense glaucous patch veils the sun, even at midday. A long, low growl slithers furtively out of the distance, like a pliant stick which insinuates its entry by a series of twists and turns. The miraculous squall catches the laggard child, naked and unawares, far from the hamlet.

When they had been on the road for nine weeks, according to the exact calculations of Jo The Juggler who alone had retained a precise idea of time, the two Rubenists and the sapak noticed that the clouds were beginning to accumulate for the storm of their arrival at Ekoumdoum. Well then, on that morning at the approach of noon, the sun having not quite yet reached its zenith, Mor-Zamba's entire being suddenly manifested the same signs of perplexity mixed with jubilation that can be observed in a predator whose quivering, turned-up nose has just caught the scent of a distant quarry in the gallopping folds of a passing breeze. He could be seen stopping in mid-stride and raising his hand as if signalling his companions and the porters to stop; he tilted his head first to one side, then to the other; he turned around several times, ponderously and with a constant tendancy to enlarge the circle of his movements; finally, the others were amazed to see him hold out his two hands as if he wanted to clasp some beloved person to his breast, and they heard him exclaim, "Great and ageless trees, your assembly has no equal anywhere in the world, I know it; spacious thickets, my friends, you put yourselves on display in swelling spirals that are not unknown to me, although I am not quite perfectly acquainted with them. Yes, you saw me pass by this very spot nearly twenty years ago. I was no more than a child then, and the chains of slavery crushed my loins, not to mention the rifle barrel that kept poking me in the back. You see me today going in the opposite direction, free, tutored by suffering, having miraculously escaped death, having myself killed a man with these hands—my own hands which terrify me on certain days, oh, my friends. . . ."

"Come on, are you serious?" protested Jo The Juggler, who had just rejoined his companion and set down the package of guns, from which he had not wanted to separate himself that day. "You repent of having killed a raging Saringala, not even in cold-blood but in the confusion of a desperate hand-to-hand combat that was more like a free-for-all than an attack? You insist on regretting that act of purification and public service? Well, that's promising. All right, that's enough; we'll talk more about it later. But that isn't everything, grandpa. How many days' march are we from your place?"

"Three or four, five at most, if it's Ekoumdoum you're talking about," replied the giant.

If friendship is a fruit ripened by the warmth of the sun, dissension might well be the relentless, cunning worm that tunnels an ever deepening cavity in it. Thus, even when, from the outside, it excites admiration for its colors and its appetising curves, it is crumbling imperceptibly on the inside, eroded by a treacherous maze of tunnels and undercut by the persistent gnawing of a termite. What doctor of the lucid sciences could shed light on these dark shades in time to diagnose and arrest the progress of a disease that is always fatal in the long run? For the second time and with a remarkable frequency under the unusual circumstances of the journey, discord had just, almost noiselessly, carved a niche in the rock cementing an alliance between two men who until then had been all the more attached to each other, because

85

they were so completely dissimilar. And fate decided that their disunion should twice find nourishment at the same source, which filled one of them with bitter loathing and plunged the other into ecstasies of joy.

During the rest of the day, Mor-Zamba manifested all the signs of an extreme emotion which, instead of diminishing, grew as the hours passed. He soon arrived at the point of proposing to the two other Kola-Kolans that they make a detour to Tambona, a city which had remained something like a distant star, bright and mysterious in the fog-enshrouded memory of the wandering child; besides, they had just discovered by accident that it was but a day's journey away, perhaps no more than a few hours. Since the moment of truth was approaching for their undertaking, they could reflect at leisure there on the proper course of action for them to adopt. On hearing it mentioned, the three companions themselves became aware of their own emotion as well as their exhaustion, and they readily agreed that several days of reflection and relaxation would do them a world of good.

Tambona had been an almost mythical city when contemplated from Ekoumdoum, where in former times its very name had echoed in the wandering boy's ears like all the names of places favored by Heaven and yet not entirely inaccessible; it was renowned in all the southeastern provinces of the Republic for the privilege of having been endowed with a charm that had for a long time remained undefinable to Mor-Zamba, but he easily unriddled the enigma of it as soon as the two Rubenists and the sapak had arrived there and dismissed their porters.

Unlike Ekoumdoum, Tambona had not been slipped under a wrinkle in the jungle, but spread out in an immense agglomeration and exposed to the open air, where all its parts were displayed with a certain imagination. The city grew out of a center that consisted primarily of several counting houses where light-skinned persons bustled about, their race and origin, as the Kola-Kolans discovered, having remained a perpetually unanswered question for the Tambonans themselves, who were after all the founders and owners of the premises. The latter were affable and even prosperous in comparison to the inhabitants of other

86

cities in the area, which happened to be the most wretched in the entire Republic, but among their fellow citizens, their reputation provided an astonishment motivated more by admiration than by envy.

Far from the center of town on a pleasant hilltop where a single sweeping glance could embrace the valley into which the crouching city was extending tentacles that were sometimes long and thin, sometimes short and fat, the travellers often came to visit an establishment that distinguised itself by the immaculate cleanliness of the grounds, the large number and judicious placement of buildings that were filled with charm despite their plainness bordering on poverty, as well as the discretion and polite diligence of its occupants. Jo The Juggler could not help thinking of his former master Sandrinelli, alias The Gaullist, when he observed the sense of authority (reserved but devoid of arrogance); the sad, almost disillusioned, disinterestedness; and the unpretentious self-denial of the European couple who directed and had no doubt founded what the Rubenists soon recognized as a Protestant mission. Both husband and wife, whose hair was beginning to grey at the temples, had extremely rosy complexions, in striking contrast to the merchants in the valley, whose swarthy faces were more like those of the mulattoes in Fort Negre. The couple led a steady, industrious, peaceful life which drew emotional expressions of admiration from Mor-Zamba, enchanted by what seemed to him the full measure of harmony, rustic simplicity, and an activity that was both useful and ennobling.

On Sunday, an unadorned, mud-and-wattle chapel—where the sunlight entered in profusion and a raised ceiling eliminated any impression of superfluous mystery—welcomed a crowd composed equally of the curious and the faithful, some of whom had become experienced in choral singing through the force of habit and others by virtue of mystical rapture. Of all the sights in Tambona, that was the one which, from the very first day, had plunged Jo The Juggler into the deepest abyss of perplexity: his never-sleeping mind immediately calculated the use to which the Rubenists could put a community so well disposed toward the Creator and his creatures. To Mor-Zamba, who would not pardon him his cynicism, he usually responded with meaningless wisecracks, but one day he finally announced in solemn tones, from which the cult of the enigma was not, however, completely excluded: "You might not believe it, Bumpkin, but since I met Hurricane-Viet, I'm no longer the same person. Among other wierd experiences, it sometimes occurs to me as it did to your brother (for, as far as I'm concerned, he is your brother forever, no matter what you say), I mean, like it happened to him that night—try to remember—I too am being transported a hundred years, two hundred years, into the future. It's true, all at once, I'm in another world which I can touch with my finger, so to speak, a world in which I have to believe. Our people are there in their villages, freed from the Sandrinellis, the DeGaulles, the Saringalas, and the Baba Touras; like all the other people of the world, they're preoccupied with achieving their own political or personal goals; they're working, they're laughing to celebrate the birth of children, and they're weeping in sorrow at the death of friends and relatives. In short, they've become very ordinary people. Tell me, grandpa, do you think it will be easy for them at that time to imagine what difficulties we, their ancestors, went through to liberate our race. Right now, we're taking on a good deal of pain and suffering without any reasonable hope of ever profiting from it. In the end, we're working for the benefit of people who will never be grateful to us for anything, because there will be no one to tell them our history, our own history. Damned Hurricane-Viet, will we ourselves ever know the true story of your life, the story which you didn't have the time to tell us? And I'm not even talking about what is going to happen next."

The Rubenists agreed to regard Tambona as a potential Fort Negre, rather than as a miniature version of it, as Mor-Zamba had originally been tempted to believe. It was the same recipe, the same constellation of elements, the same symbols, the same drop of milk whirling about in the middle of a sea of black coffee, and yet Tambona and Fort Negre appeared at first glance to be two different worlds at opposite ends of the universe. In contrast to Fort Negre—a

crucible of blood, hatred, and convulsive spasms—
Tambona seemed desirous of presenting itself as a
haven of charity and even brotherly love.

"A drop of milk in a sea of coffee, to be sure,
to be sure," Jo The Juggler often commented in his
new-found and intermittent wisdom, "but has the color
of the water ever been sufficient to make the reputation of a lake? It's more a question of germs than of
quantities. Wait a little while until a Sandrinelli
or a Maestraci is thrown in there like the virus of a
devastating epidemic. Is that moment still so far
off? It's the presence of crocodiles that makes
rivers and their banks so dangerous. They say that
germs travel quickly, that they're carried by the
wind, and that under such conditions viruses can
become crocodiles. It wouldn't take much for Tambona
to actually become a little Fort Negre. If that
happens, my good fellow, I'm telling you the truth
when I say that everything would be lost. Will
everything be lost?"

After having tried without success to approach
the missionary couple, the travellers, although full
of self-confidence, finally resigned themselves to a
liaison with the servants; they had only a minor
setback to regret, but it caused them a good deal of
disappointment at first. As Jo The Juggler gave the
servants good advice about their own situation, they
agreed to repay his services by revealing the sorts of
intelligence that kept the Rubenists providentially
well informed. It was thus the Kola-Kolans learned
that, by going upstream on the monthly motor launch,
one could reach Ndogmetano, a sizeable town, almost a
city, after a ten-day trip which was interrupted each
day at nightfall; that was where the merchants went to
get their supplies and sell the produce from this
area.

According to them, Ekoumdoum, although unreach-
able by boat, was located downstream from Tambona; the
rapids which began almost on the outskirts of the city
frequently barred the course of the river, rendering
it unnavigable for a long way in that direction. From
time to time a few dauntless traders—of the sort
which no obstacle can turn back and in whose company a
white man, well-known as a daredevil, occasionally

89

travelled--left on foot with the intention of reaching Ekoumdoum. They engaged porters, or else they themselves carried their bundles on their heads. At first they walked for four days along the shore of the river, passing beside a succession of rapids for about half the trip; after that, they joined forces to rent a raft or a native sampan made from a little cabin perched above two canoes lashed together; that is how they usually got to Ekoumdoum. The servants of the Adventist missionaires knew of no other way to reach Ekoumdoum; they did not believe that one could get there on the highway.

In their opinion, and they confined themselves to what they had heard, because they, of course, had never actually seen such a distant, unprepossessing community, Ekoumdoum had not undergone the slightest change; civilization had not yet found its way there, to the extent that the people remained hopelessly attached to their ancestral customs, extremely prim-itive and even, to speak bluntly, quite savage. It had even reached the point that their employers, the Adventist missionary couple, became convinced, after long years of mere suspicion (as is fitting for scru-pulous people who fashion their lives in the image of Christ), that the Ekoumdoum were cannibals. No one in his right mind ever went there, unless he had an urgent need for money and wanted to dispose of a few ampules of bad penicillin at an exhorbitant price, or deworming pills for children, or other all too fre-quently adulterated products from a rude pharmaceu-tical stock, for that was the sort of merchandise which arouses the greatest interest among these back-ward and brutish people. The travellers would do better to renounce their insane enterprise and look for paths which led to communities that were more hospitable to commerce.

As soon as the Rubenists' questions grew more detailed, however, the Adventists' servants became muddled, inaccurately bringing together the names of clans with no relationship to each other and falling into a state of confusion.

"These people are dolts who get everything all mixed up," the sapak finally said one day, completely out of patience. "It's a shame we weren't able to talk with the missionaries themselves. All the same, the business about cannibalism . . . !"

The giant took considerable pains on all the following days to reassure the adolescent by tirelessly laying out for him the refinement and even the consummate graciousness of manners and customs which characterized the Ekoumdoum. The sapak wanted nothing more than to agree with him, but in exchange he insisted that Mor-Zamba satisfy his restless and insatiable curiosity about the Ekoumdoum, a curiosity which translated itself into a mania for posing questions somewhat in the spirit of an inquisition. Jo The Juggler could obviously not allow such an amusing incident to pass by unnoticed; he therefore turned it to good use by bestowing on the giant the new nickname Cannibal, and until their arrival at Ekoumdoum he gave it preference over all the many others he had concocted.

It was simple for the giant to expose the absurdity of the cannibalism accusation, which was, he said, quite typical for the frenzied imaginations of missionaries; he needed merely draw his companions' attention to the similarity in many respects between the customs of the Ekoumdoum and those of the Tambona. Both were administered, for example, in the same fashion. Everything seemed to be under the control of a chief who remained inaccessible and virtually invisible, no doubt a man of dubious origins, perhaps even a stranger who had been imposed on the Tambona community by the colonial authorities, just as Mor-Bita had been arbitrarily placed at the head of the Ekoumdoum; fear, time, habit, and submissiveness eventually guaranteed his acceptance by a society that had been turned upside down. There were no police, outside of two or three unsavory individuals sporting grimy uniforms, a sort of palace guard or, more accurately, orderlies devoted to the master's person and enjoying the most perfect leisure to stroll indolently through the village—a leisure guaranteed them by the mild disposition of the local populace. The fact is, however, as the Rubenists did not fail to notice, that no crimes were committed here, nor were there any thefts or brawls—just like Ekoumdoum, insisted Mor-Zamba.

"Well, what do you know," observed Mor-Kinda, "it's good to know all that, it sure is."

When they left Tambona about a month after their arrival in that city, the Rubenists took with them a wealth of reflections well suited to their enterprise and an escort of four volunteers recruited at Tambona by Jo The Juggler with the aid of a well-tested method. The latter didn't express the slightest interest in the travellers' plans and never inquired about them, probably out of a lack of curiosity; if they had been less passively submissive, they would perhaps have dissuaded the Rubenists from acting upon their decision to reach Ekoumdoum by road in preference to the usual route, which would have taken them first along the river until the last of the rapids and then placed them in all tranquility on an ordinary raft floating from one shoreside village to another until they reached Ekoumdoum.

In the beginning, the road proved full of hazards: the traffic there was heavier than the Rubenists could have anticipated; there were even tractors pulling long, flat-bed trailers loaded with logs, although they appeared at wide intervals to be sure. Because it was necessary to avoid the danger of police controls or even of arousing simple curiosity, they travelled only at night, thereby subjecting the Tambonan auxiliaries to a hardship they could neither understand nor appreciate.

The worst, the almost unthinkable, occurred when they arrived at a fork in the road and, after a full day of inquiry, realized that the branch eventually leading to Ekoumdoum passed through an ominous opening in the forest, reminiscent of a crude swath cleared by a single file of frightened elephants. It was a poignant scene and even a quite alarming one for Mor-Zamba, who knew the epic story of an engineering feat that deserved to called a road.

The right-of-way was disappearing beneath frizzy waves of high, luxuriant weeds and tufts of underbrush sprouting from the ditches on both sides; all that somehow miraculously remained in the middle was a meandering ribbon, hardly less ravelled than a thin strand of rope, a trail where wild animals suddenly found themselves face-to-face with the men who came to hunt them there in preference to the groves and thickets of the nearby forest, men who shot them on sight at point blank range. From the embankments on either side a wall of vegetation rose abruptly, vertiginously, to a point where the trees, stretching out their monstrous limbs and intertwining them, plaited a densely woven arch that was occasionally pierced by holes through which the sun filtered, almost, one might have said, as if it had been eaten by moths. The mildest rainstorm hammered on the canopy like the thundering footsteps of giants, and people held their breath when they heard it burst and collapse in cascades; after one such agonising avalanche, the debris crashed to the ground close to the travellers, coming within a hair's breadth of knocking them unconscious. It had undoubtedly been a very long time since any vehicle had dared venture this way, and according to a hypothesis put forth by the sapak, who was displaying a jaunty self-confidence, the last one must have foundered like a galleon of olden times on route to the West Indies, and its skeleton undoubtedly still rested on the bottom of some descending slope several meters beneath the waves of underbrush.

Details that a child too unfamiliar with progress had not even noticed in the past, now pained Mor-Zamba like the brandmarks of a curse that continued to afflict Ekoumdoum, even though the road itself might still justify the pride of those who lived along it. No bridges spanned the rivers, only rough hewn, poorly fitted treetrunks thrown every which way; sometimes one of them had collapsed, leaving holes opening into an apparent abyss in the very middle of an art work already excessively rustic. As in the past, the roadbed had been gullied by the turbulent, torturous run-offs of rainwater, and it was filled with potholes that impeded the progress of even the most sure-footed and unencumbered pedestrains. But now it was by continuously tramping in the dusty high grasses and floundering through the marshy places that they were ocassionally obliged to negotiate their way, like marmosets, defying the laws of equilibrium. Mor-Zamba gradually realized that the road had not even been finished before it had been abandoned, no doubt shortly after his own capture.

During their inquiries at the fork in the road, they had heard it estimated that approximately eighty kilometers remained to be covered before reaching Ekoumdoum; taking into account the difficulty of making headway, they had originally anticipated walking for about a week. However, two days after they had entered the miserable section of road, the elephant track suddenly seemed to improve, almost as if by miracle, and they were able to increase their pace. Unanimously convinced that they were finally beyond reach of the Republic and its authorities, they travelled only during the day, although they did take advantage of even the last rays of sun, refusing to request shelter from the peasants until nightfall and making certain to leave again the next morning well before dawn.

As they approached Ekoumdoum, the villages became less frequent and more sparsely populated, sometimes even resembling temporary camps; it was as if the desert, like some sort of leprosy, had infected the countryside, inexorably gnawing away isolated villages in the same way leprosy nibbles away at the extremities of one's fingers and toes. The travellers were unable to appreciate the full scope of this phenomenon until much later in Hurricane-Viet's native city, where they were to encounter adversaries who would stop at nothing. Indeed, as soon as the harvest was over, some villages were apparently abandoned by the entire clan from a larger town which, although it could not rival the power of Ekoumdoum, nevertheless exercised, in imitation of it, successive and opposing effects of attraction and repulsion upon the scattered small communities in its immediate wooded surroundings. At certain times of the year, these families withdrew to the guardian city to such an extent that they seemed to become integral parts of it; at others, they spontaneously wandered away, no doubt obliged to do so by the exigencies of subsistence.

The Rubenists now parted company each night with their auxiliaries in order to discuss the tactics they would adopt upon their arrival at Ekoumdoum. Mor-Zamba had initially proposed that they simply introduce themselves at the outskirts of the city and enter without further ado: hadn't Hurricane-Viet predicted they would be carried off in triumph?

"It's clear you don't know the story of the man who wouldn't turn around," threw out Jo The Juggler, laughing derisively by way of commentary.

After having amply relished the dumbfounded expressions on the faces of his two friends, who were even more baffled by this new riddle than they had been by the previous ones (although they suspected another cock-and-bull story calculated to mystify them), the former servant of Sandrinelli, alias The Gaullist, finally condescended to enlighten them.

"Let's see, let's see now! The man who wouldn't turn around is a fable that's in the air wherever there is a wise man who's worth his salt. Once upon a time, there were two brothers who suddenly decided to see the wide world, but first they insisted upon seeking the advice of their father and their mother, submitting to each in turn various hypothetical situations in which the vicissitudes of life might, as they imagined, someday place them. Among other questions, they posed the following one to each in turn: 'Suppose I'm on a deserted path and hear stealthy footsteps behind me; what should I do?' 'Well, in that case,' suggested the mother with a smile, 'you should continue calmly on your way. The world is but sweetness, harmony, and affection, my beloved son. What good does it do to be afraid? Always entrust yourself to Providence.' 'My son,' replied the father with a set jaw, 'turn around quickly with your weapon raised; strike to kill and don't show any sign of mercy, or else your own life will be taken from you. Our miserable world is crawling with perverse and wicked people. Night and day, never forget to be on your guard. Always be a real fighter, my son.'

"The elder of the two young men took his father's advice, the other his mother's. The first, victorious in times of peace as well as in times of war, became a leader of men even before the age of maturity. The other was captured without a struggle by pirates who scoured the coast in search of slaves. For that matter, he was the first black man ever transported to America and sold at a public auction on the fairgrounds there; how many others followed and, because of him, experienced the same horrible fate!

95

"It is true that, having secretly entered Kola-Kola, the most well-known section of our capital, on the night before the first of January when independence was to be declared, your brother Hurricane-Viet, the great leader of men who has waged war in every clime, came on the sly to see you and assure you that, if you returned to your city, Ekoumdoum, you would be carried off in triumph, despite the conflicts of the past. I myself was present at your reunion and could not help overhearing these remarks.

"But remember that, when Hurricane-Viet made that prediction, he was under the influence of twenty-year-old memories. Is everything still the same today? Does passing time carry away no more than its freely swinging arms, like a traveller without bags? Where is your usual prudence, grandpa? Can you tell what might have happened to Ekoumdoum in such a long time? As for me, the scenario I imagine is quite different from yours. All of a sudden, you appear like a spectre from the past in the city of Ekoumdoum. Contrary to your expectations, the inhabitants of the city decide quite simply that, rather than welcoming you with open arms, they will huddle like frightened rabbits in their holes. Just remember, you saw that happen thousands of times in Kola-Kola when Ruben was up against the whites and their friends. With the clodhoppers around here, it'll be the same story as with the half-starved rogues down there. Nobody can do anything about it; people are made in such a way that they will remain eternally in their burrows to avoid the necessity of taking sides, especially when they're overcome with fear.

"And they will be overcome with fear. Why? Listen. Perhaps the old chief has died and rejoined for all eternity his unknown ancestors in the kingdom of the Essamdziki? Perhaps his heir has succeeded him, a young man of intense passions, fiery and unpardoning hatreds, and boundless arrogance? Do you think he will simply hand his throne and all the other emblems of his third-rate power over to you, as if he had been waiting all his life for that blessed moment? Realizing your intentions and knowing that some confrontation will sooner or later pit you against each other, wouldn't he want to make the first move? And

that's the wild beast into whose maw you'd so willingly jump in the hope that the Ekoumdoum would decide in
your favor and carry you off in triumph.

"No, grandpa, the Ekoumdoum, who are reasonable
people, will await the outcome of the battle and then
declare themselves for the winner. What would happen
to us, if we adopted your suggestion? At best, they
would first strip us of our arms, and when we were as
bare as earthworms, they would seize us and throw us
into the depth of some dungeon which the ambitious and
cruel young chief had just had built and of which we
would perhaps be the first occupants. Then, one
night, while a storm was breaking and thunder rolling
over the city, that mad and perverse individual would
have our throats slit, and the next day he would allow
the rumor of our escape to circulate. This story is
not just a bad dream; don't forget, that's how Baba
The Sot always deals with his rivals.

"Even leave out the possibility of dying, for I
don't know what that entails—actually, people would
have to be capable of dying a number of times before
they could speak with any authority about death. On
the other hand, I'm absolutely certain I didn't go
through all the trouble of assembling my fine arsenal
just to let some blooming young cannibal come along
and take it away from me. No, no, that's out of the
question. Why not go deliver it up to him right away
in a sublime gesture of allegiance? Keep in mind,
grandpa, the story of the man who wouldn't turn
around, the man who was captured by pirates, transported to America, and became the first to be sold at
public auction on the fairgrounds there; just think
about the dreadful pathway into misery that his weakness opened for so many of our brothers. You have to
fight, grandpa; everything depends on knowing how."

"For heaven's sake!" exclaimed Evariste the sapak
one day, suddenly abandoning the conspiratorial tone
the Kola-Kolans adopted in such debates. "For
heaven's sake, let's create an underground army.
That's what our journey is all about; it's our sole
purpose, the only reason for our being here."

Jo The Juggler was careful to refrain from
commenting on the sapak's suggestion; he purposely
left it dangling in order to savor the spectacle of

97

the adolescent indulging himself in an all-consuming
dream, and he didn't do it out of scepticism, as
Mor-Zamba believed when he confided in them two days
before their arrival at Ekoumdoum: "Evariste's suggestion isn't such a bad one after all. Living for
weeks in the depths of the jungle isn't as hard as
people are led to believe. Jo, you remember I've
often told you how Hurricane-Viet and I spent one,
perhaps even two, months all alone in the forest. Do
you remember?"

"One or two months in the forest, that's obviously quite an accomplishment," remarked Jo The Juggler
in an ambiguous tone of voice.

"Listen," Mor-Zamba resumed, "it would only take
me a few days of searching through the jungle to
rediscover the place where we stayed, and the two of
us were far from having the equipment we now have at
our disposal. It's very simple; let's get rid of our
auxiliaries, and that will already free us from the
presence of all witnesses and the possibility of their
committing an indiscretion. Since we'll probably not
find a hamlet or even a temporary encampment between
here and Ekoumdoum, allow me to offer you a new
resting place each night in a hut that I will have
built in a few minutes, using only my own fingers and
the materials at hand. In that way you yourselves can
judge how easy it is to carry out Evariste's
suggestion."

In actuality, they came across a deserted encampment several moments after Mor-Zamba had pronounced
these words; moreover, it being too late to dismiss
the Tambonan auxiliaries, they had to wait until the
next morning to do so. But from then on, it is true,
the Rubenists only slept in the fragile shelters that
Mor-Zamba erected in several minutes each night as
they watched him, utilizing only the raw material
abundantly provided by the surrounding forest. Yet in
the end it was Jo The Juggler whose expansive eloquence and bold imagination succeeded in convincing
the others to adopt his tactics; in his own terms,
they consisted at the beginning of being physically
present in Ekoumdoum without placing themselves at the
mercy of the volatile young chief, an individual who
was no longer the slightest bit imaginary to him.

That could only be done by entering the city incognito in order to observe things at a leisurely pace, to ask questions if necessary (very tactfully, that goes without saying), and perhaps, thought Jo The Juggler secretly, to undertake several brilliant initiatives which would dumbfound the enemy and oblige him to lower his guard. As Evariste the sapak well knew, it was a plan that had been adopted a long time ago in the mind of the delinquent from Kola-Kola; he had so little doubt that his companions would accept it that he had begun to execute it more than a month earlier, when he procured a gandourah and all the accoutrements of a Muslim believer.

Finally, on the eve of their arrival in Ekoumdoum, Jo The Juggler disguised himself as a Hausa holy man with a spacious cotton gandourah, a string of heavy beads, and a straw hat perched on the summit of a turban that covered his skull. At the very end, he placed the inevitably original touch that he hoped would be admired by a perceptive observer as his own personal signature, for to this costume he added a pair of frosted glasses through which he could see without being seen. But this time the expectations of Jo The Juggler were cruelly deceived by Evariste the sapak, who did not prove to be the shrewd and occasionally sarcastic but, for this very reason, formidable and irreplaceable admirer he had been during the long march. Far from filling him with joy, the new avatar of the delinquent from Kola-Kola augmented the confusion and aggressive tension which progressively overcame the adolescent as the goal of their journey approached, like a fateful day one hardly believes in but continues to fear.

They didn't meet a living soul that day, and what is more, their day's journey was cut short by an unanticipated thunderstorm followed by a number of heavy showers. Jo The Juggler and Evariste the sapak for once unquestioningly obeyed the injunctions of their older companion and remained all afternoon and all night entrenched in the hut pieced together by Mor-Zamba, who adroitly made use of the forest the way an acrobatic swimmer makes use of the water, disappearing behind a tree, only to reappear beneath a bush. A brief virtuoso sortie gave him the leisure to

catch several red-eyes, bream, and bleak whose fresh-
ness sparkled in the air; he cooked them Ekoumdoum
style, seasoning them with a great deal of red pepper
and a touch of salt, wrapping them in banana leaves,
and roasting them right in the ruddy embers of a large
wood fire; with the cassava which remained from the
previous day, he regaled his two companions in such a
manner that their doubts about favorable omens for
their mission grew less and less.

Mor-Kinda had endeavored to steel himself against
emotional considerations since their departure from
Fort Negre, but he silently marvelled at the practical
talents of that enormous creature possessed of such
manual dexterity and having such ready access to
reflex actions that had by necessity been neglected so
long.  Diverting his gaze as soon as the giant appeared to be looking in his direction, he never tired
of observing his companion without attracting attention himself, and he discovered another Mor-Zamba,
gigantic but nimble, heavyset but at the same time one
would have called him slender or even svelte, as well
suited for slithering among the brambles as for
gliding through the vines, scaling a tree trunk,
tracking down poisonous vermin, and ferreting out some
edible fruit.  His quivering ears and watchful eyes,
the perpetual chewing of a colossus whose stomach is
never completely full, his thoughtful face, infrequent
words, and invariably productive activity inspired his
two younger companions with a feeling of security that
plunged them into a mild euphoria in the midst of the
persistent drumming and pervasive rush of water from
the deluge.

Early the next morning, after having served the
two younger men a last meal of highly seasoned fish,
Mor-Zamba suddenly announced to them, "All things
considered, here's where we should go our separate
ways, my good fellows."

There ensued a final discussion calculated to
permit the three Kola-Kolans to outline, with a mini-
mum of precision, the first act in their conquest of
Ekoumdoum and to examine closely its more risky aspects.  Mor-Kinda, also known as Jo The Juggler, was
given carte blanche to execute the delicate but indispensable manoeuvre of entering the interior of the

city incognito, seconded by all the good fortune that unforseen circumstances might allow and assisted by Evariste the sapak. Mor-Zamba, who might have been prematurely recognized if he had showed himself in Ekoumdoum at that time, was at first supposed to remain hidden in the forest to avoid exposing his comrades to all the dangers inherent in such an awkward situation. There he would arrange the necessary caches for the safekeeping of their abundant supplies and prepare a refuge to guarantee their security in case a disastrous turn of events placed the two scouts in urgent need of beguiling the enmity of a numerically or physically superior antagonist, or in case any other unfortunate circumstances happened to arise. After a brief but unusually animated dispute, which was, however, resolved without dissent, it was decided the two scouts would carry no guns with them, that being the only reliable prescription for avoiding the catastrophic temptation to use them prematurely.

The two scouts reduced their load to several objects which would be inexpendable once they arrived in Ekoumdoum; these they packed in a bundle, purposely kept modest in size and given a rather soiled or even filthy appearance in hopes they could thereby protect themselves against the brazen greed of some overly clever peasant.

Mor-Kinda ordered the sapak Evariste to put on the tight-fitting, rough grey linen tunic he had bought for him, although he took great pains to stain it beforehand with red laterite mud scooped from the drainage ditches beside the road until it appeared to have been rudely worn by the relentless abuse of a long march. As far as his own Muslim holy man's garb was concerned, it hardly needed such treatment; without the slightest artifice it already sported several enormous red spots of its own, and Jo The Juggler maintained they gave it just the right effect.

"It's your play now, my good fellows," finally declared Mor-Zamba, on whom his recently acquired prestige as a man initiated into the pitfalls of life in the forest had conferred a heightened authority. "Rest assured, I'll never be further away from you than your own shadow, looking after you, even when you don't know I am there. And as soon as all of us together make the decision, I will come out into the open and put the finishing touch on the success of our noble mission. To meet with me, whatever day it might be, one of you should slip down to the road in the middle of the night when everyone else is asleep; at that moment the hoot of an owl will sound, and you have only to walk in the direction indicated by it. Good luck, fellows. And above all don't forget the man who would not turn around."

"You can count on us," replied Jo The Juggler.

When Mor-Kinda and the sapak Evariste once again found themselves in the middle of the overgrown road, walking side-by-side and even drawn rather closely together, they could not help but make the following truly remarkable observation, which surprised them at first, then puzzled them, and finally filled them with a profound anguish, although it later came to symbolize, perfectly in their eyes, the collective mentality of the Ekoumdoum: people they saw coming toward them from a distance suddenly disappeared before reaching them, as if they had vanished into thin air and merged with the surrounding nature; after a few minutes, the two Kola-Kolans heard voices behind them, and when they turned around, they thought (judging by the number and collective profile of the group rather than by the quite rudimentary and undifferentiated clothing of the individuals in it) they could recognize the peasants they had seen walking in front of them several moments earlier. Obviously the peasants had left the roadway and hidden behind the underbrush to give themselves more of an opportunity to observe the strangers at their leisure. One time, however, instead of precipitating themselves into the somber recesses of the adjacent forest, a large group of natives, who appeared at first sight to be quite young, jauntily continued walking toward the Muslim holy man and his disciple, on whom he leaned for support because of his advanced age, or perhaps due to some mysterious infirmity. The two strangers stopped, no doubt preparing to engage in a peaceful conversation, but the boisterous group of young peasants suddenly split into two units, the members of which simultaneously quickened their pace and, putting on expressions to go with their rags, adroitly passed on

102

either side of the Kola-Kolans by a manoeuvre characteristic of practiced huntsmen; their heads were
lowered as they went by, some scaling the embankment
with great agility and others shaking their heads
negatively to make it clear they had no desire to
become acquainted with strangers.

"Real cannibals, my word," muttered Jo The
Juggler with a sigh. "Where in the world have our
wanderings taken us, you and me both, my dearly
beloved sapak?"

# PART II

Father Van Den Rietter's Folly

# CHAPTER 1

"It was," Jo The Juggler loves to confide with nostalgia and retrospective amazement these days, "it was as if someone had blindfolded our eyes and then ordered us to go hunting for wild boars."

"Speak for yourself, Commander," Evariste the sapak occasionally retorts. "It was much worse than that. When you go out to hunt wild boars, commander, even with a blindfold over your eyes, you are at least fully alert. No, it was more like one of those dreams which come with the half-light of morning, when an awkward position of the head or arm or something else prevents the sleeper's eyelids from closing completely: you're not really dreaming, but you're not really wide awake either. You would like to swing abruptly into one of these two states by an exercise of will, but the other seems irresistably to carry you off. Do you know that feeling, commander? You see, there are days now when I ask myself if our reconnaissance mission shouldn't have consisted first of all in establishing contact with the old woman, Hurricane-Viet's mother. It would have been so easy! When you were playing fortune-teller and witch-doctor, it would have been enough to insinuate to any of your clients that you saw a proud young warrior among her relatives—a tall, slender soldier holding a gun in his hand and sowing terror among the whites in their own country. In the end, you could have said that or anything else; I'm certain they would have brought the old woman to you. As a matter of fact, why didn't you ever do that?"

"Why? That would have meant showing all our cards from the very beginning, eh, taterhead. The same as saying straight off to anyone who wanted to listen: 'Tell me, how does one get into the Chief's bedroom? I have a mission to strangle the monster in his bed. . . .' Why not tell them that right away? That's what poor Ezadzomo did, and you know very well what happened to him. And besides, shut your mouth; let me tell you my own sad story first. As I was saying, I had a blindfold over my eyes, and I had to go hunting for wild boars; that was pretty good after all, now, wasn't it? When I said wild boar or wart-hog, I could just as easily have said elephant or python; what do I know? Anyway, I reach out blindly in all directions. Poor me! When my hands come to rest on something, how do I know if it isn't a giant viper or an _ayang_ as aggressive as any of your beasts of prey?"

"Hold on a minute please, Commander. Speak for yourself, because, as for me, I know something about it. Can I say a word? When you touch a reptile, especially when you don't expect it, you have a feeling as disagreeable as it is terrifying; it's flabby and springy and at the same time, flat and rounded, smooth and rough, cold and moist; it's a nightmare. No, that's not exactly it, I tell you; it was as if neither your dreaming nor your waking eyes could focus on anything. That's not such a bad comparison either. You try to raise your hand to your eyelids, wanting to rub them, to take the stiffness out of them, but now it's your arm that's stiff; your whole body and all its members are paralyzed, locked in the iron grip of some ingenious torture device. There you are at the mercy of the enemy, defeated before having even begun to fight; its sheer panic."

The fact is that, for anyone capable of encom-passing with a single glance the various turns of fortune in their compaign against the chief and his allies, everything happened as if our Kola-Kolans had indeed been defeated at the beginning, before they could even engage in battle, as frequently occurs in projects undertaken in the expectation of an easy victory that can be achieved almost without striking a blow.

Refuting in advance the myth imagined by the sapak, the unknown and its thousand grinning forms did not paralyze them any more than the shadowy whirlwinds of their first night on the road had done. In his usual fashion, Jo The Juggler was even stimulated by the occasion as he approached Ekoumdoum in his most dazzling incarnation, sporting all the attributes of a prominent follower of Allah, down to a submissive young disciple carrying all the accessories of a fervent devotion and walking with precision in the exact footsteps of his master.

They entered the city along a rudimentary sand and gravel terrace that now enabled the travellers to reach the first houses without undue effort, not at all as the wandering child had done nearly thirty years previously, when he stepped across the ditch beside a pebble—strewn roadway. There it was that our two travellers, fearing to appear overly anxious to impose on the hospitality of the local inhabitants, installed themselves at a leisurely pace, like men never troubled by thoughts of greed.

Wearing frosted glasses to hide his true age, the self-styled follower of Allah squatted ponderously on a mat, which had been spread out with slow, solemn movements by his young disciple, and immediately began his ablutions. Already a row of naked and ragged children had formed at some distance; they came running madly from all directions, shouting "Hausah!" like a password, but then, suddenly, they froze, and the cry remained lodged in their throats. Standing up, the obsequious young disciple handed his master the implements of his rite as they were required during the course of its progression. At first, the old Muslim wiseman repeatedly beat his right hand against his chest with great pathos, often raising both arms toward the sky in a gesture of supplication; suddenly, he prostrated himself in a paroxysm of allegiance to Allah, facing the audience of children (who now formed a steadily growing mob) and not the Prophet's native city, as he should have done. It was truly an unprecedented spectacle, and it did not fail to attract the adult inhabitants of Ekoumdoum, who sporadically and with a decided air of superiority descended from the city in small groups, their sole purpose being to reassure themselves that their children were not in danger.

During all his endless bowing and scraping, the follower of Allah kept the enormous straw hat firmly on his head, for at the last moment it occurred to him that a good Muslim from the sect to which he supposedly belonged would have had a shaved head, far different from the elegant Kola-Kolan's bushy mop of hair; in this manner, he conjured up an incredible vision that left the adult inhabitants of the city completely bewildered, torn between puzzled admiration and an irrepressible urge to laugh. To beguile them even more and throw them further off the track, the many-talented follower of Allah undertook to entertain them with one of those nasal intonations which no one but a disciple of Mohammed knows how to produce and which later prompted the sapak to declare that only a miracle had prevented him from succumbing to what would have been an extremely ill-timed burst of laughter.

"Kuba, kuba nin Allah! Saraka kusirina malam ahia, kusirina malam ahia, kusirina malam ahia, kusirina malam ahia!"

As a matter of fact, the young disciple recognized these words (the meaning of which remained a mystery to him) as the familiar cry of a beggar from John Holt Square in Fort Negre: for many years, thousands of schoolboys had listened to this curious refrain before continuing on their way to school, where they competed with each other to see who could imitate him with the greatest technical skill, and that is how the beggar in the gandourah had become, for them, one of the best-known figures in the capital.

"Kuba, Kuba nin Allah! Saraka kusirina malam ahia, kusirina malam ahia, kusirina malam ahia, kusirina malam ahia. . . ."

Jo The Juggler emitted this strange incantation with such fervor and such charitable overtones that his eloquence must have moved the souls of everyone present, because their circle, so far away at first, gradually contracted around the two travellers. Heads were arranged in tiers: the closest rows of spectators, the youngest children, were lost in ecstasy,

110

while the adults in the background looked on alternately with skepticism and astonishment.

It seemed to the devout Muslim that his ritual, conducted in the midst of a disconcertingly obstinate silence on the part of the audience, would soon pass beyond his knowledge of Islamic liturgy and sweep him down the perilous slope of improvisation. Even when he observed the spectators whispering their impressions into each other's ears and, for the first time, experienced a feeling of uncertainty about his own position and the best way of directing the course of events, he did not break into a cold sweat. The providential invitation, which he expected but of which he had just begun to despair, actually did materialize in the same miraculous fashion he had anticipated, almost as if he had staged it himself.

A procession of older women, carrying the traditional baskets of firewood and provisions gathered in the fields, had paused in front of the two strangers, contemplating the scene which their completely unexpected presence had bestowed upon the entrance to the city. Judging by the expression on those faces, where one could discern a maternal instinct that had been frequently taxed but never exhausted, Jo The Juggler immediately realized that they were not going to melt like fools into the crowd of idle bystanders. Making use of her elbows, one of them lost no time in advancing toward the two faithful Muslims; an incarnation of the toothless old witch who haunts the dreams of imaginative young children, she was the smallest and thinest of them all, the one who had doubtless been most cruelly ravaged by time. Tears running down her cheeks and overwhelmed by pity, she proclaimed as she opened a path to the two travellers: "My God! My God! Don't you see that these poor men are begging you to give them something to eat? It's probably been days since they put anything in their stomachs. How could they have known that, when they came in this direction, they would walk for such a long time without finding a single inhabited village? Who could have told them that all the other clans had gradually withdrawn back into the city? Who knows but that one of us is at this very moment holding out a hand to receive a scrap of food, something on which to survive for yet another day among indifferent foreigners in a strange land? Have you forgotten that some of our own people have emigrated to Mackenzieville? Perhaps they too are now suffering the pangs of hunger."

Suddenly awakened from their ecstasy, the spectators in the front rows, the youngest of the children, snorted with displeasure, sneered, and began to grumble in apparent disdain for the old woman whose intrusion had broken the spell. Behind them, the oldest ones did not stand on ceremony as they invited each other to witness the presumptuousness of old crones who imagined that everyone in the world dreamed only of eating and that food alone was certain to bring peace and happiness.

The toothless old grandmother persevered, confidently wagering that her interpretation of events was correct; she approached quite near the strangers and even placed her hand on the shoulder of the young disciple, who was more submissive and docile than ever; to judge by his long, skinny arms and legs or by his clothes, covered with dust and even with splotches of mud in spots, he had undoubtedly suffered the most from lack of food and long days of walking.

"Where are you from, little fellow?" she asked him. "Do you have a mother? Answer me, little one; does your mother have the slightest idea what is happening to you?"

Instead of answering her, the sapak, who knew his role quite well, alternately lowered his head and stared vacantly into the old woman's eyes, like a child who was well-mannered but, being unable to comprehend the language of his hosts, was sick at heart for having to forego the pleasure of conversing with them.

When the old grandmother's questions became more pressing, the master himself felt obliged to intervene, with a good deal of difficulty to be sure, because he spoke the language of the Ekoumdoum quite imperfectly. Gesturing expansively toward the sky with his hands, he explained that he was a man of God who was fulfilling a sacred vow by undertaking a pilgrimage that would only be completed when his own life came to an end; the brief and wretched passage of the pious man through this vale of illusions is but an

112

endless quest for absolute perfection, which is Allah, the only God and he of whom Mohammed is the prophet. The Muslim wiseman added that Allah would bestow his eternal protection and shower countless blessings upon the dwellings and cities where it came to pass that he, El Khalik, servant of Allah, might stay even for an instant. The master continued, claiming that, despite a youthful appearance, his disciple too had attained such a degree of serenity that no vicissitude of life could ever again catch him off guard and that, whatever the date and place of his own death might be, the child, as his worthy spiritual heir, would follow in his footsteps, taking up the staff of his eternal journey and enjoying the protection of Allah, the only God and he of whom Mohammed is the prophet. No matter how defenseless he might appear, the unblemished servant of Allah has no more fear of the open road than the tiniest ant has on paths that are incessantly shaken by the brutal tread of the hunter and even the devastating thud of the pachyderm.

Thus spoke El Khalik, servant of Allah, the only true God and he of whom Mohammed is the prophet.

While the decidedly loquacious Muslim wiseman was holding forth in this manner, despite a quite imperfect knowledge of his listeners' native language, a natural event added to the enchanted atmosphere that enfolded the situation. In a setting where the Rubenists had already noticed how early the sunset usually occurred, an enormous storm cloud, followed by a continuous roll of thunder, obscured the city as it suddenly covered the forest like the tight-fitting lid on a giant cauldron. The sapak still remembers how he glanced furtively at the watch Jo The Juggler wore on his wrist and saw that it was no later than four o'clock. Dusk and even night, so to speak, had already fallen, and beneath the double menace of rain and darkness, an instinct for self-preservation prosaically interrupted the celebration of the Rubenists' first encounter with the peaceful citizens of Ekoumdoum, a remote and little known canton in the young Republic where Baba Toura, familiarly called The Sot, Baba Lush, or Massa Bouza, had reigned autocratically for he past three months.

The two pious servants of Allah were taken to the

toothless old woman's wretched house, where several families linked by the customary laws of hospitality came to lavish upon them all the careful attention owed to strangers who were being welcomed for the first time among the Ekoumdoum; it was just as Jo The Juggler had imagined it. At the moment of conducting them at last to the resting place reserved for them, the toothless old woman, who had been overcome with pity for their supposed difficulties earlier in the day, asked Jo The Juggler the following question, which had probably been burning on her lips since the beginning of the evening: "Stranger, did you really say that the inhabitants of a house or city would be eternally blessed if you stayed with them?"

"Have not the slightest doubt, venerable and saintly woman; from this moment on, you shall be protected by Allah," declared Jo The Juggler, solemnly rising and extending his right arm. "Dankal bino, dankal bino. El Khalik knows everything, because Allah placed his hand on the shoulder of his servant El Khalik, just as El Khalik himself reaches out the hand that rests upon the shoulder of his young disciple, not to lean upon the boy's weakness, but to give him confidence and certainty. Dankal bino, dankal bino, from this moment on, venerable and saintly woman, your house shall be blessed unto the thousandth generation—I mean for ever and ever. As long as rivers slither toward the ocean, as long as winged creatures fly through the air and reptiles tunnel through the damp earth, your name, my gratitude, and the benediction of Allah shall resound each morning as the star of splendor appears on the horizon at Mecca; it shall be heard wherever my fate takes me, and it shall accompany me even beyond the grave."

Her face distorted with emotion, the old woman burst into tears and cried out with joy and gratitude.

When they were finally alone in the place where they were going to spend the night, the sapak asked his older companion in an impatient, angry tone of voice if he didn't think he was going too far, all things considered.

"Hey, you still don't understand anything, do you, little rascal. In matters of superstition, you can never do too much for these hicks; that's what

114

we're placing our bets on, understand? The long march we just finished has taught me a great deal; what about you, little rascal? In the end, you see, there are only two ways to lead people where you want them to go. First, there are guns; in the beginning I really believe in them, and I still do—don't get me wrong— but a bit less than before, because, if you think seriously about it, little rascal, you know what the trouble with guns is? Well, they dull your wits; you think you're invulnerable, and then you stop laying plans. You stop paying attention to details. You always have to lay plans, don't you, little rascal? You know what happens to a guy who doesn't lay plans? Well, he's done for. The trouble with having guns is that you no longer believe it necessary to think things out and lay plans for the future. In such a case, there's always someone laying plans, someone who will eventually succeed in making off with your guns. Do you remember the militiamen we out-witted one night? They weren't men any longer, but brutes who were at the mercy of the first person who came along, provided he had an idea in his head. On the other hand, superstition is something else. In the first place, the people always love you, whereas the guy holding a gun makes himself hated. And then, you always have to think ahead, come up with new ideas, give unexpected twists to your scenario; in short, you're always on the alert, never napping; that's a good thing, it is. If I understood correct-ly, Hurricane-Viet wouldn't approve; according to him, you should never deceive anyone. What! Even military strategy would be forbidden? There would no longer be any way to make war, or love either, or even to hunt real game, because, after all, hunting is a continuous deception; think about it a little. Well then, we too are hunting after a fashion; how are we going to succeed without deceiving people? You see what I mean?"

"This wasn't the way I imagined it," said the child.

"In any case, at the point we're at now, the main thing is not to lose nerve, but to follow through to the end, don't you agree?"

"I don't like to see people deceived either,"

115

grumbled the sapak, turning away, "unless it's to relieve their suffering."

"That's it, little rascal, tell me what needs to be done."

That very night as the sapak was sleeping soundly, like a child worn out by fatigue and emotional exhaustion, Jo The Juggler boldly groped his way through the darkness to meet Mor-Zamba at the road. He triumphantly recounted the success of the stratagem he had conceived to inveigle them into urging him to accept the city's hospitality.

"You see," he said, "I didn't want to put myself in the position of someone who has to ask; I don't like to ask. It depresses me; what more can I say?"

Completely absorbed in his own dreams of action, he responded quite inadequately to Mor-Zamba's numerous questions, which were, however, eloquent testimonials to an emotion that he controlled only with the greatest difficulty. Even on the basis of his friend's chaotic and incomplete revelations, Mor-Zamba had just realized that the people of the city were lodging the sapak and the former delinquent from Kola-Kola in his house, the one he had built with his own hands twenty years earlier; he said nothing to his friend, insisting only that he describe in detail the place where they were staying.

"In any case," Jo The Juggler told him, "it would be a mistake for you to come there, for you would be running a great risk of being seen and recognized. To enter the hut, you have to spend a long time in front of the doorway. It's got a thingamajig that I never saw before, although you ought to know all about it, because after all this is your place. Well then, instead of a door, there are bits of wood placed on top of each other and held up by two poles that stand like columns on either side of the opening. As you can see from here you need to lift up the bits of wood one at a time, and that can take a while. Other than that, there's no reason to complain; it's big, and there is even a private room where one can escape, for example, from the indiscreet glances of casual visitors."

"And the roof?"

"What about the roof?"

116

"Is it in good shape? Did you see any holes in the thatching?"

"The thatching? What are you talking about?"

"But of course! The roofs of houses are made of thatch in these parts; didn't you know that? According to the thickness of the mats--that is to say, the resolve of the craftsman--the roof withstands the inclemencies of weather for longer or shorter periods of time. Rain, for example, carves ravines in it and even, after a while, leaves gaping holes."

"Ah, yes, I see what you mean, but I didn't pay any attention to that, you understand?"

"It isn't a moonlit night, however," acknowledged Mor-Zamba.

We wove mats thicker than anyone before us had ever done, he thought; it was a beautiful piece of work. I would love to see how well it has withstood the rains for all these years.

## CHAPTER 2

The process of becoming reacquainted with the
trees, the forest, and the jungle remains etched in
Mor—Zamba's memory, to judge by the way he occasionally brings it up; it was a delightful time during
which his euphoria was intensified by the possession
of an abundant stock of supplies which he had cached
in various places and which facilitated the giant's
work—to the point where he regarded it as so much
child's play.

As for the two scouts, their impulsive youth-
fulness made it difficult for them to suffer the jolts
and deafening crashes that greeted the beginning of
their stay in the city; it was almost as if they were
making their way through the whirlwinds and water-
spouts of a hurricane. Beneath the disguise of fervent believers so absorbed in the pious exercises of
their faith that they hardly paid any attention to the
restless movements and vain desires which constitute
the existence of ordinary citizens, they became completely engrossed in the painstakingly scrupulous
observation of an adversary who seemed nebulous at
first, and then mysterious, simultaneously ubiquitous
and elusive, lackluster and iridescent, voiceless and
menacing.

In the beginning it was with the older women,
their best friends, that they learned to play their
cards close to their chests. Every evening the women
arrived in a group to bring them their dinner, and
they never left without having spoken at length to the
strangers who devoted themselves to such a mysterious

religion and who promised them more indulgences and even more material rewards than Father Van den Rietter.  Nearly all of them were widows, and they spoke of Van den Rietter almost as if he occupied a missing husband's place in their thoughts.  In him they naively exalted the brave and skillful hunter whose gun never discharged in vain, the faithful friend who had gone back home to Europe but did not forget them and eventually returned to his flock, the administrator who had introduced them to prosperity.

"Well, well!  What do you mean?" Jo The Juggler asked them one day, hoping to hear them describe the mission and the rapid growth of an establishment which, as for him, he intended to visit secretly before long.

Of all the good works attributed to Father Van den Rietter, the widows seemed to derive the greatest sense of pride from the advent of Brother Nicholas, who had arranged to supply the city with the utensils that symbolized progress in this part of the country and were sold at the mission in a large bazaar which Brother Nicholas opened three times a week.

"Stranger," they said to him, "can you imagine what we were before the arrival of Brother Nicholas? The vilest kind of wild animals, wood-lice, but certainly not human beings.  We had to wait a whole year to obtain the cotton remnant we had been dreaming about, and even then it was only sold to us at an outrageous price by the band of thieves who came here to pillage the fruit of our labor.  Then Brother Nicholas arrived; every month he takes his boat to Mackenzieville and brings us back a plentiful supply of all the good things that abound in civilization. Indeed, he is at Mackenzieville this very moment; it won't be long before he returns, and then the whole city will take on a festive air, because the return of Brother Nicholas is always a blessing for the city."

That evening the widows had brought and offered their guest the calebash of wine that traditionally added spice to the evenings in Ekoumdoum, but the follower of Allah, a veritable incarnation of sobriety and detachment, had hardly wet his lips in it, although he frequently urged each of his friends to pour herself another glassful.  A general liveliness

119

ensued, and under its influence the old women, who had previously been quite reserved, appeared more inclined than usual to let themselves go. Returning continually to the two missionaries, the conversation little by little touched upon all sorts of subjects, but particularly upon the endless line of skilled craftsmen Brother Nicholas brought from Mackenzieville each time he went there in his boat. More than the cabinet-maker, more than the carpenter (nevertheless recognized as being quite competent for his ability to turn out apprentices in a short time), more than the bricklayer (so highly esteemed by the missionaries that his services had been exclusively retained by them), more than all the other professional men installed within the walls of the establishment founded by Van den Rietter, the widows waxed ecstatic over the skill of the tailor, and they were quick to agree that the most recent illustration of it was the amwalli dress that Ngwane-Eligui had worn to mass on the previous Sunday; this point was made after a debate, of which Jo The Juggler remembered the following extract for a long, long time:

"So he was the one who made that dress, that masterpiece?" one of the widows had exclaimed. "I said as much myself at high mass the other day as I was looking over that little wench."

"Who else could have made such a dress?" had said another widow. "Next to that fellow, all tailors and particularly the ones from around here ought to hang their heads in shame: they have an excuse, it is true; their profession is quite new in these parts. Ah, what were we before Brother Nicholas? Nothing, nothing but moles, as Father Van den Rietter so often tells us."

"I'll have to have a dress like that made for me, and in amwalli, as soon as Brother Nicholas returns from Mackenzieville and provided he was inspired to bring back tons of amwalli," a third widow had declared, for it was evidently the cotton fabric of preference for the women of Ekoumdoum, and Brother Nicholas' stock never lasted more than a few days. "God, our Father, allow me to have such a dress made for me in amwalli before I die, even if it only serves to wrap up my miserable remains."

"She won't have worn it for long, poor girl!"

"You mean to say she won't have paraded about in it for long; nothing prevents her from wearing it in her husband's palace, at least for her own pleasure."

"Why is that? Did Father Van den Rietter give her back? Didn't he want to keep her?"

"What? You didn't know?"

Soon other sorts of local inhabitants came, in the wake of the widows, to strike up friendship with the two followers of Allah, because the sweetness of their manners and the intensity of their piety had quickly spread their reputation throughout the city. With the exception of the young girls, who almost always stayed with their brothers during their daily round of activities, the children were among the most eager to crowd around the wise, serene Moslem who remained seated on a mat, like a tailor or a whirling dervish, sometimes inside the house, sometimes outside on the narrow embankment. Occasionally the follower of Allah would take a child's hand, solemnly regard the lines on it, and, shaking his head, proclaim to the little man whose skull was clean shaven and whose smile immediately froze on his lips: "Allah! I see there, behind you—oh!—a large man, an immense man with fiery eyes and a grim smile; he is brandishing a tapered machete which could be deadly, if the occasion arose. He is a man whose mouth echoes with gurglings of hatred and envy. Who is he, my child?"

"He is my uncle, of course!" replied the child. "He is angry at my father, because the wild game never runs into his snares, but always into those of my father. Well, he says it isn't natural and claims my father has cast a spell on him. That's why he is filled with hatred."

"Dankal bino, dankal bino," interjected Jo The Juggler once again, "and yet I have never been in your home. El Khalik sees everything. El Khalik, the master of Nouredine, walks hand in hand with Allah."

"Who is Nouredine?" asked the children in unison.

"And who is the master of Nouredine?"

"I am the master of Nouredine."

"Is that so? So instead of saying, 'I walk hand in hand with Allah,' you prefer to say, 'The master of Nouredine walks hand in hand with Allah?' Do they

121

always talk like that in your place?"

Before long all sorts of people wanted to have their fortunes told by the follower of Allah. That was particularly true after the young people of the city began to pay a daily visit to the two pious Moslems, following the lead of a dandified individual and, to the great satisfaction of Jo The Juggler, staying on endlessly. Their leader must have been a young man, or even a very young man, because Mor-Zamba did not recognize him after having listened carefully to a detailed description of him. At every hour of the day he was equipped with an ancient accordion on which he always played the same melody. He was a tall, well-proportioned, more or less slender fellow who presented himself in such a way that people would take him for a man from the large city, where he had indeed lived for a short time, as the Rubenists soon discovered. He sported a bushy head of hair invariably styled with meticulous care, dilapidated plastic sandals, a pair of threadbare khaki shorts, a sleeveless undershirt, a watchband without a watch on his left wrist, and a noteworthy shock of hair on his chest, to which he drew additional attention on special occasions by donning a patchwork sports shirt which he studiously refrained from buttoning.

The accordionist, whose name was Mor-Eloulougou, appeared on the scene toward the end of the afternoon on the day Brother Nicholas returned from Mackenzieville; the celebration predicted by the widows was in full swing, enlivened in particular by the mission school children who could be heard singing in many parts of the city. Encumbered by his tuneful instrument, Mor-Eloulougou himself seldom opened his mouth, but with the group accompanying him he did exchange a few comments, the aggressive tenor of which secretly astonished Jo The Juggler, who was unaccustomed to such verbal indiscretion on the part of the Ekoumdoumians. That very morning, the public crier had crisscrossed the city to remind people of a regulation which still, as he emphasized with a firmness bordering on intimidation, remained in effect and required that all game taken on the right-hand side of the river, the side where the city itself was located, had to be shared equally with the Palace; this

122

included fish and birds as well, the only exception being nestlings, the crier had added, repeating the final phrase a number of times. Upon hearing the protests triggered by this announcement in Mor-Eloulougou's youthful entourage, Jo The Juggler was amazed to discover that fishing and hunting, vital activities for the inhabitants of the city, were sacred in their eyes and that, according to the judgment of the youngest among them, the Chief, who was already guilty of usurping the throne, had compounded his crime by seeking to interfere with them.

When Jo The Juggler, desiring to know more about it, tried to encourage their rebellion and stimulate their confidence in him by asserting that Allah, the only true God and He of Whom Mohammed is the Prophet, had always stipulated that people should share rather than hoard their resources and that killing one's brother was the same as depriving him of the food he needed for survival, it seemed to Sandrinelli's former servant that their anger subsided rather quickly, and he accused himself of having blundered. In the agitated commotion of their initial intrusion, each new arrival who entered the house of the pious Moslems to join the crowd surrounding the accordionist approached him joyfully and said, "Well now, where do matters stand? Is it on for this evening at least? It would be just the right day."

Without extricating himself from his musical ecstasy, the accordionist drew the edges of his lips into a very expressive pout, which to a stranger might have signified disgust but which Mor-Eloulougou's indiscreet questioner interpreted in the following manner: "You don't say! It's all set? Is that true?"

"Obviously, look here!" exclaimed not the accordionist himself (he was too imbued with the importance of his role to deign interrupting the performance of it), but one of his followers. "Obviously, it's all set! What did you think? That she was going to resist him? That one? She would certainly have been the first."

"That's not ture!" retorted the new arrival. "Don't say that about Ngwane-Eligui; I won't believe you. She is not like the others; she at least is a

123

tough one. The first guy who has her runs the risk of causing a real brouhaha."

"But who's talking about her?" the accordionist's spokesman said with annoyance, as his leader remained lost in his endless refrain. "As for me, I was talking about Ngwane-Assoumou."

"Oh, yes, her. I agree; I'm perfectly willing to believe you. You'll have to admit it's a fine enough catch, although it's far from being worth Ngwane-Eligui."

"Go on, Ngwane-Assoumou hasn't even been there for ten days; that's pretty quick after all, isn't it?"

"Yes, yes, I agree, of course, of course, but after all, it's not worth Ngwane-Eligui. Well then, tell me; how did you like her?"

"Not so good!" proclaimed the cavernous voice of Mor-Eloulougou, finally emerging from his rapture and at the same time causing the din in the room to sub-side abruptly. "Mon Dieu, there was water everywhere; I don't like that. And then, she really cries out too loud; no, that bothers me. You want her? Yes, yes, yes, it's easy, you know."

On this subject as well, the young people replied laconically or evasively when Jo The Juggler attempted to fathom their secret, or else they simply admitted to him with a laugh and a lewd wink that "it is a strictly local affair; that's the way we keep our-selves busy around here. We get even with the Old Chimpanzee that way. The Bedridden Chimpanzee and his hordes take everything from us; well then, the rest of us take the remainder from him, and the ramainder is already quite a bit."

"For God's sake! Who is this Ngwane-Eligui?" thought Jo The Juggler helplessly. That night he extracted from Mor-Zamba the authorization to carry a fairly large sum of money around with him, although the giant considered his initiative, whatever it might be, both dangerous and premature; he only gave it to him several hours later, after he had gone to fetch it from his nearest cache.

The next day Jo The Juggler announced to his friends, the widows, that Allah, having decided to reward them for their hospitality, had inspired him as he slept with the idea of presenting each of them with a swatch of _amwalli_ so they could have the dress of their dreams made for them, and he gave each non-plussed old woman enough money to pay for the cotton cloth and the tailoring. During that evening they consumed more palm wine than usual, and they sang many songs, which, for that matter, included impious laments and ballads looming suddenly out of the dark night of traditions that Van den Rietter had so often ridiculed; above all, they confided a few secrets to the stranger, not very explicitly to be sure and, moreover, communicated in muffled tones, but secrets nonetheless.

That little wench Ngwane-Eligui's presence in the royal dwelling must have been quite a trial for the wretched Chief; she was the master-of-the-city's most recent acquisition. As wild as she was young and beautiful to the point of being provocative, she had at first refused to obey her father, hadn't she? After all, it is natural that youth should abhor fondling the wrinkles of age. To prevent that from being an obstacle, they offered to let her enter the bed of the son, whose flesh was firm and vigorous; he was a slender, handsome young man who had returned but two years previously from Batarẽ, where he had lived for some time while completing his apprenticeship. It always happens that way; besides, it's no more than good common sense. If a woman doesn't want to marry the older generation, well then let her take the younger one, and that is what they were proposing to Ngwane-Eligui. But as it turned out, the little scamp also refused the son with the same impassioned obsti-nacy. Well, what to do? Bestow that superb child, as one usually does with an ugly speciman, upon some servant as a reward for his fidelity? Sheer madness. Allow her to take refuge with Father Van den Rietter at the mission after she had barely arrived in the city? The master and his son could hardly bring themselves to do that.

The following day, the numerous children who came to visit their friends El Khalik and Nouredine stayed with them from morning until evening; the two stran-gers fed them as they had never before been fed at a time when their mothers were still at work in the

125

fields. Desiring to prove how much he really wanted to entertain them, Jo The Juggler ordered many plates of rice and fried fish brought out for them, provisions that had been purchased at the mission and prepared very early in the day.

Suddenly and with the customary seriousness he reserved for such occasions, he bent over the hand of the most boisterous child, and accompanied by a chorus of joyful exclamations, he announced, "the master of Nouredine knows everything; El Khalik sees everything, because El Khalik walks hand in hand with Allah. Dankal bino! Dankal bino. . . . Let us see what is happening in the depths of your little palm, my good man. Oh, la, la. Well then, you are going to be a big massa, you are, a great commander; under your orders you will have hundreds--what am I saying-- thousands of people, if, at the right moment of course, you agree to attend school. I see you tall, handsome, and covered with gold braid. Perhaps you are a colonel, but no, it is more like a provincial governor; yet, a great governor, that is what you are going to be when you grow up. But before that, what do I see there right next to you? Ah, look at that! Young women. Yes indeed, and very beautiful ones too! They seem to be enjoying themselves enormously in your company. . . ."

"That isn't me; it is more like my brothers!" exclaimed the child, while his youthful companions burst out laughing. "It's surely one of my brothers, and the young women are those who belong to the Old Bedridden Chimpanzee."

"Is that so?" said a machiavellian Jo The Juggler. "How is it possible?"

"Oh, yes," replied the child, "my brothers often claim that the Bedridden Chimpanzee's presence here is a blessing, because without him, as they say, they themselves would have died a long time ago."

"You're kidding. . . ."

"But it's true, because, like they always say, the Bedridden Chimpanzee came to us and created an incredible stock of females. Would you like to know how he does it, the Old Bedridden Chimpanzee?"

According to the remarks of the children, the Chief appeared to be a sort of comic monster, upon whom position and money had conferred the power to realize some of his wildest dreams; he was also like an hereditary target toward which their blows should later quite naturally be aimed, as if hurting him would not be a crime but, on the contrary, an unequivocally meritorious act.

"Yes, indeed!" resumed the boisterous little boy amidst the uproar caused by his brothers, who sometimes applauded him and sometimes booed the Chief. "Well, the Bedridden Chimpanzee is very rich; he has piles of money in every corner of the Palace, you know? It is a huge house that Brother Nicholas had made for him, an immense house with many rooms and banquet halls. Well, he also has lots of servants, a whole army of servants and even a police force down there in his own section of town. So he sends out his people to every part of the country, very far from here and even into places where the people don't speak like us; it is true, the Bedridden Chimpanzee has wives who arrive here without knowing our language; afterwards, they learn it of course and even speak it quite well, because our language is simple, but very beautiful."

"Yes, it is a very beautiful language; I agree with you completely. But when the Bedridden Chimpanzee sends his servants to all parts of the country, what do they do there?" asked the wise Moslem.

This time, another little boy, equally boisterous but afflicted with a mild stutter, replied, spontaneously taking up where the preceding orator had stopped. "Their pockets are filled with money, and when they see a pretty young girl, but very, very, young, you know, because the Bedridden Chimpanzee prefers them like that, although not too small, because then the parents might not agree! Well, they run after the young girl; they catch her, they take her to her parents, and they say to the parents, 'Does this child belong to you? How much do you want for her?' Then the parents reply that they want tons of money, and you know what? The Old Chimpanzee's people pay cash on the line."

"That's fantastic!" exclaimed the follower of Allah as he clapped his hands together. "And what happens next?"

127

"Next?" continued the little stutterer, "they travel a bit further, catch another very beautiful young girl, and so on and on it goes. In the end, they bring them all here and take them to the Palace. The Bedridden Chimpanzee then organizes a great celebration. The other old men of the city all go to the Palace, where they are offered things to eat and drink and everything. And the Bedridden Chimpanzee has himself carried into their midst, and he announces, 'here are my new wives!' And he gives them more things to eat and drink."

"What a remarkable man this Bedridden Chimpanzee must be!" observed the wise Moslem.

"Well, yes, but even he has problems sometimes," said a boy, who was somewhat older than the others and already had the voice of a man. "My mother says young women these days are no longer like they were in her time."

"What do you mean?"

"Well," the boy went on, "they no longer accept old men; they want young ones. My mother says it's because times are changing, and young women are changing along with them."

"What then?"

"They run away and take refuge at the mission; sometimes they try to cross the forest, but they never succeed. They are always caught again by the Old Chimpanzee's men."

"Not always!" the other children protested in unison.

"With one exception, but only one!" the adolescent corrected himself.

In less than two days, Jo The Juggler's ingenuity had enabled him to trace the profile of a serious social crisis brewing in the city of Ekoumdoum. The situation was actually far more bizarre than the Rubenists could ever have imagined, for among the men of influence in the city, not a single one had avoided implicating himself, more or less intimately, in the impending disaster.

In the eyes of the young people who congregated around Mor-Eloulougou the accordionist, Van den Rietter himself was extremely suspicious, since he kept thirty young women in his establishment, according to some—forty or even more, according to others. Did he confine himself to the charitable offer of an asylum for unfortunate fugitives? Or did he simply want to share in this manna from heaven?

"It is true," they admitted, "that he always takes pains to find them a good husband among the bachelors of the city, and as soon as he finds one, he loses no time in taking him to the Old Chimpanzee and obliging him to sign an affidavit of his indebtedness to the Chief. It is true, it is true, but after all is it proper for him to concern himself with those sorts of things? And for that matter, why does he keep the young women at this place for such a long time before arranging their marriages? Of course, he pretends to give them religious instruction; he makes them attend mass every morning. Of course, but the rest of the time, they are cooped up in isolated brick houses, where no one keeps an eye on them. That is serious, especially at night, eh; it is very serious. The proof. . . ."

It is true that, according to every one's testimony, the wives of the Chief—those in the Palace as well as those at the mission—had attained such levels of licentiousness that they thwarted all obstacles, fanning out through the city each night and rejoining the vigorous young men with whom they carried on notorious liaisons. Not having abandoned all hope of keeping them within the bounds of propriety, the old master and his eldest son were never lacking in imagination. Their special court was, for example, almost constantly in session: fines for the obstinate, imprisonments for the strong-willed like Ngwani-Eligui, beatings and even long months of forced labor in the Chief's fields for the most debauched; nothing worked.

However, like an open wound that constantly spreads as the day goes by and eventually eats away the entire organism, covering it with horrible, puss-filled sores, a marital frenzy increasingly plagued the old man as time carried him closer to the edge of the grave; this obsession had easily been passed on to his eldest son, the only one living with him at that time in the strange sort of fortress which Brother Nicholas, an architect whose willingness to please

129

exceeded his imagination, had created from the rather simple and even seemly house that Mor-Zamba had known as a young man. It is that maze-like structure which the oldest inhabitants of the city, in their undying respect for authority, persisted in calling the palace. Constituting an immense section of town, countless subsidiary dwellings clustered in no particular order around the master's residence and accomodated a remarkaable assortment of women, wives, wives' relatives, and other single females whose status was hard to define; exacerbated by youth, their frustration exerted so much pressure on the bamboo enclosure that it was literally bursting at the seams day and night.

"Don't you see?" Jo The Juggler repeated obstinately to a skeptical Mor-Zamba. "Let us consider only the following aspect of the situation: in Ekoumdoum every fledgling youth's dreams of love converge on the section of town occupied by the Chief. You'll never make me believe we can't at least turn this inevitable osmosis to our account. The train is being made up, grandpa; we'd better not miss it. Or if it has already left, it can't be far; we'll catch it on the run."

The sixth sense of Sandrinelli's former servant told him that the motive for their little drama already existed in the person of Ngwane-Eligui, whom he now pictured as a young and untameable tigress, relentlessly attacking the bars of her cage as the equally inflexible pikestaffs of her jailors flashed back at her.

The Rubenist scouts disguised as Moslem believers had not been in the city for more than a few days, but already their house was never empty; the widows regularly succeeded the accordionist Mor-Eloulougou, who was always surrounded by his followers. Not infrequently others inserted themselves between the two groups; sometimes it was the young children, sometimes less familiar visitors who arrived unannounced from the upper city and even, on one occasion, from the Catholic mission. Already tired of the constraints imposed by his mask and feeling trapped inside it, Jo The Juggler began scheming to give himself more elbow room; he discreetly endeavored to establish more intimate contacts with his visitors, and it was naturally among the friends of the accordionist that his habitual talents worked miracles: a vague promise to one, a small present to another, an allotment of cigarettes to those who had previously been accustomed to passing a rare fag-end from hand to hand, freely flowing brandy on some days—it required no more to transform the devout Moslem into a new pole of attraction and even a vital new center of activity, comparable if not equal to the Palace and the mission, thereby rewarding the patience of the lower city, which had become somewhat neglected since the barely finished road had been abandoned by motorized vehicles.

Already Jo The Juggler could no longer doubt his visitors' steadily increasing willingness to oblige, especially that of the accordionist Mor-Eloulougou's friends, who completed for him the story of Ngwane-Eligui's case. All over the city people were taking bets; some swore she seemed so untameable she would never be broken that year, while others insisted she would soon be domesticated, if not by the father, hardly capable in his present state of performing such a feat, at least by the son, a rough-mannered, vigorous fellow who was well equipped for the task and had, moreover, vowed to take her by force—a procedure with which he was amply acquainted. For the moment, there was not the slightest doubt that she had been victorious in her resistance to them. She had been seen quite recently by witnesses from outside the Palace: covered with bruises, her face swollen, she appeared as if drunk with the blows that had rained upon her; in any case, she had confided that Zoabekwe had beaten her every day like a wild animal, almost beneath the very eyes of her parents, honest people from a town located several days away by foot and by boat, on the other side of the river toward Mackenzieville, an important settlement that had been founded just beyond the border separating the young Republic from the neighboring colony. Unable to break the young woman by threats or by torture, the palace had sent for her parents, asking them to cajole their child and convince her to adopt a more reasonable attitude. They had promised to make use of time which, in the long

131

run, always reduces the ardor of rebellious daughters. Meanwhile they were being treated in a princely fashion; in every respect they enjoyed precedence over other guests; they received the best food and the best room, and they did not have to work, in contrast to the father's and son's other parents-in-law, who were pointedly invited to help in the fields and plantations if their stay extended beyond a few days.

But Ngwane-Eligui laughed at her parents' entreaties; for her, their presence was not a reason to give up, but an unexpected breathing space, since she felt certain that, as long as they were there, she would at least not suffer the ultimate cruelty. While all this was taking place and shortly before the arrival of the Rubenists, people had been suddenly and quite seriously disquieted by a rumor that had begun to circulate; according to it, women who had been married against their will would before long be authorized to leave their husbands without paying any retribution. As for Ngwane-Eligui, she was in any case determined to run away from the Palace; if that happened, people were unanimous in thinking that Zoabekwe would certainly not hesitate to kill her.

"What is the accordionist's role in this whole affair?" asked Mor-Zamba, who suspected that the rogue was, as usual, hiding a part of the truth from him.

"If I only knew!" replied Jo The Juggler. "He refuses to talk about it. I don't have any doubt he is in contact with her; that's easy enough. He wants her; that's for certain. But how far would he go?"

Jo The Juggler's audacity gradually returned to him; first to the old widows and then to the members of the accordionist's entourage, he posed the following question, which was not devoid of temerity: "Suppose that Zoabekwe's behavior suddenly revealed his intention to commit murder on the person of Ngwane-Eligui. What do you think Father Van den Rietter would do? Would he simply close his eyes, or would he oppose the Chief and his son? For that matter, what does he usually do to protect the poor women he doesn't keep at the mission? After all, he is a friend of the Chief."

"Imagine the distress you are causing us, gentle stranger," responded the widows. "Essentially, it is

132

a question of tact, of diplomacy. Father Van den Rietter is a saintly, self-sacrificing man, but he has no interest in parading as the schoolmaster of an older person, who is, moreover, the master-of-the-city. He doesn't want to humiliate the chief by rebuking him in front of his subjects and his servants. Things might happen like that over there in his own country, but here in our country, he knows perfectly well he should not act in the same way. Well, what do you want him to do, generous stranger? He still had to reprimand him, but he does it gently, very gently, as if speaking to a young child, because he is apprehensive about frightening him away."

"Father Van den Rietter so often talks secretly with the Chief. What would they be talking about, if not justice? Our Father Van den Rietter is a just man. To tell the truth, he is the very incarnation of justice; he is the messenger of Jesus Christ. When he comes among us and arbitrates between widows and the brothers of our deceased husbands—those greedy, unscrupulous men who look upon us as their property—doesn't Father Van den Rietter pronounce in our favor every time? It's common knowledge that he is the guardian angel of widows. Every time he states peremptorily, without fear of anyone and without the slightest concern for sparing the feelings of whoever might be involved: 'If a woman loses her husband, let her be free from that moment on.' Those are the strong words our Father Van den Rietter pronounces every time. You can say that he knows what justice means, our Father Van den Rietter does. Unfortunately, he is powerless to apply it when our Chief himself is involved. But as he often says, that isn't his fault, it is the fault of our own customs, and Father Van den Rietter can do nothing about them. He is a tactful man who doesn't want to transgress against our customs and humiliate the Chief by rebuking him in public. That's the sort of man he is, generous stranger."

Thus spoke the widows.

"Father Van den Rietter a man of justice and compassion?" exclaimed indignantly the chorus of young people in the accordionist's entourage. "What a joke! The Bedridden Chimpanzee and Van den Rietter are two of a kind, accomplices you might say; that's for certain. Van den Rietter would never take it into his head to compete with the Old Chimpanzee, and the Old Chimpanzee would never dare infringe on Van den Rietter's territory. Van den Rietter would never apply the same laws to the Old Chimpanzee as he does to us. Where is justice then? Ah, they're birds of a feather, those two. It's no accident that there is a mysterious young mulattress at the mission. Tell me, my good men, have you ever seen a mulattress fall from the sky? And in your opinion, my good men, how does one make a mulattress? If I am not mistaken, the mulattress, like the mulatto, issues from the coupling of a black woman with whom, eh? I'm asking you, my good men. You'll notice that black women aren't exactly rare around here, but the rest, eh? Do you know many of them? Tell me. Well then, you're lucky."

Suddenly the accordionist let go of his trusty instrument in a petulent gesture of annoyance (Jo The Juggler asserts these days that, if those standing next to him had not come so quickly to its rescue, it would indeed have fallen to the ground and, probably, been broken beyond repair); he then rose to his full height in the middle of his troops. Sandrinelli's former servant had experienced many things during his agitated life, but he was still struck by the pathetic turn of events that evening, which until then had been quite ordinary.

"Brothers," declared Mor-Eloulougou with the solemnity that is so well suited to tribal chiefs in moments of great emotion, "dear brothers, let us speak seriously for once, mon Dieu! Let us finally be men. For before today, have we been anything but children? What exploits have we accomplished up to now? While others learn how to track the passage of a leopard in the jungle, we Ekoumdoumians are keeping vigil over the first itchings in our crotch. And as soon as our rod stands up, we take hold of it like a spear, and once night has fallen, we rush toward the forest of the chimpanzees, I mean toward the Old Chimpanzee's harem, on the outskirts of which we lie in ambush, waiting until some female, escaped from the zoo, slips through the lattice-work enclosure and joins us.

134

Hardly has she inserted us between her muscled thighs than we have already found relief. And the next day, the entire city reverberates with our cry of victory."

"I myself, I who am speaking to you, why do you respect me? What is my prestige among you based upon, my brothers? You have accorded me the flattering reputation of being the scourge of the great hunting preserve, the wolf in the great sheepfold. And it is true I have preyed upon each wife of the Bedridden Chimpanzee and reduced her to a moaning victim. But now, enough of this childishness, mon Dieu! There are other games for us to play now—man's games, war games, games of blood, and perhaps of death as well. But, dear brothers, I hope I am not making a mistake; we are really men, aren't we? If that is true, we have to free Ngwane-Eligui. Otherwise, as you well know, our only resource will be the tears we shed for her. We have to snatch that unhappy child from the claws of those wild animals, because Van den Rietter, the only man who could have saved her, preferred to humor his friend, the Bedridden Chimpanzee, by returning the wretched child to him.

"And since fate has smiled on us by sending a true friend among us at the very moment when we needed him most, a rich and powerful man, a man of experience, a wise man—I mean El Khalik, the follower of Allah—let us ask him in all simplicity to lend us his aid. How many times has he told us that Allah is great and that Mohammed is his Prophet! How many times has he revealed to us that Mohammed, inspired by Allah himself, always advocated sharing and not hoarding, equality and not injustice. After all, this city is our home, and since the Bedridden Chimpanzee has shown himself to be a profoundly unjust man, a base money-grubber, a thief as it were, well then, let's get rid of him and send him back where he belongs. El Khalik, servant of the great and glorious Allah, will you help us? What advice will you give us, stranger and friend, you whose praises are being sung by everyone now that they know about your generosity toward our elderly widows?"

It is true that the elderly widows of the lower city were already competing with each other to see who could be the most zealous in spreading the venerable

135

Moslem's praises to the four corners of Ekoumdoum; they proudly displayed their dresses, quickly made from the amwalli, that highly coveted cotton fabric which the roguish Kola-Kolan's experienced eye had immediately recognized as checkered linen from Vichy. Each old woman had chosen an original combination of colors--blue and white, black and white, pink and white, red and white, yellow and white, and so forth-- to the point that they seemed like whitewashed children, dressed in a smiliar fashion but without, for all that, wearing the same uniform.

"How much did you pay Mor-Eloulougou to deliver that grotesque speech?" Mor-Zamba burst out angrily when Jo The Juggler related the bizarre turn of events to him.

"But you haven't understood a thing, grandpa!" Jo The Juggler retorted indignantly. "I had so little to do with it that, for the moment, his remarks completely bowled me over myself. I had to rub my eyes to make certain that I wasn't dreaming, although I have to admit my joy knew no bounds when I leaned over to the fellow standing next to me and asked him in a whisper, 'But if the chief, I mean the Bedridden Chimpanzee, isn't from here, where is he from?' and he replied, 'That is just it, nobody knows, but it is high time he returned. In any case, it is not our fault he's here; let him sort things out with the people who put him in power.' I have been overtaken by events a number of times, but in this instance, that would be an understatement. You see, the Chief is done for, just like Baba Toura. Sooner or later, he will have to make himself scarce, or he will be mounting the gallows. You see, he is like a referee on a football field in Kola-Kola. Remember. If everyone doesn't accept him from the very beginning, it won't be long before he is thrown out, usually to his detriment and with a great deal of commotion. Speak about being overtaken by events, I was overtaken by events. You can say that again, for in the end, grandpa, what can I preach to them from now on? Van den Rietter can continue to babble his nonsense about a certain Jesus Christ. He imagines it is all very mysterious, because he doesn't believe it himself; nothing is easier than pattering on endlessly to people about things one doesn't believe in one's self. It's a game; it's like talking to women, if you think about it. But as far as I am concerned, it's a question of common sense; everyone necessarily recognizes the truth of my gospel. Justice? They know it very well, at least as well as we do."

"But, my poor George, you certainly realize that your friends were drunk."

"Wait a minute, wait a minute! As for me, I don't have anything against drinking when it gives people back their virility and especially when it gives them back their common sense. As for me, I'm not going to judge the various paths by means of which people come to the good fight; I see that they are beside me, period. That is all that counts."

"Ah, well, do you want me to tell you? I will bet you haven't seen the last surprise yet. With all that, you still haven't laid out your plans for me. You're probably going to declare war on the Chief, aren't you?"

"Just about! Listen to me for a moment, old man. All the time I was waiting for a woman, a child, a young man with poetic inclinations, or any other inhabitant of the city to spontaneously mention you or Abena. On the strength of what Hurricane-Viet told us, I thought the people here were obsessed with your two names; I thought there was no one but the two of you on their minds. But, old man, I had to bow to the facts; it is not like that at all. I told you so. Hurricane-Viet was mistaken, don't you see? We need to devise a different scheme from the one which consists of simply showing up and saying 'I am Mor-Zamba!' That would be too easy. If people were waiting for you twenty years ago like a Messiah, ah well, that is all over now . In other words, if you decided to show yourself, it would be a catastrophe. The Chief and his son would gobble you up in a single bite, and that would be the end of the whole story. Admit it would be a shame!"

"For you."

"Don't worry about me; my story isn't going to end as soon as that; if it were a book, this would only be the beginning, barely the first couple of pages. Listen to me: we must organize our young friends in the city."

"And then?"

"Then? It'll be quite simple. One night we will enter the Chief's section of town, en masse in a single movement or by infiltrating it in small groups during a several-hour period. Oh, that can't be too difficult. They say there are only two guns in the chief's house, his own which he no longer uses (if he ever did) and his son's, which he only brings out on rare occasions for parades, because he is, it seems, a very poor marksman. In the confusion of the first few moments of the invasion, we will immediately take possession of the two guns, and the trick is turned."

"Yes, but we need the missionary's Winchester 30-30 above everything else."

"Ah, yes, I've got a little idea about that too, grandpa. Just listen: once the Old Man and his bastard son are neutralized, who is going to declare himself the legitimate chief? You can't guess? Ah well, it is a certain Mor-Zamba. And what rule is he going to promulgate without further ado? That private individuals are no longer authorized to have firearms within the confines of the territory of Ekoumdoum. Van den Rietter will not want to place himself in the position of being treated as a rebel against legitimate authority. Those people are like that; I know them."

"And you think it will work?"

"And why not? It worked well enough for Baba Toura and Sandrinelli, even though they were already sinister criminals. As soon as The Sot was named Prime Minister, didn't everyone bow down to him?"

"Everyone except the P.P.P."

"Yes, oh well, I would certainly like to see that here. Everything will work quite well, provided you are keeping our guns ready in the nearest cache at the appointed time."

It goes without saying that, as usual, Jo The Juggler was concealing from Mor-Zamba the decisive and, for that matter, the most dangerous part of an enterprise that was already in the process of being executed. Instead of replying to the accordionist's urgent appeal for assistance, the former delingquent had announced he could not make any decision before

138

having consulted Allah, adding that he would do it immediately. For a while he had shut himself in the other room of the house, the narrowest one, the one which served the two travellers as a bedroom, but he soon called Mor-Eloulougou to his side, and in his presence alone, he had engaged in a thousand grotesque gestures amidst the dancing shadows which a murky flame cast throughout the room and into which, one might almost have said, he himself sometimes seemed to merge. Finally, he had taken Mor-Eloulougou's hand and brought it close to the oil lamp; after having studied the palm by tilting it first in one direction and then in the other, he had confided to him: "Dankal bino, dankal bino! Here is what I have to communicate to you on behalf of Allah. Dankal bino, dankal bino! The master of Nouredine is in the power of Allah, as an infant is in the power of its father. Here is what Allah is having communicated to you: if you want to save Ngwane-Eligui, as you have every right to do, oh noble youth, you should go wherever there are firearms in Ekoumdoum; take them, and hide them among your friends. Thus deprived of their strength from that moment on, the torturers of the woman you desire, the woman you have promised to save, will acquiesce in all your demands, whatever they might be; then you can snatch the innocent Ngwane-Eligui from their claws."

Dismayed at first, the accordionist did not take long to regain his wits and discover that the oracle was assigning him a mission which, if he thought about it carefully, lay quite within his grasp. Mor-Eloulougou himself had at his disposal a willing legion of urchins who could go anywhere in the city without arousing suspicion, even into the Bedridden Chimpanzee's neighborhood, where they were frequently called upon to perform menial tasks for which they were paid (in a very miserly fashion, to be sure) and into the Catholic mission where, as schoolboys, choirboys, and occasional houseboys for the two missionaries they were tolerated until late at night. The mission watchdog itself had become so accusomed to them that, if it encountered them at night on the grounds of the presbytery, it wouldn't even bark. All that remained was to devise a ruse to enable the

139

youthful members of such commando groups to carry off their booty without being caught after they had infiltrated the premises which would be their theater of operations.

"Mon Dieu!" said Mor-Eloulougou then, striking himself on the forehead, "all they have to do is park themselves in some nook and wait for the right moment to sneak off with the guns as soon as the Chief's neighborhood and the Catholic mission have fallen asleep."

"What are the chances that the victims will notice the theft in the meantime?" asked Jo The Juggler in a stern tone of voice.

"We will have to pose that question to the children; they are quite familiar with the habits of those people."

"For a country bumpkin, that fellow is pretty sharp," thought Jo The Juggler after the accordionist had left.

Now, that very night shortly after leaving Mor-Zamba, Jo The Juggler, who was eager to do something, suddenly decided to effect his first reconnaissance mission in Ekoumdoum. On the pretext of not wanting to miss an opportunity to inure him to the hardships of war, he woke up the sapak, who had just fallen asleep, and helped him recover his senses in a hurry by giving him a wash-basin full of cool water, into which the youth's head could be plunged over and over again. Maintaining their bearing as militant Kola-Kolans ready for anything that might occur, tense in their watchfulness, doubled over as a precautionary measure, they traversed the city, timidly curled up in the night with its thousand folds and its millions of infinitely branching, mysterious algae. Not a single sentinel, no night watchmen, no guards. How far away Kola-Kola was! After midnight, Ekoumdoum seemed to be a place that was abandoned to the first invader who might come along. They didn't even meet a stray dog, which might have counted as a living being, or the shadow of a furtive lover.

With use, their sixth sense, dulled by the easy life of a several week stay in the city, had begun to revive; they caught themselves feeling their way with their eyes, looking with their ears, reconnoitering with their nose. Once again filled with bold abandon, they did not hesitate to venture within Van den Rietter's compound, which they identified by its high, rough-hew wooden fence; they clambered across it in full knowledge that they were coming dangerously close to the priest's residence. They were looking at a building with enigmatic lines when they heard the barking of a bellicose creature obviously headed with great determination in their direction. The two spies from Kola-Kola took to their heels and barely had time to clear the barricade, as before, like a pair of thieves escaping by the skin of their teeth from the legendary ferocity of the missionaries' German shepherd.

"Ah, yes, my poor fellow, that's promising!" said Jo The Juggler by way of commentary when they once again found themselves alone in their lair.

In summary, here is the information filtered from the jumbled mass of facts the schoolboys had delivered the previous day. Van den Rietter paid a visit on the Bedridden Chimpanzee every Sunday evening and stayed late. After returning to the mission, he went to his office, which had been installed in an outbuilding more or less removed from the actual presbytery; there he worked or read his breviary until midnight or one o'clock in the morning. He then repaired to his room, but only to lie down and fall asleep. Now, that was where he kept his rifle, behind a wardrobe and leaning casually against the wall. It was uncertain whether Van den Rietter verified the gun's presence each night before allowing himself to be overtaken by sleep; the young adolescents doubted it. "In any case," thought Jo The Juggler, "the main thing will already have been done by that time."

As for Brother Nicholas, he had no interest at all in his guns, having made use of them but once, to the best of the adolescent boys' ability to remember. A woman, who had been going toward the fields rather too early in the morning, stumbled across a sleeping antelope and returned to inform the missionaries, reputed to be great hunters and to have a weakness for venison, but she encountered only Brother Nicholas, who immediately picked up his gun and hurried to the spot indicated by the distracted woman. When Brother

Nicholas arrived, the antelope was still sleeping, and the missionary had to do no more than fire on the poor animal at point-blank range. That was certainly the only trophy of his hunting exploits in Africa.

Yet it remained indispensible to establish precisely the number of guns held at the Catholic mission, the census of those at the Palace having already been summarily tabulated, in order to be sure that the commando charged with appropriating them would not overlook anything. Mor-Eloulougou and his usual entourage could only acknowledge their perplexity: they agreed that, in all probability, the two missionaries had more guns than they habitually put on display; nevertheless, for their part, they had not, until that moment, had any particular reason to concern themselves with the armaments of those two men, for they had never dreamed of confronting them in battle.

The schoolboys, many of whom demonstrated an extraordinary capacity for observation, asserted that in their opinion each missionary possessed not only a high-caliber weapon—that is, a Winchester 30-30 for Van den Rietter and, for Brother Nicholas, a Robust double-barrelled rifle—but also several firearms that were much smaller and even quite tiny; they gave an amazing description of these guns, but it was so imprecise and halting that their elders had to inquire how they knew it was a matter of firearms and not the kinds of imaginary objects those people often take pleasure in possessing.

"During certain times of the year, at dusk when the birds of prey begin to fly in whirlwinds above the city," the adolescents replied, "Father Van den Rietter, who was the more enthusiastic and, for that matter, the more skillful hunter of the two, stations himself in the clearing around his residence, in the schoolyard, or in any other place that might be appropriate for such an exercise; then Father Van den Rietter fires them, although he waits patiently each time until one of the birds passes directly over his head." The most striking thing was to see Father Van den Rietter clasp his two large hands together to hold a gun of such miniscule dimensions. Moreover, he frequently hit the mark, and all at once the bird,

abruptly losing its forward momentum, fell into the
dust. Although they had never seen Brother Nicholas
engage in this exercise, the schoolboys claimed to be
convinced that he too had one of these guns; to
believe them, every European necessarily had one of
them, a guarantee that their enemies would be unpleas-
antly surprised in the case of a close combat. If
that wasn't true, how could one explain the utmost
self-assurance that is always and everywhere displayed
by those people.

Sandrinelli's former servant understood that the
schoolboys were trying to describe pistols or revolvers, arms which can be held in one hand or completely
concealed, when they are miniaturized, in the fist of
a big man like Van den Rietter.

In response to a question by Jo The Juggler, the
adolescents indicated which of them would, in the near
future, have the privilege of being permitted to enter
the missionaires' rooms at the residence; then they
were sent away. All evening long, Jo The Juggler and
Mor-Eloulougou successively called the privileged ones
in to them; the wise Moslem overwhlemed them with
presents and lavished them with even more abundant
promisies; he asked them to determine the number of
firearms in the possession of each missionary as well
as the exact places where they were kept. They
thought the adolescents should devote a good week to
the search, for it would not do to rush them and risk
committing a foolish blunder.

Jo The Juggler was already rubbing his hands
together, undecided whether to be more grateful for
providential circumstance or for his truly unexpected
friends in Ekoumdoum; in any case, he was happy to
have set an incongruous and somewhat unfamiliar but
multitudinous team on the right track.

## CHAPTER 3

A truly amazing incident took place, however, and once again placed everything in question at a time when the most suitable adolescents had already been recruited by Mor-Eloulougou in preparation for the planned operation; the youthful troops had been subjected to rigorous training, and they had been extensively conditioned each evening by mystical harangues, seasoned with a ceremony bordering on magic and administered by the master of Nouredine, the servant of Allah. It is perhaps not devoid of interest that, when this new turn of events was faithfully recounted to Mor-Zamba by Jo The Juggler, the giant immediately characterized it as ill-omened.

Was it an overwhelming, senseless, unmanageabley intractable crisis? Had she, as Jo The Juggler affirms (and he is better informed on the subject these days than anyone else), had she foolishly allowed herself to be taken in, when she heard reports of Mor-Eloulougou's overly flattering braggadocio? Whatever the case may be, one morning in broad daylight, Ngwane-Eligui deliberately defied the Palace by leaving the house in the Chief's compound, the house where she had been confined as a result of the special court's provisional verdict condemning her to prison until her fate could be definitively decided. She left without a word, without a glance at the old woman who was supposed to be watching over her; such a departure was against all rules of propriety, and it at first petrified the old woman with horror, then filled her with indignation, and finally cast her into

144

a state of puzzled bewilderment. And this is the most extraordinary, the most impertinent, the most presumptuous, the most troubling, and even the most poignant aspect of the affair, although it was also the most risky, the most audacious, the most amusing, the most juvenile, the most spontaneous, and even the most reassuring: without hurrying, Ngwane-Eligui crossed the city and moved in the direction of the road, addressing a kind word to each person she met, pausing to chat at one point and to answer an exclamation of surprise at another, caressing the chin of a child or bestowing on him an innocent smile which revealed the full flaming brilliance of her pearly white teeth, or raising her hand in a gesture of recognition to a pregnant sister perceived from a distance.

News of the scandal had soon set the city ablaze; it seethed with excitement and then boiled over. The most intrepid inhabitants rushed to the main thoroughfare to catch a glimpse of this incredible creature and even to gaze at her close-up; others prudently took up positions in the doorways of their own houses.

"What, Ngwane-Eligui!" the aged women of mature judgment called out to her, "how could you have the cheek to leave the master-of-the-city's compound without his authroization? How could you run away from the prison to which the well-known verdict of his court has condemned you? Where will you find refuge from now on? Will Father Van den Rietter agree to reverse his decision? Or, poor child, unfortunate girl afflicted by heaven with too much beauty, have you then decided to pursue unhappiness forever? Who will give you shelter now, poor Ngwane-Eligui?"

"There you are, free at last, Ngwane-Eligui!" the older men exclaimed ironically, always ready to use an act of valor as the pretext for a witticism or a moral fable. "One or two more young wives like you for our Chief, and sure enough, everything in the city—houses as well as men—will be turned upside down."

"Don't worry, Ngwane-Eligui!" the young people from Mor-Eloulougou's faction assured her in a tone of voice which nevertheless betrayed a touch of doubt. "Don't pay any attention to the mumblings of old people who have been worn down by grief and sorrow. Follow us, beautiful Ngwane-Eligui; come take refuge behind the impenetrable wall of our bare chests. What man will be bold enough to follow you into the bosom of that terror-inspiring enclosure."

As if Ngwane-Eligui had been waiting for their audacious proposal or had been informed of it well in advance, her ceremonious descent actually did lead her toward the house where the young people in Mor-Eloulougou's faction habitually gathered each day; there she was greeted with a thunderous cacophony of drums and rattles, triumphal hurrahs, and even war-songs, although these days it is said that, once they had installed her like a young newlywed, they refrained from taking any particular precautions and didn't seem to worry about any sinister possibilities.

It is a fact that, during the next few hours, Mor-Eloulougou and his friends, sometimes in raptures of enthusiasm and sometimes silent with brows knit, offered the city a sequence of scenes which left it absolutely breathless. During this performance, which was unlike anything we had ever seen before, mysterious secret meetings alternated with proclamations that sent onlookers into a frenzy. Because Ngwane-Eligui had finally been able to escape from the lair of the monstrous old man, it was quite natural that the finest sons of the authentic Ekoumdoum race (from which so many heroes and worthy successors of Akomo had issued during the city's glorious past) should offer her the inviolable refuge she deserved. When he came to pay his daily visit on the saintly Moslem, Mor-Eloulougou himself burst into resounding roars and seconded them with gesticulations calculated to inspire terror in anyone who saw them, although perhaps considerably less alarming for those to whom they ought to have been addressed, entrenched as they were in the upper city, far from the saintly Moslem's house and at least two or three kilometers away from the road.

An even more curious circumstance could be observed as the day began to wane; whispered cunningly from one individulal to another, suspicion grew that a retaliatory attack would be carried out before night-fall against Ngwani-Eligui and her newfound protectors by the guards from the Palace. Instead of closing ranks around the fugitive and, as promised in their

146

initial excitement, erecting an impregnable fortress around her sancturay, Mor-Eloulougou's group dissolved for once and scattered throughout the city, preferring in the end to gravitate toward the lodging of the devout Moslems, who were rendered speechless by the extraordinary flexibility of their strategy. It is not irrelevant to mention that by this time even the most naive observers could have detected a number of signs which would have enabled them to foresee the imminence of the impending drama. Swarms of children succeeded each other like waves, inundating the main thoroughfare which, after leaving the road, extended completely straight between the houses on either side, rose imperceptibly with the slope of the hill, lost itself momentarily at the top of the knoll where a small forest jealously concealed the palace (that is the reason why the Chief's section of town was called the Forest of the Chimpanzees), and then reappeared, not quite the same but not entirely different either.

Children throng to uncommon occurrences more eagerly than grasshoppers to ill-fated harvests that have been scorched by the heat of the sun, and these riotous invasions usually announce the approach of a wedding procession or a funeral. Standing near the thresholds of their own houses, as they were in the habit of doing, the adults seemed to be holding themselves in reserve. If the women were already bewailing the agony that was about to consume their sister, flesh of their flesh, their husbands' faces betrayed a quivering smile redolent with that sensual, manly submissiveness that speaks volumes about the passionate tenacity that humankind has always needed in its struggle for survival, as the entire history of our species demonstrates and regardless of what Jo The Juggler might say to the contrary.

All at once the sapak, who had also stationed himself in the doorway, heard distant shouts from the direction of the upper city. "They are coming!" Echoed an infinite number of times and expressed in countless different but equally concise forms, this announcement rolled toward the road like a hailstorm of debris clattering ominously down a steep incline. Driven almost in spite of himself, as if drawn toward the scene of a dramatic event, the child from Kola-

147

Kola ran to the place where innumerable curious
bystanders had already gathered. In the distance, he
saw a platoon of remarkably tall men, brandishing
spears and cutlasses and marching in closed ranks.
Advancing with determination but without haste, they
were preceded by a brutish sort of fellow wearing a
cruel, spiteful expression and armed with an enormous
whip that he cracked from time to time by waving it
violently through the air; a few moments later the
sapak learned that it was Zoabekwe, the son of the
chief, commonly know as The Bastard, although he
himself never knew why.

The platoon appeared quite well informed and
moved without hesitation toward the house where
Ngwane-Eligui had thought she would find refuge, but
by that time it had been deserted by everyone except
the unfortunate young woman herself.

"Come out of there, Ngwane-Eligui!  Run away,"
her sisters exhorted the young woman from all sides,
for, scattered among the bystanders, they listened
only to their own compassionate instincts.  "Flee from
here, Ngwane-Eligui!  Or is it true that you have
decided to die?"

It is true that the sapak saw her from a considerable distance, but he swears that she remained
exactly where she had been sitting, stubborn, obstinate.  Others who were not afraid to approach the
doors and windows of the building testify that she
never raised her head, even when Zoabekwe, who was
ominously cracking his whip, stormed like a thunderbolt into the fortress where she should have been able
to thumb her nose at her hateful tormentors.  She
barely flinched when Zoabekwe's monstrous whip lashed
cruelly across her back and ripped it open, or when
The Bastard suddenly grabbed her by the head, dragged
her into the courtyard, and threw her into the dust so
he could publicly vent his spleen upon her with his
sinister instrument of torture, and after it had been
shattered to pieces by The Bastard's frenzy and sent
flying in all directions, he beat the poor woman
senseless with kicks and blows from his fists.  Likewise, it has been established beyond the shadow of a
doubt that her dreadful ordeal drew neither cries of
pain, nor moans, nor pleas for mercy from the unfortu-

nate young woman, even though she seemed to have departed this life at the moment when The Bastard's men gathered her up, inert like a log of wood, and carried her away. The sapak still remembers that Brother Nicholas' old Fiat was at that very moment proceeding, as usual, quite slowly up the main thoroughfare, obliging the crowd of bystanders to part with muttered curses before it passed beside the procession that was carrying the inanimate Ngwane-Eligui and moved gradually away.

"That certainly won't be the end of it," Mor-Zamba had observed, after listening to an account of that disturbing incident. "That won't be the end of it; if you stay, you'll see—you'll have to pay dearly for your connections with that band of irresponsible braggarts."

"Too bad! I'm staying," replied Jo The Juggler.

It was good that he did, for during the days that followed, the Palace demonstrated not the slightest intention to retaliate against those who had rashly declared themselves the guarantors of poor Ngwane-Eligui's freedom or against their friends, the strangers at the other end of the city. Everything suddenly seemed to have returned to normal the following day after the Bedridden Chimpanzee and The Bastard had driven Ngwane-Eligui's parents away, because their advice and admonitions had proven equally incapable of restoring the young woman to the path that would have lead straight to the father's bed or, failing that, to the bed of the son.

"This time, it is going to be done," the older men of the city concluded in an ambiguous tone of voice. "This time, she is going to give in. Zoabekwe is not wrong to use a firm hand. If the cock wants to tame the hen, let him stop beating around the bush. It is certainly all over this time, for it is true that nothing works as well as a firm hand, at least in such matters."

Far from reassuring Jo The Juggler, the emergence of this attitude irritated him beyond belief. Perhaps he had never before experienced such a confused state of mind. Without formally breaking off relations with his allies, he decided to hold their common projects in abeyance and look for other friends in the city.

149

"Didn't I tell you so?" said Mor-Zamba triumphantly. "I have learned by experience that the
foreigner who arrives in a strange country will be
immediately besieged by people who are not among the
most desirable in the community; the latter are always
held back by their modesty, the most beautiful flower
of the heart, and if the heart were a garden, it would
also be the most fragrant. To reach them, a newcomer
first needs to crawl through the underbrush and suffer
the thorn pricks inflicted on him by the knaves and
fools who never hesitate to embrace him at once. I
advise you to adopt the following strategy: make use
of the sapak, and send him out to explore the human
jungle of Ekoumdoum, as I did long ago; maybe he will
discover gardens that have until now remained hidden
from us behind the thorny, yellowish underbrush."

It was thus that the child from Kola-Kola began
to venture by himself among the local inhabitants; as
an obedient servant, he went to the spring to draw
water for his master, thereby encountering the
children who were performing the same task at the same
time. On the first few occasions when he appeared,
the little girls ran away shouting, "Hausa! Hausa!"
while the young boys came up to him, feeling him as if
he were an extraordinary creature of some kind and,
finally, addressing a few friendly, joyful words to
him. The sapak was under orders from Jo The Juggler
never to answer them or anyone else, but to confine
himself to a foolish smile or, at most, a nod of the
head to indicate assent or denial. His height and his
loping stride sufficiently intimidated his young
friends so that none of them exhibited the least
desire to harrass him. When even the young girls
allowed themselves to be won over by the new arrival,
it often occurred that the Rubenist schoolboy from
Fort Negre passed unnoticed through the unruly throngs
of urchins in Ekoumdoum.

It did not take the sapak long to make a discovery in the upper city and to tell Jo The Juggler
about it. "You would think that all of the activity
in the entire city takes place up there," he said.
"For example, the missionary is always going back and
forth through that part of town on his bicycle."

"Which of the two? The older one or the younger

150

one?"

"Is there an older one and a younger one? As for me, I only saw a fat one without a beard and a thin one with a beard."

"Brother Nicholas is the fat, clean-shaven one, and Father Van den Rietter is the thin, bearded one; that is why they call him Soumazeu."

"Well then, Father Van den Rietter is the one who can always be seen parading around up there; he talks to the people, he goes into their houses, and he settles arguments between fathers and sons, between husbands and wives; he scolds the young people and the little children. In fact, whenever he sees a naked child, he orders him to get dressed immediately."

"Is that all? You didn't see anything else?"

"I also ran across a man, or rather a young chap—let's call him a young man—and he was making fun of Mor-Eloulougou and his clan. Not at all behind their backs, you know, but to their faces. He is someone who can't be very fond of Mor-Eloulougou and his followers. In addition, he is a spirited fellow. I offered him a pack of cigarettes, and there he is falling all over himself to thank me. Then he asks, 'Why me?' Naturally, I don't say anything. That is when a somewhat older woman, probably his mother, says to him, 'Why you? Listen, it's obvious; he has become a friend of your younger brother, who doesn't smoke. If your brother had been a smoker, for heaven sakes, the tobacco would have been offered to him. These people are generous, but they don't know how to speak our language; well then, put yourself in their place. To demonstrate their friendship, they give presents, like the package of cigarettes. The little fellow likes us, he does.' That is what the mother said to him."

"Excellent!" observed Jo The Juggler soberly. "If you continue to do work like that, little fellow, you might possibly go far, you know?"

The next day, the sapak offered a bottle of local rum to the same young man, who had become more than ever intrigued and, despite his mother's explanations, fascinated by the personality of the wise Moslem who was no doubt behind the advances made by little Nouredine, his disciple. Being unable to restrain his curiosity any longer, he came to the travellers' lodgings at the beginning of the evening with the intention of speaking to El Khalik. It goes without saying that he stumbled upon Mor-Eloulougou and his followers, with whom he exchanged, in a most brotherly fashion and much to the Rubenists' astonishment, a series of taunts and jests filled with hidden innuendoes. The sapak had been mistaken; the young man who had aroused such hope in him had merely been expressing an insignificant mockery and not a profound disapproval of the accordionist and his clan. Many times the Rubenists had the same experience, and in the end they had to bow before the facts. Far from having enemies in the city, Mor-Eloulougou and his clan comprised the avant-garde, the spearhead which was indeed sharply pointed in a way, but which also typified the mentality of the younger generation.

"Even so we need to get to the bottom of it," Mor-Zamba concluded when the problem was submitted to him once again. "It ought to be simple. Listen! Tell the accordionist you can not support the projects drawn up in concert with him unless he somehow justifies his unforgivable cowardice. It is imperative for those people to explain themselves. I think I understand, but ask them the question anyway."

"We certainly wanted to protect her, all of us did. That unfortunate little young woman!" Mor-Eloulougou replied to Jo The Juggler as he sought to justify his curious absence the day Ngwane-Eligui was almost beaten to death.

"Who, you?" Jo The Juggler queried him sharply.

"Well, yes, we the young people, all of us who feel it is not fair for an old man to abduct so many women from all over the place and cage them in his compound as if it were a zoo. Only, the elders came and told us during a secret meeting that they didn't approve of what we were doing. 'One doesn't side with a woman who wants to leave the husband who is her master. It is one thing to meet secretly with a woman who already belongs to another man; it is another to assist her in her efforts to run away; it would be better to help the husband recover his property, even by brute force, if necessary; desiring to act in any other way would make you guilty of a sacrilege; it

152

would be just as bad as allowing a dead friend or relative to rot in the sun without proper burial.' That is how the elders spoke to turn us from our intentions. Otherwise, we would certainly have made all the necessary arrangements to protect Ngwane-Eligui."

"Just as I thought," declared Mor-Zamba when these remarks were reported to him.

"Yes, but as for me, that doesn't facilitate my job," said Jo The Juggler bitterly.

It took Jo The Juggler very little time to contrive the procession of buffoonery and roguish travesties that were obviously called for under the circumstances. The following night, he detained Mor-Eloulougou and those members of his clan who, after him, appeared to be the most influential. In the bedroom of his house and concealed from the eyes of all other witnesses, the rogue improvised a ceremony that was as interminable as it was absurd, as ominously sinister as it was tedious, appropriately calculated in short to weaken if not neutralize the critical acumen of the spectators as well as their instinctual capacity for moral and physical resistance; he ran through its various stages with a diligence and sense of gravity that nothing seemed capable of disturbing.

Because everything has to come to an end, Jo The Juggler finally armed himself with an extremely sharp-edged clasp-knife, the quite involuntary gift of Sandrinelli, alias The Gaullist. Operating with infinite skill and by means of short, abrupt, almost aerial slashes, he succeeded in making a barely perceptible incision on the back of each participant's hand; that is how the charlatans did it at Fort Negre, when they claimed to be offering the simpletons a protection against snakebite. Then, one by one, he collected the drops of blood on the blade of his knife as they formed like pearls on the incisions, and he gradually mixed them all together in the palm of his left hand. To crown his performance, Jo The Juggler dipped his thumb into this liquid and, Mor-Eloulougou's fearful hesitation notwithstanding, went over to place it on the tip of the young man's tongue, where it left a large red dot; he again dipped his thumb into the liquid formed by mixing the spectators' blood together and placed it on the tip of another young man's tongue, and he repeated the process until each of them had participated in this sacramental rite, in spite of their obvious revulsion.   Finally, he himself submitted to it.

"Now," Jo The Juggler announced, addressing himself to the participants and speaking in a sepulchral tone of voice, "we are united by a sacred bond. From now on, we comprise a mystical family, to which each of us owes absolute fidelity in all matters, beginning with the secret of our plans to attack the greedy old man.   If one of us betrays the secret, Allah who is great and of whom Mohammed is the Prophet will attend to his punishment.  Allah sees all things, all places, all times.  If one of us knowingly reveals our secret to a third party, even if that third party is one of the elders of the city, let him be cursed and struck down by Allah.  If one of us takes it upon himself to talk to an elder without paying careful attention to the subject of their conversation on the day of the attack or on the eve of that day, let him be cursed and struck down by Allah.  If one of us permits himself to lie down with a woman and to sleep with her at the risk of revealing our secret in his slumber, let him be cursed and struck down by Allah. . . ."

The child from Kola-Kola, Evariste the sapak, who is in the habit of not mincing his words these days, generally argues that Jo The Juggler himself sabotaged his undertaking when he introduced an atmosphere of superstitious frenzy that would soon explode like a bomb and blow up the scaffolding they had raised with patience and not without intelligence and good judgment.   Jo The Juggler contends, on the contrary, that the sham ritual produced a very profound impression on the young peasants; the very next day he discerned a greater sense of seriousness in their facial expressions, a more reflective tone in their remarks, a less nonchalant attitude in their bearing:   they were no longer the same men, at least for a few days.

For proof, he cites the magnificent success of the operation from a logistical and technical point of view.  During their long, dull, dismal, and, for that matter, embittered lives, very few professional military leaders have the opportunity, as Jo The Juggler himself points out, to experience such a triumph.

It is an undeniable fact (about that we can all agree!): the looting of the guns took place precisely according to the plan conceived by Jo The Juggler, Mor-Eloulougou, and his companions, certainly not the least prodigious accomplishment during that lugubrious chain of event. Abetted by unforeseen delays resulting from the Ngwane-Eligui affaire, Mor-Eloulougou's young spies had had ample opportunity to complete their mission and report back, with all the desired precision, on the number and location of the guns. As for the four adolescents who had been chosen to conduct the operation itself, they were divided into two groups and intensively drilled, clearly demonstrating the lucidity, the composure, the ingenuity, and the finesse which were expected of them and which would hardly be superfluous for undertaking a task that everyone considered difficult and dangerous.

It was in the Chief's compound that the fledgling commando advanced with the greatest ease, for visitors from outside could only be detected with great difficulty in the Forest of the Chimpanzees; it was quite poorly lighted at night, and during normal times a continuous flow of exchanges between it and the neighboring parts of the city took place until very late at night. At the mission, in contrast, it had been necessary to bribe the clergymen's servant and official choirboy without revealing too much to him; a gangly, awkward fellow who had been furnished from the Chief's compound, he was effeminate, always a bit bewildered, and smitten with veneration and a dim-witted fidelity for his masters, but however shaky his collaboration might have been, it proved decisive.

The children took possession of the two known guns at the Chief's residence, but all told they carried away a half-dozen from the mission—the well-known Winchester 30-30 carbine, two revolvers (one of which was a miniaturized model), and a pistol from Father Van den Rietter's quarters as well as the Robust double-barrelled rifle and a miniature revolver from Brother Nicholas' room. Obeying the orders of their superiors, the adolescents from the two commando

155

groups then burrowed into dark, hollow recesses, waiting patiently for weariness, sleep, and lust to arrive and open the way for their escape. As soon as they thought it safe, they all left the danger zones where they had successfully carried out their missions, rejoined several older colleagues who had hidden themselves near the base of the buildings at the Catholic mission or in the Forest of the Chimpanzees, and calmly delivered the carefully wrapped guns they had been carrying like the most ordinary bundles under their arms. These young people in turn had merely to take cover at a prearranged spot in a nearby woods until Mor-Eloulougou and his two most trusted lieutenants arrived and guided them to a cave across the river, where they concealed the guns so well that it would have been vain to think of anyone ever coming by and discovering them.

How did the already anticipated apotheosis suddenly become transformed into a disaster, the impressive monument into a pile of rubble, the incredible procession into a rout, the clear sky into the confused din of a cyclone, the bursts of laughter into moans and cries of pain? Holding all the trumps and assured of his own mastery at the game, Jo The Juggler was busy, although he remained calm and collected, as was fitting on the eve of a great battle; he distributed the various roles, enumerated his overall strength, reviewed his troops, visited the caches, distributed weapons, and began the countdown. The moment of the attack was fast approaching; he had scheduled the fateful clash at midnight, an ideal time, as it seemed to him, for Ekoumdoum's glorious rendezvous with its own long overdue liberation.

Jo The Juggler was convinced that, when all was said and done, the whole business belonged to the most elementary category of military exercises. He would lead the attack; that had been agreed upon from the very beginning, so to speak. In the middle of approximately thirty strong, hefty lads armed to the teeth and under the orders of two trusty lieutenants, Mor-Eloulougou and the gigantic Mor-Zamba, the former servant of Sandrinelli would march at the head of his confederates, a compact mass bristling with pikes and spears.

"Several warriors in the front ranks will of course have to be granted the privilege of bearing arms," Jo The Juggler said to himself during the rare breaks he accorded himself. "It is absolutely necessary in order to give the defenders the impression that they are faced with a crushing defeat, but they must certainly not try to use them. In any case, they will have received neither the training, nor the ammunition to do so. Only Mor-Zamba and myself, dressed in full military uniform, will be equipped as a precautionary measure with ammunition, ready if need be to make our guns speak for us."

It was hardly necessary to pass through a gate to enter the Forest of the Chimpanzees, for despite the bamboo fence, it was perpetually open to accomodate the schemes of every truly determined male and every shameless female. En masse, the attackers would suddenly pour into the Chief's residence from every entryway. Perhaps a few preliminary shots would be fired right away by Jo The Juggler and Mor-Zamba to make certain that the inhabitants would be immobilized with terror, although this point had not yet been settled, for Mor-Zamba had succeeded until then in withholding his assent.

Once the Palace had been taken, they would assemble all the able-bodied men from the Forest of the Chimpanzees in the smallest possible number of rooms; they would be placed under the guard of several impromptu soldiers carrying guns and reporting to the sapak, who was seldom lacking in vigilance, composure, and moral discipline, as Jo The Juggler well knew. The sapak too might be wearing a uniform, if it came to that, because he did have one, although Mor-Zamba had not yet given his consent on this point either.

For Jo The Juggler, all that remained was the delivery of the guns he expected shortly before the fatal moment. He himself had an appointment on the roadway in several hours with Mor-Zamba, who on this occasion was going to bring all the guns he had been holding in safe-keeping. At the same time, a very small team of young men from Mor-Eloulougou's clan would enter the forest at nightfall, go to the cave where the booty recently taken from the authorities of Ekoumdoum had been cached, and bring it under the

157

cloak of darkness to the house of the devout Moslems. The fate of this humble detachment was about to thrust those contending for power in Ekoumdoum into a rare position of reciprocal ignorance—the anguish and perplexity on one side balanced by the hatred and constantly growing fear on the other. The first indication of the debacle occurred, however, in a situation which should have been advantageous to Jo The Juggler, although in reality it only served to inject an element of confusion into the subsequent course of events. The three men in the detachment were returning toward the city with the guns, but when they had no more than a few hundred meters to go before emerging into the open, they were suddenly deafened by an uproar so unusal that, overcome by suspicion, they turned around and retraced their steps, running back along the same path they had just taken until they stopped, completely out of breath, and hastily composed themselves, deciding to hide the guns temporarily near the spot where they happened to be at that moment—in a nondescript clump of shubbery that their own panic and an extreme lack of visibility prevented them from marking in any way.

As a matter of fact, the rout was already complete in the city, and Jo The Juggler's troops, even those from his general staff, were preoccupied with trying to save themselves. How had it been possible for this to happen?

The traitor, the miserable sycophant, the hateful Judas who did not even receive thirty pieces of silver from his illustrious patron, was a young conspirator belonging to Mor-Eloulougou's group and a full-fledged member of the mystical fellowship established a few days previously by the revered follower of Allah, El Khalik himself; moreover, he had been fully initiated into all the secrets of the conspiracy. To Jo The Juggler's great misfortune, it turned out that this faint soul (we no longer even mention his name in Ekoumdoum) was also the much too beloved son of a mother whose adoration for Father Van den Rietter went even further than the cults that faithful Catholics dedicate to their most venerated saints. A widow who was still young, in possession of all her teeth, and quite desirable, she was constantly being harrassed by

158

a brother-in-law, her dead husband's sole heir, who was tormented by the desire to take advantage of his rights over her--rights associated with tradition and with the dominant sex. Against a woman who persisted in refusing his demands, this man had invented the most circumstantial tale of licentious behavior, accusing her of the basest depravity in an alleged relationship with a man from the Chief's compound, a stranger entertained secretly every night at all hours before he left at the first crowing of the cock, a stranger who no doubt heaped presents upon her. As usual, Father Van den Rietter had been asked by the widow, enraged with indignation and self-righteous anger, to arbitrate between her and her brother-in-law; the man had accepted Van den Rietter's verdict in advance, although he was not a practicing Catholic. Because the justice of the Chief was quite justifiably held in contempt and inspired no confidence in anyone, it had now become an almost universally accepted practice for the Ekoumdoumians to endure more or less stoically the missionary's cunning and ingratiating interference in their most intimate affairs.

Now, several days earlier, Father Van den Rietter had rendered a double verdict in favor of the widow; he had not only demolished the rejected suitor's fabrications and expunged her supposed fornications from the record, thereby restoring her honor to a faithful member of his flock, he had also once again rigorously proclaimed a truth he had decidedly taken to heart: that every widow should be a free woman over whom no one is any longer justified to claim the exercise of any natural right whatsoever. This tenet of the faith pleased not only the accused in the present instance, but all the other widows of Ekoumdoum as well and even all the other women of the city, for, as they themselves declared, they too were condemned to become widows someday. And that is why the exonerated defendant and the other widows of Ekoumdoum and even the other women of the city (condemned, they admitted, to widowhood) were consumed with fervor for Father Van den Rietter.

Now then, forgetting the blood oath he had sworn before the venerable follower of Allah and obeying only his filial piety, the widow's son, troubled for a

159

long time by a guilty conscience, suddenly blurted out the overly burdensome secret to his mother, who was horrified and preached to him in the following manner: "My son, what a vile sin you committed by participating in that abominable masquerade! How you have profaned the sacred mysteries of our faith by tolerating their disgusting aperies. My son, no matter how serious your mistake might be, you will undoubtedly be pardoned for it, providing you run immediately to our dear Father Van den Rietter and humbly confess it to him."

It must have been about four o'clock in the afternoon when Van den Rietter learned about his loss and that of Brother Nicholas, about the plot itself as well as its many and serious implications. He rushed into his fellow countryman's room, but he of course did not find him there. Brother Nicholas was a zealous man who was almost always busy working with his hands, a makeshift ecclesiastic who had no breviary to read, no inclination toward mystical meditation, and hardly any interest in telling his rosary; why would he have been in his room at a time of day he quite reasonably regarded as the most suitable for physical activity in the open air? Overcome with fear and anger, Soumazeu, the man in the white cassock, had soon bicycled around his establishment in search of his superintendent of public works, feverishly questioning everyone he encountered and, for the first time, giving the bystanders who saw him the impression that he was a hunted man. All at once, they saw him descend the main thoroughfare of Ekoumdoum at hair-raising speed, disregarding the muddy holes and even the gullies which cut across it, skidding on the thick bed of gravel, dancing skillfully with his feet to regain his balance, and thus freeing the pedals to turn dizzily like the blades of a propeller.

When he reached the road, he turned right, taking a section of the highway that had been restored by Brother Nicholas for the use of his old Fiat truck; one kilometer down the road, Van den Rietter's companion was directing an army of half naked workmen armed with shovels and working in a sand pit; on some days, he remained there with his men for a long time, inappropriately late according to Van den Rietter, who

160

advanced the debilitating climate of tropical Africa as a reason for categorically condemning of any excess of zeal. That is where he found his countryman.

"Brother," he said to him almost as an aside, "what do you have in the way of guns? A Robust hunting rifle and a side arm?"

"A little revolver, yes; that's it all right. Why do you ask, Father?"

"Well, you should know that they have been stolen from you!"

"What are you talking about? Bless me, by whom?"

"By the niggers of course!"

"The niggers? Which niggers? Certainly not ours? Well, in that case, Father, I must admit that I am not following you. Tell me whatever you like about our niggers—that they climb in trees, that they are descended from monkeys (as if they ever left that stage of development!), that they eat each other in the form of steaks or roasts or stews. Whatever you like, I won't argue. But stealing guns! What would they do with them? The very idea! That would indeed be the first time in the history of Christianity that niggers have stolen guns."

"Brother, it would be better to come with me immediately so we can investigate this business together."

Bathed in the barely subdued crimson glow of the waning day, they presented quite a spectacle as they made their way up the central thoroughfare again; more anxiety-ridden and tense, Van den Rietter went ahead on his bicycle, pedalling like a ballerina and applauded by the scattered groups of onlookers, who were beside themselves with admiration to see so much energy in a man of his age. Brother Nicholas followed at a considerable distance in his ancient truck, groaning under its load of sand; he was advancing at a snail's pace, but with the roar of a thousand elephants trumpetting in unison, for the clergyman had made it a practice to climb that hill, though quite a gentle slope, in first gear, the only ratio in his transmission that inspired absolute confidence in him.

This scene did not fail to plunge the conspirators who saw it into uncertainty and a frightened anticipation of misfortune, for they had become con-

161

vinced that an unknown factor was slipping into the round of iniatives and rejoinders which they themselves had set in motion and which had perhaps by now become sheer madness.

Despite their knowledge of the forest, an inherent familiarity with it so to speak, we still find it strange these days that not a single one of the native Ekoumdoumian conspirators thought of seeking refuge in the tangled maze of the jungle or in the somber depths of a leafy thicket. They had cause to regret it, for with the exception of the small detachment that had been surprised at the edge of the woods as their gun-transport mission was being carried out, no one escaped the ravages of the raid conducted that evening by Van den Rietter at the head of a veritable regiment, composed of guards from the Palace as well as mission employees who were normally utilized for other tasks but had been transformed on this occasion into rude mercenaries.

The arrest of the Rubenist militants disguised as devout Moslems was made in a way that was not free from ignominy for these two favorites of the Christian widows. Like a true regimental commander, Van den Rietter, who had rolled his white cassock up to his knees, was the first to rush into the house; he was brandishing an enormous electric torch which swept every nook with a blinding flash of light; having timorously gathered there at dusk, the travellers and their friends were petrified. Jo The Juggler was still trying to save appearances by maintaining his role as a disciple of Allah jealously attached to the rites and attitudes prescribed by the Prophet himself; seated tailor-fashion in the middle of the house, he was hieratically telling his large string of beads, while his lips seemed to have fallen victim to a fit of fervent mumbling.

"Get up, Hausa!" thundered Van den Rietter. "Go ahead! Get up, my good fellow!"

Jo The Juggler imperturbably continued his ostentatious show of piety.

"Carry this clown away for me," Van den Rietter ordered in a calculatedly derisive tone.

Immediately a thousand arms shot forth from all sides, grabbed the Rubenist, shook him, bruised him, and then lifted him like a bubble raised by a puff of air; never lacking in rebellious spirit, the delinquent from Kola-Kola was flailing his legs in a ridiculous fashion, attempting to struggle even under such conditions; a grotesque, highly unequal combat ensued, and during the course of it, the manipulations of countless strongmen with the zealousness of drugged gorillas had quickly torn his Islamic vestment from him, despite its fullness and the numerous folds which should have impeded the accomplishment of their enterprise. Unfortunately Jo The Juggler, who in this respect was also no doubt obeying some commandment or other from the Koran, proved not to be wearing anything beneath his gandourah and his baggy trousers; thus, it was in a condition approaching innocence that the Moslem holy man was taken away by Van den Rietter's guards, who carried their prize by holding it above their heads, as if in burlesque and savage triumph; the good-for-nothing rogue from Kola-Kola continued to do everything in his power to raise his head, perhaps in the intention of determining what possible recourse remained open to him, while the brawny chaps who had captured him were demonstrating a decided preference to display the most well-rounded part of his person.

As for the sapak, he was no longer anything but the breathless and quite miserable prey of a dull-witted, limping giant who had grabbed the child by the collar of his tunic and was dragging his stiffened body along behind him or raising him off the ground and holding him momentarily at arm's length as if to exhibit him by the light of the torches that illuminated the night. This strange procession passed through most of the city before entering the Catholic mission.

In their misfortune, the two travellers at least had the consolation of being confined together in a spacious, unseasonably cool room in the presbytery, a room in which the experienced eye of Sandrinelli's former servant had no difficulty recognizing the distinctive characteristics of a boss's office. For a long time, a very long time, they thought they heard the hubbub of a disciplined but numerous and widely scattered mob animatedly coming and going in the neighborhood of the presbytery and even beyond, probably throughout a large part of the mission compound. All at once, someone screamed like an animal that had just been struck a violent, possibly fatal, blow; issuing from a powerful set of lungs, the cry rose to an incandescent pitch and then broke off abruptly, choked in a brief death rattle that was even more heart-rending.

"That must have been how they did it to the black slaves in the American South," observed the sapak in a quavering voice. "Won't it ever come to an end?"

"Be quiet!"

Yet it was the silence—an ambiguous subsiding of all unusual sounds into the undecipherable calm of an ordinary night in Ekoumdoum—that now filled the sapak with despair as he endured his first real trial as a Rubenist militant without, however, relinquishing his learned, somewhat gloomy eloquence.

Much later, Van den Rietter turned the key in the lock and unceremoniously entered the office; he had a surly expression on his face, but his hair was combed, his lips were rosy and damp like those of a man who had just finished eating, and his cassock was folded back in the conventional manner. He had barely installed himself in his chair, when he reached his hand toward the bottom of the desk, from which he withdrew a bottle of Martell and a glass that he poured one-third full and held between two fingers, as if offering it to a guest, while he himself slowly raised his eyes to look at Jo The Juggler.

As naked as a worm, the rogue was seated on the chilly tile floor; his hands and arms were tied across his back in such a way that his shoulders were painfully twisted behind him. Despite the torture, Jo The Juggler had not completely lost his self-confidence, and without flinching, he stared back at this new kind of enemy, who reminded him of Sandrinelli in a curious way; nevertheless, he could not prevent all his bodily signs—the quivering of his Adam's apple, the momentary gleam in his madly dancing eyes, the movement of his lips—from betraying his desire. The missionary mused to himself, "Well, well! He is a toper, this guttersnipe! Maybe that is his weak point. Let's see if we can do something with it." And without taking

164

his eyes off the prisoner, he suddenly tilted back his head and savored the cognac with a roll of his tongue: Jo The Juggler's Adam's apple had been shaken by an incredible vibration, as if it had been subjected to an electric shock, and the missionary said to himself, "Here's a fellow who drinks, although he doesn't like the taste of alcohol. A queer chap! And a dangerous one."

Having stood up, he once again poured the liqueur into the glass, filling it to the half-way mark this time; he took several steps toward Jo The Juggler, leaned over him, and wafted the glass of alcohol beneath the prisoner's nose, but, aware that he had been found out, the latter had promptly resumed his role of martyred dignity, of innocence abandoned without recourse to arbitrary persecution by the powerful of this earth.

"Tell me, you little son of a bitch," muttered the missionary, whose whole face was grinning with pleasure, "you like that stuff, don't you? You are an odd sort of Moslem and a fine son of a bitch, eh? Tell me you want it, my cognac. Tell me, tell me, and the glass is yours. No? You don't want my cognac? You really don't want it? You like my guns better. Where did you hide them? What were you planning to do with them? Where are you from? Both of you? From Mackenzieville? Is that it? Have both of you come from Mackenzieville? Why? To sabotage things here under the pretext that independence has been proclaimed on our side of the river? It's another attempt by the English, isn't it? Go ahead, speak, you son of a bitch! Are you from Mackenzieville?"

The missionary only interrupted his questioning to wave the glass of cognac beneath the chin of Jo The Juggler, whose suffering began to translate itself into beads of sweat that formed here and there on the pure ebony surface of his face.

"Independence? Ridiculous! They haven't even heard the word here at Ekoumdoum; moreover, I will do my best to make certain it stays that way as long as possible. You can assure your masters over there about that, if you ever get back. Is that it, eh? Is it really the English who sent you? To sow trouble among our peace-loving souls? How did you get across

165

the river, you son of a bitch? You know, my good
fellow, you shouldn't put on airs; I don't advise it,
for I do know how to deal with you people; I have the
ultimate weapon for making you talk. And if you think
I will hesitate to use it this time, you are mistaken;
I can immediately remove any illusions you might have
on that score."

Van den Rietter continued in this fashion for a
few moments without drawing any response from his
prisoner. Then, scarlet with rage and suddenly
impatient with the failure of his first tactic, the
missionary abruptly dove toward Jo The Juggler's
thighs, grabbed his testicles, and began first to
squeeze them, then to twist them as a means of
extracting a confession from the prisoner, already
suffering the cruel torture of his unnatural position
and the ropes that sawed into his arms or bruised
them. Showing the whites of his eyes and biting his
lips in pain, the Rubenist militant emitted a heart-
rending scream that expressed an unbearable suffering.
It disturbed the sapak more than anything he had ever
heard; it was as if Jo The Juggler, speaking to him in
a secret code, had addressed the following message to
him: "Do something, little scamp, or else it's all
over for poor Jo!"

Van den Rietter's lips were pulled back over his
clenched teeth, saliva foamed from the corners of his
mouth, and his eyes were starting out of his head;
with each squeeze, with each twist, he shouted, "Are
you going to talk, you little bastard? Where are you
from? What do you want from me? Where are my guns?
Who sent you here? Are you going to talk, or shall I
go on?"

The sapak was weeping, humiliated, full of compassion, profoundly upset like a child who sees a
torturer go to work on his own father. Van den
Rietter had just begun to torment Jo The Juggler
again, and another even more terrifying outcry had
just issued from the prisoner's lips; then, suddenly
overcome with furor and taking advantage of the fact
that he had been left completely free of any re-
straints, the sapak hurled himself at the missionary,
on whom he applied the fighting technique most commonly employed by the sapaks of Kola-Kola, a crushing

166

butt of the head to the enemy's forehead. One would
have said that Van den Rietter had been shot at point-
blank range; he toppled over like an enormous mass,
without a word, without a gesture, a real disjointed
jumping—jack. Still sniffing and quite taken aback,
the child leaned over the large motionless figure
stretched out on the floor.

"Well done, sapak!" exclaimed the rogue. "Now,
quickly, look in those drawers, find a knife, and cut
this bloody rope."

"Look, there is a pair of scissors on his desk."

"Hurry, help me; I can't take it any longer."

"Do you think he is dead?" asked the sapak as he
was cutting Jo The Juggler's ropes.

"Nonsense, he's a tough one, that fellow."

"Well then, shall we kill him?"

"We don't have time, you rascal, and what's more,
you know very well we don't have the right to decide
such things, at least not all by ourselves. If that
weren't the case, my dear sapak, you wouldn't have had
to ask me twice. Let's get out of here."

Before leaving the room, however, Jo The Juggler
did not forget to grab the neck of the missionary's
cognac bottle and take a few generous swigs from it;
when he had already reached the doorway, he even
returned to the desk and emptied as well the glass
that was still half full.

But as fate would have it, at the very moment the
two Rubenists rushed across the threshold, Brother
Nicholas was crossing the verandah; he saw them and,
after a brief moment of surprise, understood that the
feverishly distracted attitudes of the fugitives
bespoke the ill treatment they had just inflicted on
his countryman.

"Good God! There are the thieves! They are
escaping!" he shouted. "Over here! Quick! Help!"

Because they were unfamiliar with the immediate
area, and because they were paralyzed by the haunting
memory of the German shepherd whose barks were echoing
somewhere, reinforcing their image of him bounding
through the darkness and already preparing to pounce
on them in a murderous rage, and because they were
preoccupied with not being separated by the vicissitudes of an improvised, tactically vulnerable retreat,

167

the two Rubenists were soon submerged beneath the mob of employees who had come running at the clergyman's call. Once they had been captured, Brother Nicholas explained with numerous stammerings and stutterings that, even if they had assassinated Father Van den Rietter, he did not want to keep these ferocious wolves within the walls of an establishment devoted to the service of God.

"Go hand them over to the Chief and Zoabekwe then," he concluded, completely out of breath. "At least they will know what to do with them; besides, they have ways and means for that sort of thing. Ah, no! Mad dogs and ravenous wolves have no place here with us. We are men of God, we are. What these fellows need is a good little firing squad: bam, bam, bam, and they will never be heard of again. That's how one deals with mad dogs. Hand them over to the Chief and his son, as you did with the others a little while ago. Bam, bam, bam. . . ."

The Rubenists and their guardian angels were already far from the presbytery, walking along the path to the Forest of the Chimpanzees, but they could still hear Brother Nicholas, now probably fussing over Van den Rietter, as he riddled the night with his bam-bam-bam like a broken machine gun. His obvious panic elicited several jokes and even a few muffled laughs from the prisoners' escort. Jo The Juggler, although usually quite harsh in his judgments, claims these days that he was astonished to hear one of the lackeys mutter the following remark: "If that man is a servant of God, it must be a God who loves to hear the language of guns."

Having thus fallen into the hands of their worst enemy, Mor-Zamba's companions were immediately subjected to a very rigorous regimen, although it was far from their worst fears and expectations, which had been rather senseless in a way. It was understandable that the guards frequently came to beat them, that they were permanently confined to absolute darkness, and that they were left to wallow in their own excrement and urine, but why were the Bedridden Chimpanzee and The Bastard apparently treating the news so lightly? By the third day of their imprisonment, they had still not appeared before anyone, nor had they been subjected to even the most cursory interrogation. It seemed as though father and son expected nothing from the cruelty inflicted on the prisoners, unless it was the pleasure of listening to the moans and wheezes that accompanied their suffering.

In regard to the place where they were being held, they had been able to acquire only a very limited knowledge of it during their first three days there; it must have been a rather spacious, low-ceilinged room with rough-brick walls in some spots and pitch-covered ones in others; the walls themselves were so massive they evoked images of being buried alive at the bottom of a steep-sloped embankment. Their guards, who were also their torturers, seemed to arrive from the left by means of a serpentine passage that probably connected with other rooms like their own, where, instead of a door, there was a narrow fissure half sealed by a low wall; after having lifted the wooden latch, the guards had to draw their legs laboriously one after the other over the small cement wall. Completely out of breath, they carried torches or, very infrequently, a cheap hurricane lamp, so that one could see them advance across the room on their toes, muttering terrible oaths whenever they stepped on a pestilential little clump or in a filthy little sea. They threw themselves on the prisoners and beat them with fists, bludgeons, and rattan switches until the poor wretches wept bitterly or roared and brayed like wild animals, because they could no longer stand the pain. Far from sinking into despair and despondency, the sapak became more and more insolent and aggressive, spitting on those vile creatures as they beat him and even offering himself the pleasure of insulting them, which of course only intensified their zeal. Once, between two torture sessions, Jo The Juggler recalled the child's eyes, swollen half-shut from the beatings, and his bruised little face as he had seen them by the light of the guards' torches a few moments before, and he said to his young comrade, "Good God! What a mess I've gotten you into, my poor fellow!"

"Don't worry about me!" the sapak from Kola-Kola replied somberly, proudly.

"You know, you little scamp, I thought I'd seen everything: the shakedowns, the endless lineups in the basements of police stations in Fort Negre, the long months and even, on occasion, the long years of imprisonment, the toubabs' humiliations; I've experienced all that. But a brave little chap from Kola-Kola taking his beatings more calmly than a seasoned veteran—I didn't think it was possible, really. You are a splendid fellow!"

"Yes, but I would trade all that for a bit of sweet revenge on those sons of bitches. Isn't there any way to get out of here?"

"Go ahead and tell me what you are thinking."

"I have noticed that those pigs are always drunk," he confided to Jo The Juggler one night. "Wouldn't there be some way to knock them out completely?"

At that very moment they thought someone was silently lifting the wooden latch; a shadowy figure drew its legs with difficulty, one after the other, over the small cement wall, but there was no heavy breathing. Apparently someone else had followed the same line of reasoning as Evariste the sapak, but perhaps with greater consistency and a better appreciation for the realities of the Palace. A glowing match now moved about in the darkness and revealed the coils of a fire dragon consuming itself instantaneously. The incredulous prisoners then heard a woman's voice whisper to them, "I come to save you; it isn't very difficult. Come on, and above all don't become frightened or upset like the dishrags from around here. I have seen to everything. Don't you know people do as they like in the Palace by passing out a few cuttings of hash here and a few drops of ratafia there? The guards are a bunch of old pigs! Without taking anything they are already half asleep; well then, just think! In any case, you have understood me; everyone is sleeping, and for a long time to come. As for you, just be content to follow me, and everything will be all right."

There was indeed a serpentine passage hollowed out to the left, but they turned right, climbed a narrow stairway, and crossed several hallways that the two Rubenist thought must be part of the Palace; they did not have time to examine the place, for that is where the shadowy figure handed each of them a pagne, which they wrapped around themselves in the fashion of native Ekoumdoumians. Then, for a long time, they stealthily slipped between houses, keeping to the darkest places.

The shadowy figure led them into a dwelling where they could wash themselves hastily and fumble about for a morsel of food by the extremely feeble light of coals that were on the verge of burning themselves out in the corner.

"I am Ngwane-Eligui," whispered the shadowy figure, addressing Jo The Juggler. "Are you afraid of being beaten?"

The former delinquent hesitated, still dumbfounded by what had happened.

"Tell me that you are not afraid of being beaten," resumed the young woman. "A man should not be afraid of being beaten, nor a woman either, for that matter. What is a man who is afraid of being beaten? Less than a pile of excrement! Take a look at the dishrags from Edoumdoum; they immediately revealed all your secrets, because they were so afraid of being beaten. It seems you wanted to assassinate the old monkey? Why didn't you tell me about it? When you come back, don't forget to let me in on your plans, whatever your reasons might be. Let me guess. Don't tell me. There was a pretty girl in your village; you had been engaged to her since childhood; you went to find work at Mackenzieville; then, one day you discovered that the girl's father had sold her to the old monkey? And you came here to avenge yourself; you're right, he had to be killed. Tell me that you are not afraid of being beaten."

"Personally, I am not afraid of being beaten," pronounced Jo The Juggler without conviction, still overwhelmed by the loquacity of his questioner. "Only, you see, I am not alone; this child is with me."

"Oh, listen, you don't have to tell me that story. This is no more a child than you are a Hausa. I was never fooled by your disguise, although I admit it was a very clever one."

"You are right. It is true; I am not a Hausa,"

confessed Jo The Juggler. "But as for him, he really is a child; I swear it."

"Well then, tell him to go into that little shed, there to the left, and to stay there for a little while."

As soon as they were alone, the young woman took the Rubenist by the hand and led him over to a bed, where she obliged him to lie down, next to her at first and then on top of her. But as soon as Jo The Juggler, who was never at a loss in such matters, had begun to apply himself in earnest like a man over-coming the awkwardness occasioned by long months of abstinence, she stiffened, scratched him, bit him, and appeared to refuse; she resisted so strenously that Jo The Juggler laid down his arms before having reached his goal.

"Well then, it will be for next time," she said without bitterness.

"Can it possibly be true? You still haven't gone through with it? What sort of a creature are you then?"

"Yes, I know, down in the city everyone thinks that it is all over, that I have gone through with it, but I am telling you that, as for me, I'm not afraid of being beaten; I am strong, you understand? They can beat on me like a drum, but if I have to go through with it, it will never be with them. Remember what I am telling you; it is my last word. And now, it's time for you to get out of here; things are going to start buzzing all over the place. What an incredible idea to have wanted to snitch their popguns; I would certainly have liked to see their ugly mugs when they found out; but that's not the way to go about it; you only had to tell me and not those dishrags, one of whom immediately rushed off to spill everything to that Van den Rietter fellow; the widow's son is the one responsible for that fine deed; it's a dirty trick. I too am from a village near Mackenzieville, but on the English side of the border; they had to cross the river to buy me. Let me join forces with you to gain our revenge, do you want to? There are orange groves all along the bamboo fence, but there is also a single tangerine tree. You can recognize it even in the darkness; it is the smallest one. Between

172

its trunk and the slats of bamboo, there is a tiny crevice. If you return, there will always be a message there for you. I know how to write a bit; what about you? You too can slip me a message from time to time. I know you are coming back."

Allowing themselves to be guided by Ngwane-Eligui's recommendations, the two Rubenists carefully avoided the risks of walking along the main thoroughfare or in its immediate vicinity; instead, they stealthily crossed the belt of banana plantations behind the houses in order to rejoin Mor-Zamba, who had been lying in wait at the edge of the road since the disaster and observing the city night and day. With no apparent sign of emotion, he led them through the woods to the nearest cache, where the two escapees found clothes and boots waiting for them.

"How did you know we were going to get out of there?" asked the rogue.

"I knew nothing at all; I was hoping."

Without even giving his friends the opportunity to catch their breath, the giant ordered them to start moving again. While his comrades were running into tree stumps and bushes beside the path, stumbling over logs that had fallen across their way, or becoming snagged on low-hanging branches that obstructed their passage, Mor-Zamba was advancing freely and easily with long, loping strides. He quickened the pace as soon as the sun came up, inundating the rare clearings they encountered and splattering the underbrush with splotches of dazzling whiteness.

It seemed to his two companions that their forced march was lasting forever. The child complained that his boots had become braziers in which his feet were roasting; following Mor-Zamba's advice, he took them off and tried to walk barefoot. But his torment became even more agonizing when he had to flounder through the icy mud of a swamp that lay beneath a gloomy ceiling of thickly plaited tree branches. It was then that Jo The Juggler rebelled. "Hey, are you going to stop?" he said, losing his temper. "The child can't go any further."

Mor-Zamba put the child on his back like a nursing baby and forged ahead again, followed by the rogue, who gritted his teeth to avoid breaking out in tears. The giant was obviously sacrificing everything to his well-known mania for escaping in a desperate hurry; what good would it do to try stopping him or even slowing him down? All at once, Jo The Juggler realized that they had left the scarcely beaten path they had been more or less arduously following until then and that they were venturing through a kind of bushy undergrowth with a few sparsely scattered trees; here, as it was growing dark, Mor-Zamba himself almost seemed to be guessing at his path, sometimes retracing his steps, sometimes pausing to orient himself.

Finally, they arrived at their destination, a marvelously camouflaged hut, an immense nest whose shapes and contours and various shades of green undoubtedly blended into the surrounding maze of inextricable thickets during the daytime. It was a veritable miniature fortress, erected by Mor-Zamba and reflecting the strength of a giant, the skill and knowledge of an experienced woodsman, and last but not least the bold imagination of a streetfighter from Kola-Kola. Bamboo beds, a fireplace for cooking meals without allowing the smoke to travel very far, abundant provisions, wooden plates and spoons, sturdy lattice walls made of tightly woven fresh bamboo and covered with panels of tree bark, observation posts from which to watch for the possible approach of an enemy—nothing seemed to be lacking for their comfort or security.

It was not until the next morning that the two older men began the discussion necessitated by recent events, but when they did, it lasted all day long and proved extemely painful to Jo The Juggler, although Mor-Zamba's indictment was tinged with ambivalence, because he felt trapped between the natural demands of courteous treatment for a valorous comrade overwhelmed by misfortune and the justifiable revenge of a prudent moderation that had been flouted for all too long. For his part, Jo The Juggler was a good sport, allowing himself to be regarded as a defeated combatant but manoeuvering constantly to avoid being branded with infamy.

At first they concentrated on establishing the inventory of lost equipment. Van den Rietter's search had been a regular pillaging expedition, because the missionary must have seen each object as a clue which, if properly examined, might reveal its secret to him. For this reason, he had whipped through the place like a hurricane, the devastations of which Mor-Zamba himself had verified with his own eyes, for he had been unable to resist the temptation to inspect in person the causes and consequences of the wrath and fury he had so clearly seen from the road, while at the same time paying a brief visit to his own house.

"What are you missing?" asked Mor-Zamba.

"Everything I had on me, of course."

"Which is?"

"Don't worry, nothing but trifles: my watch, the combination pen and pocket flashlight, the sandals, and the clothes, and all the bedding. And also a bit of cash, not much, just enough to impress the local peasants. Not a single gun; you can rest assured on that score. Ah, wait a minute! The sons of bitches. . . . My clasp-knife."

"To that you have to add all the sapak's clothes, his sandals, and his bedding. With one thing and another, it begins to add up. The widows loaned you some cooking utensils, I believe, and a few others items as well, if I remember correctly. Well then, when I was there, not a single soup spoon was left. You see, your plan wasn't worth much; didn't I tell you that? You were wrong to play with fire that way and trust your lucky star. You think you are playing football on some empty lot in Kola-Kola; you gambol about performing pirouettes and playing practical jokes on the enemy, but at the same time you are ruining everything, confusing the issue, and doing a real disservice to our cause. Don't you think it's about time you stopped?"

"All right, I should stop, true enough. After all, this expedition is primarily your affair; there is nothing to say, you are the boss, you should always have the last word. I agree completely. But even so, I won't be told I never take anything seriously. Never take anything seriously? Me? Who foresaw we would probably not have to confront the old Chief himself as much as his son, an impulsive and cruel individual who is totally preoccupied with himself? Perhaps it wasn't me? Who predicted that the givens

of the Ekoumdoum problem were bound to have changed
fundamentally since the time of Hurricane-Viet?"

In detail, he then recounted the exact circumstances under which his troops were routed, placing
great emphasis on the betrayal of a single conspirator
to prove definitively, as he believed, that the basic
assumption behind his strategy had been the best one:
above all Mor-Zamba had needed to avoid showing himself, at least during that phase of the operation.
"If you had a better idea, you should have told us
about it. There is still time, you know?" concluded
the rogue.

In response to the giant's silence and having
regained a portion of his liveliness and self-
confidence due to a good night's sleep and Mor-Zamba's
excessive scrupulosity, Jo The Juggler offered to tell
a new episode in the life of his favorite heroes, the
two well-known brothers who, before going out into the
wide world, went, separately and one after the other,
to consult their mama and their papa; he entitled the
episode, "The man who refused to go upriver." But
this enticingly enigmatic title did not even pique
Mor-Zamba's curiosity, for contrary to his usual
custom, his countenance remained inscrutable. This
time the two brothers posed the following question to
their genitors: "Suddenly confronted by an incredibly
large, deep river with a treacherous current, our
traveller sees neither ferryman, nor anyone else who
might help him across. Nevertheless, he had to get to
the other side; people are waitng for him there; his
honor and his fortune hang in the balance. What
should he do?"

This is what the father said: "Walk along the
bank, my son, and go upriver toward the source.
Approached in this way, any stream can be crossed
sooner or later, because there is always a ford somewhere, or a brave ferryman; it is up to you to find
them. Walk along the bank then without giving up;
follow the tread of water toward the place from which
it springs." Such was the father's reply.

"And what did the mother say?" asked Mor-Zamba
with annoyance, as if someone had just awakened him.
"What did the mother say? Hurry up, get on with it."

"Hold on, grandpa; what are you offering me?

Tell me, do you want me to try my hand one last time? You do, don't you? Thank you. The mother replied more or less in this manner: 'In such a case, my dearly beloved son, wisdom decrees that you should arm yourself with patience, sit down to wait in the shade of a nearby forest, and meditate upon the billows rolling by; beneath the caress of your gaze, the undulating wave is like the back of a sleeping animal. Petted and cajoled in this way, every stream will ultimately reveal its secret. Of course, the wait may seem long, even very long, but it will suffice to arm yourself with patience.' This is what the mother replied; is that what you wanted?"

"What then?"

"What then? Can't you guess the rest? The elder of the two brothers followed his papa's advice and successfully did everything he set out to do, no matter how hopeless it seemed at first. As for the younger, he paid too much attention to what his mama said, and what do you suppose happened to that dolt? Naturally, he never succeeded in anything, because he foolishly wasted his time waiting for his desires to realize themselves, something they never did. It's stupid, but so is the life slipping through our fingers; try to imagine that the waves flowing between the strand and the cliff hold no unfathomable mysteries."

"And now how do you plan to go upriver to Van den Rietter's source?"

"I thought of nothing else during my confinement in the Bedridden Chimpanzee's dungeons, my good man. It is very simple; all we have to do is put everything on the line—an attack with guns in our hands, a real battle. We are not that much inferior to them, come on!"

"It's just as I thought; you have gone completely crazy!"

Drawing upon an urgent and spirited eloquence that was hardly habitual with him, Mor-Zamba undertook to make a case for common sense. According to him, the missionaries enjoyed an overwhelming, twofold superiority, even when the Chief and Zoabekwe were left out of the picture. In the first place, they had better weapons, a good number of them, and even for-

177

getting for a moment the expertise of the marksmen, these alone thoroughly outclassed the Rubenists' eight popguns. In the case of a frontal attack, what happens? Each of the white men takes one gun in his right hand and another in his left; they fire at least three times without reloading—that is, without stopping—and they easily cut down six men in a few seconds, while the Rubenists are killing three at most. And there are the attackers, annihilated in the first assault. For what is the firepower the mission-aries would be facing? The Rubenists would have to reload their guns each time, except perhaps the minia-turized revolver, but its range is not very spectac-ular. And what is there to say, if one also takes into account the skill and experience of the two missionaries, no doubt efficient, well-trained sol-diers who, like all whites, have been subjected to an apprenticeship for war since their earliest childhood.

"I saw the Soumazeus at the garrison in Oyolo," he continued ardently. "During the war, they were mobilized like all the others; they performed the same exercises, followed the same regulations, and believe me, they were not the least enthusiastic. I am telling you it is sheer folly to attack those people."

"So, aren't they the ones we will be going after? And if I told you we already had friends there? And what friends!"

Jo The Juggler finally described, in great detail, the circumstances under which they had been liberated and even those immediately following their actual liberation. But Mor-Zamba apparently persisted in failing to understand how the young woman could facilitate an attack on the city by three ragtag Rubenists, one of whom was a child.

"But of course, listen to me. We coordinate our plans with Ngwane-Eligui; such and such a day, she lights fires at several houses in the Forest of the Chimpanzees, and why not in the Palace itself?"

"Why not indeed?"

"Once everything is burning and the people, overcome with panic and fear, begin fleeing in all directions, crying and shouting, then we enter into action. We go after the missionaries; it is the easiest thing in the world, because they make good

178

targets at night."

"Assuming they show themselves. And what if they don't show themselves?"

"Impossible, grandpa. And therein lies my genius. They will be obliged to show themselves; they are the true martyrs of the city, especially Van den Rietter, who is, moreover, the most belligerant of the two."

"We take them prisoner, and then what?"

"Listen, grandpa, that's wonderful, isn't it? Prisoners, prisoners! What next! Why not also organize free elections under the supervision of Baba Toura? You could turn the occasion to good account by spontaneously dedicating—to his greater glory—the fine work you will have accomplished, and you won't even be asking for anything in return."

"Well then, you kill them, like that; three movements in double time, and they chirp their last!"

"Well, what's wrong with that? Aren't we at war?"

"To do it right, it might be better to explain that to them before we kill them; perhaps they don't know we are at war with them."

"You have understood absolutely nothing, grandpa—nothing, nothing at all. What about them? When they came to our part of the world, did they explain to us that they were going to make war on us? Didn't they arrive declaring that we are all brothers? Does that stop them from making war on us? All brothers, all brothers, I don't give a damn what you say. Do you remember what old Van den Rietter dared to say in front of us? That pig, he said, 'Independence? Ridiculous! They haven't even heard of the word here at Ekoumdoum; moreover, I will do my best to make certain it stays that way as long as possible. . . .' There, what do you have to say about that? A toubab who dares to say such things isn't making war on you? Really? Frankly, I don't know what you need. And I haven't even told you the rest of it."

"George, my friend, my brother, I think I understand; just imagine, only a moment ago I was still in doubt. Now then, George, my brother, it is your turn to listen to me, and you must realize that I too am speaking very seriously. So, I am telling you it is

out of the question to kill the two missionaries; as
long as I live, I swear it shall not be. It isn't
that I like them any better than you do, George. When
they captured me twenty years ago at Ekoumdoum, Van
den Rietter was already there in the city; from one
end of it to the other, he was a witness to that
miscarriage of justice, and he neither raised a finger, nor said a word in my defense. Do you think I
don't know that he secretly wants us to remain
shackled forever in the chains of slavery? All of
them want us to be subject to them, always.

"But George, my brother, why have you come to
Ekoumdoum, so far from Fort Negre, so far from that
city which is still undoubtedly your favorite place in
the whole world? To lighten the burden of the people
or to bring them additional sufferings? Think about
it for a moment. Wiping out those two missionaries
here at Ekoumdoum—do you realize what that means? It
means you are making an irrevocable declaration of war
on Sandrinelli, on Maestraci, on Brède, on all the
toubabs who constantly surround The Sot and dictate
his every step to him, and on all the others I haven't
mentioned. You know as well as I do that the dominant
characteristic of those people is their long memory;
they never forget. Time can pass, and days can succeed each other with what appears to be a monotonous
regularity, but one truth abides, and you can rest
assured of that: those people will be digging tunnels
below the surface, like termites; they will be
approaching by tiny steps, imperceptibly but inexorably, like ants; if necessary they will creep along
centimeter by centimeter; they will rebuild the road,
section by section; they will send lumbering engines
of death; they will come as far as Ekoumdoum, and they
will find you."

"What then?"

"That is easy for you to say, George, my brother,
but you do not know them as well as I do. You have
seen them in their homes, next to their wives or
surrounded by their children; they are loving husbands, smiling fathers, beings who are more or less
human. You have seen them in their offices, buried in
a dossier or issuing orders with jaded arrogance to
their black subordinates. But you have never experi-

enced them during times of war--for instance at a highway construction site--consumed with repressed hatred and a desire for vengeance, biting their lips in frustration, cruel, frenetically singleminded, relentless."

"We too will be prepared; we can put up a stiff resistence. We will make war on them. After all, why not?"

"Their tanks and armored personnel carriers have a destructive capacity that exceeds your wildest imagination; with such engines of war they will crush you in an instant."

"Is it so certain?"

"They will annihilate the innocent inhabitants of the city, and even the stray dogs and rats, with bombs dropped from airplanes, if necessary; they will flatten all the houses and set fire to the rubble after having doused it first with gasoline. That is how they are, exactly how they are. What good would it do to arouse their vengeful instincts? Whatever they preach, they do not turn the other cheek and allow it to be slapped; that is what they prescribe inside their churches, but on the outside, it is a different matter. I have no idea of the state in which Hurricane-Viet expects to find Ekoumdoum when he returns, but as long as I am alive, I want to preserve this city intact for him; it was the cradle of his birth. Let him find it standing as he left it so he can make use of it, if he wishes, or sacrifice it as an offering to the sacred cause, if he desires."

"It is terrible, grandpa, what you have just said there. Do you realize it amounts to renouncing all initiative?"

"Of course not, George! Do whatever you like, but don't rub out the two missionaries."

"What are you afraid of, grandpa? Fort Negre is almost two thousand kilometers away; there are no roads which anyone could use to travel from there to here; there isn't even any regular communication between the capital and Ekoumdoum; by the time Fort Negre becomes aware of anything at all, we will be organized; we will have established a line of defense from which we can easily beat back any attack. People survive aerial bombardments by digging holes in the

181

ground. A bit of daring and imagination, what the hell! In any case, some day sooner or later you will have to settle your account with Baba Toura."

"Perhaps, but I have said my last word. Whatever you want, except the assassination of those two."

"That's easy to say."

# CHAPTER 4

Meanwhile, scenes marked by an anguish and confusion at least equal to those revealed during the dispute between the two Rubenists in the forest were taking place in the city of Ekoumdoum. The escape of the prisoners was not noticed until ten or eleven o'clock in the morning. The son of the Chief, Zoabekwe, commonly known as The Bastard, was so distraught that he fell into a frenzy and started to manifest all the external signs by means of which people usually recognize the onset of madness.

As soon as he began to regain possession of himself, he formed the intention of inflicting an exemplary punishment on his guards, whose guilt seemed self-evident to him. He was very quickly obliged to abandon that idea: there was a lack of any logical sequence in their stories, and it was impossible to establish with certainty which of them was supposed to have been on duty at the alleged time of the escape—impossible to determine who was generally responsible for assigning guard duty, or even what criteria had been used in making the assignments. Everything apparently took place in a careless abandon, a joyful anarchy, a good-natured spontaneity (behind which, unbeknowst to the master, there smoldered the bitter resentment of the incompetent and the lazy), and a relentless animosity toward the prisoners at night.

The Bastard then thought about all the women living in the compound, for they could freely and indiscriminately move about anywhere in the Palace, having access to the living quarters as well as the rooms reserved for administrative and ceremonial purposes; it would be like looking at a sandpile through a magnifying glass. He suspected the adolescents from the city, for there had never been any question of prohibiting them from entering a district where their countless services were indispensible. He suspected everyone, but he knew almost immediately that he would be unable to implicate anyone in particular.

As long as the former happiness and insouciance had reigned in the Forest of the Chimpanzees and even after a penchant for capriciousness among the master's young wives had begun to transform itself disastrously into a spirit of recalcitrance, its inhabitants had lived in a confused togetherness, a tangled maze, an absolute chaos. It had always been difficult to distinguish among the father's wives and those of the son, relatives who had come to visit these women or even live permanently with them, servants' wives and their daughters of all ages, as well as local women whose links with the Chief's wives were encouraged by tradition and who were often present within the confines of the compound. Likewise, it was customary for the children of the city—even those well on their way toward puberty—to overrun the fashionable section of town during the day. But these crowds of people, this coming and going, this constant ebb and flow, this inextricable jumble of humanity rendered these august premises more like a fairground or a caravansary than the residence of a man who had been placed at the head of an enormous city and was exercising uncontested authority there.

Especially during the night among the shadows whose grotesque dances were being orchestrated by the flame in an occasional oil or gas lamp, the undulating songs of the young women, mothers swearing countless oaths as they ran after their overly mischievous children, adolescents who had come from the city and were secretly carrying illicit messages, and even lovers stealthily slipping into the heart of this anthill that seldom became calm before ten o'clock in the evening, one might well have believed that the primary advantage of the powerful is their privilege of being the focal point for the joys and intrigues of

184

a family whose ranks never stop growing. Who could have imagined the tragic chain of events during which so much happiness would be plunged inexorably into the abyss?

Enraged by his impotence, The Bastard rushed to prostrate himself at Van den Rietter's feet, for the missionary had quickly recovered from the aftereffects of his dramatic encounter with the Rubenists, whom he more than ever persisted in regarding as British agents.

"Help me, father," The Bastard implored. "Come to our rescue, for if you do not, what will happen to us? But first of all, explain it to us: What is happening? Where is it leading us? Who helped them escape? Who shall we punish? Who shall we spare? How can we put a bit of order in this whole mess? Who should we trust? Who should we distrust? And why? Or why not? Where am I? Where should I go? What should I do?"

"Calm down, my son, calm down!" replied Van den Rietter. "Above all, don't panic; that would be the best way to lose the match when you should be playing a cautious game against a ruthless opponent. Who are those people? Agents sent by Mackenzieville of course, that is to say by the British, overcome by jealousy at seeing us reconcile what they call independence with the friendship and gratitude of the people on our side of the river; they were hoping for the apocalypse, a bloodbath, complete chaos; in short, they wanted to play the same trick on us they had played so often and so successfully in Syria, in Indochina, in North Africa.

"For the moment, they still have not pulled it off here; get that into your noggin, my child. Yes, they have guns; perhaps they have our guns, and we are completely naked; they know we are at their mercy, and they are no doubt going to lauch a surprise attack on us any day now, possibly even within the very near future. But all is not lost, if we lose no time in getting ouselves organized. No matter how well armed they are, a handful of men against a city with thousands of inhabitants is condemned in advance to failure, unless there is a fifth column in our midst.

"Well then, are you going to put things in order

at your place, my child? I think it is necessary,
absolutely necessary; the survival of us all is at
stake, not to mention the preservation of the great
work that has been accomplished during these past
twenty years. I am going to give you some painful
advice, although it is unavoidable. But first, are
you sure you have your father's approval?"

"He will agree. He is a cripple."

"A cripple indeed, but jealous of his prerogatives."

"Leave it to me, father."

"Now, that is a better way to put it, my boy.
Well then, from this day on, never forget: I am
depending on you and on you alone. Agreed?"

"Agreed, father."

"Very good. Let's get down to business then.
The primary cause of the disorder and anarchy at your
place, my boy, is the overcrowding. There are too
many people in your compound; it is impossible to keep
so many people around and still maintain a strict
surveillance over all of them."

"What can I do?"

"What can you do! What can you do! Listen here,
you can do everything, because you are in your own
place. Yes or no, are you really in your own place?"

"I am really in my own place, father."

"Good, then you can for once break with a venerable tradition by chasing the superfluous people from
your section of town: parents-in-law, near and distant cousins of parents-in-law, servants and mistresses of parents-in-law, and I won't even mention
the rest. When you think about it, my child, what do
you have to gain by giving a damn about all those
people? Nothing, nothing at all. It is between you
and your tradition: one of you has to go. It is up
to you to choose. Well then, what will it be?"

"All right, father, I am sending them away."

"Will you have the courage to do it? I am
warning you, it will be hard."

"I will be firm, I promise you that."

"Bravo, my child. Next, you need a real police
force, but I am the one who will attend to that. Even
so, I can explain it to you. Until now, your men
never actually constitued an army, but only an undis-

186

ciplined mob. As our first act, we will organize them into a hierarchy and name a commanding officer, then several assistant commanders, then the immediate subordinates, and so on down the line to the bottom rung of the ladder. Thus, in case of a momentary setback, we can easily determine who was not equal to his task, and we can punish him in front of everyone, as an example. In contrast, you should shower your best men with presents and prestige, place them in the spotlight, give them the opportunity to shine. There are not fifty-six different ways of doing it. As I just said, my boy, I myself am going to take a hand in the matter. But, my child, it is urgent, very urgent, believe me, because it won't be long before the others show themselves."

"Father, why don't we go and buy guns in Mackenzieville?"

"Oh, certainly not that, my child! Anything but that. You don't want us to give our enemies the pleasure of seeing us lose our nerve, do you? Is it necessary for us to shout from the rooftops that we have allowed a bunch of wandering ragamuffins to strip us of our weapons? What are you thinking of? Their malice and sarcasm are lurking in wait for us over there. Nothing will escape them, not even the smallest gleam in our eye or the slightest change in the usual inflection of our voices. No! Brother Nicholas will go to Mackenzieville in his boat as usual, and the sooner the better, for we must not hesitate to show ourselves. Naturally he will attract the gaze of every police informer the British have in their pay. As usual, however, he will unload the sacks and baskets filled with our customary produce. As usual, he will load the provisions and other things that respond to the habitual desires of the peaceful souls in our community. He will carry his head high, maintaining a serene and slightly nonchalant expression on his face and walking about unconcernedly, like someone who is not at all worried about anything in particular. He will make a show of his extreme self-confidence, of his beatitude in short. And above all he will not buy guns. In that way, if the British expected to see us fall apart after the blow they have just inflicted on us, they will be severely disappointed. Go and begin to implement the necessary measures, my boy; the others won't be long in coming. Maybe it will even happen tonight."

After the arrest of the conspirators, the interrogation of Jo The Juggler's allies was conducted without respite or pity, but even ten days later, it had failed to produce any results that might justify a hope of ever finding the stolen guns again. The local leaders, Mor-Eloulougou and his accomplices, had, to be sure, put up a very feeble resistence before making satisfactory confessions, humbly requesting forgiveness for the error of their ways and solemnly promising never to take them up again. But although they had acknowledged their complicity in the theft of the guns, they declared themselves unable to account for their disappearance and indicated by name the three members of the small detachment that had been charged with retrieving them from the forest and bringing them to the leaders.

These auxiliaries had stubbornly eluded the investigations of Zoabekwe and Van den Rietter, who requited their impatient fury on the person of poor Mor-Eloulougou, suspected of having committed all sorts of invidious acts. One can imagine the accordionist's relief when, tiring of the hardly reassuring company of the usual forest creatures and despondent at the prospect of having to subsist any longer without a warm meal, the three fugitives reappeared and surrendered to their judges, Soumazeu and The Bastard. They told their story with a candid willingness to please: overcome with panic when they realized that the conspiracy had been betrayed, they had thrown the guns into a thicket which they had failed to mark in any way; as a result, they regretted having been unable to identify it shortly before their return to the city, because they would have liked to have brought the guns back with them. They had been hiding in Nature these past few days, but having grown weary of combat, they opted for a return to the hearth.

This confession had prompted Van den Rietter to organize one search after another, scouring vast expanses of forest and exhausting his employees and friends, particularly Zoabekwe, whose flabbiness and inherent laziness were revealed in all their splendor.

188

Yet each day his efforts proved as vain as they had on the preceding one.

Van den Rietter's repeated but fruitless searches finally convinced Ngwane—Eligui that the tale of guns jettisoned out of haste and fear in some obsure thicket was no more than a stratagem to fool the two missionaries and Zoabekwe by diverting their attention from the possible future initiatives of their invisible enemies. She also persuaded herself that, since the two strangers were henceforth alone in the possession of guns which they undoubtedly knew how to use, they would return as soon as possible to harrass the authorities, who were now terrorizing the entire city, or even, quite probably, to strike a single decisive blow. However, although she always remained awake to the utmost limits of her resistence to fatigue, each night brought her an additional share of incredulous disillusionment. In the darkness, in the silence brought about by the system recently imposed by Van den Rietter, she perceived none of the expected signs. The mailbox near the tangerine tree collected her own messages, and, to her despair, only her own.

How can it be, Ngwane—Eligui said to herself, that men who are highly spirited and armed to the teeth can equivocate for such a long time in the face of a few decrepit old men without guns and commanding a harmless herd of sheep? In the young woman's imagination, the two strangers, perhaps overwhelmed by loneliness, were restricting themselves to a wooded area on the outskirts of the city (probably no more than few spear casts from the Forest of the Chimpanzees), contenting themselves with furtive nocturnal excursions into the city itself, prowling about in a cowardly fashion like hyenas, and dodging the police patrols like frightened dogs with their tails between their legs. They didn't have any nerve either, the dishrags; it had been her last hope.

To buck up their courage, she made a sport of sowing confusion into the complex apparatus installed by Van den Rietter and, in reality, responsive to his command. One day she ran across an undernourished dog or a wandering cat and gave it a violent blow with a stick, or else she sneaked up on the animal late at night and poured a kettle of boiling water over it,

189

producing a frightful scream; another day she bribed a young boy and sent him into the darkness to blow off one of those remarkable firecrackers which even the smallest children in Ekoumdoum excelled in fabricating out of a few matches and a nail, out of nothing at all, really; on still another day she had a hunter, who had just returned from the forest, spread the news that he had seen the footprints of strangers in the sand or mud of a river bank, a cliffside, a clearing.

On each occasion, Van den Rietter's police apparatus swung into motion; brandishing spears, swords, and clubs, his men quickly occupied the suspicious area, swarming through the surrounding houses and searching them with feverish, convulsive movements while their companions were taking up positions on nearby roofs or seeking cover behind a bush in the Forest of the Chimpanzees; or else Van den Rietter, displaying an aggressive boldness, took personal command of a group that devoted itself to long hours of searching the area designated by the revelations of the hunter.

The true balance of power between the official authorities of Ekoumdoum and those whom Ngwane-Eligui now referred to only as "the strangers in the night" was thus lost on everyone, even the young woman herself, for although her intuition was consciously unorthodox, she was far from suspecting the ironic paradox of a situation that was, to say the least, quite uncommon. The guerillas were certain that their enemies had easily recovered the precious loot Jo The Juggler had momentarily succeeded in appropriating without, however, taking definitive possession of it. Zoabekwe and Van den Rietter were gradually led by the futility of their searches to conclude that they had been the victims of a hoax and that their guns had definitely fallen into the hands of their enemies. Yet the anger inspired by that idea could not be vented as freely as they may have desired; that would have been the equivalent of revealing their panic in broad daylight and allowing a flattering reputation for imperturbability and absolute self-confidence to become tarnished.

However, the inhabitants of Ekoumdoum did not fail to detect the increasingly profound ravages effected each day in Van den Rietter's personality by the madness which had struck him during the earliest moments of his drama, but which had initially smoldered for a long time, like a fire in the underbrush, before bursting suddenly into flame. Before this time he had been a hardy, enterprising pioneer; now he suddenly became an impatient, domineering tyrant. More tenacious than remorse and as persistant as an obsession, he transformed himself into an infinite number of persons, as one might have said, for he was present everywhere in the entire city at once. Constantly accompanied by an aging bicycle that was covered with a reddish-brown patina but remained in excellent condition, his own elongated profile on a sturdy frame, his white cassock rolled up to a pair of hairy thighs around which the flaps of his generous khaki shorts fluttered animatedly, his long beard with tinges of grey, his two beady eyes lurking behind ramparts of wrinkles and bristles, and his more or less thinning but still purplish red hair, he no longer looked the part of a hard-working neighbor, but of a returned fellow citizen in a way, of an occupier in a word, of a barbarian to say it all.

His speech, which had only been steady before, became clipped and metallic. Until then his face had merely been impenetrable, like a great wall that discourages the overly bold, but now it grew more pointed like the tip of a sword, penetrating people's hearts and souls and hollowing out caverns where inertia, doubt, and debacle were entombed. He who had previously visited the Chief only at infrequent intervals and had never evinced more than a polite, almost shamefaced benevolence toward him, suddenly besieged the master-of-the-city as well as his son Zoabekwe, commonly known as The Bastard, and cloistered himself with them to elaborate the plans of battle. When he reappeared, he would be shaking his head (in astonished disbelief no doubt), clenching his fists (in impotent rage certainly), moving his lips and mumbling both a prayer and a defiant challenge to the God whom he had served with such devotion and who nevertheless seemed to be abandoning him.

Instead of flocking to him and surrounding him as they had formerly done, the children now scattered

191

like frightened birds at his approach; if he by any chance caught them unawares, he was no longer greeted with a clarion-clear "praised by Jesus Christ, father" in his own language—a salutation which not long before had sent him into raptures of pride and melancholy—but by silence, embarrassment, and, perhaps, curiosity tinged with compassion.

"It is strange," he confided wearily to Brother Nicholas as soon as the latter had returned from Mackenzieville, where he had gone on schedule. "It is strange; you could almost say that there is a vague touch of hostility in the air."

"Let us be serious, Father," his fellow country-man replied. "You are imagining things, because we have not found our guns."

"Nevertheless, I am not so sure . . . ! The expressions on the children's faces, the studied indifference of the adults; some days I ask myself if they don't know, if they aren't in on the plot."

"So you think it must be a plot then? And at least some inhabitants of the city must be accom-plices? No, father, that sort of thing could never happen here, not with our niggers! Listen, you know these people quite well. You yourself have always told me they were completely harmless. In the end, we will get our guns back, set your mind at ease; as for me, I believe it is somewhat of a bad joke; you'll see; they would undoubtedly admit it, if our friend Zoabekwe would help them along a bit more forcefully."

"That is all he does, and he doesn't use the back side of the spoon."

This was the climate in which the first initia-tives inspired by the Rubenists' new strategy were carried out from their base of operations in the forest. Far from having succumbed to despondency after the recent defeat that had proved so discon-certing and mortifying to him, Jo The Juggler had drawn a new enthusiasm, a paradoxically heightened spirit, from it, even while keeping well within the narrow boundaries imposed on him by Mor-Zamba.

As he discussed the situation with Evariste the sapak, a former schoolboy embued with history and the knowledge of books, Jo The Juggler began to see that pitched battle was not their only recourse and that they could replace it with a more profitable and no less deadly tactic, for psychology would play a larger role in it. By spurring each other on and passionately amending each other's suggestions, they had spent several days drafting a bold proclamation. The sapak had recopied it in his most attractive calligraphic hand on the large sheets of paper with the "République Fran{aise" letterhead that Sandrinelli's former servant had pilfered from the June 18 school complex. Reproduced a number of times in this fashion, the text of the proclamation read:

Respectable and respected inhabitants of the great city of Ekoumdoum:

We are the men of Commander Abena, the son of Ekoumdoum, your noble brother who went to war twenty years ago and is today on his way home, impatiently awaited by you, as we all know. And it is in the name of Commander Abena, the noble son of Ekoumdoum, that we are addressing ourselves to you, respectable and respected inhabitants of the noble city of Ekoumdoum.

Commander Abena has fought victoriously on five continents and successfully confronted people of all races during his long epic journey. Each time he happened to find himself among people suffering beneath the cruelty of chiefs who usurped lands, wealth, and women, he liberated them from their hateful rulers and ended oppression by passing his sword through its body.
But during all this time, Commander Abena did not forget that his own people were still groaning beneath the cruel oppression of a chief who usurped land, wealth, and women just like the other chiefs against whom he had fought on five continents. However, Commander Abena had to arm himself with patience and wait; he had to count the years, he had to count the months, and he had to count the days, because he could not act before the time appointed by fate.
Respectable and respected citizens of Ekoumdoum, the time is about to arrive. Thus, at the moment when you read this proclamation, your noble son will be on his way home, and nothing will be able to stop him.

He is finally coming to liberate his own people; he is coming to liberate you, noble inhabitants of the great city of Ekoumdoum, to drive out the usurper, and to end oppression.

Prepare yourselves therefore to fight at our sides beneath the banner of Commander Abena, the noble son of your venerable soil. You will soon receive precise instructions; we ask you to adhere strictly to them. While you are waiting, be alert. Never let your eyes be unoccupied; never let your foot rest upon a spot that has not been inspected in advance; never let your ears fail to notice the least crackling. Let your heart be made ready to welcome the return of Abena and to celebrate at the same time the independence that has been waiting far too long outside the gates of your city. Commander Abena has himself dispatched independence in the vanguard of his army as a harbinger of his return. The storm is going to break.

Respectable and respected citizens of Ekoumdoum, that is what

Commander Abena, your noble brother, has sent us to tell you.

Jo The Juggler then announced that he would go by himself to Ekoumdoum, where, under the guise of darkness, he would use bamboo staples to post copies of the declaration in the most appropriate places. Considering the delinquent Kola-Kolan's lack of familiarity with the requirements of life and travel in the jungle, the presumptuousness of the idea caused Mor-Zamba to laugh derisively, and he decided that all three of them would make the journey. After leaving the next morning, they walked slowly and sometimes even dawdled along the way, as if the giant had wanted to savor the pleasure of initiating his young friends into the secrets of guerilla warfare. At the half-way point, they stopped at a hut that was similar in more than one respect to their general headquarters, although it had the singular advantage of serving in addition as an ideal depository for the supplies of food requisitioned from the Ekoumdoumians' fields, at least a half day's march away but on the other side of

194

the river, which meandered in such a way that its path provided a constant source of surprise. Undoubtedly the most learned of the three, Evariste the sapak, possessed the most relevant sense of dialectics, and he observed that the guerillas would soon be floundering about in the most undesirable state of confusion, if each of these hideouts were not given an appropriate name; for that reason, he proposed to confer the same appellation on each of them, varying only the number appended to it; for example, he would call the large general headquarters they had left that morning Fort Ruben I, the hut where they were at that moment spending the night Fort Ruben II, and so forth. The proposal was adopted without opposition, and the sapak's systematic approach was universally well received, even eliciting a word of praise from Mor-Zamba.

They arrived in the vicinity of the city as dusk was falling and took cover in a thicket beside the road to wait until it was sufficiently late. To assure the greatest possible freedom of movement, Jo The Juggler had inveigled permission to carry out the poster-hanging mission by himself, and when he first crossed the city, he did not encounter a living soul, just as he expected. He posted his sheets of paper primarily on the mud walls of the school buildings; he quickly attached a single copy to an outbuilding at the mission, sufficiently far from the presbytery to avoid the necessity of confronting the missionaries' German shepherd. He finally betook himself to the Forest of the Chimpanzees, where, with joy in his heart, he tacked one on the wall of the enclosure. Regarding that part of his mission as completed, he then thought about Ngwane-Eligui and sought to locate the distinctive tangerine tree she had elevated into a mailbox. He carefully walked along the bamboo palisade, stopping at each tree along the way and estimating its size, although the darkness obliged him to rely less on his vision than on his sense of touch and smell. All at once, he thought he had found his tangerine tree; seeking definitive proof, he crouched down and made certain that its slender trunk plunged into the ground like a fence post, straight and perfectly smooth, without the protruding root

195

structure characteristic of the orange trees.

Finally convinced, the Rubenist was just bending forward to stand up when Van den Rietter, dressed completely in black while assuming the night watch, glimpsed what he thought was the shadow of one among the many shameless lovers who aroused the ire of Zoabekwe; he pounced upon it and literally impaled his broad, hollow chest on Jo The Juggler's recently shaved, leaden skull. Like projectiles crashing together, the two men slammed into each other with the entire force of their momentum, and they both fell backwards to the ground, but Van den Rietter, once again knocked unconscious by the head of a Rubenist, remained stretched out in the dust. Overcome with anxiety, the rogue quickly stood up and immediately took to his heels, fleeing through the banana plantations and scraping his body on all sorts of underbrush, but he did not even pause to catch his breath until he had finally reached the road. Good-bye to Ngwane-Eligui's messages and the information which might have changed the face of Ekoumdoum at a single stroke—like the nose of Cleopatra, as the sapak Evariste always mysteriously adds at this point in the story. For the young woman had very recently posed them a question which, no doubt, would indirectly have revealed the fact that the authorities of the city were still looking for the guns which had been stolen from them, and that meant they would have been at the mercy of a surprise attack by the first person who came along.

Today when anyone asks Jo The Juggler what he would have done, if he had received notification of the absurd situation, he invariably waxes indignant that anyone would dare pose him such a question. "Me? Well, I would have charged, deaf to all warnings of danger and blind to all obstacles, with the ball out front. No matter what the idle braggarts tell you, no one has yet discovered a way to inspire enough courage in an unarmed man to enable him to crow in front of a gun that is ready to spit death at him. I would have locked those gentlemen up, along with the Bedridden Chimpanzee, on the first floor of the Palace. To make Mor-Zamba happy, I would have fed them, coddled them, and fattened them up like eunuchs, but they would have been very closely watched, and during all this time, who would have been changing everything in Ekoumdoum? Well, we would, all of us . . . like now, eh."

"Yes, but much sooner," the sapak habitually retorts at this point, "and with a great saving in sweat, suffering, and even blood."

"Why, of course," Jo The Juggler concludes, "of course it was a stroke of bad luck, but who do you think you are telling that to!"

When Jo The Juggler had rejoined his friends and told them the outcome of his mission, a brief discussion convinced them that, as a result of his latest misfortune, Van den Rietter could be expected to mount a draconian vigilance during perhaps the next ten days, more or less; therefore, it was futile and even dangerous to venture into the city before at least that much time had elspsed; Jo The Juggler could take possession of Ngwane-Eligui's messages as soon as Soumazeu had relaxed his guard. The Rubenists returned to Fort Ruben I, but by a different route, permitting the two younger Kola-Kolans to learn even more about the forest and to become acquainted with another hideout, also halfway between Ekoumdoum and Fort Ruben I, although it was primarily intended by Mor-Zamba as a weapons cache. The sapak baptised it Fort Ruben III, and the name was immediately accepted by his two older companions.

Of all the tracts posted in various parts of Ekoumdoum, it is astonishing that only one escaped Van den Rietter's sweeps through the area and actually found its way into the hands of the people; even then, it arrived by such a long and circuitous route that its fate is perhaps more worth telling then any other. The school principal had undergone an extended apprenticeship at Betara, quite far from his native city, but it had done nothing to eliminate either an absentminded listlessness that verged on obtuseness or an obvious poverty of imagination; he was the one who noticed the sheet of paper posted on the mud wall right next to the door of the little office he entered each morning a half hour before ringing the bell that announced the beginning of classes. He mechanically skimmed the tract without ever actually seeking to grasp its meaning or, more importantly, its possible

197

ramifications; he then handed it to the youngest of his colleagues as if it were some frivolous extravagence from the arsenal of pranks and practical jokes appropriate to the incomprehensible turn of mind characteristic of childhood. This young man brought the curious document to the attention of other young school teachers, and their common puzzlement continued to grow with the passage of time and repeated rereadings of the text.

They were in the habit of talking with Brother Nicholas, a white man who seemed frank and open to them, in any case less distant that the ordinary model, for he occasionally agreed to explain, for their benefit, the exquisite sophistication of European customs and the profoundly humane morality of Christian civilizations in general. They went to consult him and request that he unravel the mystery of this text. Brother Nicholas seized the sheet of paper, pretended to glance through it, and asked for a few hours to study it at leisure in his won room. However, having discussed the matter with his fellow countryman Van den Rietter, he already knew it was subversive propaganda disseminated by fiendish agents sent by Mackenzieville to sow discord among the peace-loving peoples who, occuying this bank of the river and having been placed by Providence under the benevolent protection of the French, wanted nothing more than to remain as they were. When he entered his room, he stuffed the sheet of paper into a drawer; several days later, simulating great embarrassment, he announced to the young school teachers that he had had the misfortune to lose the document they had loaned him. As chance would have it, the missionary made these remarks not only in front of the young school teachers, but also in the presence of a very young brother of one of them, a small boy who worked as an occasional servant for Brother Nicholas and who, while cleaning the stout clergyman's room that morning, had opened a drawer and glimpsed the notorious tract lying there. The child remained silent, but later, as soon as an occasion presented itself, he took possession of the document and gave it to his brother.

When the young school teachers became aware of the lie told by Brother Nicholas—a man who had seemed

so frank and open to them and not at all distant--they
were intrigued; they spoke about it so much among
themselves that it finally occurred to them to go and
confide the whole matter to the elderly mother of a
certain Abena, who had left the city and gone to war
twenty years ago, according to local accounts, although people had only heard speak of him once since
that time, from the lips of an old missionary, a
crippled war veteran who had doubtless been on the
brink of senility and feeble-mindedness. Thus it was
that the incident finally reached the larger public of
Ekoumdoum: surrounded by a halo of the prestige
associated with legend; intensified by the frustra-
tions, the silences, and the mystifications of the
powers that be; quivering with the delirium of fervid
imaginations; inclining toward the feverish surreality
of fables; swollen with visceral feelings of anticipation; bloated with extravagant hopes.

The figure of Abena, the enigmatic son of
Ekoumdoum whose memory had faded with time, suddenly
reemerged in an almost meteoric flash. It seemed
incredible that everyone had not immediately recognized him by the information given in the now famous
declaration, that there existed Ekoumdoumians, even
nursing infants, who were not instantaneously carried
away by the familiar epic ring of the name. The city
itself experienced a paroxysm of confusion and fantasy, as people sought to establish the relation
between its missing noble son and those who had
written and disseminated the magic sheet of paper.

In the first place, who were they? Was it
indeed, as the majority soon came to believe, the two
travelers disguised as Moslems who had recently spent
some time in the city--a small man who sometimes spoke
in terrifying tones, sometimes in honeyed, affection-
ate ones, and a tall, slender adolescent with thin
arms and legs and a sad face? What in the world had
happened to them after their wonderful and mysterious
escape from the deepest dungeons in the Palace? Had
they fled far from the city, far from the country
perhaps? But maybe they were prowling about the
countryside at that very moment? And why might they
not be hiding somewhere in the city, in the home of an
accomplice? What sorts of friends could they still

199

have after the arrest of Mor-Eloulougou and his group? To clear the matter up, would it not be best to establish secret contact with the prisoners?

In the climate produced by ths collective exaltation, a mad though popular spirit of agitation was born, and it must have been the immediate cause of the discomfiture suffered by the Chief and his protectors, the cause of their fall, slow but inexorable, momentarily delayed by guile, postponed by violence, and yet never truly exorcised. Thus, it was not without consternation that people all over the city soon knew about an incident which would have been unthinkable before and which the adults, curiously enough, mentioned only when whispering into the hollows of each other's ears. One of the Chief's wives (according to other sources, it was one of The Bastard's) caught the urchins of the city raiding her fields. Instead of following conventional practice and running away, they calmly pursued their impudent handiwork, and because the young woman had been unable to restrain herself from railing at them, they had even addressed several obscene gestures to her at first and then a few threats, the meaning of which remained obscure as some people vainly fired volleys of questions through the wall of silence maintained by others. "Just wait until Abena come, and we will make you, and everyone like you, throw up," they had dared say to her.

The mystery of the expression "throw up" was even more intriguing and unsettling at the Palace, because the incident repeated itself, setting other children from the city in opposition to other wives of the Chief or The Bastard, both of whom desperately but fruitlessly racked their memories in search of the slightest suggestion of extortion or theft.

Other threats, more vague perhaps but repeated and backed by gestures, were voiced in the presence of those who lived at the Palace, creating such a heavy atmosphere that certain of the Chief's men, recruited from distant tribes and not even sharing a common language with us, could not resist for long and humbly requested authorization to take leave of their master, because they knew all too well that they had been the instruments of our oppression and would incur our vengeance if the wheel ever turned; it is true that their request was denied, for they never had the courage to explain themselves in all sincerity, torn as they were between the insubstantiality of their alleged reasons for wanting to leave and the dramatic implications of their plea. It even happened that children from the Chief's residence came home in tears, revealing that they had heard themselves being taunted by their playmates from the lower city with a strange and no doubt insulting rebuke: "Dirty foreigners! Just wait until Abena comes, and you will pay with your skin."

It is no less strange that their mothers never divulged this provocation. Zoabekwe soon made it clear to Soumazeu that he could no longer take any endeavor to heart unless a solution were finally found for the drama which, as far as he was concerned, belonged categorically atop the list of serious problems facing the city: none of the previously adopted measures had succeeded in cooling the ardor of lovers on both sides of the enclosure; quite the contrary, it seemed as if such measures had only fanned the fires of their passions.

"There are not thirty-six different solutions to the problem, my child," Van den Rietter replied to him. "Replace your bamboo fence with a mud wall. Take all the people you still have and put them to work on it; I am telling you, take all of them. I will throw in my people. With a little show of energy on your part, you'll see, it'll be done in a week."

The structure did not fail to impress the inhabitants of the city, and it was indeed completed in a week, but its architects soon realized that it was only fulfilling its purpose quite imperfectly: to enter or leave the residence according to the caprices of their young hearts, lovers merely needed to replace the breaching technique, as old as carnal desire itself according to Van den Rietter, with the equally venerable one of climbing.

The cracks in the edifice of power became increasingly evident with an unexpected restiveness that emerged among the Chief's former wives, who were being housed by Van den Rietter at the Catholic mission. They had always declared themselves satisfied with a fate that at least protected them from the

whims of masters whose possessiveness knew no limits.
But now they suddenly began to demand the option of
returning to the enclosure they had detested so
intensely just a short while ago. They were claiming
they wanted to recover the semblance of a home in this
way, for since they were no longer anyone's property,
they felt abandoned by everyone, scorned almost, and
quite useless. The inconsistency of this behavior was
already enough to inspire serious doubts in a bachelor
hardened by the study of theology and the untiring
pursuit of piety, but Van den Rietter became firmly
convinced that his pupils had been possessed by
devils, when they dispatched a delegation to him
several days later with a message that was delivered
to him more or less in the following words:

"Van den Rietter, our Father, forgive us for not
having always shown you the complete honesty that
children owe their father. If we desire to leave the
mission for good, it is not to return to the Palace,
as we falsely maintained at first, but to go and lose
ourselves, without further ado, among the ordinary
people in the city of Ekoumdoum; we want to live there
with the men of our choice, but without asking them to
acknowledge any indebtedness toward the Chief, for it
is up to us to repay the money that made us the property of the Chief; we will do it by working in the
fields like all the other women in Ekoumdoum, where
land is not scarce; like the other women, we will
entrust our produce to Brother Nicholas' boat so that
it may be sold in Mackenzieville, and with the money
earned in this fashion, we will reimburse our master.
However long it takes, we will do it, provided you
allow us to live quite simply among the men and women
of the city; our happiness is to be found under these
circumstances and not in that sterile prison where you
confined us—with our consent in the past, it is true,
but only against our wishes in the future. Allow us
to leave, Van den Rietter, our father."

Van den Rietter answered their petition with an
imperious and categorical refusal. One night these
ladies, who were not at that time subjected to the
least supervision, scattered in all directions and
were received without further ado at various housholds
in the city, where an underlying and never fully

202

suppressed resentment against the Chief still smoldered among Ekoumdoumian patriarchs attached to the
integrity of ancestral traditions, and it vouchsafed
the women several dazzling testimonies of sympathy and
even friendship, if not solidarity with their cause.
The next day the missionary, at the head of his men,
had to search all the houses of Ekoumdoum one after
the other and to verify the identity of each woman
living there; he led them back like a herd of sheep to
their section of the mission and organized a formid-
ible police force to guard it, just like the one he
had deployed around the Forest of the Chimpanzees.
But in this case as well, the local dandies did not
lose heart; on the contrary, one would have said that
their frenzy grew in proportion to the obstacles
raised around what they regarded as their natural
prey, especially now that, as everyone said, Abena was
coming back, for if Abena was going to right all
wrongs, didn't that mean he was going to eliminate all
deprivations? For that matter, how could one be
deprived without thinking one's self the victim of a
grievous wrong?

Van den Rietter and Zoabekwe were from then on
closely linked together and seldom showed themselves
publicly, except in each other's company; which of
them made the decision to suppress at all costs the
phantasmagoria behind the effervescence that was
threatening to engulf the entire city? No one can
deny that, properly speaking, the murder itself was
attributable to Zoabekwe, commonly know as The
Bastard, because he clearly stained his hands with
blood when he took upon himself the execution of a
task against which his father had, however, always
warned him, explaining that such a crime would necessarily call down a blood curse on their family and
sooner or later summon in its wake the only possible
expiatory response, another crime. It is no less true
that Van den Rietter was always careful to distance
himself in public from the vortex of violence into
which Zoabekwe allowed himself to be drawn; he even
announced more than once that the thought of such
heinous acts made his blood run cold with horror when
he was alone in bed at night; he added that the conduct of the young man, who was, moreover, under the

protection of his father, had unfortunately been inspired by an authentically African tradition, a thousand-year-old heritage, against which he, the white, the perfect stranger, was powerless, even if he wanted to fight against it.

It was under similar circumstances and in remarks of this kind that Van den Rietter's dissimulation betrayed itself. In certain matters, his shrewdness and dexterity easily put us off the track; in others, we had the impression he was not making the slightest effort to conceal his cards, as if he thought we were too stupid to distinguish one from the other or as if he no longer had anything in reserve to cover his nakedness, his duplicity. This is how it was on that tragic occasion. For if Van den Rietter's foremost worry was the fear of not exercising sufficient restraint in dealing with our tradition, and if his most ardent desire was to preserve its purity forever, would it not have been better for him to have stayed away from our part of the world altogether, or to have left immediately after arriving, as it were, by accident? Indeed, how had he expected to bring the Christian principles he carried in his luggage into harmony with our ancestral beliefs, unless the latter were somehow modified? And as far as that goes, what had he been doing during his twenty-year stay in Ekoumdoum but mocking our customs, belittling them, making us ashamed of them as if they were barbarisms, and sometimes even forbidding us to engage in them, as had been the case with dancing by moonlight—a practice we eventually abandoned, and that is the equivalent of saying we unlearned it, after having tried for several years to devote ourselves to it far from the city in clearings specifically cut from the depths of the forest for that purpose? The youngest school teachers knew the missionary quite well, and they declared later that Van den Rietter had only used this specious line of argument to justify himself for being constantly together with his friend and yet not exerting the pressures that might have diverted The Bastard from his sinister plans. Retrospectively perspicacious, even these young people have today finally discovered the truth, deductively, by asking the questions that should have occurred to any man with common sense.  Didn't Van den Rietter actually desire the spilling of blood as long as he himself did not become tainted by it?  Was he not the instigator, the one who placed the gun in the murderer's hand, the one who, more than anyone else, deserves to be branded with the infamy of the crime?

Although the methods of supervision and defense implemented in the Chief's compound and the women's quarters at the mission had proved singularly inadequate to dampen the spirits of the audacious and the recalcitrant, they had so impressed The Bastard that he took it into his head to build a fortified wall around the entire city as a means of countering a possible incursion by the "British saboteurs," as he called the Rubenist guerillas with whom he, like the two missionaries, was continually obsessed.

"You can not be thinking seriously about such a thing, my son," Van den Rietter told him as he burst out laughing.  "You would have to put the entire population of the city to work, and that means keeping them under restraint for weeks, months, perhaps a whole year; where is your army of policemen?  Don't you know that one armed man for every three inhabitants of the city would scarcely be enough?  Well then, figure it out.  Let us even assume for a moment that you succeed in putting up your Great Wall of China; what then?  Do you think that people who are accustomed to coming and going freely will agree to let themselves be penned like sheep?  All at once and without any advance preparation?  They would go out of their minds, my child; maybe they would start smashing everything; there would be a riot, a general insurrection.  The point is that there are plenty of people in your little town, even when nothing is happening; well then, can you imagine a riot down there?  In such a case, the British at Mackenzieville are the ones who would be gloating.  You have a mania for failing to see the obvious, my little fellow; it is a bad habit you should eventually give up.  People can be controlled much better by emotions than by fences; what is more, it is a method that saves time and, above all, money."

Because the dull-witted and simple-minded Zoabekwe still did not seem to understand, Van den

205

Rietter looked the Chief's son straight in the eye and made his point explicitly, "I know an emotion which definitely keeps people in check—fear. Fear, do you know what that is?"

"Yes, father."

"I doubt it, but act as if you did anyway. Frighten the hell out of them once and for all; then, come tell me if it doesn't neutralize them better than a wall. Fear, my child, is thousands upon thousands of invisible bars, steel bars, carefully interwoven steel bars. Do you see what I mean? A man who is afraid is a fenced man, a paralyzed man."

Zoabekwe carried away that image with him the same way a healthy man unknowingly picks up the apparently harmless germ of a fatal disease: he continues to believe himself as solid as a rock, even as the ferment of decay sets in and begins to sap his strength. His languid blood no longer circulates from the heart to the extremities and back to the heart without spreading devastation throughout the body and burbling beneath the influence of its muted fermentation, no matter what he may think. His damp, flaccid skin imperceptibly swells with foul humors, while he remains convinced that his breath is sweet enough for kissing his friends. If he were unaware of his illness, what doctor would he consult?

Now, shortly afterwards and perhaps even on the same day as the conversation that has just been reported, it so happened that one of Zoabekwe's wives, undoubtedly the ugliest and most jealous one, approached The Bastard, lavished him with cajolery, and promised to tell him a remarkable secret, if he would only give her a present, the value of which was, after extensive haggling, finally established as three thousand francs. Curiosity, desire to implement decisive measures at a critical juncture, and impatience to exercise a stintingly accorded authority eventually overcame The Bastard's legendary stinginess, and he paid the required sum. It was then he learned that Ngwane-Eligui, not content with merely scorning his bed, had not hesitated to incite the women to revolt, those in the Forest of the Chimpanzees as well as those at the Catholic mission; it had been at her instigation that the latter had insisted upon leaving the mission and had in fact departed to go and live among the inhabitants of Ekoumdoum under the pretext that their happiness could be found there.

"That girl," muttered The Bastard when the woman had finished. "She is unquestionably the favorite daughter of Satan, a real she-devil; I no longer have the slightest doubt she will do anything to cause problems for us. But what is to be done? Listen, for the moment watch her closely, keep your eyes open, constantly observe her little game, and remember her friendships in the Palace, her contacts with people outside, and her tricks for communicating with them. Everything you learn should be faithfully reported back to me. If you serve me well, you will not be wanting for presents or money; count on me."

The poor woman's twisted venality had just given The Bastard one of the keys to real power, and he was not going to relinquish it in the future. As an informer, the ugly one displayed a zeal that exceeded all expectations, to the point that her reports enabled them to flush Ezadzomo from his hiding place beneath the bed of a Chief's wife, who in this instance proved to be no other than Ngwane-Eligui the Younger. And that is what was doubly and fortuitously aggravating in the case of this adolescent with a notoriously tumultuous past.

Already regarded by the police and the Palace spies as an unruly chap, an unredeemably depraved troublemaker, Ezadzomo was a repeat offender in such matters and a regular customer at the special court, which had put him through the gamut of its penalties—from a simple fine to six months of hard labor on a plantation. "Was he not an ideal victim for the punishment that would dumbfound the city and confine it forever within a wall of terror!" said The Bastard to himself. Instead of bringing him before the court, he would throw him temporarily into a dungeon at the Palace, while waiting for inspiration to suggest the most appropriate torture and the most suitable moment for inflicting it.

Since he was gradually entering into the spirit of his office at that time, Zoabekwe devised a plan to bribe other women from the Palace in order to make sycophants of them; he chose the ones whose coquet-

207

tishness seemed to mark them as easy prey for would-be lovers. He did not reveal his good fortune to Van den Rietter until he had ascertained that his success was exceeding his wildest dreams.

"Congratulations, my child," exclaimed the missionary as he embraced him. "You see, you are making progress. Magnificent, absolutely magnificent! There is no other word for it. Come, have a drink with us. You don't even know what you can do now, do you? Apply your method to the whole city. Why not, hmm? You are going to do more than merely confine them behind a wall, my son; you are going to tie them up in little packages, chirp, chirp!"

Always ready to learn despite his acknowledged progress in the art of governing, The Bastard did not fail to follow his mentor's advice, actually weaving a net around the city, a rough, loosely knit one at first but one which became increasingly refined and tight-meshed in the course of time—the first network of spies, informers, and stool pigeons that had ever plagued a community of Bantu peasants, undoubtedly among the most peaceful people in the world. The pay received by these men and women was paltry; besides the novelty of participating in a perverse game, they were above all motivated by the intoxication of being able to harm others in secret and with impunity.

It is rather difficult these days to depict the ravages which Zoabekwe and his master effected in this way on the spirits and souls of people. They knew almost everything they wanted to know; they even outwitted the best ones. An unfamiliar wind chilled petulant impulses and stunned audacious ones. Lovers were muzzled by telling them about their own affairs or even fantasies caressed only in the intimacy of their dreams; even the most harmless braggarts were reduced to silence when they heard repeated the exact words of boasts they had made the previous night in confidence among people who were above all suspicion.

In contrast, the two confederates sought to reconcile the patriarchs, venerated by the Ekoumdoumians; they flattered their attachment to tradition, or, if the old men continued to take umbrage at the growing ascendancy of the rulers, they tried to destroy their reputations by placing them in the embarrassing situation of having to satisfy in public the disgusting or demeaning desires they had until then gratified in secret.

Despite everything, these old men were heartened by the complaisance of the city's masters; they met one day and expressed their astonishment that young Ezadzomo, who was no more than a child, had not yet been judged in the usual manner for having violated the master-of-the-city's sacred enclosure and repeatedly paid court to one of his wives, and, moreover, that the young man had been held incommunicado since his arrest some time ago. They resolved to initiate a procedure they had not dared undertake in years; they wended their way in a procession to the old Chief, in front of whom they expressed their concern. The bedridden old man convulsively sat up in bed and declared, with indignant surprise and between fits of coughing and spitting, that he knew nothing at all about an extremely important case in which a young scatterbrain had dared reach a decision without consulting him, the true master who was still alive, very much alive. Summoned with great urgency, The Bastard—the young scatterbrain whom Van den Rietter had not hesitated to take under his wing—acknowledged the facts brought forth by the patriarchs, while barricading himself behind reservations that he only relinquished grudgingly when backed into a corner by paternal curses during the course of a scene which the venerable, but really quite faint-hearted, representatives of the city even today characterize as "very pathetic" to the accompaniment of several strokes on their white goatees.

It was decided without further ceremony that the young Ezadzomo would immediately be freed. When he reappeared in the city, he was as grey as an injured man who had rolled in the dust with pain for a long time, emaciated, exhausted by hunger and the darkness of his cell, and, like nearly everyone else in Ekoumdoum, ignorant of the murder plot that was being hatched against his youthful innocence.

It was not without anger that The Bastard saw himself deprived of a prey whose reputation as an unrepentant blasphemer had, moreover, been crowned with the incomprehensible partiality of his dear

Ngwane-Eligui, that she-devil who, by thwarting his efforts to subdue her, had rendered him inconsolable—him, the son of the master-of-the-city. To imagine that she had tendered her loins to that snotty-nosed brat! Was it believable? Thinking to lend credibility to the quickly launched rumor of a general amnesty, he also had the still imprisoned local conspirators released on the evening of the same day. He invited Mor-Eloulougou and his most trusted lieutenants to a private banquet, and as soon as the wine had begun to fuddle the minds of the young people, he proposed that they place their intelligence at his disposal in exchange for privileges which he detailed for them slowly, one by one, to seduce them for certain without giving them time to reflect. When the people of Ekoumdoum allude to this regrettable incident these days, it is fashionable to speak about the trap into which immature young people were bound to fall—young people who, furthermore, had just left prison and undoubtedly believed they were playing for their freedom. The fact is that, from this very night on, The Bastard and Van den Rietter had no better spies in the city, at least none who were more zealous, than the former allies of Jo The Juggler. As long as the accident of their destinies had placed them in a camp where the partisans only had blows to receive, their natural caddishness had but all too cruelly bridled their malevolence and their cowardly aggressiveness. With what delight could they now give free rein to these instincts, guaranteed of impunity from the most corrupt torturers and assured of unconditional approval from the powers that be. They launched themselves even more frenziedly in pursuit of Ezadzoumo, because the accordionist secretly held a grudge against him for having taken advantage of their detention to triumph over him in the race for Ngwane-Eligui.

When he was still a very young child, Ezadzomo had displayed an inclination for hunting and an aptitude for life in the forest—qualities which aroused the interest of Mor-Afana, the most renowned practitioner of those arts and, in the memory of Ekoumdoum, the only man capable of capturing a giant viper alive after attacking it frontally, although he had unfortunately reached the evening, if not the dusk, of his life and was in search of disciples to whom he could bequeath his secrets. The aging man had taken the urchin under his wing and little by little inculcated in him the two principles to which he had resolved to limit his initiation. "In hunting as in warfare," he said to him one day, "the one who strikes without closing his eyes does not have long to wait for victory to come." Applying this adage, the child had practiced anticipating his antagonist's next movement and even divining the plan of action that was germinating in his head. Despite the perpetual laugh that brightened his face, nothing his opponent thought or did escaped his attention, constantly on the alert.

Another day the declining old man confided to the small child, who sat up to listen: "In hunting as in warfare, the one who sees without being seen has the best chance to survive alone." Thus, beneath his air of a disconcerting will-o'-the-wisp, always in the mood for an impious prank, there was concealed a young man endowed by dint of practice with infinite patience, a young man capable of spending long hours stationed along the presumed path of his adversay, lying in wait until his prey finally turns up and, unaware of the danger, offers itself to his rapacity.

He hardly possessed an excess of these two qualities, clear-sightedness and watchful quiescence, when it came to serving Ngwane-Eligui soon after she had indicated to him that she had chosen him from the pack of voracious wolves pursuing her; it had sufficed for her to forward the following message to him: "It is impossible that the two strangers have gone far from here. Find them and come tell me about it as soon as you can." Concealing himself in one place after another, wherever his instinct told him the two strangers might pass, he had kept watch for endless hours without growing weary, although he was occasionally relieved by his inseparable companion. It was lost effort; to compensate for his failure on that count, he had easily outdistanced Van den Rietter, The Bastard, and their men in the race for the lost guns; having found them, he had simply hidden them in a different place. At first he had hesitated to inform the young woman about them, but he eventually decided to do so.

"Incredible!" she had whispered, transfixed with amazement. "Listen well: leave them where they are, but hurry and find the two strangers; then I will keep all my promises. Come back often and tell me how you are doing. But I swear that as soon as you have established contact with them, on that very day I will be yours."

When he was released from prison, she made it clear to him that she was renewing her oath.

Well then, Ezadzomo, who had quickly, almost miraculously, recovered from his detention, and his faithful companion once again adopted the practice of scouring the mysterious forest with its thousands of croaking sounds. Like the entire younger generation of Ekoumdoumians, they were fascinated by instruments of war, and before each excursion into the woods, they went to worship at the shrine of what had almost been the booty of Jo The Juggler. They held each gun in their hands, weighed it, contemplated it by running their eyes over it from one end to the other and back again; finally they took aim with it. Each day witnessed a slight increase in their boldness; they surprised themselves by taking the guns apart and putting them back together again. They spent hours there, and their absence did not fail to intrigue their pursuers, who were spying on them from a distance.

Mor-Afana knew Ezadzomo quite well, having been his master in the art of hunting (the most noble of all arts in the eyes of a true Ekoumdoumian), and here is how he today describes the young man who disappeared so tragically: "He had two virtues which make a man invincible, but he was afflicted with a fault that, by itself, was capable of undoing him in the flower of his youth. I became aware of it one day when he was accompanying me on the other side of the river; we had penetrated to the heart of the desolate jungle. Trying to cut a taut vine above my head with a single blow of my machete, which had grown quite thin with use, I made a wrong move; as it happened, the blade glanced off the elastic surface of the vine and made a gash in my left hand; it happened more quickly than I can describe it. Torrents of blood immediately spurted forth and ran down my arm. In vain I begged the child to urinate on my wound; he was shaken with sobs, he embraced me effusively, he tore at his forearms and then at his cheeks as he cried out to me, "My God! But you are going to die; soon you will be no more than a corpse stiff and cold; then they will bury you and put you in the ground like the slip of a cassava root; I will never see you again, and never again will I walk with you in the jungle!' It was in vain that I told him, 'No, no, my son, you are wrong; I run no risk at all, provided you urinate there, on my wound.' Nothing to be done; he had tensed up with despair. Despite all his good will, he was unable to produce a single drop of urine; he suddenly lost his head and was completely carried away.

"Wherever you may be, my poor little one, your compassion was your downfall. It was if you went mad when you visualized the suffering of those you loved. You were like a lion with a tender heart."

It would be impossible to find a better description of the drama which constituted the trial of Ezadzomo and his inseparable companion Ezabiemeu and which resulted in an outcome that proved fatal to the two young people, no more than children really. It is true that, overcome with compassion at seeing the poignant spectacle of suffering that Ngwane-Eligui seemed to be presenting, the credulous young man flew into such a rage of despair that he burst into a torrent of invectives against the Chief and his family, and the patriarchs in the audience were powerless to interrupt it, despite the chorus of moans, pleas, and exclamations of fright and horror in which they sought to drown the voice of their headstrong protégé. Afterwards, when the venerable old men left the courtroom in a group, they were haggard, trembling, and terrified, as if they had just witnessed the breaking of a taboo, in comparison with which the act of making love to one's own mother would have seemed a trivial pecadillo.

Ngwane-Eligui had only been called before the court as a witness. Today it is firmly established that she had not been beaten before entering the hall of justice, nor had she been in any way threatened with such treatment. Perhaps the guard made a pretence of preparing to administer one or two swats of his fly-whisk to her buttocks, but that was merely a symbolic gesture to remind her that a woman should adopt a reverent, humble attitude upon entering a courtroon and appearing before an assembly of men convened by virtue of powers granted them by the master-of-the-city. No one had expected the young woman's entrace to trigger the explosion that occurred before their very eyes. When Ngwane-Eligui appeared, she was groaning, and her cheeks were bathed with tears, her hair bedraggled, her face distorted with pain, as if she had been subjected to torture all night long and all the preceding day as well.

Ezadzomo undoubtedly did not know that all women who are guilty of infidelity or impropriety use the same technique to move their judges and ward off the punishments they have incurred. He was probably unaware of the fact that, in this sort of comedy, Ngwane-Eligui had the reputation of outshining all her sisters in the wide world and that, since her arrival in Ekoumdoum, she had saved herself from the wrath of her masters, justifiably annoyed by her unremitting scorn, only by holding them in terror with the refinement of her artifice. In any case, as soon as the court expressed the intention of beginning its questioning, everyone saw her suddenly throw herself violently on the cement floor, where she rolled around, kicking her legs wildly and accompanying her performance with heart-rending screams.

Now then, unable to endure it any longer, the young man, who was no more than a child, broke into a vengeful indictment, of which, as misfortune would have it, only the most alarming snatches crackled above the hubbub of a general panic: the Chief was a usurper; his hands were red with the blood of his predecessor, the true master-of-the-city, the legitimate chief of Ekoumdoum; for decades, the blood of the city's legitimate master had never ceased crying vengeance; so that justice might finally be done, the city was impatiently awaiting the imminent return of Abena, the noble son of Ekoumdoum, the hero who, having gone to war twenty years ago, had faced people of all races on each of the five continents. . . .

Unbeknownst to the one who uttered these remarks and his inseparable companion, who, as was fitting, approved them in public, such words were inexpiable and sealed the sorrowful fate of the two defendants. As the patriarchs hurriedly left the hall of justice, a closed session was declared in an atmosphere of such confusion and unreality that the missionaries never obtained an intelligible version of the incident after their return from Mackenzieville, where both of them had gone by boat two days previously, as if on purpose. Thus, Zoabekwe concealed from them the actual reason for his implacable hatred of Ezadzomo and Ezabiemeu; he confined himself to informing them that the two defendants had publicly avowed their mortal enmity toward the Chief and his family, another way of admitting, he contended, that they were indeed in the service of the Mackenzieville bandits, who had obviously entrusted the stolen guns to them for safekeeping. As far as Van den Rietter was concerned, he had made up his mind on this subject a long time ago: as a result of playing soldier by pretending to practice their marksmanship with the Winchester 30-30 carbine and above all by taking it apart, the two young people had disengaged the breech, but Soumazeu had convinced himself that they had damaged it intentionally, the sort of crime that was quite characteristic of British treachery.

Until the very end, the two Europeans were thus going to know nothing about the true nature of the profound crisis that had placed Ekoumdoum in conflict with its master; this situation had always existed, although the two somnambulists had failed to recognize it, because they had been so steeped in their own preconceptions that they had always considered it uninteresting and, for that matter, pointless to follow the meanderings of the soul of a city in the heart of Africa, provided of course that it was firmly under their control. They discovered the truth at a moment when it was much too late to do anything about it, and that was indeed the most fitting punishment for their self-induced hallucinations.

As early as the day after the trial and long before they had actually disappeared, the city seemed resigned to the loss of Ezadzomo and Ezabieneu, two patients who were apparently beyond the help of any medical treatment from then on. It sometimes happens that a person forgets an arm or a leg that has fallen asleep; he is surprised to hear himself suddenly remarking that this inert thing is part of his own body and not some foreign object, bleached and dessicated by the vagaries of the weather; he regards it with mixed astonishment and horror, staring at it and then suddenly turning away his eyes. Ezadzomo and Ezabiemeu were like two of the city's limbs that had permanently fallen asleep, and a mute, at least apparently indifferent Ekoumdoum had turned its eyes away from them once and for all, in such a way that the only remedy of surgical science seemed to be amputation.

Yet it did not occur in quite the expected fashion. It is a fact that about three or four weeks after the trial, a rumor suddenly spread through the city and informed people that the two companions, as inseparable as always, had escaped from their cell in the prison. The inhabitants of the city were seized by a curious restiveness, simultaneously impassioned and mechanical, rebellious but without the slightest sense of wonder. At the head of their men, The Bastard and Van den Rietter conducted futile sweeps through the surrounding forests to accomodate themselves to the round of mystifying rites that comprise the substance of power. With all the liveliness of a masquerade, the search had been proceeding for three days when a fisherman, whose boat was going upstream along the shore, perceived two bodies of young people, no more than children really, floating side-by-side and moving slowly away from the underbrush that overhung the water. Then it was that anger and a desire for vengeance roused the youngest of the men, by far the most numerous as well as most of the women and all of the children; the Palace and the presbytery trembled. For three full days and three whole nights, a rush of tears, lamentations, and rolling in the ashes seemed to push the city close to the edge of mutiny. Then a touch of weariness gradually rendered people susceptible to the words of the older men and women, whose increasingly dubious impartiality had not yet destroyed their quite exaggerated reputation for wisdom and perspicacity. The fact is that their whispered remarks would have been incapable of antagonizing either Zoabekwe or Van den Rietter. The cause of all their misfortunes, the original curse, dated indeed from the arrival of the two travellers, those bandits who called themselves followers of Allah and who had introduced it into the body of the city, like a drop of poison that was going to upset the entire organism, and they had been seconded by that detestable Ngwane-Eligui, that bird of ill omen, that sensuous mirage whose scintillating seductiveness continued to turn the heads of young people like Ezadzomo and Ezabiemeu, who were no more than children.

It is also a fact that, being unable to lay their hands on the actual offenders who were quite secure behind the ramparts of fortresses bristling with guns and Janissaries, the people gradually inclined toward throwing the harmless innocents, pointed out to them by the prophets of the acceptance of evil, as fodder to their desires for vengeance, more exasperating to them than the cries of hungry children. It was not rare to hear people curse the two missing strangers, formerly devout Moslems whose popularity had once been so widespread; outside the Palace, people whispered that the malevolence of fate toward the city might perhaps be appeased by sending Ngwane-Eligui back to her own people; inside the Palace, her co-wives spit at her as she passed, and someone slapped her in the face.

There even came a time when the learned preachers of resignation to the allegedly immutable order of things could freely indulge in their teaching without fear of encountering anyone to contradict them. "How those two boys could have escaped, the poor fellows!" they declared. "How could such words have been said, spoken, pronounced without their author being immediately struck by lightning? What would people think in that case? What would the good people have thought? That anything at all can be said with impunity? At that point who would still be willing to restrain his tongue? Who would want to deprive himself of the pleasures of blasphemy? Let us hope they have taken their sacrilegious talk into the grave with them and that it will never again see the light of day. Let us bury our faces in the lap of forgetfulness, where we lived happily in the beginning."

Under the influence of such preaching, the bruised, broken, despairing city withdrew into itself; even the dogs, more skinny than ever, seemed to reappear during the day only when they were hugging the walls. Father Van den Rietter and Brother Nicholas experienced a feeling of peace for perhaps the first time since the day when the theft of their guns had been discovered; at least that was the appearance they gave in public; as a matter of fact, they could once again be seen attending to their usual activities in absolute tranquillity. Soumazeu once again began to reconcile fathers and sons, widows and brothers-in-law, orphans and their guardians. Brother Nicholas once again used his wheezy old truck to transport sand and other materials necessary for building the brick church that was beginning to take shape over on the other side of the city, next to the mud and wattle chapel, although the construction was proceeding so slowly that even the youngest children expressed doubt they would ever live to see the completion of that monument. Regally, unconcernedly he drove across the city, now nearly as silent and haggard as a cemetary and scarcely less deserted, while a thousand simultaneous whinnies of his motor re-echoed in the distance. He seemed not to have the slightest suspicion that each and every person who watched him drive by expected him to be suddenly struck by some misfortune—a tree blown over on him by the force of a tornado, an unanticipated fall into a ravine, a lightning-like stoppage of his heart as the result of a violent sneeze. Indeed, what can bring about the death of human beings, if not misfortunes that are as cruel as they are unforeseeable, blows struck by a destiny more powerful than all humanity combined?

All the same, that is what Mor-Zamba was explaining to Jo The Juggler and the sapak Evariste at that very moment. "It is true," he proclaimed to them, "that the order of men, frequently condemnable and occasionally intolerable, cries out for rebellion, even armed rebellion: that is the path blazed a short while ago by the immortal Ruben; it is what Hurricane-Viet was teaching recently, yesterday so to speak. But what good does it do to violate the natural order with the dogged perseverance that Jo The Juggler brings to such a task? Harrassing his enemy instead of sleeping at night, disguising himself as a true believer and usurping the appearances of a religion he does not profess, implicating innocent children in the abominable act of stealing guns, diddling a woman beneath her husband's roof, perhaps even in the room next to his own—what could follow upon so many pro-fanations, except more profanations, more sacrilegious acts, like the mysterious murder of two men who were very young, children almost?"

"Mysterious, mysterious," retorted Jo The Juggler with a mocking laugh, "not as mysterious as you think. Listen, I will read Ngwane-Eligui's message: 'The two men, children almost, who had been caught by surprise in possession of the stolen guns, were murdered by The Bastard; he must have had them poisoned before throwing their bodies into the river to make it look like a drowning. That will be your fate if he ever catches you; he has succeeded in turning the city against you, and against me. My fate will perhaps not remain in doubt for very long. Watch out for your-self, but please do not go too far away, and indicate your presence in some way.'"

Jo The Juggler had, as a matter of fact, re-entered the city of Ekoumdoum on a pitch-black night just after the two bodies had been discovered in the river. By virtue of his consummate guile and vigilance, he had succeeded in outwitting the guards and militiamen with whom the darkness had now been peopled by Van den Rietter's suspicious imagination and Zoabekwe's morbid presumptuousness. "Ekoumdoum has indeed changed!" reflected Jo The Juggler, both amused and annoyed at having underestimated the enemy. The tangerine tree was now leaning against a mud wall instead of a bamboo fence. During its construction, Ngwane-Eligui had visited the spot to repossess all the messages that had accumulated in her quite rudi-mentary mailbox; she now came very late each evening to slip a single message into the hiding place, and she returned very early each morning to retrieve it,

if it had not been removed by the intended recipient,
as had always been the case until now.  By groping
patiently in the crevice between the tree and the wall
(it was barely perceptible to his sense of touch), Jo
the Juggler eventually felt and withdrew a scrap of
paper that had been folded several times and skewered
with a bamboo shoot.

"What do you think about her suggestion of not
going too far away, grandpa preacher?"  Jo the Juggler
asked Mor-Zamba.  "Me, I am for it.  What about you?"

They did not have the leisure to debate the
question at length.  It must have been during the
afternoon of the same day that the sapak was bitten by
a snake whose venom was regarded by the people of
Ekoumdoum as extremely dangerous, almost always deadly.  The Rubenists were staying at Fort Ruben II in
the intention of gathering provisions from a farming
area that belonged to the Chief and could be reached
in a half day.  Having arrived in the vicinity of the
fields after a long walk, the three guerillas had
parted company, each of them moving to the site of his
particular mission.  The sapak had been charged with
acquiring a supply of sugar cane, a simple task.  For
the past several minutes he had been moving along a
path frequently used by the peasants, although he had
little fear of encountering one of them, because it
was Sunday.  Nevertheless, he was depending on his
sense of hearing more than on all his other senses
combined; he jumped at the least crackling sound and
held himself ready to vanish into a nearby bush if he
heard voices or the characteristic swish of someone
walking through the undergrowth, the shrubs, or the
branches.  The gloomy thickets gradually gave way to a
more open forest, dotted with areas where thinly
scattered trees or tangled scrubwood indicated that
formerly cultivated fields were lying fallow.

As often happens to people when they recall
dangers from which they somehow miraculously escaped,
the ex-schoolboy from Kola-Kola usually laughs and
cries at the same time while recounting how he found
himself in an area of transitional growth when a
brilliant rush of amber sunlight streaming across the
edges of a dark shape created a fringe of chiaroscuro
that was speckled with white dots literally dancing on

all sides and completely disorienting his sense of vision. It suddenly seemed to him that he was floundering in a wriggling mass on the ground, a sort of gigantic, amorphous, furious undulation. He thought he must be crossing a rivulet hidden beneath the underbrush, although it was a curious rivulet, running transversely across the hillside. He jumped back when he saw the eddy of variegated bluish-greens, reddish-browns, blues, and pale yellows. Without realizing it, he screamed in horror for several moments after stumbling across the cottony, flaccid yet elastic body of a giant _ayang_; the frightening sensation gave him wings as he rushed away, screaming more hideously than ever. He thought the monster was in turn looming up behind him.

"He must have been resting there," Evariste is in the habit of explaining, "calm, relaxed, you see. When he heard me coming, he undoubtedly decided to leave, but he was too lazy and didn't do it quickly enough. At that moment I arrive like a simpleton; my ears are wide open, but not my eyes, and that is a big mistake in the forests around here. I do not know what other forests in this wide world are like, but I really learned what needs to be done in this one. All right, I hear him drawing himself together at my heels, no doubt annoyed that I stepped on him. Besides, what is there to say? At Kola-Kola, you know, when a Mameluke is chasing you . . . try to imagine it. Before his hand comes crashing down on your shoulder, one might almost say that you heard his arm shoot out; probably a sharp release of breath just before he reaches out his arm, or maybe it is merely a puff of air, but what is certain is that the person being pursued hears it. Well then, that is exactly how it happened. At nearly the same instant, I felt his clammy skin gliding across my right leg, brushing it lightly; I had the impression it was like an arrow missing its mark; I tripped, but I continued on my way, because I figured I had escaped unharmed. I was still holding my machete. There I was in the sugar-cane field; I cut a stalk, even though I am shaking like a palm tree in a tornado. I am getting ready to eat it, when Mor-Zamba shows up and says to me, 'What happened to you? You were screaming as if you had been suddenly changed into a chimpanzee.' Well then, I tell him about my little escapade. All at once, his face clouds over, and he says to me, 'How are you feeling now, right away?' I reply to him, 'Oh well, not bad, not bad, but that's funny; my right foot has just now begun to hurt; it is probably a thorn I brushed against.' Mor-Zamba doesn't say a word; he takes my foot in his hand without having to take anything off my feet, because I still could not stand to wear those damned boots that Mor-Kinda was determined to get me to wear, despite my objections. He claims that, if I had conformed to this elementary form of discipline, I would not have been bitten or that I would have been saved by the boot's fabric. On the other hand, Doctor Ericsson said he was not sure, but there is nothing to be done; the Commander always has to bring back his laurels. But what is certain is that my right leg had swollen so much in the next few seconds that it looked like a young elephant's paw; the edema had invaded everything—toes, heel, ankle, everything."

The largest blade in Mor-Zamba's enormous multipurpose pocketknife had been specially sharpened in anticipation of such accidents, and he used it to cut the incision he had so often practiced at the Colonel Leclerc forced labor camp near Oyolo, where snake bites were common; above the knee he placed an improvised tourniquet made of vine. He took the sapak in his arms and headed in the direction where Mor-Kinda should be; after responding to the prearranged signal, the latter appeared almost instantaneously.

"We are leaving for Tambona," Mor-Zamba told him in a tone of voice that brooked no opposition. "We will be on our way as soon as we have assembled all the necessary equipment. Evariste was bitten by a nasty little beast, and we have nothing to treat him with on the spot. We will only need blankets and money, but they are at Fort Ruben I. I am going there, and I will be back in a few hours. The Raleigh is cached near the road, which can be reached from here by a shortcut. If the child is thirsty, give him some of your rum to drink; that is what they recommend. You can begin immediately for that matter; make him drink some, even if he doesn't want it."

When he returned, shortly after midnight no doubt, the moaning child said to Jo The Juggler, "I am going to die, no? Tell me that I am going to die."

"What an idea!" replied Mor-Kinda, who had, however, already been convinced of the sapak's own prognosis by the child's burning fever, by the alternating fits of delirious exhaustion and spasmodic quivering which seemed to indicate that his condition was critical, and above all by the monstrous edema that was engulfing his leg and had now reached the knee.

"Liar!" the adolescent muttered. "I know I am going to die. What difference can it make to admit it? Only, it is stupied to die before. . . ."

"Before what?"

"But look here! Before having given those bastards a good licking in return for what they gave us. When some character slaps a licking on you, you have got to give it back to him; that's all. Otherwise, there is no justice. That's certainly true: if you can't pay back a licking, then you are no longer in the game. Remember, at Kola-Kola we always paid back the slaver's Mamelukes for their lickings, and those of Baba Toura too; that was the right thing to do. It is stupid to die before paying them back."

"Shut up, you are talking nonsense!"

The Rubenists got underway as soon as day began to dawn; they reached the road well before nightfall and retrieved the Raleigh, enabling Mor-Zamba to ease himself from the burden of the sapak, whom he had until then been carrying on his back. Although some of the mechanisms were horribly rusted and a flat tire obliged them to travel on one rim after the second day, the bicycle readily supported the weight of the young patient, who remained seated on the baggage-carrier, his right leg attached to the frame by means of a splint and his left one dangling above the pedal on the same side. By walking almost constantly, day and night, they arrived at Tambona three days and only two nights after their departure. Moaning constantly, growing more and more exhausted, having drunk little and eaten less, the child at least kept a firm grasp on the breath of life, and that in itself seemed miraculous to Jo The Juggler, who was hardly suspect-

ible to superstitious beliefs. Even the advance of
the edema had stopped; Mor-Zamba contended that it had
receded, although Mor-Kinda was not ready to believe
anything unless he heard it from an authorized source.

They went directly to the Protestant mission, and
as soon as they had explained to the black servants
that the adolscent had been bitten by an _ayang_, these
two individuals, who had proved so reticent during the
Rubenists' first visit, immediately ran to look for
their master, whose skin was the color of milk. The
man examined the sapak for a long time and finally
declared: "This is indeed the first time I have ever
seen anyone get off so easily; it's true he is a young
lad and you two have cared for him admirably: the
splint is perfect, and the incision is properly done.
All the same, if he was really bitten by a giant
_ayang_, the beast couldn't have had much venom; she had
undoubtedly just made use of it. Otherwise, this
little fellow would have been dead within several
hours, whereas now he is completely out of danger."

The two missionaries gave orders for the child to
be carried into the mission infirmary, and while the
man was still attending to him, they expressed a
desire to know where Mor-Zamba had learned to dress
snake bites. He briefly told them his story, concealing the hardly pacific reasons for his return to
Ekoumdoum and any other details that might have
shocked those good-hearted whites.

"Well, well!" mused the missionary after having
listened attentively to his tale. "Perhaps someday I
will take a trip through your part of the country."

"I am not sure it would be a good idea," remarked
Mor-Kinda, "because there is already a Soumazeu down
there. . . ."

"Oh, is there?" said the missionary, laughing
good-naturedly. "And what difference does that make?"

"What difference does it make? That one is
jealous of his borders, he is! The arrival of a
_Simsimabayane_ would not necessarily send him into
raptures of delight."

"Nevertheless, there are many rooms in the house
of the Lord," the Protestant missionary declared
thoughtfully. "That Soumazeu doesn't know how to
treat snake bites, eh?"

"Apparently not," replied Jo The Juggler. "In any case, he is not at all equipped for that sort of thing."

"Yet that is where one needs to begin," said the missionary. "Those people are rather odd. Is he a Frenchman?"

"You guessed it," answered Jo The Juggler.

The next day, the missionary, who had offered to put up the two Rubenists, addressed Mor-Zamba, "My name is Dr. Ericsson, and I am a minister in the Adventist church. I would like to offer you the following deal: I take care of your young brother for nothing, and you assist me until he recovers. I will send you in my place to care for people here and there in Tambona country. You have enormous hands, but you are also quite dexterous; that is rare. You already know how to give an intramuscular injection; with my help, you can quickly perfect your technique for giving intravenous ones and undertaking other minor treatments. You see, once you return to your place, you will be able to ease many pains. Our accounts will be even as soon as your brother is well again. What do you think?"

Without the slightest hesitation, Mor-Zamba accepted Dr. Ericsson's all too tempting offer. In several weeks, he learned much more than he had during his long years of captivity in the Colonel Leclerc forced labor camp. There he had only been a male-nurse with the clandestine avocation of caring for thousands of comrades, even though he bore no official responsibility for them. Now he could enjoy the title that accompanied his occupation and even more. In addition, Ericsson was anxious to sanction the competence of his new associate, and he did not hesitate to entrust his motorbike to him, enabling the former inmate of the Colonel Leclerc camp to accomplish his professional interventions several dozen kilometers away from the Protestant mission by traveling along arduous tracks that were nevertheless endowed with firm, if not solid, right-of-ways. His good working knowledge of machines and even his mastery over them delighted Ericsson, who had forgotten, probably because he failed to understand, the endless episode of his apprenticeship as a truck driver for a black

225

businessman in Fort Negre.

Unbeknowst to Ericsson, Mor-Zamba sometimes went beyond the role that had devolved on him, and it occurred under the most moving circumstances. Confronted with the unexpected death of a patient and the relatives' desire that the minister's assistant assume the full duties of his superior, Mor-Zamba many times saw himself constrained to open the Bible, read a verse or two, and even add a few commentaries of his own, relating them to the dead person's character and to the bystanders' hopes for continued good health in a province that had recently been stricken with misfortune. Spread by a virus that Dr. Ericsson believed to have come from elsewhere and perhaps even from abroad, a flu epidemic was decimating the Tambona people, who, because they were more diverse, more widely scattered, and divided into a larger number of clans than the people of Ekoumdoum, were also less easy to supervise and control. After a long and vexing period of trial and error, Ericsson had finally discovered the best way to attack the virus that was responsible for the epidemic, but he lacked a sufficient supply of medicine and recommended dividing a single dose of antibiotic so that it could be used to treat four patients.

From his catechists in the villages surrounding Tambona, Ericsson got wind of the fact that his best male-nurse also worked wonders by delivering commentaries on the Bible at local burials. "That fellow is a jewel," he said to himself. "Yes, but even so, it is awkward. He would at least have to be baptized. Yes, but how could I broach the subject without hurting his feelings or even upsetting him? And then what? Impossible to make a simple catechist of him. Let us wait and see; it is a phase in the evolution of our west-central Africa . . . ? Of course, he would have to learn a bit of English. Although a humble pastor in the heart of Africa would sooner have need of faith, enthusiasm. . . ."

Although not having been invited to participate in a profitable enterprise by Pastor Ericsson, George Mor-Kinda, more commonly know to his friends as Jo The Juggler, had not fallen in his own esteem, quite the contrary. Following the adage according to which a goat must graze where it is tethered, the former delinquent from Kola-Kola, although well aware of the paradoxical ambiguity of so-called popular wisdom, resolved to try his luck at the city's petty commerce, apparently quite active, swarming with shamless confidence men, gullible simpletons, blustering shopkeepers, and all sorts of other people who reminded him of Kola-Kola. With the as yet virtually untouched capital he had requisitioned from the June 18 school complex, he acquired a small stock of cheap goods, especially salt, the most sought after commodity in the marketplace at Tambona; each morning he went there and spread out his wares in a rudimentary booth. Immediately installed, shouting more loudly than any other vendor, his face hidden beneath a large straw hat with the brim raised on one side and lowered on the other, he launched into a burlesque patter that soon attracted a crowd of people around him.

"Oksinn! Oksinn! Oksinn! Truly oksinn, but that doesn't say everything, for I am giving it all away, passing it all out. This is the great and long awaited give-away. This is your lucky day, young man, fair lass, beautiful woman. Look here, this box of salt; my comrades sell it? Ah, well, as for me, I am giving it to you for nothing, word of God! Just trouble yourself to hold out your hand, and it's yours. You don't believe me? Try it anyway, my lovely woman. For nothing I am giving away the salt of good soups, the salt of good stews, the salt which makes little husbands loving and tender at night, my lovely woman, the salt which leads to caresses, the salt which makes even sterile women give birth to beautiful children. This is a miracle salt; come closer, fair lasses, you who are looking for loving and faithful men. This is a miracle salt for miracle men, men who are great lovers and faithful husbands at the same time."

When the sapak had been restored to health, he was unable to choose definitively between Jo The Juggler's business—too noisy, turbulent, and, if scrutinized closely, more than a little disturbing— and Mor-Zamba's activities, in which he thought he smelled the obsessive sanctimoniousness that had bored him stiff during a misunderstood and humiliating childhood. One day he accompanied one of them, the next day, the other; most of the time, however, and especially when he had unearthed a book or a European illustrated magazine, even if it were several years old, he remained at the mission to indulge himself in reading, the activity he loved most of all.

The three Rubenists met frequently. Dressed in khaki, sporting the same straw hats, and wearing boots (with the exception of the adolescent, who always put on plastic sandals), they nevertheless presented the image, not of soldiers fighting for an austere and desperate cause, but of elegant dandies strolling down the colorful streets of a sprawling village that was undergoing increasingly rapid change and acquiring a certain prosperity, just the opposite of Ekoumdoum, which, moreover, they were making every effort to forget for the moment.

# PART III

Moonlight Also Sets Fires

# CHAPTER 1

The revenge that fate held out to the three Rubensists, defeated despite their prodigal displays of bravery, first appeared in the unexpected, almost facetious, guise of a petty annoyance at a carnival. Instead of instigating and channeling the subsequent rush of events, our three heroes were, more often than not, going to be carried away by it, and even when the balance of power shifted to the detriment of their enemies, the Rubenists were going to appear overwhelmed, to the point of lacking flexibility and a sense of initiative. A perceptive observer would have been able to see that they were as awkward and indecisive as a man who, although seated upon a magnificent steed, knew nothing about horsemanship and was unqualified even to be holding the reins in his hands.

In any case, that is what has often been insinuated by George Mor—Kinda, also called Jo The Juggler and, since the happy ending of that curious adventure, The Commander. He tells how two brothers engaged in a fierce rivalry were given to understand that a hidden treasure would be discovered in the depths of the woods by the one who demonstrated the greatest zeal in looking for it, as long as the search was carried out at a time when the heavens were ablaze. Night was falling at the moment this prediction was made, and the first of the two brothers settled down to await the thousand fiery fingers of dawn. In the clear lunar radiance that cut soaring lines through the luxuriant geometry of the scene, he saw no more than a dull gray monochrome overlaid upon a dream. Nothing

231

moved him--not the star's coquettish wink as it dis-
apperared gracefully behind a cloud and abruptly
returned with a playful impetuousness, nor even the
persistent humility in its fixed gaze; he fell asleep.

"As far as his brother was concerned," Jo The
Juggler then concluded, "he suspected that moonlight
also sets fires; he immediately went to work, and his
insight was rewarded when he discovered the hidden
treasure and appropriated it for himself."

"What exactly does that mean, Commander?" the
sapak always asks at this point in the fable.
"Explain it to us."

"Since our arrival in Ekoumdoum," Jo The Juggler
then continues, "the unappreciated star had been
constantly winking at us. What signals it sent us as
soon as we arrived in the city! Remember! Following
its disappearances behind the cloud of our neglect,
each of its sudden reappearances echoed like thunder,
down to that miraculous lightning bolt that illuminated our escape from the hidden depths of the Bedridden Chimpanzee's dungeons. Wasn't it necessary for
its persistence to follow us as far as Tambona, where
it shattered the confounded scales that were obscuring
our vision, even though we knew the teachings of the
immortal Ruben and the less immortal Hurricane-Viet?"

"There shall be no revolution without the participation of women on an equal footing with men!" the
sapak Evariste then pronounces sententiously. "But
just exactly what does that mean, Commander? To tell
the truth, I'll bet you are like me and know nothing
about it at all. The old buzzards from the counsel of
elders claim it would be a real catastrophe, if women
were allowed to have their say. I will admit that I
am like you and do not see why it should be that way.
At least on that point we are in agreement, you and I,
and I think we are right. That is certainly true!
You are right; considering the condition of our race
and the point it has reached, things could not be
worse. Well then, what sort of curse could the women
bring down upon us? For without them--I mean, without
their having done anything--we were already a race of
slaves. On the contrary, I am, like you, betting that
things will improve."

"The old buzzards are never lacking in arguments

to prove to you that women are a curse. Count on them—and on the other one who is in the process of swinging over into their camp. What a bumpkin!"

"He is strange, that one! And it didn't start today. Don't you think he was already a bit strange during the entire course of our long march?"

"Who wasn't a bit strange during that whole business? You, by any chance, you little rascal?"

It all started again with the unpleasant sensation repeatedly inflicted on the pedlar Jo The Juggler by what he at first thought was a ragged band of impudent young girls. The first time he saw them, he was struggling mightily to gain the crowd's attention on a normal market day; not many people were there, and those who were seemed more inclined to gawk than to open their purses. He felt as if he were being stared at and even appraised by a defiant mob of young girls who at first glance resembled all the others who arrived each morning from the villages surrounding Tambona to sit in the open air and offer their families' traditional produce for sale; as usual, they were wearing very little; he found them too dumpy, too countrified. When he looked at them more closely, they seemed to have more of a greyish tone than the average people who could be seen in the market, like the Kola-Kola schoolchildren who, living far from their mothers, were untidy and poorly nourished. Above all, their lips were dry, and their eyes were tinged with yellow. The next day, the group of young women had grown, and they continued to observe him with the same mysterious expression on their faces. The following day was a festival, and when he again found them camped in front of him, the vendor from Kola-Kola was truly puzzled. A number of times he interrupted his patter and was surprised to find himself stuttering and his brow furrowed with anxiety as he furtively scrutinized the mob which now encircled him and whose bold stares conjured up the nightmare image of birds peering fixedly at a carcass that hunters were about to abandon to them.

This veiled aggressiveness seemed even more palpable to him, when the sapak Evariste, who had just beaten a path through their densely packed ranks, rejoined him next to his stall. Speaking in a lowered voice between two professional harangues addressed to the crowd of idle onlookers, Jo the Juggler described the situation to him.

"In my opinion," reflected Evariste somberly, "those children are holding something against you, some sort of shady deal, an overcharge on a cup of salt for example, or perhaps a package of Bastos sold at a higher price than somewhere else. A thousand little nothings, of course, but you know how thick-headed these peasants can be. Expect the unexpected from them. Maybe they are thinking of fixing your clock. They are simply waiting for the best moment. You think you only have a few young girls to deal with. The tactics of war, my dear fellow. The boys are lurking in ambush somewhere right around here. A little signal, and bam! You suddenly have a hundred of them on your back. What weird people! Just let them try something, and we will give them the most memorable round of their lives, all right?"

"You are out of your mind," grumbled Jo The Juggler. "You no longer think of anything but quarrelling and fighting. You want to take on a hundred of them all by yourself; who do you take yourself for? Zorro?"

He immediately launched into an empassioned, lively, solemn harangue which passed over the wall of adolescents and addressed itself to a rather substantial matron, from whom, to tell the truth, the sometime pedlar expected at that moment to derive no more than a purely tactical advantage: assuming that the portly woman yielded to the seduction of his eloquence and the desire to approach his stand, he imagined her bursting like a bulldozer through the rampart of young peasant girls in whose midst he was beginning to feel trapped. The fact is that the enormous individual calmly allowed herself to be harpooned and undertook, with elephantine grace, to breach the wall of adolescents who separated her from the object of her desire, while Jo The Juggler looked on, more and more delighted as the pachyderm moved forward victoriously.

Curiously, the young girls did not seem at all vexed by the mastodon's intrusion; on the contrary, one would have said that they were amused by it; they did not offer the slightest resistance to her advance,

234

if one disregards the somewhat oscillatory inertia that is inevitably present during this sort of encounter between such obviously opposed forces of nature. They suddenly seemed to take advantage of the tumult to scatter joyfully in small groups, chattering and gesticulating animatedly. Yet it did not take long for them to reappear, one of them munching on a groundnut wafer, another on a corn fritter, another on a banana fried in palm oil—all tidbits that could be bought in the market. Still engaged by the portly woman with a soft, mellow voice and a languorous expression in her eyes, Jo The Juggler and the sapak could for the moment ignore the return of the adolescents.

When they were finally free, the marketplace had been largely emptied of its usual inhabitants; the customers were returning to their homes; the peasants were on their way back to their villages and hamlets; their day finished and their merchandise packed, some of the vendors were heading toward an antiquated motor vehicle that would be proceeding to another festival, while others moved toward a covered shed where they would leave their bundles for the night. Soon there was no longer anyone around the two friends except the mute, mysterious mob of young girls, whose gaze seemed to have become more leaden as their vigilance intensified.

The two Kola-Kolans in turn started to wrap up their petty wares, straining to appear nonchalant, like people without a care in the world. They took their bundle and carried it to the shed where it usually remained until the following day. Then, swinging their arms and walking in their customary fashion, they began moving toward the neighborhood where they were now living. Grouped in virtual military formation, the adolescents, who had been waiting in the distance, marched off in pursuit of them, remaining quite far behind at first, but gradually narrowing the gap. The two Rubenists never stopped discussing the situation, although their faces continued to be monuments of imperturbability; they decided to slow their pace and allow themselves to be overtaken so they might discover the key to the riddle. In response, the impudent young girls paused in their march, observing the pair with a gaze in which the Kola-Kolans believed they could read an unusual state of excitement, and that disturbed them even more. They once again quickened their pace to a normal rhythm, shaking their heads with condescension, as is appropriate when dealing with a childish prank that could not possibly have the slightest importance. In turn, the adolescents marshalled their forces and moved forward again, not without quite prudently exerting themselves to make up for the delay, since they were probably afraid of losing the trail in some alley of Newtown, the suburb they had•just entered and an area reserved for non-Tambonans. They were soon in sight of the Rubenists' house.

As often happened, Mor-Zamba was standing in front of their dwelling on the tightly packed dirt road that served as the major thoroughfare of Newtown, where the passing of a motorized vehicle was an unusual event; he was on the lookout for the appearance of his two companions, for he knew it was time for them to return. As soon as they came into view, he welcomed them from a distance with manifestations of joy and tenderness that could not have left the slightest doubt in the adolescents' minds about the bonds uniting this enormous giant, whom they didn't know and who frightened them, with the two pedlars, whom they had willingly harrassed for their own amusement.

Seized with panic, as if the ogre were preparing to gobble them up one after the other, the battalion of young girls broke ranks with a crafty suddenness; lowering their heads, dropping their arms, and stiffening the look of determination on their faces, they abandoned themselves to a stealthy retreat, and it became the two younger Rubenists' turn to take off in pursuit of the young girls; they had soon overtaken them.

"This is a very odd sort of joke," the two young men said to them. "What in the world has gotten into you? What game do you think you are playing?"

"Well, well, you really don't recognize us, Nouredine?" one of the girls said in an ironic tone of voice as she approached the sapak, stroked his cheek, and then moved her hand slowly through his hair and across his neck. "But it really is you, isn't it,

Nouredine? No chance of a mistake, it is really you?"

"How could Nouredine recognize you?" another cried out in a burst of laughter. "Nouredine has changed so much that he is no longer Nouredine, so to speak. He even speaks our language to perfection. You learn quickly, my little Nouredine."

"Don't you know that the followers of Allah have special gifts?" a third young girl declared emphatically.

"Honestly," continued the first adolescent, a short, little woman, more pudgy than the rest and with hair cropped close to the skull. "Honestly, Nouredine, you don't recognize your friends from Ekoumdoum? Yet it was only a few months ago that you came every day to join us at the fountain; at dusk, you were always carrying a stone goblet you had just filled with water for the ablutions of your master El Khalik. Do you remember now? By the way, one might almost say that the individual standing right next to you is precisely El Khalik himself, although he has shed the flowing robe in which he made such a comical appearance."

"Why, indeed, it is El Khalik himself!" the adolescents mimicked repeatedly.

"Allah is great, my good people," the first and unquestionably the boldest of the girls exclaimed. "Allah is great and El Khalik is his prophet."

"You have uttered a blasphemy, you unfortunate creature!" scolded Jo The Juggler, rolling his eyes like some grotesque carnival character. "It is not El Khalik, poor El Khalik, who is the prophet of Allah, but rather Mohammed."

"That doesn't make any difference, " retorted the short, little woman. "What have you done with your flowing robe? Are you no longer the man of Allah?"

"Of course, of course, my child," replied Jo The Juggler. "It is not I who have changed, but Allah. It is true, my children; Allah is no longer what he was."

"You claim to come from Ekoumdoum," the sapak finally interrupted. "That is the most extraordinary, and perhaps even the most ridiculous thing I have ever heard. Well, as for me, I don't believe a word of it."

"What proof do you need, Nouredine?" shouted the young girls in unison. "The most recent news about your friend the accordionist? He has become one of The Bastard's henchmen, a member of the Chief's militia, charged with barking at the heels of his own brothers on the construction sites of the Bedridden Chimpanzee and Soumazeu. We can also tell you about Ngwane-Eligui. To tell the truth, nothing has changed for her. At least almost nothing. . . ."

What additional words were said, actions performed, and gestures exchanged as their reunion moved toward its turbulently emotional culmination, none of the principals is actually capable of saying these days, as if they had never entirely extricated themselves from that whirlwind. The same thing happens to the wretched victims of a devastating cyclone; groping about with desperately feverish, instinctive motions, they seek to ward off the disintegration of their homes; they clutch fitfully toward their parents, their children, their faithful companion; when everything becomes calm again, the dawn reveals a group of automatons rehearsing the vital motions that saved them, yet quite incapable of describing in detail what they had been doing.

What secrets did Ngwane-Azombo and her sisters begin by revealing to them? Why had it immediately been a question of that in particular among so many equally urgent matters? What decisions were made? How was the linkage established between actions and words?

According to the sapak Evariste, it goes without saying that the adolescents told them first about the revolt of the mothers. As he says, this sequence evolved quite naturally, and the story of this unprecedented event at Ekoumdoum imposed itself on them after the name of the unfortunate Ngwane-Eligui had been mentioned. Thus, the young girls had informed them how Ngwane-Eligui had been cooling her heels in isolation, hatred, and quarantine at the Forest of the Chimpanzees and that she had only acquired her freedom, providentially in a way, as a result of the epidemic and the numerous fatalities it had almost immediately occasioned, despite the presence of countless certified healers in Ekoumdoum. In the end, it

238

had indeed been necessary to call upon the young woman who had already impressed the mothers shortly after her arrival in the city and at a time when insults were being literally heaped upon her, for even then she had successfully exercised her bonesetter's talents on the sprains and dislocations of the city's children and adolescents; people said it was a natural gift, passed from generation to generation in certain families of her tribe. The Bastard willingly allowed her to leave her prison, but only when accompanied and kept under surveillance by two Palace women, chosen from among those who were most hostile toward her.

Ngwane-Eligui had barely entered the house of the first sick child, when she demanded that all the men who were present must leave. As soon as the women were by themselves, she had asked them to leave her alone in a closed room with the little patient and the grieving mother.

"I will try to help your son," she whispered to the mother, whose face was bathed in tears. "I brought you a few herbs, and in a moment I will tell you how to prepare them. But first, remember this, and remember it well: there is little chance that your son can be saved. I know that what I am saying is extremely cruel, but we are facing a serious crisis; the survival of Ekoumdoum itself is at stake, and not only the life of a single young child. Convey my message to the other women in a few minutes, after my guardians and I have left. Above all, don't tell them that you heard these things from me; I hardly need to explain in detail what will happen to me if you do. Listen to me then. Haven't you noticed that this epidemic tends to strike male children? It is a plot, my dear sister, yes, a plot. If you allow the crows and all the other pests to dig up the seeds in your fields and eat them, where will you be the next day, the day when the crops are scheduled to be harvested? No matter how rich a city might be in full-grown men, how many years will it take for that city to cease reproducing and to wither up like a tree without roots, if it is suddenly deprived of its youngest generation of males? How many years will it take for it to disappear, abandoning its fertile lands to strangers? This disease is unknown among us, because its cause lies elsewhere; it is a foreign curse. Remember that, and remember it well."

"What do we have to do?" the mother asked in a voice that quavered with unbearable anguish. "Penicillin? They don't want to sell us any in Mackenzieville; that is what Brother Nicholas told us. They say, 'Go ahead and ask your French masters for penicillin, since you love them so much you want to keep them at all costs.' The people of Mackenzieville don't have any feelings."

"That is simply not true; Brother Nicholas is an out-and-out liar. Pencillin is only dispensed at Mackenzieville on the advice of a doctor; the English taught them that it is too dangerous a medicine to be placed in everybody's hands. If you show them a letter from a doctor who says that you need penicillin and that he will administer it to you, then they will sell you penicillin in Mackenzieville. And that is the truth. But unfortunately we don't have a doctor here at Ekoumdoum. It would have been better if Van den Rietter were a doctor rather than a vobiscum. What good does it do you that he tells you 'vobiscum, vobiscum' every morning, while your children are growing stiff in your arms?

"Listen well to what I have to say: perhaps all is not lost for the people of Ekoumdoum, although it might be for the children who are already suffering from this cursed disease. Tambona is about a week's trek from here, and it is possible that medicine is sold there on the open market; there are almost daily connections between Tambona and a major city; by contacting a trader in Tambona, even if we dare not push on to the big city ourselves, we should be able to obtain some penicillin. I will say the same things all afternoon long to the other mothers of sick children. Try to get together as soon as possible, at first among yourselves and then with the other mothers, who ought to realize that all the children in the city are threatened, with the possible exception of those at the Palace; and finally you should discuss it with the rest of the women in the city. . . ."

As Ngwane-Eligui had predicted, the ravages of the cruel disease did not abate. Gradually coalescing into a group and emboldened by the sight of their cohorts, the mothers of Ekoumdoum had gone to The Bastard one day and pleaded for him to put together a caravan that might go to Tambona and procure the necessary medicine. Zoabekwe had of course sent the mothers away after having denied their request in the following terms: "Already I don't have enough men for all the tasks I need to confront; where would I find men to send off to Tambona?" The mothers had then said with sadness in their voices: "Why not free our young people, those noble descendents of the founders of Ekoumdoum, those whom you are making work like slaves to clear your fields?" The Bastard had then replied, not without rancor this time, "Free your children? That is completely out of the question. They are prisoners—the whole city is a prisoner—to pay for the crime of having given hospitality to two double-dealing strangers without telling me about it. All of you are confined behind the steel bars of an enclosure that is invisible perhaps, but inexorable. If I let them escape from their cage, who will answer to me for their loyalty?"

The mothers then took it into their heads to solicit Father Van den Rietter's religious, amicable, and prestigious sanction for their initiative; they therefore made their way in a procession to the pres- bytery, where Soumazeu made the following remarks to them: "Pay careful attention to the wise counsels of the man whom God in his infinite goodness has placed over you and whose father, elected by your city, is, moreover, still alive. If you want things to run smoothly in your city, never forget that, in the final resort, he is the one on whom it is appropriate for you to rely. No, believe me, my poor children, it will serve no purpose to send people to Tambona. Let us resign ourselves to the fate which God has given us; let us accept His will. Come to Sunday mass tomorrow morning; we will pray together so that God might make His desires better known to us."

It was truly more than the mothers could bear. The next day the Christian mothers unanimously decided to abstain from going to mass, and they called upon all the other women, whether or not they were Christian, to follow their example, and that is precisely what most of them did.

241

Having assembled shortly after daybreak, the women of the city had devoted the entire Sunday morning to a careful examination of the cruel words Soumazeu had uttered the day before. As time passed, tempers had flared during this impromptu court of inquiry; the confusion in people's minds had gradually translated itself into denunciatory allegations, as if the "salt" of the city of Ekoumdoum had only then begun to understand Van den Rietter's true nature.

"It is true then?" one of the mothers had soon declared in a tone of heartbroken surprise. "Has The Bastard really been plotting with the missionaries to reduce us to slavery once and for all by exterminating our young male children, the spearhead of our future city, the support of our old age, the guarantor of our forests and rivers? Is it really true, all that has been said? Is it really true that they emptied vials of hideous germs behind our houses one night in order to overwhelm us with epidemics? Is it really true that the epidemic decimating our sons results directly from these intrigues?"

During the day, it might have been said that the women's furor rose through one half of the sky as the sun was sinking in the other. One could hear the mothers beginning to howl in pathetic, quavering tones, like a chorus of dogs bewailing death; others could be seen rolling in the dust, tearing out their hair, or covering themselves with ashes as a sign of despair. At the onset of evening they came together in a menacing horde, armed with torches which danced frenetically in hundreds of hands and appeared to be setting the city on fire. Not a single man displayed any desire to join the ranks of these slaves who were determined, for the first time in the history of the city, to stand up to the master.

Tumultuously they entered the Palace enclosure and declared it occupied until an audience with the old chief himself could be arranged. It was not without panic that The Bastard envisioned the necessity of accounting to his father for the management of the city and, what is more, of doing it in front of witnesses who were in such a mood that they could easily have contradicted him and even brought accusations against him.

242

"If it is about the caravan," he said to the
women, "why don't we discuss the matter and try to
reach an agreement among ourselves, rather than
bothering an old man whose strength is failing?"

It still took many long days of palaver and even
of haggling over details, for The Bastard sometimes
blew cold to extricate himself from the onslaught of
his assailants and sometimes hot in response to
demands that they be granted access to the old chief.
In the end, it had been necessary to settle the
matter; at one point, Zoabekwe, who claimed to be
making his final concession, succeeded in imposing a
solution which was unprecedented in the history of the
Ekoumdoum, and he cut short any further discussion by
insisting that they take it or leave it. Although the
resulting situation was a novel one, it signalled the
defeat of the master: some young girls from the city
of Ekoumdoum were authorized to form a caravan and
make their way to Tambona; only, Zoabekwe would place
one of his men in charge of them, entrusting him with
the mission of protecting these adolescents during
their entire journey and leading them back, safe and
sound, into the fold. A few moments later they knew
that the man would be Ndogdam Tsibuli, an individual
who, although devoted body and soul to The Bastard,
hardly inspired a great deal of confidence.

It is on this last point that Jo The Juggler's
version most expressly contradicts the story told by
the sapak Evariste. According to George Mor-Kinda,
the adolescents' first disclosure, the one they immediately made to the three Rubenists, actually involved
Ndogdam Tsibuli, and with good reason. From the very
beginning, he had noticed a sort of chronic apprehen-
siveness among them, as if they were afraid of being
followed or observed from a distance. Furthermore,
during the first few moments of their tempestuous
reunion, he, Jo The Juggler, had not been surprised to
see Ngwane-Azombo's face suddenly grow dark as she
lowered her voice and warned, "Be careful! Ndogdam
Tsibuli might not be far from here at this very
moment; perhaps he is watching us." In reply to
which, Jo The Juggler had asked the young girl, "But
who in the world is Ndogdam Tsibuli?" Ngwane-Azombo
had begun to explain that he was one of The Bastard's

henchmen, a thief, an unscrupulous man, but she was speaking more and more slowly, and she never stopped turning her head to cast a glance in one direction or the other, like a little puppy that had just received a beating. That was why the Rubenists had decided to invite the band of young girls into their house, which was indeed close at hand, although the guests were so numerous they had to crowd against each other to find a place to sit on the chairs and mats in the large, cement-floored living room.

There they had put the finishing touches on the portrait of the rather hateful man whose discipline had been inflicted upon them by The Bastard; they emphasized his depraved and salacious tendencies, the exhorbitant requirements of which he had persistently attempted to impose upon them during their juourney. In fact, the crowning example of his perfidy had just occurred three days previously, when he had decided to confiscate all the money which they had been ordered to use for buying medicine in Tambona and which they had deposited with him as they earned it.

For they had earned it, and earned it with great difficulty. Each adolescent had received a twenty-pound basket of ground nuts from her mother, and she had been obliged to carry it on her back for the whole seven days of their journey. Then, once they had arrived in Tambona, they had had to come to the market every day, displaying their produce in the hot sun and extolling its virtues to people who were much less eager to buy than were the inhabitants of Mackenzie-ville, which was, after all, a far more populous and wealthy city.

Ndogdam Tsibuli had waited until the last batch had been sold and the money deposited with him before announcing the conditions of an odious blackmail attempt. Thus it was three days ago that he had said to them, "even when you find medicine to buy, I will not give you back this money unless you first give me satisfaction. Think about it: the sooner you decide, the sooner you can buy your medicine, and the sooner we can all return to Ekoumdoum. Decide for your-selves. I will be waiting patiently. . . ."

Along with their protector, who hardly merited such a title, they had been living in a neighborhood inhabited by native Tambonans, although it was not difficult for temporary residents to rent a whole house in that patchwork jumble of adjoining structures. It was there that Ndogdam led the life of a pasha; sleeping all day long and most of the night, he only roused himself to feast upon canned fish, swill down great quantities of corn beer, or smoke hashish. The children were afraid that soon nothing would be left of their hard-earned money.

Jo The Juggler had listened to the adolescents' story with a serious expression on his face, and when they finished, he had said to them, "Listen, children, first of all we are going to feed you; your stomachs appear to be as empty as the look in your eyes, and your voices are beginning to crack. Well, first of all we are going to feed you something to give you back your strength, because you are certainly going to need it. Then, you should return to your protector, as if nothing has happened. Tomorrow or the next day, after we have given you the signal, tell him that you have made your decision. Preferably in the middle of the day. From that moment on, don't leave him any respite; overwhelm him with his favorite dishes and his favorite drinks. We will take care of the rest. But the most important thing is this: in the meantime, prepare youselves to break camp at any moment and move off in the direction of Ekoumdoum."

In short, Jo The Juggler had been unable to resist the temptation to make use of the ruse that had already earned him so many triumphs. Mor-Zamba had access to the sleeping powder in Dr. Ericsson's pharmacy, but he refused for a long time to abet the dubious undertakings of Jo The Juggler, who only overcame the giant's scruples by dint of diabolical perserverence. On the appointed day, he supplied the adolescents with tiny pellets, which The Bastard's henchman unsuspectingly swallowed in the food and drink they served him all evening long. One or perhaps even two hours before midnight, Ngwane-Azombo and three other envoys from the adolescents' camp came to tell the Rubenists that Ndogdam Tsibuli had just collapsed and was henceforth at their mercy. A lively debate immediately ensued, and the guard's death was decreed over the strenuous objections of Mor-Zamba; as a result, he refused to participate in the execution, which he characterized as a cowardly assassination. At this point, Jo The Juggler assured the adolescents: "don't worry; Mor-Dzomo, our friend here, is a Protestant minister, a Simsimayabane. As soon as these people hear the slightest mention of blood, they go into a daze. Don't be uneasy; he will just have to get over it."

Accompanied by the sapak Evariste, who was equipped with several lengths of rope, and the young girls, Jo The Juggler, who had made all the necessary arrangements in advance, crossed the burgeoning town under cover of darkness and soon reached the house where Ndogdam Tsibuli was lying stretched out on the ground.

He said to the adolescents, "The honor is yours, my young women! I would like to see if you can be good for something." Besides a natural zealousness that undoubtedly stemmed from their desire for vengeance, they were so numerous that they executed his orders without the least difficulty. They bound the prisoner's hands and feet in such a way that it would have been futile for him to struggle; they popped an enormous gag between his widely gaping jaws, and a number of them forced it into his mouth by pushing savagely on it. Finally, they tightened the sapak's leather belt around his neck until it was completely constricted, and they would have held it like that for the rest of the night, if Jo The Juggler, who was observing the condemned man's convulsions, had not told them a few moments later: "He is dead; you can let go. Ah, my children, we have just done a wonderful thing together! It would perhaps be better not to brag about it too much yet, at least for the time being, until the day when we shall have inflicted the same fate on Zoabekwe and his chimpanzee of a father." The fact is that the militants from Kola-Kola had just, for the first time, killed an enemy in cold blood.

That very night, the adolescents and the Rubenists got underway for Ekoumdoum. Seeking to console Mor-Zamba and rouse him from a disconcerting melancholy, Jo The Juggler never ceased repeating: "In any case, you know? We didn't have a choice.

246

Whatever it costs, we have to preserve the advantage of surprise. Otherwise, goodbye revenge, and goodbye victory! Well then, try to imagine what it would be like if he were alive. What contortions and juggling acts we would have to go through to avoid being seen, or recognized. . . . In short, it would have been just as well to give it all up immediately. And why not go back to Fort Negre right away?"

"And what is more," interjected the sapak, "they don't give it a second thought; why should the rest of us worry about it?"

If Mor-Zamba is to be believed, Ngwane-Azombo and her sisters first spoke to the Rubenists about the dreadful epidemic. As a matter of fact, what would have been more natural? The image of one's own people being abandoned to the terror of such a tragedy is an obsession which would haunt anyone. It is true that, from the first moments of his encounter with the adolescents, he thought they seemed to be tormented by a chronic anxiety; a shiver must have been continually running down their backs at the memory of the devastating epidemic that had already lasted for more than a month and claimed at least fifty little victims without giving any signs of releasing its stranglehold. It only struck nursing infants and very young children, usually of the masculine sex, as if it hoped to dry up the city's vitality at its source by harvesting its most recent growth.

For the first two days, the stricken child vomited at irregular intervals; then, he stopped taking food and slowly sank into a sort of lethargy as he fell victim to a burning fever, under the influence of which his quivering little body shook and, from time to time, emitted a weak but sudden cry of pain. The nasal passages were not blocked, although a colorless, watery fluid flowed abundantly from the nose. Soon an irreversible loss of weight set it; the eyes turned back into the head; the arms and legs remained motionless, in a haphazard arrangement, reminding one of a disjointed jumping jack. These developments occurred during a two or three week period. Then, all at once the sick child became restless, twisting about slowly in his bed, turning his head first in one direction and then in the other, the symptom of a pain

247

that was all the more heartrending because it was
silent. In the end, after several barely perceptible
little spasms, an unexpected stoppage of breath indicated that the young sufferer had just passed into the
other world. Such was the description of the illness
as reported by the adolescents.

Abandoning his two friends to their plans, the
details of which he no longer recalls these days,
although he unhesitatingly declared them to have been
reprehensible in nature, Mor-Zamba had rushed to Dr.
Ericsson and described the symptoms to him.

"It is the flu!" the missionary gave his diagnosis, insofar as the term diagnosis applies under such
circumstances. He added that, at least in this form,
such ailments were unknown in the provinces of Africa
and that it had undoubtedly come from Mackenzieville
and beyond, from Europe and Asia, continents where the
flu virus was capable of inflicting formidable damage
upon people who were better nourished and, on he
whole, better protected by advances in medicine and
public health. "With our people here, we have reason
to fear the worst," he finally concluded, as if
speaking to himself.

Mor-Zamba doubts that, when Dr. Ericsson proclaimed the virus had been imported from Europe or
Asia, he had meant to imply, as Jo The Juggler and
Evariste the sapak subsequently concluded, that he too
was accusing Ekoumdoum's masters of having knowingly
and deliberately spread the disease in the city.
However, it is true that Dr. Ericsson conducted himself in this situation as if he were once again bent
upon doing the opposite of what his brothers, the
French missionaries at Ekoumdoum, were doing, for they
were his rivals, no matter what he thought. His
generosity amazed Mor-Zamba and even his two comrades,
when they were informed of it, although the Rubenists
already knew better than anyone else the extent of his
charity.

He outfitted them with a rudimentary medical kit
that was primarily composed of hypodermic syringes and
needles for administering shots as well as cotton,
bandages, compresses, and forceps for dressing open
sores. Unaware that they themselves already had some
medicine, he also furnished them with a large consign-

ment of it, including a small amount of penicillin.

"It is really not much," he confided regretfully to Mor-Zamba, "but if you know how to go about it skillfully, you can save dozens of children with this tiny amount, and why not even more? In desperate situations, don't hesitate to divide one capsule into two or three doses. According to the circumstances and results, be generous at some times and frugal at others. No one actually knows the potential strength of antibiotics on populations that have never used them before and are therefore quite sensitive to them; I am convinced that people can work veritable miracles here. Who knows but that a single small drop of antibiotic injected into the rump of a small child might not be enough to save him in certain cases?"

If people in the audience expect at this point to hear about the group's departure or if they are curious about factual matters, like the fate reserved for the merchandise of the occasional pedlar George Mor-Kinda or the actual condition of the Raleigh, none of the three Rubenists will provide balm for their anxiety. Ngwane-Azombo, on the other had, will perhaps satisfy them. She alone seems to have been struck by the peculiarity of the material circumstances that surrounded those three final days, spent in the unreal anticipation of an execution and a noctural escape from Tambona. According to her, the Rubenists carried off the remarkable feat of coordinating the preparations for their departure with the measures being taken for the purpose of rendering The Bastard's henchman incapable of doing any further harm; they did it so successfully that everyone was ready to march at the exact moment when Ndogdam Tsibuli was taking his last breath. At no time during those last three days at Tambona did the young girls' movement between the Rubenists' residence, where they came to obtain their instructions, and their own house, which they shared with the bully whose orders they obeyed, arouse the suspicions of that detested individual; the announced change in the young girls' attitude toward him had filled him with confidence to the point where he saw the smallest details of each act only as new assurances of heretofore unknown pleasures. Not until the last day, and even the last few hours before the nightfall that was going to prove fatal to Ndogdam Tsibuli, did the Rubenists finally assemble their numerous possessions, among which was indeed the merchandise that Jo The Juggler had been hawking just a short time before; everything was divided into tiny portions that the adolescents parceled out and packed in their baskets under the eyes of their unseeing protector. It was thus, as Ngwane—Azombo makes clear, that on the path leading from Tambona to Ekoumdoum there were always two Rubenists with their hands free while the third was effortlessly pushing the Raleigh, which had been repaired ever since the vanquished partisans' first days in Tambona.

But whoever the narrator might be and as long as the story is being told separately by each participant, the audience will always have to tolerate a forgotten detail, an obscure point, and even, here and there, an unexplained break in the action or an incomprehensible turn of events. The audience itself is therefore obliged to redress these deficiencies either in the midst of the action or, more frequently, with some displacement in time, because a new episode, a hitherto unclarified detail, or an unanticipated allusion abruptly comes along to clear up a shadowy image that had been left behind long ago, just as a traveler who suddenly raises or lowers his torch often illuminates a thicket that had until then been shrouded in darkness.

What would happen if the various protagonists wanted to reach an agreement in order to offer the audience a coherent narrative of the events? Perhaps they would convey a better sense not only of its meaning, but also of its sequence and continuity; perhaps they would slow the momentum to a snail's pace, smooth out the steep slopes, and fence off the precipices. But before that occurs, they would have to battle it out so hard among themselves that they would run an enormous risk of alienating each other permanently and never reappearing before the court.

In any case, at the very instant when Ndogdam Tsibuli passed into the other world, the Rubenists and the adolescents once again took the road toward Ekoumdoum, but from this point on, they constituted a free community, united by a memory of the blood that

250

had been spilled and invincible in their high spirits and self-confidence. Their extremely cautious eight-day march took place without incident and brought them within the environs of the city that had been decimated by the epidemic; during this time, the three guerillas had the leisure to learn in great detail about the nightmare into which Ekoumdoum had sunk since they had been cut off from it by the sapak's accident and their precipitous retreat to Tambona.

# CHAPTER 2

The discovery of Ezadzomo's and Ezabiemeu's bodies in the river had been followed by the most ominous and cruel period ever experienced by the inhabitants of Ekoumdoum; for that matter, the city's unfortunate situation must have persisted and had perhaps even grown worse—the young girls said they were trembling in advance at the thought of plunging back into a hell more frightening than the one that Van den Rietter's teachings had rendered familiar to them.

One might have said that the masters of the city had conspired to take advantage of Ekoumdoum's torpor to conjure our awakening as far into the future as imagination could carry it. How far away it all seems now—the massive betrayals that followed the escape of the two strangers, the invisibe barrier, the prison of terror in which the inhabitants of the city had found themselves penned from one day to the next, even without the stigma of close confinement. It was the era of the bagnio.

In telling their story, the adolescents expressed mock astonishment at the extreme docility and even the complaisance with which, they said, the male inhabitants of Ekoumdoum had accommodated themselves to the whims of a few individuals (several of whom were bent with age), rather than showing themselves to be models of ancestral pride and images of manly courage, as tradition would have it. They explained how the new prisoners had, on many occasions, seemed to consider it a point of honor to anticipate the perverse desires

252

of their tormentors, although a collective flick of the finger would have sufficed to overwhelm them in less than an hour. The young girls continually punctuated their report with exclamations pronounced in tones of joy strangely mixed with contempt. "And to think that women, when they are very young, have the stupidity to envy individuals of the opposite sex! Imagine little girls dreaming of becoming little boys!" they exclaimed from time to time.

Each day it became increasingly obvious that Van den Rietter, barely concealed behind Zoabekwe The Bastard, was the only master, the true master of the city: he saw everything and imposed his will on everyone; he inspected the troops and probed the depths of souls; he examined people's acts and intentions; he controlled life and even death. He seemed to gorge himself on the management of human affairs the way others tirelessly surfeit themselves on food or drink—like the old Chief who, they said, wallowed in the caresses of his young wives at the risk of bursting like an overinflated cow's bladder.

Soumazeu had begun by dividing the city into districts and placing each of them under the jurisdiction of a man who was by nature hostile to those living there. It was in this way that people from districts in the center of Ekoumdoum, the original nucleus of the city and the cradle of our most illustrious ancestors, had experienced an alarming and painful revelation of the hatred borne them by the small clans on the plateau, their satellites since time immemorial. To the eyes of the undiscriminating stranger, the members of these clans could be confused with us; in actuality, they were different in more than one respect and had lived for a long time in the forest surrounding our city; there they clustered together in small villages of thatched huts. Ekoumdoum had spread out and even swollen to abnormal proportions in such a way that, instead of dividing into a family of cities, as frequently occurred elsewhere, it had gradually lured its satellites closer and then immobilized them, so to speak, keeping them confined to an area above the city and far from the road, on a remote plateau where their hamlets were scattered among ponds and woods in the midst of an enormous swamp. A reservoir of wives for Ekoumdoum, which was actually but one clan among many, although bloated to the point of obesity by the forgotten vicissitudes of its own history, these clans had, during the course of centuries, woven a tissue of interrelationships with us, a network of kinship and cousinhood which we regarded as indestructible and impossible to untangle, but in which Van den Rietter, infallibly guided by time and his diabolical mania for hunting down the secret weaknesses of human beings in order to subjugate them more effectively, had eventually succeeded in discovering tumors of resentment, the eternal bane of the weak, abandoned by nature to the unwitting tyranny of the strong. Ulcerated each day by the friction of the giant's presence, his dependents were secretly disconsolate over their own dwarfism.

Promoted to the ranks of night watchmen, guards, and overseers in our districts, these men did not wait long to flaunt their desire to avenge themselves upon us; as soon as they took office, they called us together, and with their faces distorted into ironic grins, they declared to us, "From now on, you should not even think of passing yourselves off as descendents of a noble city's heroic founders. There are no more founders, let along heroic ones, and there is no longer a noble city. You are nothing, because you have never been anything."

The most hateful of these spies were those recruited in large numbers by Van den Rietter and The Bastard from among the mixed populations in the Chief's compound or at the Catholic mission—thugs and bullies, helots, sons-in-law and cousins-by-marriage of the Chief or his son. Zoabekwe's inertia and domestic indecisiveness had prevented him from clearly distinguishing among his own and his father's people by sending away the majority of them, as he had promised Van den Rietter, but the two associates now congratulated themselves on this show of impotence, recognizing that the most recent course of events was offering them the longed for means of extracting some profit from a population that had until then been somewhat of an embarrassment. Having nearly always come from further away than Mackenzieville and occupying a position halfway between slave and free man, these animals were so foreign to our beliefs and customs that they could not even speak our language or else spoke it so badly they massacred its syntax and grammar, like Ndogdam Tsibuli, who had been spying on the young girls during their trip to Tambona and whom they had just strangled to death, after having drugged him to sleep. In our districts, these men behaved as if they were occupying forces intent upon imposing their own outrageous law in a country that had been conquered by force, like boors perpetually between two gulps of wine or two puffs of hashish, like lechers lusting to fall unexpectedly upon solitary women and even little girls.

The presence of numerous arrogant, greedy alguazils in the midst of our young people at a time when they were not yet completely insouciant about their honor had soon produced a scuffle, and Van den Rietter used the incident as a pretext to carry out a plan that had doubtless been elaborated far in advance. He had proclaimed that all Ekoumdoum's troubles stemmed from the chronic laziness of its younger men, exempted from the obligation to work by an absurd tradition that was completely unknown in any other part of the world. When work becomes a natural habit for young people, like getting up in the morning at sunrise or going to bed at night, peace and harmony would be certain to follow. With the Chief's authorization, he, Van den Rietter, would take it upon himself to inculcate that salutary discipline in a city that was woefully lacking in it.

He immediately set the day on which it would henceforth become mandatory for every male citizen who was neither head of household nor school pupil, and with the exception of those who happened by any chance to be engaged in some regular productive activity, to present himself by eight o'clock at the Catholic mission, where roll would be called and everyone assigned to the site of a land reclamation project that would give him the opportunity to place his strength at the service of his beloved chief, symbolic embodiment of the city of Ekoumdoum. At the same time, Soumazeu had the town-crier announce that it would be highly appropriate to revive a hallowed

255

ancestral custom that had lapsed into disuse long before the arrival of the wandering child, although its shameful abandonment, as Van den Rietter informed us, could only lead to the decadence of our people. For that reason, the younger men of the city would henceforth be obliged, as in times past, to open each planting season by clearing the trees and underbrush from a large plot of land, which would, after the removal of roots and stumps, be divided into fields that each of the Chief's or The Bastard's wives could then have cultivated by the women in her entourage—usually relatives who had come to live with her for a while.

At that moment, we suddenly realized that Van den Rietter had taken advantage of the invasion, the districting, and the constant surveillance of the city to provide himself with inventories, reports, and any other data that might help him establish a strict accounting of Ekoumdoum's male population—of all ages.

The young girls were right when they said it was all decided on the first day of the labor project. The atmosphere was tense, and the young people who presented themselves at the mission early that morning wore expressions in which resentment contended with curiosity, as on the face of a fiancée who is being married against her will. They could be seen standing in the courtyard of the presbytery, waiting patiently and holding their felling swords under their arms or in their hands. Everything seemed so dreamlike, so unreal, so implausible that a persistent rumor circulated through the assembly; according to it, Soumazeu had staged the whole affair as a practical joke, a sort of farce, undoubtedly to determine the extent of his ascendancy over the minds and spirits of the Ekoumdoumians. The hypothesis of a trial or test seemed to be partially confirmed at eight o'clock, when it was announced that Father Van den Rietter had been temporarily delayed and would join his troops at the work site in about two hours. Our young people were led there by a handful of overseers who made a show of taking command.

Finally they arrived at the site of the work project, a vast hillside that sloped imperceptibly toward the river. When their warders instructed them to begin working, our young people looked so humiliated and annoyed that it seemed for a moment as if they were on the verge of rebellion, but that was not to be, and they could be seen complying with their orders, although quite unwillingly. Supporting themselves by placing their left hands on the long poles designed for that purpose, they lifted their machetes lethargically and then ponderously leaned over until they appeared to be broken in half, their heads buried in the underbrush; indeed, they chopped with an assiduously calculated awkwardness, more often than not allowing the flat side of their implements to land on the tangled vines in the bushes.

Van den Rietter actually did appear a little before noon, and he must have been struck by the workers' silence and their lack of enthusiasm, but he betrayed no sign of annoyance, probably aware that it would be imprudent at this stage to aggravate the young people, for if they revolted, the whole city would revolt with them. In any case, he did not need to survey the scene for more than a few seconds to realize that, although his mobilization order had been formally addressed to all the young men in the city, only about half of them had actually responded.

"Many people are not here today," the missionary shouted, making certain that he could be heard by everyone. His hands were on his hips, his legs spread apart, his lips pressed tightly together.

As one after the other of our young people interrupted their feeble efforts, they successively turned their expressionless faces toward Father Van den Rietter.

"One might almost say," continued Van den Rietter as soon as all the young people had stopped working, "one might almost say that a goodly number of your brothers are reluctant to come and work for your chief. How do you explain the fact that so many people are absent?"

The missionary posed this question several times, although he always formulated it differently, yet his only response was the same repeated assault of vacant stares. Finally an anonymous voice answered him, "Who could have given you the ridiculous idea that we were ever anything but reluctant to work for the person you call our chief."

Shot like a stone from the sling that an innocent child was brandishing in his hand, this reply scored a direct hit on the missionary, who seemed to waver under the shock. Another stone cast by an equally cruel hand might well have sufficed to bring down Van den Rietter by opening the eyes of that presumptuous man who wanted to control everything, get to the bottom of everything, scrutinize everything, but who failed until the very end to solve the only mystery worth being elucidated, the mystery of the true relations between his friend and ally the Chief and our city. "Leaving out of consideration the mystery of woman!" exclaimed the young girls in unison, with a burst of mocking laughter, as they had already done many times after having intoned this stock phrase about the mystery of woman, a phrase that functioned as a sort of refrain in their narrative. And this time too, as always in the past, when Jo The Juggler expressed a desire to know more about the significance of this enigmatic and disconcerting phrase, they replied with animation, but without abandoning their mockery, "You men, don't rely on us to tell you our secrets. Play your roles as much as you like, and we will play ours."

Unfortunately, out of cowardice or perhaps dumbfounded by the novelty of a situation they had never before encountered, the young people allowed the subject to drop at that point, turned their backs on the bearded tyrant who had come from across the sea, and once again began to attack the underbrush with blows as futile as they were redundant.

"What! What!" Van den Rietter stammered, "Are you trying to make me believe it is not a part of your tradition to work joyfully for your chief, a man elected by the people of your city? Well then, when you choose a chief, the very least you can do, my children, is to serve him with enthusiasm."

It sometimes happens that a wayward madman stumbles into the midst of a family gathering and sows panic everywhere by mumbling incomprehensible tales, describing fantastic sights, calling upon phantoms, and muttering to himself as he becomes lost in the desolate incoherence of his dreams. At first, surprise and astonishment put a stop to the singing, immobilize the expressions on people's faces, and inspire screams of fright. But the true nature of the case soon becomes apparent to everyone, for the evidence is clear and brings with it a sense of relief, pity, or mockery. The family celebration begins anew, more lively than ever, and the madman, finally recognized for what he is, soon finds himself abandoned to his solitary phantasmagoria.

"You understand," continued Soumazeu imperturbably, "you obviously recognize him as your beloved chief. As far as that goes, how could you do otherwise? For in the end, it has been clearly established that he is your beloved chief, chosen by yourselves—I mean to say, of course, by your fathers, but isn't that the same thing? Well then, what the devil! Serve him with a bit more spirit. Otherwise, people will begin to think you don't love this worthy old man, and, you have to agree, that would be just the opposite of the truth. Don't worry about anything else, my children. Indeed, I am just now on my way to find reinforcements for you."

He went off in the direction of the city, and in addition to the troop of bodyguards who now surrounded him night and day, he took with him a few young people who had been selected from among the workers to point out the places where their brothers, having ignored his summons, might be hiding and, possibly, to lead him there, for he was determined to track down the insubordinates, as he called them, or deserters.

"Halt!" he said suddenly, when they had arrived at a marketplace in the center of the city; he held out his hand toward one of his attendants, who placed a large account-book in it. Beneath the beating sun, Van den Rietter, who was wearing tinted glasses, began to call names, and each time he did so, the young people who had been selected from among the workers were expected to furnish him with precise information. What is more, they did it most of the time, because our young people are perfectly cognizant of each other's habits, characteristics, and usual expedients. If by any chance they were incapable of satisfying the missionary, they entered the house of the young man sought by Soumazeu, or a neighboring one, in the assurance that they would at least find an old man there or a few young children who could give them further information.

Each time the secret of a hiding place was revealed to him, Van den Rietter dispatched a squad of commandos to the spot, saying, "Bring him back. If he resists, his crime is compounded." On the basis of criteria that no one could fathom, he reserved several recalcitrant individuals for himself and insisted on personally driving them from their hiding places.

"But my God! What were the adults doing all this time?" the sapak had asked the young girls at this point in their story, not hesitating to annoy his older companions with his interruption.

"The women were toiling in the fields as usual," the adolescents had replied, "and as usual they were kept in the background of the drama by the very bounds of servitude that come with their role. As far as the men were concerned, a small number of them were also away from home, attending to some sort of familial task in the forest, either by the river or elsewhere. Actually, most of them remained cloistered in their dens or lairs, occasionally stealing a furtive glance through a half-opened doorway and acting as if they were completely unconcerned by activities that had long ago become things of the past for members of their age group."

What makes our blood run cold these days (although at the time it apparently surprised no one except the young girls of the city, and no doubt their mothers, whose opinions necessarily shaped their daughters' mentalities) was that members of the counsel of elders—that is, all the old men, all the men whose advanced age was universally acknowledged—were at that very moment fraternizing with the authorities of the city, thereby sanctioning a criminal foreign tyranny over their own people. The adolescents did not fail to relate this dereliction of duty to the three Rubenists, whose desire for information about the city was insatiable.

Father Van den Rietter had, it seems, vowed not to stop until he had restored (as if the city were a parched tree in need of water) all the tendrils of its root system and all the vigor of its trunk to their ancestral rites. He had thus persuaded The Bastard and his virtually bedridden father to invite the members of the counsel of the elders to the Palace on that day and to regale them sumptuously, no matter what it might cost the greed of the one and the senility of the other. The old men had been informed of the invitation two days before, and they had greeted the honor with a show of emotion, for they remained imbued with their own empty prerogatives and foolishly attached to the customs that had nourished their childhood, doubly returned from this moment on.

They had thus gone to the Palace shortly after dawn, as had been customary in the olden days, either limping along one after the other like a parade of panting flunkeys, or skimming across the ground, cheeping and fluttering their wings like a cheerful flight of white-bleached sparrows. In this way, while their children and grandchildren were exhausting themselves and pouring their sweat into the land that had formerly belonged to their ancestors, the land which should have been the sacred trust of these old men but which the usurper had quickly wrenched from their pusillanimous hands, the supposed guides of the city were gorging themselves in the odious tyrant's palace. Confined inside the Chief's compound for the whole day, they knew nothing about the serious events taking place in the theater of the city founded by their forebears.

To draw this episode to a conclusion, Ngwane-Azombo had declared, "The men of the city of Ekoumdoum have disgraced themselves for all time!" "Yes, but who is going to tell them that?" retorted the other adolescents in unison, bursting into a chorus of burlesque guffaws, as they loved to do.

To return to Father Van den Rietter, it was child's play for the missionary to surprise the insubordinates who had remained within the city—separately or, more infrequently, in groups, seated in a cane chair at the family dwelling or simply stretched out on their beds, as they had always done until late at night; however, these were by far the least numerous.

It proved much more difficult for him when the recalcitrant individuals were fishing on the banks of

261

the river, sometimes quite far upstream or downstream from the city, often in creeks overhung with luxuriant growths of vegetation and swarming with reptiles and fish of all sizes.

The missionary's conceit had to surmount or skirt the most cruel obstacles when he attempted, albeit without success, to catch up with those recalcitrant fellows who had gone hunting in the forest. Although the crisis had prodded the masters of the city into adopting a policy that consisted of continually discouraging activities that might place male citizens in a position where they could escape supervision, there had, for all that, never until then been any question of forbidding people to hunt, even in the most remote parts of the forest. Perhaps the idea had not yet occurred to anyone; perhaps they had a vague fear that an intolerable shortage of meat might drive the Ekoumdoumians to rovolt.

To every insubordinate he had just tracked down, even if he had found him stretched out in bed, Van den Rietter declared, "that sort of activity is not on the schedule for today, my good man. Come on! Get up, you lazybones. Off to work, you little rogue, and be quick about it."

Taken by surprise, the young man abandoned whatever he was doing at the moment or hastily got dressed and followed Van den Rietter, whose train of captives continued to swell with his own contributions as well as those of the commandos he had dispatched to the four corners of the territory around Ekoumdoum with instructions to rejoin Soumazeu, rather than going to the work site, once their mission had been completed.

The young girls were still amazed that the inhabitants of our city had adopted the practice of complying with Van den Rietter's imperious injunctions, even if they had not converted to the religion he was preaching, and that was indeed the case for the vast majority of them. He had told us, "It is high time you renounced that satanic mania for flinging about your arms and legs and writhing about like raving lunatics by the light of the moon; your confounded drums make a devilish racket which keeps me awake at night!" And then, it is true, we had obeyed him and renounced night time dancing in the city itself. If

262

we were by any chance tormented with a desire to appease our atavistic instincts, we repaired to a clearing in the heart of the forest, sufficiently far from the city so that the rumbling of our drums might be dissipated in the intervening thickets and leafy foliage before coming to brush softly across the august eardrums of the uninvited guest. These days it seems like such a distant era, and so unreal!

He had told us, "It is high time you renounced the habit of allowing your wives and daughters to walk about with their breasts uncovered, erect like standing invitations to lechery. How can you fail to see that it is an indecent, barbarous custom?" And then, it is true, we had yielded, forcing ourselves, with varying degrees of success of course, to cover our women's breasts, whether or not they were standing erect.

He had announced to us, "What a scandal it is to see such young men, and healthy ones at that, get up in the mornings only to remain seated all day long in front of their houses, while their wives are breaking their backs in the bush to feed these lazy good-for-nothings who haven't the slightest sense of honor!" And then, we have to agree, we had been moved and even disconcerted by the appropriateness of this reproach, as a consequence of which, the adolescents confided in a burst of communal laughter, the men of the city had made it a rule to accompany their wives, from a distance of course, to their fields.

Because of this authoritarian, intolerant, quick-tempered, insatiable individual, we had had to give up dice, although we were crazy about the game; we even drank our palm wine in secret. Little by little, under the pretext of raising us above the level of animals, he had contrived to replace our gentle customs with absurd practices that were not even those of his own country, but merely the delirious product of his own depraved imagination, or perhaps, of some book that had been written by some morbid soul, for, as Jo The Juggler would soon demonstrate to the missionary's everlasting shame, the hallowed traditions of his country are far more perverse and bestial than our own:  don't people say that rape, theft, murder of elderly parents whose longevity delays the moment of

263

inheritance, abandonment of innocent babies, and unjustified seizures of land are part and parcel of daily life over there, although they are but the rarest of occurrences in our part of the world?

It is indeed true that, in agreeing to follow Soumazeu without the least hesitation, our young people were merely conforming to a law that the entire city had tacitly adopted since the long-bearded man's arrival in our part of the world. This submissiveness, which knew no bounds and was so incomprehensible, almost led to our ruin. Who would have believed that our young girls, adolescents who were still no more than children in the eyes of their families, would be the ones to resist?

On the other had, what is there to be said about Van den Rietter's sudden change in tactics? Did he himself know what he was doing? Or was his mind in the process of becoming unhinged, like the rusted mechanism of an old alarm clock exposed for too many years to the inclemencies of our weather? After having exhorted us for such a long time to forget our traditional practices, here he was suddenly insisting that we return to them. What sort of madness could have taken hold of him—or what sort of fear? And why did he not see that, since the essential tradition for all people is freedom, the ultimate disaster in the tradition of Blacks was to be commanded by a White and that any attack upon a people's freedom vitiates all its other traditions?

Van den Rietter reappeared at the work site early in the afternoon. Without excessive gloating, like a man who had known other successes in life, he herded a compact flock of young males in front of him, while they were apparently reduced to wondering which role it would be more appropriate for them to play-- ordinary, harmless malingerer or fearless, haughty rebel.

"Bravo, my good fellows!" he shouted, clasping both his hands above his head and addressing himself to the workers. "Bravo, my children! You are absolutely marvelous. But now it is time for you to stop, my little ones, and to come receive the reward for your zeal and your fidelity. Thanks to the generosity of the Chief and his son, and thanks in some small measure to my own as well, you are invited to the most elegant banquet you have ever seen in your lives. Listen, my good fellows: the main dishes have been simmering in the compound of your beloved chief, a worthy old man indeed, but I am the one who has taken care of the wine, most of which comes from Mackenzieville, a delight to the palate--it will absolutely amaze you. Well then, my little ones, follow me. But first give your implements to the newcomers; they are going to take your places. Let them show us then, if they are going to do as well as you have done."

And so it came to pass. In an enormous hall at the Palace, where the open sides, the dusty woodwork, and the rusty hardware reminded one of a classroom, they found themselves in front of tables heaped with countless dishes of meat in various sauces and assorted vegetables to accompany them, pitchers of red wine from Europe, calebashes of palm wine, bottles of beer from Mackenzieville. After Soumazeu's benediction, the young people sat down and ate, at first with restraint and discipline, but soon, as the alcohol went to their heads and despite the presence of Father Van den Rietter (who presided over the meal with an extreme indulgence, it is true), they no longer remained in their seats, abandoning themselves to a confused, animated gaiety and degenerating into a noisy throng.

Soumazeu occasionally disappeared to rectify some feature of the banquet, adding something here, removing something there, as if he were preoccupied with the purity of a liturgy, because in his own mind this love-feast was doubtless only the first stage in a long ritual ceremony. He reappeared suddenly with a suspicious, inquisitorial gleam in his eye; he surveyed the guests; he searched their expressions; he leaned over to verify the intonations of their voices and to assure himself that he had indeed noticed a particular individual at the work site. This was his way of protecting himself against gate-crashers who, profiting from the proverbial complaisance of their brothers, would unfailingly resort to deception as a means of sharing in the feast without having partaken of the toil. He indeed did discover two of them, and they were dismissed without ceremony. Then, carried away by his own momentum but encountering great difficulty in distinguishing one of our young men from another, he happened to vent his anger on several faithful subjects who had not stinted their efforts at the work site, and each time his vehemence inflicted a bitter humiliation on them.

As soon as the meal had been consumed, Van den Rietter sent the young people away, mounted his bicycle, and headed off toward the work site to see the other shift at work.  It was hard to believe, but a swarm of young people was milling about on the edge of the space that had been cleared by the day's work. Van den Rietter knew immediately that it was no miracle which had doubled the number of insubordinates he had tracked down one-by-one that morning.  After having passed through the mesh of his net, the more recalcitrant ones, lured by the scent of the sumptuous repast that would reward the efforts of their brothers, had eventually decided on their own accord to show up at the work site.  It is simply that the strict controls exercised over these meals by Van den Rietter had very quickly become known, and being unable to count on any ruse that might assure their presence among the invited guests, they had resigned themselves to coming and engaging in a bit of work.

The second meal took place shortly after sunset, and numerous oil lamps had needed to be placed along the walls to illuminate the enormous banquet hall.  It seems Van den Rietter wanted the Chief to show himself among the guests during the second meal, as he had shown himself to the counsel of elders earlier in the day, and to deliver a traditional oration, but they say the Bedridden Chimpanzee refused categorically, claiming he no longer had the strength after such a hard day to drag himself to a hall so far removed from his bed.  Bursting into a concert of laughter, as they loved to do, the young girls went on the explain that Van den Rietter was extremely annoyed by this breach in the purity of our tradition; it ruined his entire evening and even much of the following day, which nevertheless proved to be an apotheosis for him.

Indeed, all our young people without exception reported by eight o'clock the next morning to the Catholic mission; there they were organized into rows and directed to the work site, where Van den Rietter was sitting at a table covered with papers and waiting for them to arrive. Soumazeu undertook to call the roll by running through lists recorded on sheaves of paper that he turned over with great diligence. Each of our young people responded with a sort of pride and possibly even a hint of enthusiasm.

Then, Van den Rietter's recruits spread out across the work site and resolutely set to work. All day long it was thus possible to contemplate a scene that would have brought tears of rage, shame, and pity to the eyes of the proud founders of our city: under the cynically bemused supervision of lounging warders—a brood of men recruited among the class that had just yesterday been subject to the rule of their most noble descendants and even among the rabble of outsiders who populated the Chief's compound or the Catholic mission and who, for the most part, would have been unable to say where they had been born or what their lineage might be—the youngest and most handsome of their living descendants were exhausting themselves to clear their own land for the benefit of a master from elsewhere, while urging each other on and waxing ecstatic over the prospect of the wretched festivities that were going to reward their servile labor.

The adroit Van den Rietter was of course at great pains to avoid deceiving such expectations; in fact, he more than fulfilled the anticipation of his new troops. When he declared the day's work completed at about six o'clock in the afternoon, it was to announce that a tasty meal awaited the youthful workers in one of the mission buildings. The young people immediately rushed headlong to the appointed place, where they gorged themselves on food and drink, although the main dishes seemed inferior to those of the previous day, because they had been prepared with exotic ingredients like rice, olive oil, and zebu meat, imported from Mackenzieville and possessing an unfamiliar taste that caught their unsophisticated palates by surprise.

In addition, the missionary organized festivities which lasted a good part of the night and during the course of which he allowed our young people to give free rein to their need for celebration, sensual joys,

267

and even carnal pleasures. He encouraged them to dance, to drink, to play games of dice. It was an unabashed return to paganism in our city, and the troubling thing about it was that it occurred under the aegis of Father Van den Rietter himself.

To crown this extraordinary day, Van den Rietter addressed the following sermon to the young people of the city at the moment he was taking leave of them: "I congratulate you, my children; you are fine fellows indeed, and until now you have done excellent work. There is no reason for it to stop here. On the contrary. Tomorrow is Saturday, but as an exception to the normal rule, there will be no work, because I will be accompanying Brother Nicholas to Mackenzieville and shall therefore be unable to direct your efforts myself. Sunday as well, there will be no work, obviously. But Monday, we have an appointment at eight o'clock on the work site.

"As I just said a moment ago, you are fine fellows—gentle, kind, innocuous. That is how I like you to be, and that is how you should always behave. Allow yourselves to be shaped by your superiors, like a vase in the hands of a potter who moulds the clay as he pleases without meeting any resistance, for the least insubmissiveness in the clay would ruin the final product. I am the potter, and you, you are the clay. That is the way God has ordained it; well then, what more fitting role is there for each of us than to follow the path God Himself has laid out? To want things to be otherwise is to expose yourself to the wrath of the Creator and to the greatest of misfortunes.

"Yes, I know that false prophets recently tried to sow the seeds of discord in your innocent souls by coming and saying unto you: 'Everything must change; everything must be turned upside-down. Life will be better when fathers obey and sons command, when masters serve and servants give orders. Let us change everything from top to bottom; it will be easy, and everything will be better!' That is what they told you and what they will perhaps tell you again some day.

"My little ones, this, in contrast, is what your own common sense tells you deep inside yourselves. It tells you:  'Who will oblige masters to become servants, if God Himself decreed that they should be the most intelligent, the most wealthy, the most powerful? Who will deprive them of the possessions which their profound knowledge of science and the infinite wisdom of the Creator have accorded unto them? Who will strip them of the airplanes and other terrifying weapons which their ingenuity has bestowed upon them? Who will keep these airplanes from dropping bombs upon their enemies? Who will prevent these bombs from annihilating a hundred cities like yours at a single blow? Who will compel those who have the airplanes, those who are the masters, to give them up and transform themselves into servants?'  That is what your common sense tells you; you need only open the ears of your conscience, and this is the teaching it will always impart to you.

"Therefore, do not listen to evil prophets. When they return, tell them this:  'Gentlemen, false prophets, go your own way.  Allow us to lead our humble and peaceful but happy existence under the fatherly guidance of those whom God has placed over us.  Allow us to follow the rude yet wise traditions bequeathed us by our ancestors; they are the ones who stipulated that we should cluster around our superiors, like chicks around the mother hen, that we should distance ourselves from evil shepherds who would lead us straight toward the abyss of misery and unnecessary suffering.  Our fate is humbly to obey.  Did not God, Whose work is perfection, place the lion above all the other animals of the forest and call him king of the beasts?  Likewise, He ordained that the children of Ham should honor the children of his brothers' children and be obedient unto them, just as the animals of the forest honor the lion and are obedient unto him.'  This is what you should tell the false prophets when they return, for they will return; I am certain of that; I know them.

"Yet go now and sleep in peace; prepare yourselves for next week and the completion of the marvelous work you have so courageously begun.  And when this project is finished, we will undertake another one, and when that one is finished, we will undertake a third, and so on and on.  Together we will build a soccer stadium, a dock for loading and unloading the boat, model farms. As far as your imaginations can reach, my children; there is no chance we shall ever run out of work. . . ."

The forest-clearing project was soon completed, as was the soccer stadium, which was begun immediately afterwards. Our young people, under Brother Nicholas' supervision this time, had just started work on the dock for loading and unloading the boat, when the epidemic struck.

The group of Rubenists and young girls were only a day's march from Ekoumdoum as the adolescents broke off their tale, asserting that that had been the situation at the moment when they were leaving the city.

For them to draw this narrative to a conclusion, they needed to be prodded by a question from Mor-Zamba, whom they called Mor-Dzomo or Simsimabayane on the strength of what Jo The Juggler had told them in jest. According to them, nothing could persuade the masters of the city to interrupt the work projects, and nothing could persuade their brothers to rebel or even to slacken their efforts—not the heartbreaking deaths of small children, not the dismay of the city, not the despair of grieving mothers. One might almost have said that the entire male populace of Ekoumdoum had been emasculated. It was as if someone had injected a lethargy-inducing poison into their blood, a poison that eventually transformed them into insensible animals whose motions were purely mechanical. Nothing seemed capable of arousing them and restoring their lost sense of dignity—not the voice of a mother and certainly not that of a sister. Ruled over by Van den Rietter and his numerous battalions of alguazils, informers, spies, and guards of all sorts, they exerted themselves all day long and slept soundly at night during the week; on Sunday, they drank, danced, and fornicated themselves into a stupor.

Finally, it was the anticipated day of their arrival at Ekoumdou, and they arose well before dawn. The young girls gave the Rubenists to understand that it would now be best to leave the track they had been following until then, that is to say, the abandoned road; it was the least precaution they could take to

avoid unpleasant encounters. After having concealed
the Raleigh in a thicket, the Rubenists unhesitatingly
followed their companions into the obscure depths of
the forest, where the adolescents silently snaked
their way through the foliage like a parade of squir-
rels. They proceeded in this fashion for a length of
time that seemed interminable as well as more and more
distressing to the Kola-Kolans, with the exception of
Mor-Zamba, who had a good knowledge of local geography
and remained calm, because he could surmise the intentions of the young girls. When they finally stopped,
the brilliance of the sun, fleetingly glimpsed through
domes of leafy vegetation, seemed to indicate that the
day star was as its zenith.

"You are wrong," said the adolescents, "it will
be dark in three hours at most. That is when the rest
of us intend to enter Ekoumdoum; we could do it
sooner, but we don't attach much importance to that;
it is a matter of discretion. We would like our
mothers, who will be informed of the situation tonight, to meet and organize themselves before Soumazeu
and The Bastard suspect anything at all. Tomorrow
morning they will of course call us together and
question us about the particulars of our journey; we
will tell them a tale that the leisure of our return
trip has enabled us to construct in minute detail. We
will claim that Ndogdam Tsibuli disappeared after
having extorted from us the money produced by the sale
of the ground nuts; for that reason, we are not
bringing back any medicine. This is the tale we
concocted to serve them tomorrow when they question
us.

"In the meantime, we will have entered the city
on the sly; we will have slipped in among shadows, one
after the other, hopefully without being seen by The
Bastard's and Van den Rietter's spies and alguazils.
There is nothing to fear; it will actually happen that
way. And even if a guard or militia patrol catches
sight of one or the other of us, they will not take
any particular notice of our presence. There are so
many young girls like us in Ekoumdoum that seeing one
of them would not astonish anyone, no matter what
moment of the day or night it might happen to be.
Leaving out of consideration the depraved and the

debauched, who ever looks at a young girl?  If I go
into the Palace this evening to murder the Chief in
his bed, someone will certainly see me, but who would
be disturbed by my presence?  Who would take a young
girl seriously—the supposed shadow of her mother, the
understudy of an understudy?

"People say that you are Abena's men.  Not many
people believe that in Ekoumdoum; Ngwane-Eligui, as
for her, she is convinced; to tell you the whole
truth, she was the one who guessed you were in
Tambona, and she is the one who put us on your trail.
This is what she succeeded in having communicated to
us on the eve of our departure:   'The two strangers
are doubtless in Tambona; that is the only place where
they could have gone.  Keep your eyes peeled so you
will recognize them.  Tell them to come back at once;
tell them the city needs them.'

"Thanks to you, Abena has become the new Jesus-
Christ of Ekoumdoum, although very few people there
ever saw him and even they no longer remember him, but
didn't Abena ever teach you that accordionists are to
be avoided like the plague in our city, where it is
necessary to seek out young girls who see everything,
know everything, and can do everything, because no one
ever sees them?

"Listen well; this is exactly what is going to
happen tonight.  Shortly after our cautious infiltra-
tion of Ekoumdoum, our mothers are going to get together; under the pretext of holding a secret women's
ritual, a procession of them will come here by way of
a path that runs along the river, for at this point
you are virtually on the bank of the river.  They will
be carrying torches so there can be no possibility of
your making a mistake; in any case, they will be
guided by one of us.  They will disguise you and
surround you in such a way that, when they lead you
back to the city, no one along the path will be capable of distinguishing you from the other women.  You
will have a great deal of work on the first night, if,
as is probable, the epidemic is continuing to wreak
havoc in the city; every mother of a sick child will
immediately want to put your power to the test.  In
any case, you will change houses each night to elude
the suspicious watchfulness of Zoabekwe's and Van den

Rietter's spies and militiamen.

"Have confidence in us; we too know our way around, when it comes to being invisible; invisibility is the daily life of a woman; we are born, we grow up, and we die, as it were, in a state of invisibility. Nothing will happen to you as long as you are being protected by women. Provided you save their children (that is to say, our race, whose survival is at stake), there is no sacrifice they will not make for you. As for the rest, entrust yourselves to Ngwane-Eligui."

Despite their surprise and their reservations, the Rubenists could hardly refuse to accept this strategy.

## CHAPTER 3

When they were alone, the Rubenists initially reproached themselves for the agreement they had just made with the young girls. They doubted that exposing all three of themselves to such a risk was consistent with Hurricane-Viet's cherished maxims of prudence.

"That isn't the real question," reflected Mor-Zamba finally. "The real question is this: can we have confidence or not in the seriousness of these adolescents for the future?"

"Affirmative!" Jo The Juggler replied, "on this point, and on all the others for that matter; I didn't catch them napping once during the two weeks we have been performing the most remarkable feats in their company. I am ready to follow them anywhere."

"Well then, all three of us will have to go," decided Mor-Zamba. "A little bird tells me we shall not be running much of a risk in the midst of the women who are coming to pick us up; I even suspect the final outcome is close at hand."

"Explain yourself, grandpa," said Jo The Juggler. "Tell us how you succeeded in catching a glimpse of the final outcome before I did."

"Until now Van den Rietter has conquered everything in his path," Mor-Zamba continued. "But will it be as easy for him to put down a women's rebellion?"

"As for me, I don't share your optimism," declared the sapak. "Those girls are certainly serious, as serious as you would like. On the other hand, they have an unbelievable lack of imagination; they are real blockheads. During all the time we spent

274

together, I have been watching them constantly, I have. And I was constantly saying to myself, 'It is not possible; there must be at least one of them who will finally recognize Mor-Zamba!' Yes, yes, I know what you are going to say: they weren't even born yet, etc., etc. But that is all the more reason."

"Wait a minute, my little scamp, I don't follow you," Jo The Juggler objected.

"But of course," proceeded the sapak. "Listen. A physique like his, you will have to agree, is certainly not what people call an ordinary model; any normally constituted imagination would inevitably be struck by that. And the story of his departure, his abduction by the soldiers, that extraordinary legend, more incredible than any of those that give children visions at night before they fall asleep—has no one ever told them the story? And what is there to say about Mor-Zamba's character which—admit it—is unlike any other? His gentle voice, his kindly expression, his unwavering concern for the weakest among them, his solicitude for their well-being and their safety, his self-denial, everything about him would intrigue the first person who came along and give him food for reflection. You can't be forgetful to that extent, even twenty years later."

When Jo The Juggler remained silent, at a loss for words, it was Mor-Zamba who responded to the sapak Evariste. "That must have been what my mother thought too," he said. "Listen to a story I have never told you before, or anyone else for that matter, not even Abena, with whom I spent a large part of my childhood, although I will undoubtedly tell it to him some day. Before she died, my mother said to me, 'Above all, do not let my death stop you; follow the path that lies before you, and never look back. When you arrive at the place I have so often told you about, the place where I would so much like to have gone with you, boldly enter the city and approach the people who live there. They will only need to see you, to look at you, and they will immediately recognize their sister in this, her living image; they will take you in their arms and bathe your head in tears of affection and compassion.' Alas, when I arrived in Ekoumdoum, no one recognized me. Yet not five years had passed

275

since the departure of their sister.  Far from it.
Try returning in five years; I am saying only five
years, not twenty—you will see."

"That's true!"  Jo The Juggler agreed.  "In five
years, I'll bet you even your old man and old lady
wouldn't recognize you, assuming they are still
alive."

"And why shouldn't they be alive?" retorted the
child with a start and something like a quiver of
indignation in his voice.

"And why should they be alive?" Jo The Juggler
replied cruelly.  "Old folks are made for dying;
perhaps you didn't know that?  Listen, when somebody
has full-grown children, he is an old man and can
therefore kick the bucket from one day to the next.
Do you admit that your parents have full-grown children, yes or no?  Well then, they are old folks!
Therefore, they can kick the bucket from one day to
the next, even if they seem to be in perfect health,
just like that.  Mine too.  The old lady could kick
the bucket from one day to the next, you know?  One
fine morning and pouf!  Nobody there.  Neither seen,
not heard from again.  Well then, what about it!
That's life, my little old man.  Even so, you have to
be a kid sometime.  It isn't everything.  Let's get
down to serious business now.  We can take off these
rags we have been traveling in and put on our best
clothes, preferably something in khaki that has a more
or less military look about it.  Don't forget we are
soldiers first and foremost; it is our basic role and
the easiest one for us to play, after all.  On top of
it we will superimpose the one our female comrades
have in store for us."

"I am curious to know what it is going to be,"
said the sapak Evariste with a weary tone in his
voice.

"It won't be very complicated," Mor-Zamba
declared.  "They are going to put dresses on us or
muffle us in pagnes.  That is always how women disguise a man.  We will also have to take off our
sandals and go barefoot, like everyone else.  Have you
reflected seriously on the fact that I am going along
this time, my friends?  It is frightening, isn't it?
Speak up, I am listening.  What do you have to say

about it, my dear George? And what if they recognize me?"

"There is no getting around it, that is for certain; you have to come. Only you know how to give shots. To tell the truth, it is unthinkable for you not to come. If they recognize you, oh well, circumstances will inspire us with an appropriate plan of action. Those damned hoydens didn't leave us any latitude for our own initiatives. The bitches! And you, sapak, what advice do you have for grandpa?"

"To deploy a whole array of deceptions to conceal his face from everyone, without exception, as long as possible; for that matter, the same principle also applies to us, it seems to me. In the meantime, we will be taking the pulse of the city. Afterwards, we will decide what to do, taking all the givens into consideration. As far as the rest is concerned ...."

Actually Ngwane-Eligui the Elder, the mother of Abena, did recognize Mor-Zamba, precipitating the course of events and setting in motion the forces that ultimately brought this remarkable adventure to a climax. Yet this recognition scene did not occur for a long time. The women sent out to meet the guerillas, about twenty in number, had been chosen from among young mothers born and raised in the outlying clans of the plateau, clans that had been unaffected during the tumultuous upheavals occasioned by the wandering child's dramatic sojourn in the city, or else they were from the countryside around Mackenzieville in the neighboring colony. They were far from being able to recognize Mor-Zamba.

As Mor-Zamba had foreseen, they disguised the Rubenists by removing their plastic sandals and wrapping them head to foot in pagnes. The firebrands they had twirled in the air to illuminate the scene were snuffed out by rubbing their still glowing ends in the damp earth; then, the women led their newfound friends by the hand through the darkness, conducting them toward the city.

In confirmation of the young girls' prediction, Mor-Zamba was busy all night long in the murky light of a rather rustic oil lamp, while his two exhausted comrades abandoned themselves to sleep in an adjoining room. He had not removed a single veil from his

277

masquerade; nevertheless, his gaze filtered through a
small slit he had managed to contrive just above the
bridge of his nose, although not without donning the
sunglasses Jo The Juggler had loaned him for the
occasion.  In that way, he not only discouraged curiosity, but his colossal, almost spectral height lent
him the appearance of a formidable, mysterious, inaccessible sorcerer.  This outfit hampered his movements
slightly without restraining them.  It also proved the
ideal strategy for affecting an austere implacability
and obliging each mother to enter his infirmary alone,
her child in her arms.  Thus, far from thinking about
examining his features, the poor woman abandoned
herself to an anguished, almost horrified fascination
with the preliminary operations of sterilizing the
needle, attaching it to the syringe, removing the air,
and filling the syringe with a transparent liquid.

Her lips tautened and moved back over her gums to
reveal her chattering teeth as the needle approached
the limp buttocks of the little patient.  Her eyelids
contracted and her eyes closed in a horrible grimace
as the point of the needle broke through her child's
skin; the same convulsion that shook his body also
wracked hers; a plaintive moan issued at the same
instant from their two throats.  As she stood up to
leave and carry the prostrate little being away with
her, she sniffled in a heartbreaking fashion, and
tears streamed down her cheeks.  Without the benefit
of a complete diagnosis, Mor-Zamba suspected that the
children they brought him were affected in varying
degrees by the disease, and he apportioned the doses
according to his own judgment.  Before daybreak he had
administered about thirty shots and completed his task
for the moment.  He slept during a large part
of the following day, while his two comrades took
their turn standing guard.

After peering through the interstices of a crude-
ly assembled wooden door, Jo The Juggler and the sapak
Evariste realized they were in a house that was
located in the very heart of the city, perhaps five or
six stonesthrow from the neighborhood where they had
been housed not long ago.  Shortly before sunset, just
as Mor-Zamba was waking up, the murmur and tramping
feet of a passing crowd sent the two Rubenists scur-

rying to their makeshift observation post, from where they saw Van den Rietter, cloaked in his vestments and flanked by two large choirboys, in whose company he was muttering incantations in Latin; he was descending the main thoroughfare at a measured, formal pace and moving toward the road. At a distance of several meters he was being followed by a multitude of school children telling their rosaries under the surveillance of their young teachers, strategically positioned on either side of them; somewhat further back were the adults, staring silently in front of themselves.

Barely an hour later, the procession again made its way past the two Rubenists, but in the opposite direction. This time, between Soumazeu's group (which included a children's choir singing at the top of its lungs, in Latin as usual) and the first ranks of the mob of school children, two tall men were advancing cautiously and carrying a white wooden coffin on their shoulders. The utter seriousness in people's expressions, the contemplative attitudes of the faithful, and their tear-drenched eyes betrayed a profound collective emotion that presaged a momentary break in the day-to-day affairs of the city. That is exactly what Ngwane-Azombo must have thought, for shortly after the funeral procession had passed by and darkness had fallen, she stole into the Rubenists' hiding place and brought them some impatiently awaited news.

It had been the funeral of a Christian whom the two younger Rubenists knew quite well. She had been the liveliest, the wittiest, the most talkative, the most generous of the old widows who had adopted them by the side of the road at a time when they were still known as El Khalik and Nouredine; subsequently she had struck up a real friendship with them. She was dead, not a victim of the flu epidemic, but merely from a minor ailment of the kind that often afflicts older people. The previous night, due to a sudden worsening of her conditon, Van den Rietter had been obliged to come several times during a brief period to confess the old widow, to give her communion, and, shortly afterwards, to administer extreme unction; as a result, he had frequently passed in front of the house occupied by the Rubenists, a few meters from Mor-Zamba, who was busy giving shots to infants suffering the effects of the epidemic. In this way, the two implacable foes had been rubbing shoulders without knowing it.

Then, not without malice, the young girl described the reception the city had accorded the news of their return. With the exception of its masters, stunned by the adolescents' invented tale, Ekoumdoum had been completely taken aback to learn of the hardships undergone by these delicate youth during their odyssey. As irrefutable evidence for the veracity of their story, their emaciated young bodies had provoked an outburst of indignation among mothers, while demoralizing fathers and brothers; their gaunt faces worked on people's imaginations and depicted, better than words could ever have done, the trials which their tender years had been obliged to endure. People were dismayed by the depravity and cruelty of the man who was supposed to have guided and protected them, but who had callously abandoned them after having subjected them to a reign of terror.

The young girl also provided them with information about the prevailing state of mind in the city. According to her, the situation was not actually tense, but neither was it particularly reassuring for the masters of the city, especially Van den Rietter, who had for the first time encountered an incipient resistence among the young workers he had just launched upon the task of creating a model cocoa plantation. The young people were working eight hours a day on the project, without counting travel time, for they had to cross the river to reach the site, and they only got back, completely exhausted, at nightfall. But they no longer had the consolation of sharing a good meal in each other's company at the end of their day, because Van den Rietter had sought to hoodwink our young people by promising to pay them in hard cash, although only after the fruits of their labor had been sold to the British merchants at Mackenzieville, that is to say, at best in four years' time. At that point, our young people had openly balked for the first time, carrying their audacity so far as to demand an unconditional return to the former system of payment, which meant a fine meal prepared with strange-tasting ingredients imported from

Mackenzieville.

According to the young girl, the latest disaffection of Van den Rietter's workers could well turn into open rebellion, if the return of Abena's men were known in the city. However, on the other hand, it was foreseeable that Zoabekwe might then unhesitatingly resort once again to extreme measures.

"It is strange," the young girl concluded. "Everyone in the city seems to be convinced that something is going to happen. All sorts of rumors are running around. Several days before our return, it seems, hunters noticed larger numbers of footprints on a riverbank, as if a group of armed men had passed through the area. Others claim to have seen the vestiges of a campsite, although people say their description could just as well have been that of a gorilla nesting ground. Are you sure you are Abena's only men in our part of the country?"

"We never said we were Abena's only men in this region," Jo The Juggler responded hastily. "Commander Abena is a great general; he does not inform walk-ons like us about all his projects. If he has dispatched other troops to your city, we know nothing about it."

At this point, Mor-Zamba addressed the young girl in the following manner: "Tomorrow night we have to leave the city before daybreak; it is absolutely essential, for after I have given about thirty shots this evening (and perhaps I will have to give even more!), there won't be any antibiotics left, except for the stocks we have cached in the forest. What arrangements do you intend to make for our departure?"

"I am going to tell you," replied the little slip of a woman without the slightest hesitation. "To protect you in such a way that no one can come near you, there are three lines of women constantly surrounding you, day and night; they give the impression of coming and going, bustling about, withdrawing for a moment to tell their rosaries or attend to more intimate matters. Yet if anyone makes a move toward the house in which you happen to be staying at any given moment, he will be immediately intercepted. But obviously, if Zoabekwe overran the place with fifty or a hundred of his brutes, we could only put up a ridiculously weak resistence; that is the situation. You will therefore leave here by virtue of the same technique that enabled you to enter the city. Several dozen women will cluster around you in a compact mass and move toward the forest under the pretense of participating in a secret ritual. Observers will be stationed a stone's throw apart all along the path to make certain it is free of people lurking in ambush. You see, it isn't very complicated."

"I doubt we shall return in less than three days," Mor-Zamba went on. "Our caches are widely scattered and far from here. Besides tonight, then, let two nights go by, and on the third we will be waiting for you at the same time and in the same place. Carefully explain to the mothers that we would be unable to help them in any case, because we no longer have any medicine."

As soon as they were alone again, Mor-Zamba sighed and said, "Ekoumdoum would be wretched place, if it were not for the women. There is no question about it, women are the salt of this earth."

"It is remarkable," Jo The Juggler seconded him. "Never in my life have I felt as well housed, as secure, as safe as among these good women. It is as if I were surrounded by a high protective wall plaited with their discipline, good judgment, and sense of loyalty. But note that only the youngest ones are really in on it: that is to say, those whose age should have troubled us the most. Without getting nervous, without strutting about, without bragging, they have played the roles of spies, informers, innocently curious observers...."

"Are they worth exchanging for the characters—more stupid than malicious actually—in whom you placed your trust during your first attempt, eh, George?" asked Mor-Zamba.

"Let's be serious," continued Jo The Juggler. "How do you explain the fact that they are so different from their men? You ought to know them, you should. After all, you are one of them. How do you explain it?"

"She already told you," Mor-Zamba replied. "You should have listened to her. You see, only the women farm the land around here; they are the only ones who attend to the planting each year, and they are con-

vinced that the survival of the race is at stake. I
am telling you again: she has already told us that
herself. Where no seeds are planted, there shall be
no harvests."

"In the end, it is all rather logical," said the
sapak approvingly. "In that regard, what she told us
about the young workers commandeered by Van den
Rietter is amazing, don't you think? Frankly, can you
believe she really meant to say that the young people
would be working without the slightest compensation
from now on?"

"That is it exactly," replied Mor-Zamba. "It is
a free labor force. Nobody knows better than I do
what that means."

"In short, it is slavery then!"

"You said it, you little scamp!" interjected Jo
The Juggler.

"Always the slavery of Blacks!" exclaimed the
former schoolboy from Kola-Kola. "Like Egypt, like
America, like South Africa. It is funny; the toubabs
always do the same thing to us. Wherever there is a
White and a Black, there is a master and a slave. The
master is always the White, and the slave is always
the Black. As for me, that is what struck me as soon
as I began reading books. Why are we always the
slaves? Why are they always the masters? Can you
explain that to me, can you? I would like to meet up
with somebody who could explain it to me. Take a chap
like Sandrinelli. Do you feel yourself inferior to
Sandrinelli, Jo, do you? No, of course not. And yet
he was the master and you, you were actually the
slave; do you admit it? How do you explain that?
Yes, I know, you don't give a damn."

"I don't give a damn, me?" Jo The Juggler protested. "But have you taken a good look at yourself,
you little scamp? What good is your whining? If you
want to prove yourself a man, you little scamp, you
only have to act. Do the same thing the toubabs are
doing, and you will no longer be their slave. The
toubabs never wear themselves out with useless whim-
perings; they act, that's their secret. I know them
very well, I do. And there is one thing I can tell
you right now: no toubab is ever again going to be
the master of old Jo, and old Jo is never again going

283

to be anybody's slave. I would rather die...."

You don't have to get mad!" interrupted Mor-Zamba. "The little one was only asking you a question; that is all."

From this point on, events become marked by a sort of madness that makes their telling a virtually impossible task, so much so that it is still extremely difficult for us to explain them ourselves. How did it happen, for example, that the news of the Rubenists' presence in the city spread, slowly but irresistibly, despite the oath of silence imposed on mothers of the sick children and, as a matter of fact, respected by them? For it was at this moment that the strong breeze began blowing, the breeze that was constantly going to swell in intensity until it grew into a hurricane.

Drunkenness is at first no more than a slight disturbance of the vision, as if everything were being caressed by a barely perceptible shiver; one still believes it is possible to pull one's self together by splashing a few drops of water on one's face or pressing one's hand against one's eyes. Yet the dizziness suddenly grows worse; other people, stationary objects, the sky itself, everything begins whirling around. There is nothing to lean against as the darkness of the vertigo progresses. One has to abandon any idea of struggling against it, simply allowing one's self to be carried away by the inevitable collapse of the system. How did this vertigo take possession of Ekoumdoum? A number of different accounts were in the air, each one more improbable than the next. According to some, the decisive role was played by Mor-Eloulougou and his confederates, by now zealous supporters of Zoabekwe. They were well acquainted with the people and their usual habits in the part of the city that borders on the road, because they had been born and raised there. They supposedly took advantage of their familiarity with the area not only to unmask the fraudulence of the tale told by the young girls, but also to shadow the adolescents, particularly Ngwane-Azombo, although their suspicions had not actually been corroborated until the guerillas, having left the city before dawn and heading in single file toward their first cache, Fort Ruben III, passed next to a thicket in which they had concealed themselves later in the day. The objection usually raised to this hypothesis is that the guerillas had left Ekoumdoum before the first crowing of the cock and must by that time have been far beyond the limits of the zone in which Mor-Eloulougou and his confederates dared to operate.

There are also those who allege it was not Mor-Eloulougou and his accomplices, but the old hunter Mor-Afana who, upon hearing footsteps in front of him, had taken cover behind a clump of underbrush and seen the three Rubenists pass by. Although in his case such actions were completely innocent, the old hunter Mor-Afana has nevertheless always denied them.

Why look so far afield for an explanation that has been lying at our very feet? How long could three men, somehow sent by Providence to wrench nursing infants from the jaws of the ogre epidemic and their poor mothers from the martyrdom of despair, how long could they remain undetected in such a large city? Indeed, wasn't everything conspiring to reveal their presence? The mothers of the sick children comforted each other and asked each other questions in tones that had, until then, been unfamiliar to their families and neighbors. For a long time they had been dragging themselves about, exhausted, haggard, whereas now a flicker of understanding glistened in their determined expressions; previously furrowed with wrinkles, their faces took on a new life and even became lit up with the hint of a smile; just yesterday they had been oblivious to their appearance, unconcerned with any touch of coquetry, but now they all sported some token adornment on their wrists or ankles. Whoever happened upon them in this unwonted guise could not help asking himself, "What in the world has occurred?"

Are people troubled by a coincidence which would tend to confirm their suspicions—the fact that the anecdotes about an imaginary, narrowly avoided encounter in the heart of the jungle between the male inhabitants of Ekoumdoum and the three guerillas began to circulate on the same day? There is nothing surprising about it, when one relives the most memorable hours of that day. Upon hearing the news that the

285

sorcerer with the syringe would be gone for several days, the mothers felt the poison of despair once again rise to their heads and cloud their vision. Ngwane-Eligui's exhortations were not enough to close the icy abyss that had suddenly opened in front of them again. They gave free rein to their imaginations, feverish with hatred, for an old wound is quick to bleed. The man with the syringe had fled, frightened away by some threat from the masters of the city; he would not have gone away of his own free will without having completed his task. The foreign criminals from the Palace and the Catholic mission had thus not abandoned their plans to exterminate Ekoumdoum! Here and there, seeing one of the Chief's servants pass by, or one of Zoabekwe's militiamen, or an alguazil, or an informer, some of the mothers barked out at him, "Remember Ezadzomo!" or else "Abena will not be long!" Like a decaying carcass draws swarms of flies, these acts of hostility occasioned an influx of informers and militiamen to the neighborhood where the recent period of mourning had appeared to bring with it a relaxation of police pressure. Mor-Eloulougou and his men combed the area all day long, entering houses at will and subjecting them to a thorough search, although they were greeted by the sarcastic taunts of the mothers and their daughters, who said to them, as if in an aside, "Why so many pig snouts where there is no garbage?"

These days it is easy to understand the mistake of those who ascribe the sudden outburst of renewed zeal on the part of Mor-Eloulougou and his confederates to an imagined encounter with the guerillas in the forest.

At nightfall on that same day, one of the sick children treated by Mor-Zamba took a sudden turn for the worse; widows and wives of all ages gathered, according to the usual custom in the city, to comfort the grieving sister and stand vigil over the child until his death, the imminence of which no one was in the slightest doubt. All at once, the youngest mothers decided to form a procession and go to the Palace, where they asked that Ngwane-Eligui the Younger be allowed to come and lay her hands on the sick child, even if she could not save him. The

Bastard seemed quite embarrassed, as if he didn't know what face to put on; he had undoubtedly already gotten wind of the sullen unrest that was once more undermining the credibility and authority of the city's rulers in the so-called "road" neighborhood, over which a chronic state of insubmissiveness had settled, along with the epidemic, and he hesitated between severity and the mask of good-natured indulgence.

He equivocated at first, like a man desirous of sacrificing to a superstition, and then granted the mothers' request; their mournful procession returned slowly to the dying child's bedside. As soon as she had fulfilled the expectations of her sisters, the young woman surveyed the crowd for a long time and then groped her way toward Ngwane-Eligui the Elder, Abena's aged mother who was squatting far from the hearth in a dark corner of the room. She spoke to her in the following way: "They say there is a third man, a man of enormous proportions. No matter what they tell me about him, this newcomer remains a mystery to me. Is he your son?"

"A man of enormous proportions? Really?"

"I have the information from an absolutely reliable source. Is he your son?"

"A man of enormous proportions? No, properly speaking he is not my son, but it is hardly any different; it is even worse in a way."

"I don't understand. That man is not your son, but you know him."

"Do I know him? All I can tell you for the moment is this, my daughter, and you will have to content yourself with it: if he really is the man I think he is, and if his return to the city is no mere fable, it means the twilight of the past and the dawn of the future."

"He can change our way of life?"

"Completely!"

"Even that of the women?"

"He can do it. Listen to me, and I will tell you a secret, but don't repeat it to anyone; he can do it, because he is our true chief; the other one is a usurper from another place. He can do it, but before he does, how many difficulties must we face, how much blood shall be spilled, perhaps as soon as his presence becomes known. He is in danger of suffering the same sad fate as Ezadzomo and his inseparable companion. You still remember those two, don't you, my daughter? If such a misfortune were to be repeated, you ought to know that you might well be held responsible for it. He must be saved at all costs. What can be done?"

"First, you must assure me that he is indeed the one."

"How?"

"I will tell you tomorrow, maybe even the day after tomorrow. There will still be time, don't worry, and don't panic. I can do a great deal, much more than you think."

As impassioned, self-willed, quick-witted, and filled with hate as Ngwane-Eligui the Younger might have been, the idea that the women could confront the masters of the city in a test of strength had not yet even crossed the young rebel's mind. At that moment she was still thinking in terms of compromise, tolerance, a miraculous state of affairs originating in some sudden change of course, a violent upheaval that she envisioned only in the vaguest terms; it might last several days and be a bit bloody (why not?), but it would culminate in success. The Bastard and his father would liberate the wives who had demanded their freedom. The man with the syringe would settle in the city to save the lives of children, to treat adults and cure their various ailments, and to lavish upon his people all the knowledge he had acquired during his long years of wandering. As she later acknowledged, the women in Van den Rietter's compound would have had to beat several of their guards to death in breaking out of their prison and joining the irresistible tide of women from the city, for then the enormity of their crime would convince them that they had reached a point of no return and that women would have to assume responsibility for a rebellion their men had refused to undertake.

All at once the young woman's shadow straightened up, and she said in a loud voice, "My dear mothers, my dear sisters, are we really alone here?"

"Yes, we are alone," replied a chorus of widows and wives of all ages.

288

"Well then, listen to me. I will tell you something you do not already know; at this very moment, you enjoy an important advantage over the Palace. Having nearly reached the term of her pregnancy, Zoabekwe's favorite has just isolated herself to await the first pain of her first childbirth. The wait may well be long. This will be his seventh child, and The Bastard is hoping it will be his first son. Until the birth has taken place, Zoabekwe will avoid all acts of violence, or I do not know him; he is much too afraid that a curse might fall upon his woman while she is in labor or, worse yet, upon the unborn child, the most vulnerable of beings to any malediction. Without The Bastard's consent, Van den Rietter won't interfere with anything. Make good use of your advantage. Two days from now, after the man with the syringe has returned, show the Palace that you are ready to pay with your lives to see his work continue in the city. Show them you are willing to make a living wall around him and if they want to get him, they will have to climb over piles of your own dead bodies. With the number of children you have and with the love you bear them, you will have the strength to do it, provided you close ranks to confront the enemy. You have learned that you cannot count on your men; if you fail to defend the blood of your blood, the flesh of your flesh, who will take care of them?"

After this exhortation, the young woman once again groped her way toward Ngwane-Eligui the Elder, the mother of Abena; she leaned over to whisper something in her ear and then went over to place her hands for one last time on the dying child, before asking the youngest mothers present to accompany her back to her prison in the Palace.

What enigmatic, dramatically resolute expression was stamped on the young woman's face as she approached the sick child for the last time, a face once again exposed to the glow from the hearth, where a pile of embers was gradually dying out? Into what state of tragic immobility had fright transfixed the wiry, gnarled body of Abena's elderly mother, and what agonizingly steady gaze had it imprinted on her eyes, when, a short while later and just after Ngwane-Eligui the Younger had taken leave of the group, the flame from a log that had been abruptly thrown among the coals illuminated her as if by lightning? From that moment on people began to believe that the shadow of Abena's authority was spreading across Ekoumdoum and that the hero's men were perhaps already prowling through the vicinity of the city, if they had not already surrounded it, as rumor suggested.

The next day there was no longer any doubt about it among all the mothers who had seen their children treated by the man with the syringe, especially when it appeared that the dying child of the previous evening had not only overcome his spell of weakness, but was showing signs of regaining his appetite. And that served as an occasion for the other mothers whose sick children had been treated by the giant to testify that similar observations had been made about the condition of their little ones.

Of course, there had never been any doubt among the girls who had visited Tambona and returned to Ekoumdoum during the course of an eventful journey and who, moreover, jealously guarded their secret. Influenced by the jubilation and arrogance of those who knew, those who did not have the privilege of sharing in the secret of the gods also acquired the faith, although they lacked any tangible proof. The young schoolmasters from the Catholic mission ran to Ngwane-Eligui the Elder's house and did their utmost to make her confide in them. When she animatedly protested her ignorance, they merely regarded her attitude as the prudent fidelity of an elderly mother held prisoner by instructions to be cautious—instructions impressed upon her by a son with whom she must be in frequent contact.

At this point we did not have the slightest idea of the degree to which the enemy camp was in the grip of uncertainty, lassitude, and doubt. Without the singular emotion of anguish compounded by an undefinable hope that occasionally depressed us and occasionally raised our spirits to great heights, we would certainly have asked ourselves, "What new strategy have the masters of the city suddenly adopted? Or what strange paralysis is keeping them cloistered in their own compounds? Under other circumstances, Soumazeu and The Bastard would already have undertaken a variety of initiatives to arrest the multiplying signs of danger; they would have put on a show of force to prove that they indeed retained control over the city; to convince people that the forest was free of peril and harbored no guerillas, they would have led battalions of men in endless sweeps through the countryside; to nip any seditious impulse in the bud, they would have instituted nightly patrols, making their omnipotence felt and clearly demonstrating their clairvoyance. But they did nothing of the kind. The scene remains empty of its usual protagonists. What in the world has happened?"

Thanks to Ngwane-Eligui the Younger, a portion of the city's inhabitants knew, of course, that Zoabekwe's hands were tied by his own superstitious fears, but we were only informed after the fact that, at the same time, Brother Nicholas was seeking to convince Father Van den Rietter that he had plunged headlong into an impasse and that the best way for him to get out of it was by resigning himself to a strategic retreat.

"Believe me, Father, it is real hornet's nest," the stocky man chided him. "I am telling you again: you will ruin yourself, if you try to offer them the daily banquet they are demanding; the mission's treasury could not withstand the strain, and your ally refuses to open his purse strings. However, on the other hand, if you persist in offering them good money four years from now, do you think these young people will agree for long to work so hard? They are dissatisfied, and you can do nothing about it; soon they will become angry and revolt. How do you expect to put down a riot when so many people are involved, perhaps even from the surrounding area? Believe me, Father, your authority would not be enough this time. Well then, how do you expect to put them down? Where are your batteries of machine guns? Do you take yourself for a Governor of the colonies?"

"You are behind the times, Brother Nicholas," jeered Van den Rietter, "there are no more Governors."

"All the more reason! All the more reason! Precisely! No, I am telling you, forced labor, statute labor, is a thing of the past, even for our niggers; all that belongs to a bygone era, it does.

291

Father, resign yourself to an act of humility that will at the same time be an act of charity. Offer them one final little binge and announce you are letting them go. Take the initiative to avoid an outburst of violence. Listen, next Sunday, for example, make the announcement that you don't need them any longer. Wisdom sometimes consists in knowing how to retreat, Father."

"But I will lose face."

"Of course, you will lose face, and then! Perhaps you prefer a riot?"

In short, the situation was such that everything was converging toward a brutal collapse of the authority that was tyrannizing over us, but we did not know it. Thus, the ease of our victory was going to amaze even the most perceptive among us. Despite the fact that Ngwane-Eligui the Younger was the soul of the insurrection, she herself admits that, even several weeks after the initial stages in the uprising of the mothers, she still could not believe her eyes or her ears.

"It sometimes happened that I sat bolt upright in bed at night," she recounts, "without being able to tell whether I had just passed from dream to reality or from reality to dream.

"It is true; in a way I gave the signal. It was at my request that Ngwane-Azombo went to Ngwane-Eligui the Elder several hours before dark on the night of the guerillas' return and said, 'If you want to be one of us in the near future, prepare yourself. In that way, you can meet the man with the syringe and examine him at leisure. At this point, I will cut my message short; I will complete it tonight, if you recognize the man with the syringe.' I suggested bringing the ancient hurricane lamp that the venerable old woman had been obliged to raise very high and hold with one trembling hand at the level of a face which she ceaselessly scrutinized in every detail, sobbing to herself and whispering, 'He is indeed the one; it is Mor-Zamba! My God, how he has grown! But, yes, there is no doubt; it is indeed he....' Then little Ngwane-Azombo, who was following my instructions, it is true, completed the message in the following manner: 'Do not waste time in shedding tears; it is a question of

292

his life and those of our children—the spearhead of our city and the seeds of its future, the guarantee for the survival of our race. Go quickly back toward the city; sound the call to arms among all the wives, mothers, widows, adolescents, and even the youngest girls, provided they are old enough to help. Mobilize yourselves without delay. Make a wall of your own bodies around the man with the syringe, so he will be protected against any danger. But be careful. Let this business be ours alone, a woman's business.'

"It is true; I gave the signal, but could I have imagined there was so much anger in a woman of her age? Could I have guessed there was so much energy in a body gnarled with years and withered by waiting, behind those yellowed eyes? Could I have expected such a show of authority? How astonished I was when they came to tell me that the oldest women were the ones who had refused even the briefest respite, that they were the ones who had spent the entire night putting up the first latticed wall of interwoven branches around the two houses, that they were also the ones who, as dawn was breaking, brought stakes they had cut in the forest to erect a more sturdy palisade around the initial enclosure, proof against an assault that Zoabekwe's brutes would certainly mount upon the man with the syringe and his friends.

"I gave the signal, it is true, but as for the rest, how could I have foreseen it?"

## CHAPTER 4

At daybreak the older women were joined by the younger wives; they were bringing warm food, a first meal for the valliant troops led by Abena's mother, but rather than leaving again, they stayed. The mothers of sick children arrived in a single group after the morning mist had cleared and as the sun was climbing higher and higher into the sky, warming the city and setting it ablaze with light. They settled into one of the two houses in the little fortress, the one that was going to serve as an infirmary, while the other housed the guerillas, since there could no longer be any question of changing their lodgings every night.

The other mothers of young children arrived in scattered groups; one after the other, they sat down tailor-fashion on the well-trodden, earthen terraces of the houses bordering on the fortress, on the coarse-grained gravel of the main thoroughfare, in the dust of the adjoining yards and vacant lots.

"What good is it to go on living?" they sighed, placing their youngest child between their legs or, in the case of a nursing infant, stuffing the tip of a breast into its mouth. "Yes, what good is it to go on living, if we have to sit by and watch the extermination of our sons, the annihilation of everything that is precious to us? It would be better to die with them; in that way, nothing will remain of Ekoumdoum, because that is what the masters of the city have decreed.

We are not afraid of dying, if death allows us to

accompany our beloved children into another world."

With the approach of midday, the young girls arrived in helter-skelter fashion, as did women from all the remaining age-grades: widows who were still young, mothers whose children had all passed through puberty, wives without children. Nearly all were carrying wooden bowls or cast-iron kettles in which steam was rising from a bush-meat stew, a ground-nut soup, or bitter leaves boiled in water—dishes they passed, behind the scenes, to those of their sisters who had left home without having had time to cook for themselves.

Several hours later, the entire neighborhood, all the way to the decommissioned highway, was covered with a flood of women, whose ebb and flow had soon metamorphosed the tiny fortress around the infirmary and the Rubenists' residence into a tiny islet buffeted by the high seas. The attraction exercised by this gathering became so strong that apparently nothing in the city, not even the domestic animals, could any longer resist it. Then a bizarre incident occurred, transforming this light-hearted carnaval into an angrily writhing, convulsive mob. A regiment of furies suddenly appeared, charging down the main thoroughfare at full tilt and shouting words of defiance; as this strange band of cohorts approached, it was with a mixture of enthusiasm and disbelief that the women around the fortress recognized the prisoners from the Catholic mission. Their mouths were twisted by imprecations, their eyes glazed with hatred; their cotton dresses were ripped to shreds, testifying to their recent participation in a hard-fought battle. As soon as these wild creatures had spread out into the crowd, they inspired it with a feverish excitation and fanned the voracious flames that wreaked such frightful havoc in just a few seconds. It was no longer a question of anything but breached fences, hand-to-hand combat with the enemy, broken skulls, guards knocked unconscious and even killed. How many fatalities? Two for certain, since the women had seen their brains pouring out into the ground like blood-stained mucus; perhaps there were three, perhaps more. It was a shame that Soumazeu himself had not been within reach; they would certainly have taken care of that old eunuch.

From this moment on there were no longer women sitting and chatting in a sisterly fashion or women peacefully rubbing elbows as they came and went; there were only women urging each other on, women alternately crying and laughing as they rolled on the ground, women shouting challenges at the men (spectators who remained at a respectable distance) and accusing them of cowardice, women brandishing fists in the direction of the Palace. In a paroxysm of combative frenzy, one of the newcomers yelled the name of Ngwane-Eligui the Younger, and like a watchword, it was immediately taken up and echoed by the other mutinous prisoners, who soon began to scream, "Free her, free Ngwane-Eligui the Younger. Everyone to the Palace! To the Palace. Let us free Ngwane-Eligui."

"Why go to the Palace?" the others replied dispassionately. "Ngwane-Eligui the Younger is already with us. Ngwane-Eligui is devoting herself to the care of the sick children in the infirmary. Ngwane-Eligui the Younger is free. If The Bastard intends to come here and recapture her with the aid of his savage brutes, we will see them coming from a distance. Well then, let us arm ourselves with pikes and machetes; they shall find tigresses barring their path this time, not sheep."

"Let's not wait until they show up," continued the mutinous prisoners. "Let us make our preparations in advance. We shall erect a new wall around the fortress, of pounded earth this time."

Wishing to serve as an example for their sisters, the rebels from the Catholic mission immediately set to work, for they were well acquainted with this kind of forced labor, and the other women imitated them step by step. As time passed, the carnaval atmosphere returned, and the insurgents gradually became convinced that the rulers of the city would allow the entire day to go by without seeking to mount a counterattack; they sensed that, no matter what happened later, this lack of activity already constituted an admission of weakness.

What were the masters of the city doing during this time? We know now that the two missionaries remained closeted together all day long and discussed the situation endlessly.

"No, no, no, no, Father," Brother Nicholas said to Soumazeu. "Don't get mixed up in it. Let the niggers gobble each other up, if that is what they want to do. After all, what business is it of ours? Is that our role? We have been left behind, Father. Something has escaped us in this country. We thought we understood everything, but we have been left behind. A bit of humility, what the hell! Let them do as they please."

Zoabekwe made several attempts to meet with his indispensable adviser, but it was as if Soumazeu were absent, mute, obliterated from the face of the earth; each time, he encountered only Brother Nicholas, who addressed the helpless Bastard in the following terms: "We will send for you when the time comes, my child. You have often sorely grieved the Virgin on account of your many wives; nevertheless, pray to her, implore her forgiveness; she will intercede with her Son and ask Him to enlighten you with regard to the most appropriate course of action to follow in the difficult circumstances you are presently facing."

In the gathering dusk, a final dramatic turn of events, no less unexpected than the previous ones, occurred in Ekoumdoum, where all the inhabitants, even Van den Rietter's young workers who had rushed back from the cocoa plantation, seemed to have congregrated near the little fortress as if for a prearranged meeting. The mulattress from the Catholic mission appeared and caused such a sensation that the women who were working stopped in mid-motion, those who were dancing in mid-step, those who were singing in mid-refrain, those who were speaking in mid-sentence; those who were sitting down got up, those who were standing found some prop to lean against, those who were laughing became serious, those who were holding themselves at a distance came closer, those who were leaving returned, those who were doubting believed, those who were worried grew calm, those who were drooping with age became young again, those who were panicky settled down, those who were filled with hatred felt moved to pity, those who were growing weak recovered their strength, those who were talking nonsense became reasonable; in short, it was as if the

297

world itself had been turned upside-down.

As she advanced straight ahead with the stiff deliberateness of a sleepwalker, the women spontaneously formed a wall in front of her, grumbling in voices that cracked with emotion, "What are you doing here, you of all people?"

"Am I not one of you?" she whispered timidly without staying her mechanical pace. "Am I not a black woman?" I too want to stand watch at the bedside of the sick children in the company of Ngwane-Eligui the Younger; tell her that I have come and that I have medicine for the sick children—medicine taken from up there, for they have it, you know, they have always had it. They treated each other; they know how to give shots; they give them to each other, and they sometimes even gave them to me. I wish to devote myself, along with Ngwane-Eligui the Younger, to curing the sick children. Tell her I have come; she knows very well I am one of you."

Almost miraculously the crowd parted, opening a path in front of this strange young girl and showing her the way to the little fortress.

"I have some medicine," the mulattress repeated as she entered the infirmary after Ngwane-Eligui the Younger had come to greet her at the door, take her by the hand, and lead her to Mor-Zamba. "Yes, I have some medicine. They had some up there, so I took it. How are the little patients doing?"

"Quite well," replied Ngwane-Eligui the Younger.

"I am certain they will soon be doing better and better," affirmed Mor-Zamba. "I am willing to bet there will be no more deaths. Ericsson was right: antibiotics can work miracles in our part of the world."

"Perhaps it wasn't so serious," opined Jo The Juggler. "Perhaps it was a harmless disease. It only goes to show that you can die from a harmless disease, if it isn't treated at all."

"Especially very young children," agreed Mor-Zamba. "I am convinced people don't really know how fragile young children are and how much they need to be protected. It gives us some idea of our own responsibilities."

The following day also went by, but the authorities, although flaunted to the point of outrageous provocation, dared not show the slightest sign of life.

"You will never make me believe this is normal," said Jo The Juggler.

"Oh, but it is," the sapak Evariste answered him. "It is a deliberate strategy: I read about it in a book; they even have a special name for it. They call it, 'letting the situation come to a head.' Before independence, Sandrinelli and The Sot applied this very treatment to strikers at various firms in Fort Negre."

"Explain yourself!" scolded Jo The Juggler impatiently.

"It is simple," the sapak went on. "A strike, an insurrection, or a rebellion is, after all, like a sudden onset of fever in an ordinary person. Well then, instead of rushing into anything, a shrewd doctor might content himself with the hope that his patient is not seriously affected; he secretly says to himself, 'above all, don't panic!' All right, he waits. For one, two, three days, the sick person is bathed in his own sweat. Then, all of a sudden, the fever drops back to normal, by itself. In other words, the strikers, the insurgents, or the rebels grow tired, lose their belief in the possibility of success, begin to suspect everything and even their own leaders, often turning against them. The movement unravels; then it disintegrates completely, having died a natural death. And the trick is turned; the authorities no longer have anything to do but gather up the pieces."

"That is true; it is shrewd," observed Jo The Juggler, "and extremely dangerous. If that is really their plan, Bumpkin, you know what you have to do then? A major declaration. After all, you are Chief now. One part of the city has already recognized your claim, and, what is more, Hurricane-Viet has authorized you to act on his behalf; I will testify to that. In your declaration, you announce the overthrow of the present rulers and order them to surrender their arms."

"That is an obsession with you," teased Mor-Zamba.

"Believe me, old chap, it will work. And as far as that goes, you don't have any other choice."

For once Jo The Juggler was mistaken. On the third day of the women's rebellion, as the Rubenists had just finished discussing the strategy of "letting things come to a head" for the third or fourth time, a rumor began to spread: Soumazeu had been seen without his bicycle, without his bodyguard, descending the main thoroughfare on foot from the upper city and moving toward the highway—that is to say, toward the assemblage of women and the little fortress, which he approached in a nonchalant fashion, like a father coming to visit his children.

"No doubt about it," the women began saying to each other. "No doubt about it, he is coming here; the goal of his little excursion is us. Maybe he is coming to take back his daughter, the mulattress. If not, what cheek! What impudence! Seriously, what business does he have coming here, after all that has happened? Convince his prisoners to return to their cage? Does he really think such a thing is still possible? Oh, the shameless man. Let us hope for his sake that he has come to take back his daughter, the mulattress."

"I am not Van den Rietter's daughter," the mulattress protested when these remarks reached her ears.

"Who are you then?" Ngwane-Eligui the Younger asked her.

"I am an orphan, or rather a child who was abandoned and then taken in by Brother Nicholas. Actually I am Brother Nicholas' niece, that is to say the daughter of his brother, a businessman at Mackenzieville. In 1956, my father went back to his own country to get married. When he returned to Mackenzieville, he didn't want me any more, no doubt at the urging of his new wife. At that point Brother Nicholas took me in, and that is how I ended up in Ekoumdoum."

"Why didn't you go with your black mother?" asked the mother of a sick child.

"Because I don't know her and never even saw her, although she is still alive. After having lived together for a long time as man and wife, they sud-

300

denly separated one day; that is what people told me without ever giving any specific reason for the separation. I already know that Brother Nicholas does not intend to take me with him either; when it comes time for him to leave he will put me in an orphanage at Mackenzieville: that is how they always do it. I am one of you, and from now on I want to live like you, not isolated in the cold rooms and deserted corridors of a building from across the sea."

As he marched forward, Father Van den Rietter came under increasingly dense hostile fire from the race of women; hundreds of pairs of eyes seemed to be launching an uninterrupted stream of projectiles toward this eminent personage, who just yesterday had been admired and respected, but who was now cursed and detested, like all fathers who abuse their authority. When he was finally within earshot, the confused hubbub of voices from the crowd gradually abated, as in a dying storm, yet at the same time the faces that turned toward the intruder were set in defiance, frozen.

The error that was then committed by Van den Rietter was perhaps no more than a side-effect of the mute reproach with which an unfamiliar vestment suddenly burdened his shoulders, causing him to stumble. Perhaps he wished to regain his composure at the very moment he was seeking to reestablish contact with the women of the city. Perhaps he wished to grant a final respite to his confused state of mind. The day was already drawing to a close, and the sultry weather had brought out myriads of large insects and other winged creatures that the hawks were hunting as they cleaved the darkening sky in long swooping, zigzag flights. Having approached to within a mere stone's throw of the assembled women, Soumazeu suddenly interrupted his forward movement, planted himself firmly by spreading his legs like an gymnast preparing to execute a maneuver that required both strength and skill, flung his head back, raised his clasped hands at arm's length, pointed them heavenward, and began to swivel his whole upper body, from right to left at first and then from left to right. This went on for several long minutes until a sharp explosion resounded, although it did not take the crowd by surprise; a dark shadow simultane-

301

ously shot through the air like an arrow before crashing at Soumazeu's feet on the coarse-grained gravel of the main thoroughfare.

"Look at the cruelty and insensitiveness of these people," the crowd observed in a muted murmur. "He lets the epidemic decimate our children, he reduces our young people to slavery, he sees us being tormented by the cruelest pangs of grief, and what is he doing all this time? He plays at killing innocent creatures he doesn't even plan to eat. There in a nutshell is the cruelty and inhumanity of these people. Just wait a few minutes, and he will be preaching brotherly love and compassion for the weak."

However, Soumazeu, having reassumed his grotesque firing position, brought down three more hawks one after the other, completely oblivious to the disgust and indignation provoked by this unnecessary carnage. One of the mutinous prisoners from the Catholic mission declared in a muffled voice: "Band of savages, now you know what is waiting for you if you dare make another move! That, if you haven't understood it already, is the message Soumazeu was in the process of communicating to you. I wouldn't let that arrogant foreigner have his way, if I were a man."

More deaf than ever to the misgivings of the crowd that was watching him, Van den Rietter shot down yet two more hawks.

"Lie down with your face in the dust, you band of monkeys!" cried out the same woman. "Oh, if I were only a man! Not a man with nothing between his legs, like those around here, but a real man, a man who has something down there."

At this point, the people of Ekoumdoum had the good fortune to be present at the scene of a true miracle, an event the inhabitants of the city had been awaiting for years, for centuries perhaps, without daring to admit it to themselves, as the women were to confess between sobs during the triumphal pandemonium that broke out later. Never had anyone seen such an insignificant gesture produce so much emotion in the soul of a people, or etch itself so profoundly in their minds, or change their collective personality so dramatically. To be sure, Ngwane-Eligui the Younger's first unauthorized departure from the Forest of the

302

Chimpanzees and her stroll through the city—more
serene and mockingly disrespectful than an open
challenge—had filled us with a dread that proved, oh,
so justified. By revealing to us the abyss of our own
impotence, the abhorrent murders of Ezadzomo and
Ezabiemeu had cast us into the throes of despair. As
for the exploit of George Mor-Kinda, known to his
friends as Jo The Juggler, it reverberated in our
hearts like a signal for the birth of a marvelous new
era, like the final oar stroke which sends a little
skiff unto the shore of the promised land after such a
long sea journey that we had forgotten the year when
our ship had first been outfitted.

Standing not far from the fortress in the midst
of the women, Jo The Juggler had not failed to observe
Van den Rietter's every gesture since the moment he
had first been seen descending from the upper city
toward the road. He had watched him closely as he
planted himself on the primitive right-of-way of the
main thouroughfare, raised his two clutched hands, and
aimed at his moving target while swivelling his upper
body from the hips. After Soumazeu's first victory,
he had listened with joy to the hostile, vindictive
remarks of his neighbors, for he shared their indignation and the harshness of their judgments. He had
seen the missionary reassume his firing stance and
bring down three more hawks, one after the other.
Humiliated and overcome with rage, he had said to
himself, "Ah, yes, so far from his own country, so far
from his brothers in Fort Negre, all alone in the
middle of an African city, in the very heart of
Africa, here is another white man on the verge of
victory. One would think they were born to win,
wherever they might be! But why do they always win?
Because they are the strongest? Not so. It is rather
because they alone have the presumptuousness necessary
for winning. Where does that presumptuousness come
from? If I have properly understood what the sapak
Evariste has so often told me about their history, it
comes from the fact that they only remember their
victories. People whose history consists only of
victories eventually, in the course of generations,
convince themselves they are being protected and
destined for victory by Heaven itself. As centuries

303

pass, the children of these people begin to believe in their own invincibility. Then, bloated with self-confidence, they charge at every opportunity, and it always succeeds.

"As for us, the sapak was right; since the arrival of the toubabs, we no longer have any history, because they stole it from us. They taught us that our history was no more than having been conquered by them. It is true; we no longer know anything about ourselves and our fathers except what the foreigners have told us; that is to say, they conquered us, period. That's all there is. Under the circumstances, we develop what the sapak calls an inferiority complex. Having been defeated once (yes, but what a struggle it must have been!), we became convinced that we would always be defeated in the future. Why has the sapak so often harrassed me with that line of questioning? Yet he knows so many things; he must know the answer. What distinguishes the master from the slave? In the end, it is all quite simple: the one is convinced that he must always win and the other that he must always lose. Well then, my good Jo, it is up to you to choose: do you want to be a lord or a slave? A lord? In that case, you have to go. Charge, old Jo, terror of the Mameluks, scourge of school complexes, bane of Gaullists and other Sandrinellis, hero of turbulent nights in Kola-Kola. Even if he is called Soumazeu, no country clodhopper is going to cut short the career of a true son of Ruben, a disciple of Hurricane-Viet."

By advancing various considerations, each more relevant than its predecessor, Jo The Juggler had, with Mor-Zamba's consent, introduced several guns and a supply of ammunition into the fortress. He returned to the house, picked up a rifle, loaded it slowly and deliberately, slipped several bullets into his pocket, and left before anyone had time to see or understand what he was doing. Calmly making his way through the crowd of women, he resolutely strode toward Van den Rietter, stopped a few centimeters from the missionary, set himself as he had seen others do, raised the gun that was clenched firmly in his two hands, and pointed it toward the sky, while the women were shrieking in terror.

304

What was the missionary's attitude, what expression dominated his face, ordinarily so imperious, when he caught sight of a small man standing next to him and preparing to fire a gun? Some people assert that he was so surprised he turned to face Jo The Juggler and even addressed a few words of encouragement and good will to him. According to others, it is true the missionary actually made a quarter turn to embrace the totality of his rival's presence at a single glance, but no more than a contemptuous glimmer of curiosity lit up the passionless expression on his face; in any case, he never opened his mouth; on the contrary, his lips remained tightly pursed, as they always were when an inhabitant of the city forgot himself to the point of daring to oppose him.

It is highly probable that no one had sufficient presence of mind to observe this by now detested individual, whom we would just as soon have seen dispatched forthwith to the devil, such was our fascination with the diminutive guerilla who had come from so far away and who was perhaps going to absolve us of doubt and redeem our cowardly past. Indeed, we probably did not even look at each other, for it is quite possible we closed our eyes at the fatal moment, like a mother or father seeing a son enter the arena and begin to test his strength against the champion from the enemy camp, just after the city had placed its last hope for saving the communal honor into his hands; the opponent is known as a ferocious, awe-inspiring man, and his reputation for invincibility alone casts a pall over the frail and gentle child, whose health cost so much care and anxiety, whose colds lasted forever, and whose leg, despite the passage of time, still creaked as the result of a childhood injury.

What we will always remember perfectly is the explosion, a single sharp report, because it stirred the city to the core of its being, returning it, in a way, to its original track, from which Van den Rietter had diverted it, at a moment when it could have been derailed completely; because it still reverberated in the depths of our soul like the murmur of an eternally gushing spring in the mysterious darkness of a cave; because it continues to buzz in our ears, which it deafened like the bracingly vigorous pulsations of rejuvenated blood; because it was followed almost immediately by another sound, an abrupt thud announcing that the bird of prey brought down by Jo The Juggler had just crashed on the coarse-grained gravel of the main thoroughfare.

Who can describe the wild scenes that followed? Is it not better to resign one's self to a simple enumeration of bare facts and gestures? Jo The Juggler was immediately carried through the city in triumph by the mutinous women from the Catholic mission; their ululations were so shrill and the words they uttered so impassioned and ecstatic that they seemed to be expressing the quintessence of frenzied delirium. Except for the Forest of the Chimpanzees, the entire city spontaneously poured into the main thoroughfare; those who were at that moment in the upper city surged toward the neighborhood of the fortress like an all-devouring flood.

The men, particularly the young men, no longer hesitated to strut about side-by-side with the women, who taunted them by shouting, "Well, well, people would almost say the end of the world has come, wouldn't they? Here are slaves themselves taking it into their heads to walk upright, rather than crawling, beneath the very eyes of their master. Look at them puffing out their chests, roaring with laughter, swaggering around; people would almost think they were real men, men with something between their legs. Just look at them; they might almost make us believe they are finally determined to seize their freedom with their own hands. What are they saying? That it is true? That they only have to be put to the test? You men with sham virtues, are you asking for a test? You want a test to demonstrate once and for all that you are real men? Well then, we will call your bluff! There is your test, just a few steps away; your test is this long-bearded foreigner who just yesterday was making you toil in his fields as if he had deprived you of your virility. So we are calling your bluff. There is your test. What do you say? That you have not crossed the river and toiled in his fields and plantations since the second day of our rebellion? That is not enough. If you are really men, go and

306

snatch that popgun out of his hands. Go ahead, go
ahead.... Don't forget, we are watching you. Today
is the day when all doubt about the true nature of
your sex will finally be resolved."

After Jo The Juggler's exploit, Soumazeu had not
made the least effort to withdraw, as everyone
expected him to do; motionless, he gazed pensively at
the frenzied crowd, as a teacher might have done in
the presence of boisterous pupils yelling for no good
reason in the schoolyard. The adolescents had been
touched to the quick, so to speak, by the exhortations
of the women, and they had soon surrounded the missionary, speaking to him at first in a quite reasonable fashion.

"For a long time we have been working on your
projects, mainly at your cocoa plantation," they
declared to him. "We would like you to pay us for our
labor in hard cash, right now. Don't you know that
all work requires a salary since independence, brought
by Abena, came to the city of Ekoumdoum, our noble
city? But why do you remain silent? Why don't you
answer us? Are you dismissing our request as being
without merit, or do you consider it justified, and,
if so, are you going to grant it? You are not
answering us; you never answered us; you never wanted
to consider us as human beings. In your eyes, we are
monkeys, aren't we? Well then, why don't you also go
preach the gospel to marmosets and orangutans in the
jungle?"

"Let him give you his gun," shouted the sapak
suddenly, for, on the advice of Ngwane-Eligui the
Younger, he had mingled with the young people. "Let
him give you his gun, if he doesn't have the means to
pay you."

"That's it," echoed the young people. "At least
give us your gun, and we will consider your debt paid
in full. Give us your gun, or you will have independence to deal with."

The youthful mob was now dancing a rowdy saraband
around the missionary, but the violent intensity of
the performers, the aggressive solemnity of their
gestures, the progressive exacerbation of their
demands, the steadily increasing volume of their
voices, the enthusiasm of the applause they received

307

from the spectators—everything belied this apparent jocundity. Besides, the circle tightened around Van den Rietter, who remained more imperturbable than ever. Casting defiant glances at yesterday's master and brandishing their fists beneath his chin, the older ones seemed to be aware that they were engaging in a sacreligious game of profanation.

Without having made the slightest defensive gesture, Soumazeu soon found himself caught in the ebb and flow of a scuffle started by the youngest and smallest of his inquisitors, like a stately oak whose trunk is being shaken and whose uppermost branches made to tremble by the irregular blows of an anonymous axe. It was at this moment that Mor-Zamba rose to the full height of his stature, commanding all the authority of a mysterious, almost legendary reputation that was being spread a bit further with each passing hour by the stories, albeit still somewhat reserved, of rare survivors from the olden days, of those who had witnessed the arrival of the wandering child. The sapak began to speak, addressing himself in the following terms, not to a companion, but to a referee, a judge, a master: "There you have it: you know very well that these young people are accusing the missionary of making them work without a salary. For that reason, they demand to be paid in hard cash, immediately. It is logical, no? Very well, note that they will consider their former boss's debt paid in full, if he hands over his popgun to them. That is what they have said."

As if touched by a miraculous act of grace, Van den Rietter had shed his arrogance upon seeing Mor-Zamba; he had no intention of disputing the advantage of the giant's position or even calling it into question; he simply resigned himself to the humiliation of having to engage in vital negotiations with a stranger in his own fiefdom of Ekoumdoum, as if someone had just notified him of his own downfall. It was finally agreed by the two adults that the gun would be given to the adolescents as a sort of toy (that is to say, without ammunition) and that the young people would then cease their harrassment of Van den Rietter. Soumazeu thus removed the revolver from his pocket and entrusted it to Mor-Zamba, and he handed it to the

sapak Evariste, who was immediately besieged by a
shoving throng of the city's young people, consumed
with curiosity.

Jo The Juggler's triumphal procession had been
cut short at his own request, and when he arrived back
on the scene, Van den Rietter, who had been liberated
from the rabble, was walking away side-by-side with
Mor-Zamba, who towered head and shoulders above him
and appeared to be protecting him; they were conversing with a discretion that seemed cordial in a
way.

"What does this mean?" said the former rogue,
pointing his forefinger toward Mor-Zamba and Van den
Rietter. "You, can you tell me what this means? The
Bumpkin fraternizing with a toubab who nearly killed
me with a twist of the testicles?"

"Don't get upset, Jo," the sapak answered him.
"He is walking part way home with him like that,
because the other fellow had a bad case of nerves; our
friends over there jostled him around a little while
ago and took this away from him; look at it, Jo—not
bad, is it? Do you realize what you have just done,
Jo? But if your first shot hadn't been successful?
Because that is what did it, you know? It was either
the first shot or disaster, no matter what you did
afterwards. It is true, that is what counts with
these people: you needed at all costs to have Heaven
on your side. And the best way of demonstrating that
was for you to hit the bull's eye on your first shot.
Whew! But you did hit the bull's eye with your first
shot; that is the important thing. What got into you,
Jo? What sort of a bug could have bitten you?"

"Jo, do you remember me?" said one among the
hundreds of wide-eyed adolescents who had gathered
around them.

"No, my good fellow," replied Jo The Juggler,
"remind me who you are."

"The day you arrived, when you were still wearing
a long robe, like a Hausa, do you remember? Well,
shortly before you reached the outskirts of the city,
you ran across a group of young people, say about a
dozen. You stopped, no doubt to speak to us, but we
quickly ducked out of sight. You must have taken us
for real savages, didn't you? Well, we were going

poaching on lands reserved for the Chief, and we
didn't want anyone to know about it. What is incredible is that from now on we are free to hunt wherever
we please. That is true, isn't it?"

"I am absolutely convinced of it," replied Jo The
Juggler without hesitation. "That will all be confirmed for you by the new Chief, but it is as good as
officially declared."

"From this day forward we are your soldiers to
command," continued the adolescent, "yours and
Abena's. Tell us to do anything, and we will do it
immediately."

At this very moment, Ngwane-Eligui the Younger
slipped in beside Jo The Juggler, took him by the
hand, and led him a short distance away from the
crowd.

"I am going to the Palace with the rebels from
the Catholic mission," she whispered to him in confidence, speaking almost directly into his ear.

"What are you going to do there at this late
hour?" the Kola-Kolan asked in a worried tone of
voice.

"All of us have an old score to settle with that
brute of a Zoabekwe, who beat us so often that each of
us still bears the traces of his bullwhip on our own
bodies. Well, we are going to get even with him, and
no one can stop us. This is the best time for what we
want to do to him; it is now or never."

"We will come and help you; wait until we get
ready," beseeched Jo The Juggler.

"Out of the question! We are certainly old
enough to settle our affairs all by ourselves."

"Look here, you are all crazy; he is stronger
than all of you together. He is going to hit you with
a fist like a club; he will mow down ten of you with
each blow."

"You don't know anything; you are nothing but an
uncouth brute, like all men. If you want to bet, you
only have to say so, and you can listen to him, from a
distance of course; it won't be long before he is
braying with pain; each of us has taken an oath to
give him several lashes on the back with his own
bullwhip. However, there might be ample reason for
you to find other ways of amusing yourself. For

310

example by making a brief excursion in the direction of the presbytery. I seem to recall someone up there taking a few liberties with your testicles one night. But after all, it is your business if you think people who do things like that have any right to sleep on a night like this. As for us, we have been waiting months, and in some cases years, for this moment."

"In our case, it is the guns we are interested in. Our mission is to take charge of the guns."

"Count on me to bring you back all the guns from the Palace. Farewell."

The young people of the city had been waiting respectfully for Jo The Juggler, and when he returned to their midst, he suddenly flared up and announced to them: "You fellows want to be soldiers, eh? We will soon see about that. Now then, arm yourselves with machetes, for you are going to engage in your first battle at the presbytery, right away! We have to gain possession of the missionaries' guns. Remember this: it is a question of life or death."

"This evening?" the sapak asked.

"I said immediately," replied Jo The Juggler.

"All right, but the big dog, what are we going to do about that enormous beast?" continued the sapak. "Are you going to knock him on the head as soon as we arrive? But if you do that, you will be sounding the alarm for the two toubabs, won't you?"

"The dog?" several young men from the city said in unison. "There is no longer any dog; he died a few weeks ago. People think he was bitten by a wild animal, perhaps a snake."

"Well, well, that changes everything," exclaimed the sapak Evariste.

"General muster at this very spot in ten minutes!" ordered Jo The Juggler.

He led the sapak back to the fortress and furnished him with a rifle. "This gun isn't loaded," he confided in him. "Thus, you have nothing to fear; it will be enough simply to display it, but give me the revolver, because this sort of toy can be very dangerous."

"Tell me, had you been drinking a little while ago?" the sapak asked with an extremely worried look on his face.

311

"What has gotten into you?" replied Jo The Juggler. "Do you really think this is the best time for joking around?"

"Had you been drinking? I am not joking around."

"No, I had not been drinking, but I was drunk nevertheless, and it was your fault. You were the one who made me drunk the day we returned, or the day after that (it doesn't make any difference), for you were the one who called me Sandrinelli's slave. Well, you see, I am in the process of proving to you that I am not Sandrinelli's slave. And just wait--what happened a little while ago was only a beginning; for the sequel, just open your eyes and open them wide, you little scamp. Now the toubabs are in for a surprise, they are. So they wanted to make a slave of old Jo? Well, scamp, we shall see about that."

It is true that he too had a unique opportunity for carrying out his revenge! For example, there was the absence of Mor-Zamba, whom it was better to leave in the dark, because he could create a scandal by doing his utmost to halt the operation, whereas under the present circumstances, he, Jo The Juggler, would finally be able to execute the plan he had conceived eight months earlier for an assault on the Forest of the Chimpanzees, although a series of unfortunate events at that time had obliged him to shelve it hurriedly somewhere in the depths of his memory; with a few minor changes, however, it could easily be readopted for an attack on the presbytery.

Moreover, everything went quite smoothly, and the first great military victory of the Rubenist commando group was an absolutely flawless one--a true Battle of Austerlitz, as the sapak Evariste claims these days. Unless they had received explicit orders to be in the mission compound at such a late hour, the employees habitually spent the evening with their families or friends in the little settlements scattered throughout the diocese; they invariably refrained from coming to bother the missionaries after nightfall. As a consequence, Jo The Juggler's troops were able to carry out their leader's instructions in full, occupying the missionaries' fine residence without encountering a living soul and concealing themselves among the shadows.

The scouts' report confirmed all the suppositions of Jo The Juggler and the strategists on his general staff; the two missionaries were in the process of eating dinner; the houseboy brought in the various dishes one after the other, crossing a porch illuminated by a single electric light bulb without a shade, entering the dining room, and setting the food on the table in front of the missionaries as they requested it. The cook had put out the fire in his stove and was proceeding to the final stages of cleaning and tidying up before leaving the presbytery. That is precisely what he did after about ten minutes, and Jo The Juggler allowed him to walk slowly away, whistling to himself like a man who is perfectly satisfied with his condition in life.

As arranged in advance, Jo The Juggler fired a shot into the air, and a mass of assailants poured into the dining room, the hallways, and the adjacent rooms. Two groups of machete-wielding men had just taken the two missionaries into custody when Sandrinelli's former servant leaped into the dining room and pointed the rifle in his right hand and the revolver in his left toward the two Europeans.

"Nobody move!" he thundered, rolling his eyes in a grotesque fashion and speaking French, because people had told him that Brother Nicholas, despite a show of good will, understood the language spoken at Ekoumdoum only very imperfectly.

"What is it?" stammered that very Brother Nicholas as he stood up and raised his hands in the air. "What do you want from us?"

"I didn't say, 'hands up,'" Jo The Juggler thundered again, rolling his eyes more than ever. "I said, 'nobody move!' Sit down, fatso!"

At that moment, the commando group, led by the sapak and charged with taking the houseboy prisoner in the kitchen, entered the dining room, pushing a poor young boy, bewildered and trembling, in front of them.

"And now," continued Jo The Juggler in a tone of voice so ferocious it sent Brother Nicholas into an ludicrous state of panic, "and now tell your houseboy to go get the guns, all the guns, and bring them here."

When, despite the mute entreaty of his fellow

countryman, Van den Rietter hesitated, peering vacantly at the former delinquent as if tempted to play the card of dull-wittedness or even stupidity, Jo The Juggler fired his revolver into the ceiling above the two missionaries, startling the young boy as well as Brother Nicholas and producing a shower of plaster shards that splattered across the table cloth and the food. Brother Nicholas turned an anguished face toward his countryman, who finally articulated the following words, almost in a whisper: "Go ahead, Edward, go get the guns; you know quite well...."

Frightened and desperate, Edward opened his mouth several times without being able to utter a single sound and then left the room in the company of the commando group directed by the sapak with a technical proficiency that was an object of admiration for the general-in-chief himself. A few minutes later, the young boy, still closely guarded by the sapak's commando group, returned with the guns and placed them on the table in the middle of place settings, platters of meat, bowls of vegetables, and bottles of wine. At the very same moment, there was a great commotion in the courtyard; by the light of the unshaded bulb on the porch, Mor-Zamba could be seen cleaving the densely-packed rows of adolescents armed with machetes and entering the dining room, completely out of breath, no doubt as a result of calling to Mor-Kinda.

"Jo, Jo, Jo," he repeated. "Jo, you are out of your mind! I beg you to stop, wait. Jo, I beseech you. Ah, I have apparently arrived in time. Jo, I beg you...."

"Shut up, Bumpkin, you make me tired!" Jo The Juggler interrupted him curtly. "Don't get involved in this; we will settle our accounts later. Evariste, our list of guns, does it tally?"

The sapak calmly proceeded to inventory the guns and then nodded affirmatively in the direction of Jo The Juggler.

"Perfect, my good fellows. Mission accomplished. Time to withdraw."

"Father," exclaimed Brother Nicholas in a plaintive tone of voice, addressing himself to his countryman. "Father, make them swear they will guarantee our safety from now on. Hey, you people, do you acknowledge that you are responsible for our safety from now on?"

"And what about Jesus Christ?" mocked Jo The Juggler. "Doesn't he want to do anything for you anymore?"

"Father," moaned Brother Nicholas, "make them swear...."

"Don't worry, Brother Nicholas, I have already had occasion to speak about it with that fellow, the big one, who appears to be their leader."

"Don't panic, fatso," sneered Jo The Juggler derisively. "We won't even touch your testicles; we are not like you people. Farewell, and don't let our little visit ruin your appetite, you lucky stiffs; always well supplied, aren't you? Jesus Christ probably. It is a pity he isn't quite so generous with the rest of us."

## CHAPTER 5

Yet it had almost immediately been necessary for us to awaken from that delirious night and devote ourselves to the futile task of retrospectively separating dream from reality. Even the longest palavers with other participants in the events could not suffice to reassure the protagonists about the lucidity of their own perceptions. This was why Jo The Juggler so often had a fixed stare in his eyes the next morning at the infirmary, to the extent that Ngwane-Eligui the Younger and the sapak Evariste were frequently obliged to interrupt what they were saying or doing to lean over the previous night's original hero. "Are you sure you are feeling all right, Jo?" one or the other of them would ask him somberly.

"You are getting on my nerves!" he inevitably replied. "I am feeling perfectly all right; only, I can't help thinking about everything people are saying."

"I can't either, but I don't believe a word of it," said the sapak Evariste, going him one better and turning toward Ngwane—Eligui the Younger. "In the first plae, what could you possibly have done to overpower such a brutal, strapping fellow? They say you surprised him, all well and good! The giant was attacked from every side by dwarfs: while five or six of you were grinding his testicles (a refined mode of torture, the techniques of which are obviously known to women as well as missionaries), another five or six took it upon themselves to bite him in the calves, the buttocks, the arms, the thighs—I can see it from

316

here—and the bulk of the company set about knocking him down, holding him on the ground, and tying up his arms and legs; up to that point, I don't have any problem—I am a rather open-minded fellow—yet all of you should have black eyes, bruises, perhaps even broken arms, but you, Ngwane-Eligui the Younger, you don't show the slightest trace of having been in a fight; you must have been content to supervise the operation. But after that? People say you calmly carried him into a rather large open space (a court-yard or a banquet hall, it doesn't matter) so the largest possible number of people could witness the punishment by whiplash. Then you tore off the last rags that were covering his body. It is at this point that I no longer believe what they are saying."

"Why not?" asked Ngwane-Eligui the Younger.

"When confronted by such a violent outburst of cruelty, no one intervened?"

"Poor Nouredine!" replied Ngwane-Eligui the Younger. "How inexperienced you are! You still have many things to learn, no question about it. That is why you have to do more than read books. How often have you yourself encountered people foolhardy enough to intervene between a torturer and his victim? It is easy to see that you have seldom been a victim, or a torturer either, for that matter."

"In this way, each woman stepped forward to administer her share of lashes with the bullwhip."

"Of course! And then?"

"And then he cried out in pain."

"Not even that! He wept bitterly; he blubbered like a little boy being severely thrashed by a stronger playmate. No dignity at all. He could at least have cursed and vented his spleen. Not even that. He begged for mercy."

"And now he is lying down, his back covered with welts."

"Covered with welts, that's it exactly."

"He will never again dare show his face in front of people!"

"My word, that is his problem; you can always go and ask him."

"But what about the guns?" asked Jo The Juggler, starting like a man who has just woken up.

317

"We have them," the young woman replied. "We will give them to you in a little while. Be patient."

"And what are you going to do now?" the sapak went on.

"Be patient, Nouredine, it won't be long before you know."

When the sun was at its zenith, the rebels from the Catholic mission, having taken the town crier's place and added the two hunting rifles from the Palace to the usual accoutrements of the job, began criss-crossing the city to give notice that everyone was invited to the covered grandstand at the stadium on the next day, Sunday, when the great women's confession would begin.

"What is this business about a women's confession? And why are they carrying guns to announce it?" the sapak wanted to know.

"Be patient, Nouredine, you will learn all about it tomorrow," the young woman answered.

"Even so, it is odd that women are the ones behind this revolution," the sapak concluded.

Only late in the afternoon did Mor-Zamba appear at the infirmary. "Jo, I have to speak with you," he said in an abrupt tone of voice. "Let's step outside for a moment with Ngwane-Eligui the Younger, if she would be so kind."

"It doesn't make any difference to me," said the young woman. "Settle your men's affairs among yourselves, like we settle our women's affairs among ourselves."

"Be reasonable, I am asking you as a favor," Mor-Zamba pleaded.

"In that case...," replied the young woman, following the two men and the sapak.

"In this city," Mor-Zamba began, addressing himself in particular to Jo The Juggler, "the true custodians of ancestral authority are the old men, those who are collectively known as the council of elders. I have been holding discussions with them all day long. The elders want us to give the Whites back their guns. According to them, the Whites don't mean us any harm, but they cannot get along without their guns."

"And what do you yourself think about it,

Bumpkin? Tell us the essence of your thinking: do they or do they not mean us any harm?"

"Jo, listen to me carefully; it doesn't make any difference what I think. At this moment, I am satisfied to serve as a spokesman for the elders."

"Is that how you conceive of your role as Chief?"

"As a matter of fact, that is it exactly, if you care to know."

"Well then, you surprise me a great deal, old man. Now you listen carefully to me: about eight months ago, the sapak and I nearly got ourselves killed here; we owed our salvation to this little woman, no more than a child really, and to her alone. Were the elders also the custodians of ancestral authority at that point in time? If they were, what did they do to rescue us from the secret dungeons and from the beatings inflicted on us by the brutes from the Palace?"

"Yes, it is true, Zoabekwe did terrorize the city," Mor-Zamba conceded.

"And who helped him terrorize the city?"

"Listen, Jo, this is not the time to talk about it."

"Answer me, Bumpkin, I am asking you as a favor; I want to know the essence of your thinking. No doubt these two children would too. It seems the two Whites didn't mean us any harm, and yet they helped a robber baron terrorize the city, kill its children, and I will spare you the rest. Ah, ancestral authority in Ekoumdoum is a fine thing indeed, if the elders are its true custodians. You are free to negotiate your power with the old buzzards, but as for me, there is one thing I will never put in their hands, and that is the guns we obtained by conquest, following the orders of Hurricane-Viet."

"Can I say a word?" interjected the sapak Evariste. "After all, I contributed something to the conquest of those guns. Why not make a deal for their return? What would they give us in exchange? I read in a book that everything is negociable in the field of diplomacy, as long as the value of what is being offered equals the value of what one expects to receive. What are they offering us?"

"Nothing is equal to the value of those guns!"

Jo The Juggler declared categorically. "When it comes to those guns, as I was saying yesterday evening, it is a matter of life or death."

"You are flaring up, Jo, you are flaring up and not even listening to me," said the sapak, growing angry. "Isn't the departure of the Whites also a matter of life or death? If Sandrinelli and all his pals suddenly left, you can imagine how quickly the atmosphere at Fort Negre would change. Have you ever thought about it? Otherwise, they are going to stay in the end. And you know they always do the same thing to us again: they will discover some new scheme for reducing us to slavery."

"What you are saying there is not such a bad idea, you little scamp, not such of a bad idea at all. Well then, Bumpkin, suggest the following deal to the old buzzards: we give back the guns, and the Whites clear out."

"You are completely out of your mind!" protested Mor-Zamba.

"All right then, no guns!" exclaimed the two younger Rubenists in unison.

"It is just as I thought," muttered Mor-Zamba. "You are in league against me, and you are treating me as if I were not one of you. It has nearly come to the point where you will soon be accusing me of being a traitor."

"What are you talking about?" said the sapak. "You ought to be paid for knowing these people better than anyone else. You know perfectly well that, as long as they stay here and remain in possession of their guns, it doesn't make any difference what they promise today; they will inevitably reestablish their domination in the long run."

"I will suggest your proposal to the elders in any case; of course, they will not endorse it. If by any chance they do agree to it even so, you will give up the guns, won't you? That much is certain."

"Absolutely certain!" chorused Jo The Juggler and Evariste in reply.

"Curious fellow, that friend of yours!" Ngwane-Eligui sighed after Mor-Zamba had moved away. "If I had thought he had that kind of mentality.... What will he say tomorrow if the elders decide that

320

Zoabekwe's wives and those of his father must be returned to their former masters? And you? After all is said and done, how would you respond to such a situation? Would you suggest that those two make themselves scarce in exchange for the return of their women? Are you really thinking about giving the Whites back their guns? Are you serious?"

"Oh, no," replied the sapak and Jo The Juggler at the same moment. "We took too many pains to get hold of them. Such things only happen once in a lifetime."

"The Simsimabayane of Tambona was certainly a likeable chap, but what a dishrag he has made of Mor-Zamba, the lion of Kola-Kola," declared the sapak.

"That is what you think!" Jo The Juggler replied. "He has always been like that, but people seldom noticed it in Kola-Kola, because down there he was obliged to roar and fight tooth and nail if he wanted to survive. Things are so different here."

"I like both of you very much," admitted the young woman, throwing her arms around their necks and hugging them, one after the other. "You, at least you are unwilling to compromise. Come see the women's confession tomorrow; you will like it, word of Allah!"

The women's confession, a blasphemous public ritual conceived by quasi-satanical sensibilities, served as the occasion for Ngwane-Eligui the Younger and her sisters to show that they were not only unwilling to compromise, but passionately committed as well. They had rehearsed a liturgy, the most striking features of which had apparently been designed to dazzle the minds and stir the emotions of the spectators scattered throughout the grandstand on makeshift seats, although the rows became more and more densely packed, more and more crowded, as the day wore on.

Next to an official table where three solemn women sat facing the audience, there was another, smaller one a short distance away; seated behind it was a young school teacher from the mission, notebook at hand, inkstand and penholder within reach.

"Come to order!" one of the three women suddenly articulated in French, the one who, sitting between the two others, was no doubt going to serve as presiding judge.

It was not long before silence reigned.

321

"Who wants to begin?" the presiding judge asked at this point, her crossed arms resting on the table.

"I do!" shouted a very young woman seated among the spectators, as she raised her hand at first and then abruptly stood up.

"Come forward," ordered the presiding judge.

As in a well-orchestrated performance, the young woman came forward without betraying the slightest sign of emotion, and when she reached an open space laid out between the judges and the public, the official spokeswoman told her in an imperative tone of voice: "Turn around and face the people. And now tell us your name, slowly, very slowly so the clerk can record it in his book."

The young woman, who seemed more and more to be acting out a role rehearsed in advance, slowly pronounced her name as well as that of her father, according to the traditional way of defining one's identity during the reign of the former chief.

"What place do you come from?" asked the presiding judge.

"From the territory of Mackenzieville, like many of the others among us. That is where the procurers of the former chief came to buy me from my parents before bringing me to this place."

"Within a few months of your arrival here, you rebelled."

"Yes, I rebelled."

"Why?"

"Because I want to be the wife of a young man, a man whom I desire each day on account of his charm and the strength of his body, a man with whom I can take pleasure in making love. I no longer want to put up with the wrinkles of a filthy old man; I no longer want to be told what to do."

"But if they had offered you the son of the Chief, a young and vigorous man, would you have accepted him?"

"No, I would not have accepted him."

"Why not?"

"Because the husband of several wives is not a true husband to any of them. I would have had to wait weeks, months even, before a man took me in his arms. Not that there is any lack of men, quite the contrary.

I saw them around me everywhere, all the time, and their love-starved expressions tore at me like claws. I was like a bubbling spring surrounded by a fence— foresaken and inaccessible, pretty but useless—a spring regarded wistfully by a traveler whose throat is burning with thirst. It would be such a pleasure for me to satisfy his desire, but he is forbidden to come near me and bend down and refresh his lips in the coolness of my breast."

"And yet, didn't our fathers also have many women?" the presiding judge inquired.

"Our fathers had their customs, which were what they were, but we also have our customs, and they differ more and more from those of the past; such is life. I once knew a wise and skillful hunter who had successfully wielded a crossbow for many years, congratulating himself on its efficacy and proclaiming in all sincerety: 'What a marvelous device! How much I have skimmed from the woods and forests with it.' But one day he discovered a gun and learned how to use it; he brought back more game than he had ever brought back before. At this point, he abandoned the crossbow. 'It served its purpose,' he said, 'but the other one performs marvels.' Our fathers had many wives, a practice that undoubtedly served its purpose, like the crossbow, but as for us, something marvelous has appeared on the horizon, and it is quite rightly turning us away from age-old customs."

"Do you have a lover in the city?" asked the presiding judge.

"Of course I have a lover, and we had to invent the most incredible ruses to meet without giving ourselves away."

"Is he a married man?"

"Hardly, I would never have loved him in that case."

"Seeing that recent events have changed our situation, has this man expressed a desire to marry you?"

"Yes, he wants to marry me."

"What is his name? Pay attention, clerk, and write it down carefully. What is his name?"

When the young woman had revealed the name of her lover, the spectators, who until then had been con-

fused and distracted, burst into an applause that soon
turned into shouts of joy and triumph. Yet such
affairs had not actually been a secret; everyone in
the city had surmised them long ago, and it had even
become an established tradition to gloat over them.
But admitting them publicly without fear of punishment
suddenly lifted the veil from the miraculous transformation the city had just undergone, almost without
knowing it.

"You can do as you like!" the presiding judge
finally said to the young woman.

Heads turned and all eyes were upon her, when,
lively as ever, she went over and sat down next to a
robust and equally young man, who greeted her with a
smile. Confessions followed each other all day long,
putting the majority of the rebels from the Catholic
mission on stage; for the most part, they were very
young wives of the old chief, and they had rebelled
during the first few months of their stay in the
Forest of the Chimpanzees.

But all the confessions were not to be so innocent and harmless, in a way; early in the evening,
after the three women judges had procured a hurricane
lamp to illuminate the proceedings, there appeared
before the court a rebel who was the mother of two
small children, a woman somewhat older than the
sisters who had preceded her. Replying to a question
from the presiding judge, she disclosed: "As soon as
I refused their demands and even before I sought
refuge at the Catholic mission, they took my children
away from me; another mother has been caring for them
during the long months that have gone by since then.
However, I found my children again on the very first
day of the insurrection."

"Were these children engendered by the old chief,
your putative husband?"

"Absolutely not."

"How can you be so positive? How can you know?"

"He is too old; he never even entered me! How
could he have made me pregnant? His cock is always at
rest, dead so to speak; it is no more than one wrinkle
among thousands of others. How could he beget
children?"

"Well then, do you know who is the father of your

324

children?"

"I know perfectly well who he is; for that matter, you only have to look at them and then look at their real father."

"Tell us his name."

Although public opinion in the city suspected such things, this revelation too gave rise to enthusiastic applause, exclamations of pity, and cries of joy.

Appearing before the court immediately after the preceding witness and speaking along the same lines, another young woman, also the mother of children, bluntly raised the ante: "I don't believe age alone is involved when it comes to the old chief's inability to father children. I don't even think age has anything to do with it."

"What are you trying to say?" asked the presiding judge. "Explain yourself."

"Well, he is sterile. He has always been sterile, that man. It certainly didn't start yesterday."

"Sterile, what does that mean?" asked the presiding judge.

"Well, it means that even long ago, when his cock could stand up straight and tall, that fellow was still incapable of fathering children. In his very seed, there was some flaw. I myself don't know the details, but perhaps a doctor could explain it. Besides, I heard it from another wife of the old chief; she is much older than I am and knows more about such matters. Her own children are almost fully grown now. Well, do you know what she told me? That they weren't really the old man's children."

This crushing disclosure was tumultuously hailed by an audience whose responses varied from outraged amazement, hoots of vengence appeased, and youthfully triumphant, ringing laughter to rumblings of doubt and shame. The tempest was in proportion to the magnitude of the event; it was the first real revelation of this public confession, but what a revelation!

A man in the audience stood up and shouted, "Can this be the truth? If so, all the children of this stranger would actually be the genuine offspring of our city, the noble descendents of our ancestors? Is it possible that, in attempting to subjugate us, this man contributed to our prosperity? We want the truth. Let us be told the name of the mother whose children are almost fully grown, the woman who has just been mentioned here. Let her be summoned immediately to appear before this court."

Unfortunately, it was late, and after discussing the matter, actors and spectators agreed to meet again on the following day after work, that is to say early in the evening.

Thus it was, and during the course of this new session people heard and discussed two long testimonials, each more unimpeachable than the other; reinforced by suddenly discovered resemblances between the children of the old chief and certain local residents, some of whom had, to be sure, died in the meantime, these testimonials removed all doubt from the minds of even the most sceptical individuals.

From this point on the confessions followed each other at the rate of two per working day and no more than ten on Sundays; they were longer now, because they were being made by women who had more experience with the role of an old tyrant's wife. Other events, even when they were extremely important, seemed to take place behind the scenes of this scandalous drama in which traditional authority, doomed to an apparently irrevocable death, was gradually being dismantled. People became so obsessed with the whole business that, after a few days of absolute chaos, the city once again split into two camps, although along quite different lines this time. The first formed spontaneously and without prior consultation behind the two younger Rubenists; it included Ngwane-Eligui the Younger and the mutinous wives from the Catholic mission, the young people who had comprised Van den Rietter's free labor force, most of the Bedridden Chimpanzee's and The Bastard's wives, all the mothers of young children, as well as many widows, representing a variety of age-groups and acting out of solidarity with Ngwane-Eligui the Elder, the venerable mother of Abena, since the guerillas claimed to be his partisans. The second camp was a small minority, to tell the truth; it included above all the council of elders and its clients, recruited primarily from the satellite clans on the plateau, as well as the mis-

326

sionaries who, although they no longer dared show
themselves in public, secretly encouraged the elders
to resist what they regarded as an act of madness by
women and young people who had been led astray by
British agents. Like all those who had been serving
Zoabekwe's reign of terror, the accordionist and his
followers went into hiding among the satellite clans
on the plateau or in the thatched huts and abandoned
buildings near the Catholic mission, but their secret
emissaries frequently came to assure the elders of
their support, hoping in this manner to escape the
punishment they deserved for their participation in
the murder of Ezadzomo and Ezabiemeu.

It was in vain that Mor-Zamba strove to serve as
a bridge between the two camps.

"The council of elders is right," he said imploringly. "We have to give the Whites back their
guns, unconditionally. As long as you continue to
hold them, the entire city will want to emulate your
attitude of defiance toward the prerogatives of age
and traditional authority; disorder and lack of discipline will persist. Perhaps blood will even be
spilled. There can be no solution to anything until
these disorders cease."

"Ah, is that it?" exclaimed the two younger
Rubenists. "Now you are speaking the language of
Sandrinelli and The Sot. Restore order first, and
then we talk...maybe. Aren't you ashamed of yourself,
Bumpkin? Well, let the Whites leave first, and then
you will see order returning all by itself, as if by
magic. Otherwise, Bumpkin, as long as the Whites are
here, do you know what order is called? Slavery,
that's what it is!"

"Listen, comrades, you have to understand the
elders. They are old and tired; we have to humor
them. Everything frightens them. For example, this
endless confession of women is incomprehensible. What
exactly do they want?"

"If the elders and the Whites had given them the
opportunity to air their grievances before impartial
judges, there would be no women's confession at this
moment. The women are in the process of judging their
old husband (a repulsive, vicious, despicable character) because neither the Whites nor the Elders ever

327

dared judge him themselves."

About this time Christmas arrived. Van den Rietter's disappointed expectations had not diminished his arrogance in the slightest, for he desired at all costs to celebrate a midnight mass, as he had always done in past years; perhaps he was hoping this time to take advantage of the ardor kindled in people's souls and the compassion aroused in their imaginations by the birth of a child-God in a foul-smelling stable, between a braying donkey and a cow chewing its cud, to catch the participants' emotions by surprise and, in a way, recapture the allegiance they had unjustifiably withdrawn from the established authorities. The camp of dissidence and insurrection did not fail to sniff out the danger.

Massed at the back of the church and in the entryway, the mutinous women from the Catholic church and the young people who had placed themselves under Jo The Juggler's banner at first allowed the mass to proceed as usual. But during the invocation, they raised calebashes of palm wine at each tinkling of the little bell as it was being shaken by the choirboy, and, between generous draughts of the local beverage, they intoned a thunderous chant that provoked scattered peals of laughter: "This is the blood of our ancestors. Let us drink together, brothers and sisters; let their strength return and be amongst us."

During communion, as misfortune would have it, at a moment when Van den Rietter, holding the pyx with the consecrated wafers in his hands, had begun moving away from the tabernacle and toward the communion table, he missed the last cement step and fell sprawling, to the great consternation of the old women and very young children in his immediate vicinity, while the sanctified little discs carved from the martyred body of Jesus Christ rolled inauspiciously across the floor.

Learning of the incident, the people at the back of the church—they had momentarily lost interest in the Savior's Nativity and immersed themselves in the mysteries of a pagan ritual that traced its origins to the time before memory—rushed to the communion table, drawing in their wake a horde of idle bystanders, representing all ages and both sexes and eager to see

328

at first hand what extraordinary transformation was miraculously being wrought in a modest African temple on a floor strewn with consecrated wafers. Ngwane-Eligui's rebels and Jo The Juggle's youthful partisans approached as close as they could to the squatting priest, who was picking up the wafers one after the other before placing them reverently back in the pyx; they tugged on a fold of Soumazeu's alb or on the fringe of his stole, leaning over as if to whisper a secret into his ear and telling him under their breath: "Van den Rietter, this was a sign from God. It is all over now, and all you have to do is leave. You have even been repudiated by your own master, Jesus Christ. So, what remains for you to do here? Defiled from now on, your wafers are only good for pigs and those who resemble them."

The fact is that before Soumazeu's mishap, the communion table had been swarming with clusters of the faithful, conspicuous among whom were the employees of the Catholic mission and their families, but by the time the missionary had repaired the damages of his fall and was preparing to distribute communion, it had become astonishingly deserted.

Such unfavorable circumstances hardly prevented Soumazeu from wanting to deliver a sermon at the end of the mass, according to a tradition he himself had instituted. But, speaking in Van den Rietter's own terms, one might have said he was drinking his cup of bitterness to the lees and following his way of the cross to Golgotha. As he reached the foot of the pulpit and prepared to mount the bottom step, Ngwane-Eligui's mutinous women, former compulsory guests at the Catholic mission, and Jo The Juggler's adolescent partisans massed in front of him, barring his way and saying: "For too many years you have monopolized the privilege of sermonizing from the top of this plat-form. For once then, give the floor to someone else; your turn will come only at the end, if there is any time left and if the people really want to hear what you have to say."

Confronting his adversaries' aggressiveness and determination from this point forward with a new mask, comprised of humble resignation and infinite patience in the image of a holy apostle destined for martyrdom,

329

Soumazeu meekly remained standing on the spot they indicated to him. With his long beard recently turned completely white, with his bizarre, almost comical adornments, with his forlorn Mount-of-Olives expression, with the crown of thorns one was tempted to seek on his pale skull, he finally offered the disquieting spectacle (a bit late perhaps) of sublime self-sacrifice and flesh subdued through mortification—an image that would have won him the hearts of the city in perpetuity, if he had not for so many years remained content to play the role of ally to cruel and brutal tyrants.

Summoned by his partisans from libations that had nothing to do with mysticism or spirituality, Mor-Kinda arrived. Speaking extemporaneously, he was obviously improvising as he went along, with all due respect to Mor-Zamba, whose imagination has continued to fabricate conspiracies based on heaven knows what scenario concocted by the adolescents, Ngwane-Eligui's rebels, and Jo The Juggler.

This is, more or less, what Mor-Kinda said to the audience: "Van den Rietter has often told you he came here to teach you how to put sin behind you. He has often insisted that all the black man's misery comes from the fact he is living in sin and depravity. He has often assured you that a sin like slothfulness (in which, according to Van den Rietter, we Blacks take a great delight) does not exist in his country. I am convinced Soumazeu would have continued peddling these fairy tales for a long time to come, if Providence had not sent a man, one of our own, a son of Ekoumdoum, a fierce combatant who has lived in Van den Rietter's country, to tell us the truth about the countrymen of this individual whose lying remarks have often done you great harm.

"Well then, Commander Abena, the noble son of Ekoumdoum, a man who has fought on five continents, confronting tyrants and crushing them, freeing captive peoples, succoring widows and orphans, he will soon be here himself. Do not ask me to tell you precisely when he will arrive in the noble city that witnessed his birth; I would be unable to give you the exact date. For Commander Abena is a great general who does not communicate his long-range plans to lowly privates

330

in his army, to those who, like me, hardly deserve the honor of unlacing the sandal on his left foot. But when you see Commander Abena, he himself will tell you what he has told me, for I know him and have had long conversations with him.

"Commander Abena, the noble son of your illustrious city, will describe for you the horrifying vices, abominations of wickedness, that prevail in Van den Rietter's country: graft, theft, rape, murder, dishonesty, injustice, gluttony, the abandoning of children, the plotting to do away with elderly parents who stand in the way of an inheritance, the permanent state of war. In our part of the world, all these crimes are the exception; I call on you to bear witness to the fact. As far as their slothfulness is concerned, just listen: for hundreds of years, Van den Rietter's brothers came to our continent; they raided our villages and our cities; they stole our young girls; they kidnapped our young men and transported them by the thousands to America. Why did they do it? Ask Van den Rietter. They wanted to make our people toil on their plantations, just as Van den Rietter himself, under your very eyes, made the young people of Ekoumdoum toil without pay on his plantation. That is why people whose skin is the same color as ours are living in America today. The Holy Ghost did not transport them there. Their ancestors had not originally lived in that part of the world. Those Blacks came from here; they are our brothers. That is something you have never been told by Van den Rietter.

"Well then, what were Van den Rietter's own brothers doing, while our black brothers were working in their fields and their houses? They were playing cards; they were dancing with their pretty ladies; they were abandoning themselves to all sorts of debauchery. So, Father Van den Rietter, tell us where slothfulness abides. Father Van den Rietter, if you are truly concerned with saving a people from sin and depravity, then return to your own country. Your people have more need of Jesus than anyone else on earth; they are wallowing in drunkenness, gluttony, theft, idleness, and all sorts of other abominable vices, the very idea of which would not, in many cases, ever even enter the mind of an Ekoumdoumian.

331

"Does this mean I am saying that everything about our own ways is perfect? If so, I would be lying to you, as Father Van den Rietter has been lying to you during the many long years that have now come to an end. Terrible disorders are also gnawing away at us, although Father Van den Rietter has not helped us to cure them. For instance, let us consider polygamy. Old men on the edge of the grave, old men whose muscle is no more than one wrinkle among thousands of others, these old men buy up the youngest women, reducing young men to poverty. Is that just? If Christ had been given the opportunity to come as far as this place, if those people had not murdered him in the flower of his youth, would this not have been the first evil against which he might have crusaded.

"Dear brothers and sisters, my young comrade Nouredine has read extensively in countless books, and I learned from him that, when the governing of cities in other parts of the world passes out of the hands of tyrants and into those of the people, they begin by distributing the land to those who work it. In our city, a single man was hoarding the land; his case having been heard, the land becomes free again, as it had always been before Van den Rietter's brothers invaded our continent. In contrast, we will inaugurate a new era, a rebirth of freedom, by instituting a just and equitable distribution of women. Together let us swear a soleman oath that we shall never again tolerate more than one wife in the household of any man, particularly if he is an old man whose muscle is as flabby as the other wrinkles on his body. This is the gospel that Commander Abena called upon me to preach unto you.

"Together let us swear a solemn oath to oblige the new Chief to respect and even, at the appropriate moment, formally sanction the wishes expressed by women during the course of the confessional meetings that are now taking place in the large covered grandstand at the stadium. All right, then, repeat after me this phrase, coined by Commander Abena himself: one man, one woman. One man, one woman. Say it yourselves now."

"One man, one woman!" the crowd marked time. "One man, one woman! One man...."

Jo The Juggler shouted himself hoarse a while longer, bellowing his slogan and doing his best to carry the audience with him, but after the first minute of widespread enthusiasm, the facade of unanimity crumbled at a vertiginous rate, and soon there was no one left to chorus his refrain, except Ngwane-Eligui the Younger's mutinous women and his own young partisans, who were massed at the foot of the pulpit. The church had become transformed into a fairground, where a hundred vendors were simultaneously haranguing the people in their immediate vicinity, where crowds were forming and bursting apart like soap bubbles, where disoriented men and women were wandering about in search of serenity, ecstatic men and women spreading their jubilation, desperate men and women soliciting consolation.

"I was far from being in full possession of my faculties," Jo The Juggler later recounted. "That is the least one can say; nevertheless, it did not take long for me to realize that I was like the soccerer's apprentice who created situations he was subsequently unable to control."

Desiring to plumb the state of a public opinion that had been whipped up in this fashion by his homily and catching sight of an elderly woman moving from one group to another, shaking her head and apparently tormented by some horrifying perplexity, Jo The Juggler called out to her in the following manner: "Venerable grandmother, I see you have something you would like to say to this gathering. Come h e r e , closer, yes, up into the pulpit. Don't be afraid; the pulpit of a church belongs to everyone, but first and foremost to the congregation. Jesus never forbid anyone to come up into the pulpit; I know, because I have read it in books. Come up and tell us what is on your mind."

The elderly woman climbed into the pulpit, pausing motionless on each step to await Jo The Juggler's gesture of encouragement. Finally, she arrived at the top of the dais.

"My son, how can we believe," she pronounced each word slowly and distinctly, her face drawn, her mind apparently in a daze, "how can we believe that Van den Rietter has told us nothing but lies? No, my son, it is impossible that all his words were lies. Sometimes he told the truth. When he told us about the sufferings of Jesus Christ, abandoned by everyone and nailed to a cross for the salvation of mankind, I sensed... I knew he was telling the truth. Just like you, my son, when you informed us about the wanderings of our child Abena and about his going into exile to save us, I sensed you were telling the truth.

"Yet, from another point of view, it is true I have always, for many long years at least, had the feeling that Van den Rietter was also hiding something from us, that he was not telling us the whole truth. I really did suspect, deep inside myself, that there was a second messiah, a black messiah, like us. We certainly guessed it might have been our own child Abena; there was an underground rumor to that effect, but we were never sure, and our hunger remained unsatisfied. It was then I began tormenting myself with the question of why Van den Rietter refused to reveal this truth to us as well.

"My son, your remarks have finally opened my eyes; thanks to you, I now understand: a white prophet can only proclaim a white messiah; let the black messiah be proclaimed by a black prophet then. That is why we always need two prophets, and not one alone—a black prophet and a white prophet are needed so that all messiahs can be proclaimed equally. My son, I am glad you spoke from this platform today. From now on, both of you, both you and Van den Rietter, should climb into the pulpit every Sunday and, one after the other, proclaim your messiah and your part of the truth."

Caught by surprise at first, Jo The Juggler was beginning to devise some artifice to cut short these untimely jabberings, but, on the other hand, murmurs of contentment that rose in a swell from the crowd, heads bobbing in assent, and numerous unequivocal exclamations of approval soon left no doubt about the sentiments of the audience. Mor-Zamba, who had entered the church at the beginning of the elderly woman's speech, immediately began to make an ostentatious show of approval; an older woman, perhaps Ngwane-Eligui the Elder, having become apprehensive at the unexpected turn of events during the midnight

334

mass, had gone to warn him and ask him to participate in an important debate, while at the same time guaranteeing by his presence that the oratorical exchanges would be conducted in a disciplined manner.

Encouraged no doubt by Mor-Zamba, Van den Rietter climbed into the pulpit as soon as the old woman had returned to her seat, and he humbly took his place next to Jo The Juggler, who looked at him thoughtfully for a moment and said: "Father Van den Rietter, if you have a declaration you would like to make to us, well then, we are not going to be like you; we are not going to reserve the floor for ourselves; we are going to give it to you of our own accord. Go ahead, speak."

The priest had miraculously shed all his haughtiness, all his arrogance; without becoming as smooth as honey, his voice had nevertheless lost its barbs and it tendency to lacerate the ears of his listeners; his words were no longer laced with steel so as to cow the inhabitants of Ekoumdoum and fetter them with chains; instead of sweeping through the air like a hurricane or shaking the earth like an elephant's tread, his gestures bespoke peace, goodness, friendship, and all the other virtues which had been so absent from his behavior during the twenty years that had now come to an end. He assured his listeners endlessly that he would no longer be anything but the apostle of Christ and that in the future he would refrain from playing other roles, avoiding them as if they were the most unforgivable of deadly sins. "A drunkard's oath, " thought Jo The Juggler to himself.

When Mor-Zamba's turn finally came, he climbed into the pulpit and, without explicitly stating that he was the new incarnation of authority in the city (assuming it should have been fully understood long ago), he gave assurances that all the measures proposed by the women at their constituent assembly in the stadium would be ratified as soon as the missionaries' guns were returned to them. This felicitous conclusion, he insisted, now hinged only upon the good will of those who were illegally holding the guns; let them at last give concrete form to their so often proclaimed support of the women by facilitating their true and abiding liberation.

"Do you swear you will ratify the measures proposed by the women for their own liberation?" Jo The Juggler asked him.

"I swear it!" said Mor-Zamba.

"Then we will return the guns immediately," Jo The Juggler declared.

# CHAPTER 6

By December 26 the general assembly of Chief's wives had already resumed its daily sessions at the stadium grandstand. Now that almost unanimous popular approval of the rebels' cause, as well as that of all the women at the Palace for that matter, had been assured, the public confession soon turned into a festival for the betrothed. Ngwane-Eligui the Younger's rebels were extremely attractive young women, even when they were already mothers, and at the end of their testimony they invariably threw themselves into the arms of men as young and impatient as they themselves were high-spirited and imbued with seductive charms. Yet this scenario occurred less and less frequently as older and older women came before the court, initially summoned to testify about the lineage of the old tyrant's supposed children and eventually impelled by a sort of contagion to join the ranks of their younger sisters.

The men who had once loved them readily acknowledged the paternity of children stemming from their relationship, but they immediately alleged real or imagined promises contracted since that bygone era and then turned their backs on their former mistresses, or else the women themselves took the lead in laughing at their own past, proclaiming that although so-and-so had been a charming lover in those days, he would make an impossible husband today.

Each confession now revealed lineages that were more and more surprising, because they involved older and older children, whose resemblance to this or that male inhabitant of the city had once intrigued the curiosity of some perceptive observer before eventually falling into oblivion through force of habit. This development held the city in such a state of suspense and so monopolized people's attention that the missionaries' departure, arranged without Mor-Zamba's knowledge by Jo The Juggler and the sapak Evariste, passed virtually unnoticed. Spectators flocked to the confessions mainly in the hope of discovering who was the real father of Zoabekwe, that blood-thirsty traitor to his own people, and his two younger brothers, who were then studying at Oyolo and had not returned to Ekoumdoum for nearly a year. Their mother was dead, but people suspected two older women from the old tyrant's harem of being privy to all the secrets, all the mysteries, and the whole city was agog in anticipation of their testimony.

The large grandstand at the stadium was filled to overflowing with a tumultuous crowd, throbbing with excitement, but the two women were unanimous in attributing the paternity of Zoabekwe and his two brothers to another deceased individual, much to the disappointment of the spectators, who had taken great delight in imagining the embarrassment which the disclosure of this relationship would have caused both the father and a son whose hands were stained with the blood of his brothers and sisters. People consoled themselves by marveling at the extraordinary intuition of a city that early on had saddled Zoabekwe with the nickname Bastard.

The fact remains that, thanks to the general assembly of insurgent women and above all to the confessions of the old tyrant's wives, all the so-called children of the former chief took full possession of their true lineages on December 31, 1960, a symbolically appropriate date. Then, on New Year's day 1961, Mor-Zamba, satisfied that the missionaries' guns had in fact been returned to them, fulfilled his promise and organized a formal ceremony to bestow upon these individuals their new identity as full citizens of the city of Ekoumdoum, to give a new life to their mothers by officially declaring them free, and to marry forthwith those who had partners. Only one of the former chief's putative children, Zoabekwe, was

338

missing when the roll was called, for he dared not leave the Palace, where shame and fear held him prisoner. His wives were also emancipated, but in contrast to the old tyrant's wives, none of them had ever had an affair with anyone from the city. Furthermore, they could not help occasionally feeling the loss of a husband whose muscles had an unforgettable vigor and whose children bore the unmistakable mark of his paternity.

It immediately became necessary to help establish a new way of life for the women who did not desire to rush so quickly into marriage and among whom were Ngwane-Eligui the Younger, the mulattress, and those who had been unable to find a companion due to their age or lack of physical attractiveness. With the aid of Jo The Juggler and the sapak Evariste, who had succeeded in raising a modest police force recruited from their own young partisans, these women set up residence in the now abandoned buildings of the Catholic mission. However, the allocation of rooms and work spaces soon became a permanent cause of friction among them, and the young Rubenists suggested they call a general assembly, which, although its sessions lasted nearly a week, did succeed in defusing the latent crisis.

Encouraged by the favorable outcome of this initial experiment in free speech, the women convened a new general assembly for the purpose of organizing their daily round of activities. They divided themselves into groups of six, in each of which three women worked for one day in fields cultivated collectively by the group, while the three others were providing child care (if it were necessary), preparing meals, and doing other household chores. The next day this division of labor was reversed. They were free to receive any visitors they desired, for their comings and goings were not subject to regulation, unless a group voluntarily decided to impose a set of rules upon its members, who could themselves revoke such rules at any time. This form of social organization had only been adopted after lengthy debates and after the women had, at the suggestion of the two young Rubenists, accepted as a guiding principle the notion that it would be best in all matters to do

339

exactly the opposite of what had been done under the tyrannical rule of the old chief and the missionaries.

In the middle of the month of January, the old tyrant himself expired before Mor-Zamba had ever even dreamed of drawing any of his countless secrets from him.

"That was clever of you!" Jo The Juggler said to him angrily. "What a marvelous opportunity you missed there. Now, will you never know the truth about the death of the previous chief, your grandfather? Ever since you began courting the old buzzards, you have forgotten all your responsibilities, Bumpkin. Maybe you are counting on those deaf mutes from the palace guard to give you a tour someday through the buried mysteries of a repulsive regime which included them among its primary beneficiaries? Maybe you are also counting on them to help you confront any dangers the future holds? For instance, do you really think The Sot will wait a hundred years before sending Mamelukes to Ekoumdoum or some neighboring city—Mamelukes armed to the teeth with machine guns, mortars, and other pleasant little gimcracks and perhaps even commanded by someone like Brède, burning to have it out with his sworn enemies, the Rubenists? It is in the nature of government that any regime will seek to guarantee full control of its territory by establishing garrisons in the most remote parts of the country. If Baba Toura comes out on top in his struggle with Ruben's successors, that is exactly what he will do. And if he ever gets wind of what has just taken place here, you can count on him to give priority to Ekoumdoum. Well then, how do you expect to greet these charming guests? With a peace pipe like Indians in the Westerns? You know how the Indians ended up, don't you? Ask the sapak to tell you that story sometime; it is quite fascinating.

"Or are you planning to welcome them like a man—that is to say, by spraying them with a shower of bullets? Well, old man, perhaps it is time you began your preparations, because, contrary to appearances, this whole business is not coming to an end; it is only just beginning, if you ask my opinion. Furthermore, Hurricane-Viet is the one who said it, remember? Oh, la-la, to let the old Chimpanzee kick the bucket without pumping him for information...!"

"No one could get anything more out of him,"
Mor-Zamba assured him. "For I don't know how many
weeks, he hadn't even opened his mouth."

"Nonsense!" retorted Jo The Juggler. "I spoke to
him myself, and just a few days before the missionaries left, I even heard him talk. Imagine. That
being the case, don't try to put one over on me."

"Well, well, you never let me in on your little
secret," said Mor-Zamba suspiciously. "All right
then, you spoke with him just a few days before his
death; how did that come about?"

"And how do you think the two Whites finally
became convinced it was in their best interest to pack
up and leave, whereas they had until then been unwilling to entertain even the thought of it? Accompanied by the sapak, I went up there myself one
evening; old ruins don't strike superstitious fears in
us, not the two of us. It was already nearly dark,
and for that reason, very few people could have witnessed our arrival; perhaps there wasn't even a single
person there to observe us at that moment, except of
course the dauphin, who, as we had foreseen, was in
his rooms on the first floor; I had no difficulty
catching him by surprise there. I say to him, 'Take
me to your father immediately.' And he complies
without a moment's hesitation. When we arrive at the
old man's bedside, I tell The Bastard, what are you
waiting for? Your mission is done. You should have
seen the coward skulking away.

"Then, turning to the father, an old wreck, it is
true, but hardly in the throes of death and even
rather lively on that particular evening, I say to
him: 'Summon the two Whites as soon as possible; have
them come here to your quarters, and ask them to leave
town. Explain to them clearly that their continued
presence shrouds the city in a rumbling storm cloud
that threatens at any moment to unleash a whirlwind of
unimaginable destructiveness; let them leave and the
heavens of Ekoumdoum will once again be bathed in the
splendor of sunlight. As soon as I pause, he says to
me, 'Who in the world do you think you are, coming in
here and speaking to me this way?'

"I reply that I am but a simple soldier from the

341

valliant bands of Commander Abena, the man who brandishes the thunderbolt of independence in his right
hand as he moves relentlessly forward; I also tell him
that my two comrades and I were sent here by Commander
Abena himself, because he wanted us to pave the way
for his arrival in the noble city of his birth, just
as hints of dawn precede the actual rising of the sun,
and that Commander Abena himself, the noblest son of
the city of Ekoumdoum, was speaking to him through my
mouth, saying, 'Oh, Mor-Bita, Chief grown old and grey
beneath the strain of governance, it is true that
serious errors have been committed in your name, but
although there is nothing irreparable in your relationship to the noble city of Ekoumdoum, there is one
condition: settle your affairs among yourselves, like
a family, independent of any intrusion by foreigners.
No father, not even the most criminal one, has ever
been transformed into a member of a different race by
his own infamy; some venerable mystery of his nature
invariably renders him subject to the ultimate curse.
Who will ever be able to convert common blood into
something that is no longer shared, or turn night into
day, or make water refuse to conceal fish!'

"You see, Bumpkin, if you want to move people to
tears, it is really rather simple: you merely have to
lavish on them in words whatever has been denied them
by reality. Does that cost you anything? The Bedridden Chimpanzee began to express his gratitude--so
effusively, you should have seen it. He tried to
raise himself on his couch, but he immediately fell
back; he was sobbing and sniffling like a child overcome with the most intense remorse. He assured me I
had just spoken words of profound wisdom that went far
beyond my age. Finally, he said to me: 'You may go
now, my son, but be prepared to respond to my summons
tomorrow evening at about this time.' The next
evening, as a matter of fact, the sapak and I were
indeed privileged to witness his dramatic encounter
with the two toubabs; on this occasion, he demonstrated a sense of authority that I would never have
suspected in him. The two missionaries told him, 'Old
man, we are your only true safeguard. As soon as we
have turned our backs, it won't be long before your
enemies fling themselves upon you and slit your

throat.' —— 'No, that isn't the point at all,' he
replied, 'It isn't that simple; you are foreigners,
and you know nothing about the truth. You never
really wanted to know, because you only believed the
stories you yourselves invented. Well then, know the
truth at last: I was a chief whose throne rested upon
a dead body, upon the corpse of a man who ruled before
me in this city. He had been elevated to the position
by the Germans, and they had chosen him from among his
own people; that is why they accepted him so quickly....' Then, Van den Rietter asked him, 'Chief, now
tell us the whole truth: who actually killed that
man? Do you know?' —— 'Of course, I know, but since
my people have agreed to do me justice, I will explain
myself to them in these matters. I have confidence in
the man who brandishes the thunderbolt of independence
in his right hand as he moves relentlessly forward. I
will tell him the whole truth, insofar as I know it.
In the name of God, go away; let us settle our affairs
among ourselves, like a family. You were always
dividing us, and you discovered the most ingenious
ways to do it; your only joy, your sole gratification,
was seeing us scattered about like fragments of an
earthenware pot irreparably smashed in a fall. Go
away, in the name of God. We are tired of the misfortunes you have brought upon us....'"
    "Did he really say that to them? Are you sure?"
said Mor-Zamba, overwhelmed with astonishment.
    "Why would we tell you something like that if it
weren't true?" the sapak Evariste asked indignantly.
    "Look here," interjected Jo The Juggler, "were
there any words more appropriate to convince the two
old glue pots to pack up and leave? Tell us what they
are; we are listening."
    "All right, the Bedridden Chimpanzee said that,
and afterwards?" said Mor-Zamba, on the verge of being
annoyed.
    "What do you mean afterwards!" Jo The Juggler
uttered in amazement.
    "Wasn't there another act in this play?" asked
Mor-Zamba.
    "What other act?" retorted Jo The Juggler. "That
is to say, there was obviously another act. You know
it as well as I do; by the following day the two old

343

glue pots were beginning to pack their bags: that was the next act."

"But in any case, we now know the truth about the death of the previous chief!" Mor-Zamba burst out.

"What is it then?" asked Jo The Juggler.

"You just referred to it in your account of the Bedridden Chimpanzee's remarks!" Mor-Zamba exclaimed.

"Oh! Is that what you call the truth these days?" Jo The Juggler also grew indignant. "And that is really enough for you! Well, you are not very demanding. You don't care to know the name of the person who was responsible for the murder of your grandfather, or what torments they inflicted on him, or where they buried his body, if they ever even took the trouble to give him an honorable burial. These are merely sordid details; Monsieur Mor-Zamba's noble thoughts are now soaring far above the petty concerns of daily life."

"Why always come back to the past?" Mor-Zamba sighed.

"You have gone mad!" shouted the sapak. "Get hold of yourself, Bumpkin, if there is still time. Why always come back to the past! You speak about it as if it were a crime, not an indispensible task and a highly profitable exercise. Are you also going to accuse of us coming back to the past every time we mention the immortal Ruben's assasination at the hands of the Brédes and the Sandrinellis?"

"All right, all right, all right!" intervened Jo The Juggler in a conciliatory tone of voice. "The dead are indeed dead, as they say; let us leave them where they are. Burial or no burial, is the Bedridden Chimpanzee's present lot more enviable in any way than that of your grandfather? All right again. Let's forget the past for a moment and concentrate on the present. What are we going to do with the old man's heir apparent! I am of the opinion that he should be tried by a people's court and, after his inevitable conviction, shot in a public place."

"Shot in a public place!" muttered Mor-Zamba with a sudden start. "How can you mention such abominations without trembling? Anything. Anything you like, except shooting people in cold blood. Anything except that. Shooting people, no, no, no...!"

"Oh yes!" declared the sapak firmly.

"Ah, you too!" reflected Mor-Zamba with disconsolate compassion. "Evariste! A mere child! Has he completely corrupted you then?"

"Just think about it a little, Bumpkin," continued Mor-Kinda. "In the first place, The Bastard deserves to be shot a thousand times over, considering the number and atrocity of his crimes. But above all, old chap, what an extraordinary lesson! What a marvellous image to be etched in the collective memory of Ekoumdoum! A son-of-a-bitch sinking slowly to the ground, in public, toppled by bullets from a people's firing squad! A bandit struck down in front of everyone by the justice of the masses! Slaves at last masters over the tyrant and executioners of the man who had been torturing them! There is a scene that will haunt them at times and inspire them at others, generation after generation and for centuries to come. How do you think they went about it, breaking our spirit and reducing us to what we are now—wretched piles of rags? How do you think the toubabs went about it when they arrived in our part of the world, eh? You suppose they called our forefathers together, passed out a few bonbons, and then announced to them: 'We love you dearly; love us too, because we are so wonderful. But above all be sure to behave yourselves, children.'

"No, my good man, that is not how it happened. In all our cities, the old buzzards recount stories about it, stories that send a shiver down your spine; I heard dozens of them during the time I used to spend my vacations with the old men in my mother's village. It is true the toubabs called the people together—not (alas!) to pass out bonbons, but to select at random a few specimens from the local population and then slaughter them immediately without further ado, that is if they didn't bury them alive in front of the entire community. Believe me, this is how it happened and not otherwise."

"That is completely and utterly true!" the sapak Evariste added sententiously.

"Believe me, Bumpkin," Jo The Juggler went on, "this is a language that every community understands perfectly. It offers the image of a spectacle that

345

haunts the collective memory for a long, long time. Take a good look at your old buzzards in Ekoumdoum: it is not an illusion if they so often appear more dazed than normal; there is something in their expression, a fleeting glimmer of fear, you might say, the panic-stricken stare of those who saw, or believed they saw, the ultimate horror. From now on, this trump card needs to be placed in the hands of the people, so that our race in turn can stop bowing and scraping, so that it can lose its disheartening propensity to stick out its ass for others to kick. If we can do that, the sapak Evariste will no longer have to experience the torment of always seeing Whites in the role of master and Blacks as slaves. The Bastard must be shot in a public place; after that, Bumpkin, you will see calm being restored and peace once again pervading our blessed city."

"Let Zoabekwe be judged," declared Mor-Zamba after several long minutes of reflection and in an uncustomarily solemn tone of voice. "Let him even be convicted. But Zoabekwe will not be shot, George; I will do anything to save him from the firing squad. Anything, George, absolutely anything, have you understood me? I will publicly take sides against you; I will denounce your bloodthirstiness and your obsession with violence; I will conceal none of your maliciousness; I will cut the last thread of the fraternal bond that unites us. If necessary, George, I will declare war on you."

That is almost what happened two weeks later during the feverish, impassioned preparations for the trial of The Bastard and all those implicated in his crimes, or at least the ones who had resurfaced since the defeat of the tyrants. That afternoon, Jo The Juggler, who had soon begun to keep his plans secret from the former male nurse of the Colonel Leclerc forced labor camp, was as usual bustling about the building that had been permanently designated to house the dispensary. Not only the children stricken by the epidemic, but all sorts of patients were now being treated there. The former delinquent from Kola-Kola was surrounded by a large work party, and, with characteristically indefatigable loquacity, he was imperiously dispensing orders to its various members; they were his first friends from the city, the companions of the accordionist, who was himself still in hiding, and the follower of Allah had not hesitated to reduce them to the sad state of manual laborers and handymen, perhaps desiring in that way to avenge himself upon them for their betrayal.

He had not stinted their toils in fixing up the infirmary and its outbuildings. The thatched roof had been entirely redone; the walls had been raised and large openings pierced in them before they were rough-plastered and whitewashed. An odd assortment of furniture for storing things—wardrobes, dressers, and chests-of-drawers requisitioned as spoils of war from the Catholic mission and the Palace—was crowded into all four corners of the locale. Following the instructions of Jo The Juggler, who remembered a similar piece of furniture in Ericssons's infirmary at Tambona, the missionaries' carpenter, whose equipment and magical efficiency fascinated the sapak Evariste, had constructed an inclined examination table that the Kola-Kolans later covered with a sheet of polished metal they had obtained by cutting up the liners from oil drums that filled an entire shed at the Catholic mission.

At that moment Jo The Juggler had just spread out on this table a sickly, white-haired old man with a persistent cough; the man's left calf was being consumed by a sort of ulcerated sore, and a nurse's aide was gently pouring a stream of water over it. Then, armed with a tweezers appropriated from Brother Nicholas' bedroom, Jo The Juggler set about cleaning the puss-filled wound, as he darted glances devoid of civility upon an individual who, for him, seemed to symbolize the whole race of old buzzards. He was beginning to daub the afflicted leg with a tincture of methylene blue when the sapak suddenly burst into the dispensary. At first, he was puffing so hard he was quite unable to speak for a while.

"Listen here," the former schoolboy was finally able to articulate between gasps, "I know somebody who is going to be surprised; what do you want to bet?"

"I already know; I am the one who is going to be bowled over, no?" replied the rogue. "What is it now? Has something new happened?"

"The boat is back!" announced the sapak.

"What did you say?" Jo The Juggler blurted out. "The boat is back? Well, yes indeed, you damned sapak of my heart, I am completely bowled over; I am open-mouthed with admiration and gratitude. I am amazed, transported into raptures of enthusiasm; you had no idea how true your words would prove to be. Old Monadjo was able to bring back the boat all by himself then? Old Monadjo wasn't shipwrecked then? He wasn't overcome with panic when he found himself the only steersman on board? Sapak, this is the most beautiful day of our lives. This time it is really going to work; we will finally be able to get along without the Whites, seeing as Old Monadjo could bring back the boat all by himself and without the slightest mishap. Don't think for a moment I ever doubted him, I mean us. I always knew we would get there. Old Monadjo once told me, 'Don't worry about me, Jo, I have seen others do it!' From that moment on, I was convinced he could pull it off. I had confidence in him, believe me. All the same: the first time, that is quite an accomplishment even so. Damned Monadjo! That scoundrel brought the boat safely back to port. The first time, quite on accomplishment even so, all the same...."

"You talk and you talk, Jo, but you are not listening to me," the sapak Evariste finally succeeded in protesting. "That is just it, Monadjo is not the one who brought back the boat; it was Brother Nicholas, don't you see?"

"What do you mean, Brother Nicholas?" Jo The Juggler roared. "Brother Nicholas here again? No, it can't be true! Evariste, tell me it isn't true. Set my mind at rest; tell me it isn't Brother Nicholas who brought back the boat. You will never make me believe...."

"Nevertheless, it is true," sighed the sapak Evariste. "Brother Nicholas brought back the boat; that is the way it is and not otherwise. If you want to know more about it, Jo, you would do better to come down to the dock, like everyone else."

"God bless it!" stormed Jo The Juggler. "Won't we ever be rid of those people once and for all. Go on, grandpa, it is all over for today; go rest for a while now, and I will see you again in two or three days. In the meantime, no alcohol, no tobacco, no women. Do you understand? Otherwise, old man, you know what could happen? They might just be obliged to dig a little hole behind your house and plant you there like the cutting from a cassava root. Can you picture it from here? Come with me, sapak. Brother Nicholas.... Brother Nicholas.... What in the world do we have to do with Brother Nicholas? God bless it, what a curse!"

Brother Nicholas had indeed come back on the boat; by his presence and with a fixed, melancholy expression on his face, he was directing the noisy, disorganized operation of debarking the peasants who were entangled in the purchases ordered by their fellow citizens.

More densely packed together than a wall, the mob that swarmed around the dock and made access to it impossible was seething with rumors born in the excitement of the unforeseen and the curiosity that seeks to unravel mysteries, rumors that offered contradictory versions of the events which brought about the missionary's return to a city where he had left not only friends and admirers behind. To settle matters once and for all, Jo The Juggler and the rebel women called a town meeting, open to all the inhabitants of Ekoumdoum and held at the covered grandstand in the stadium; they immediately improvised such a rigorous interrogation of the missionary that the spectators could not help comparing it with a cross-examination.

The old man explained how, shortly after their arrival at Mackenzieville, as preparations were being made for their embarkation in anticipation of the return trip to Europe, Van den Rietter had died suddenly after eating a can of spoiled meat. Nevertheless, as Brother Nicholas insistently claimed, his companion's well-known courage and self-composure worked wonders, allowing him sufficient leisure, during his final moments of agony, to confide several tender secrets to his fellow countryman, even though he himself was well aware that his last hour was fast approaching. "Brother Nicholas," he had whispered to him, "I tell you truthfully and solemnly that I am

349

happy to die on African soil, where I have served so unselfishly and for such a long time in a place that has reaped so many good years of my miserable existence. Being unable to rest eternally in the Christian cemetary at Ekoumdoum, that beloved city in which I left behind so many children, I want to be buried here in Mackenzieville, which remains African soil in spite of the British." These were, as Brother Nicholas assured us, the last words of Soumazeu at the moment of his death.

The oldest spectators, particularly the elderly women, were deeply moved, their faces already bathed in tears; in contrast, the youngest ones laughed derisively each time Brother Nicholas, who had never bothered to perfect his knowledge of the language spoken at Ekoumdoum, confused one word with another or stumbled in a very unfortunate way over a tonal stress pattern.

Pushed to the limits of her patience, no doubt by the feelings of pity that were gradually stealing over a crowd rendered defenseless by surprise, Ngwane-Eligui the Younger suddenly interrupted the old missionary and declared, "Brother Nicholas, we extend our most effusive thanks to you for this truly disconcerting story. However, we might be moved still further, if you would finally deign to tell us the reasons why you yourself came back, because, all things considered, that is what concerns us most. Perhaps you had forgotten some object which has a great personal value for you and you wanted to get it back. Perhaps you decided in the end that it was your duty to convince your daughter to return with you to your own country? We would like to know why you came back here, Brother Nicholas."

"Why Brother Nicholas came back?" shouted Jo The Juggler, who, having just leaped up beside the missionary, was being cheered and applauded by the city's adolescents and Ngwane-Eligui the Younger's rebels. "I know why he came back, I do indeed. I myself will tell you why Brother Nicholas is here in our midst today, here in spite of us. He is not here with the intention of retrieving some object that has a great personal value for him, nor is he here to convince his daughter to return with him to his own country. Just think, that would be too good to be true.

"You do not know them; you do not know these people: they always have a desire, a passionate obsession I ought to say, for leading, for being in charge of our communities, for shepherding herds of chimpanzees like us, because that is all we are, according to them.

"But that is not the confession he is going to make in your presence. Not Brother Nicholas, oh, no! I know them; they don't admit such things, no more than they admit the little glass of brandy they pour down their gullets every night before going to bed, because that, you mustn't forget, is a sin. They don't confess their sins; they take great pains to conceal them. Whenever their behavior seems mysterious or strange to you, don't hesitate: it is simply a cover for their morbid passion to dominate us.

"He is going to tell you he suddenly remembered that old Monadjo is incapable of bringing the boat back to Ekoumdoum all by himself, despite the instructions he, Brother Nicholas, had lavished on him in vain. At that moment, he became filled with compassion for the poor Ekoumdoumians who would be waiting for days and days without any sign of their relatives returning from Mackenzieville, or else seeing them return after they had endured long weeks of walking through the forest and facing all sorts of dangers. At least, that is what he was preparing to tell you. But what dangers, and even more serious ones, did your own young girls have to confront a short while ago, young girls who had to walk to Tambona and bring back medicine at a time when the epidemic was wiping out your very youngest children! Where was Brother Nicholas then, and where was his compassion?

"Is Monadjo capable of bringing the boat back all by himself? Listen carefully: I have asked that question to Monadjo himself thousands of times, and thousands of times Monadjo replied, 'How is it possible that I could not bring it back? For a long time Brother Nicholas has been content to observe my work from a distance, meaning that I have been the true steersman of the boat for years. That is what old Monadjo himself has always told me. Do you want to hear him yourselves? He can't be very far away.

351

"The truth is Brother Nicholas would die of envy and vexation if he knew Monadjo was the sole master on board the ship, because Brother Nicholas needs to consider this contraption as an integral part of his personal heritage. But all of you know it belongs to the Catholic mission, and that is the same as saying it belongs to the city of Ekoumdoum. The boat belongs to all of you. But Brother Nicholas would die of envy and vexation...."

"All the same, let's allow the old white man to speak for himself," cried out the older women, whose voices where reinforced by a deep manly bass that echoed behind Jo The Juggler, who did not fail to recognize it as that of Mor-Zamba.

"No need to let ourselves be bothered any further by this fat old man," protested the city's adolescents, who were scattered through the crowd. "Haven't we seen enough of him? Don't we already know his charlatan's pitch in advance? Let him go back and peddle it in his own country."

"All the same, let's allow the old white man to speak for himself," repeated the chorus of elderly women. "After all, he is a human being. Why shouldn't he have the right to speak? Why treat him so inconsiderately? Your turn, Brother Nicholas! Your turn to speak now."

"I came back," Brother Nicholas began stammeringly, "I came back, because I didn't have the courage to leave."

"And why not?" shouted the city's adolescents scattered among the spectators. "What boulder is blocking the path that leads back to your country?"

"All the same, let's allow the old white man to speak for himself," said Mor-Zamba in a voice which shook with anger and which Jo The Juggler recognized perfectly this time. "Your turn, Brother Nicholas, speak up."

"It is true," continued Brother Nicholas with a fervor permeated by an apprehensive humility. "It is true that the path back to my country is blocked by an immense boulder, an insurmountable obstacle, my own age! I am too old, my children; I have lived too long in Africa, here in your country, elsewhere.... Who will be there to greet me or worry about me? What

352

would my life be like?  In a colder climate, under skies perpetually overcast with low-lying clouds, try to imagine the damp, windowless walls of a long building, the home monastery of our order.  Try to imagine the boredom of endlessly monotonous hours, all the same, all of equal length, and the feeling of being useless, of owing everything to charity, at a time when you still have strong arms that demand nothing better than to help others, to transform things, to create life.  And in five years, ten at the most, the final illness, a bare hospital room, among doddering strangers who have lost all hope, a place you only leave feet first, in a coffin or something like that.

"Well then, I said to myself, 'For a long time I belonged to a populous community and lived among friends who treated me cordially, like brothers whom I served with my daily labors and with whom I chatted for hours that never seemed long to any of us, because we were so happy to find ourselves in each other's company.  Among them, there is even a child whose blood I share, a young girl for whom I am almost a father, or in any case the only relative she knows.  I will return to Ekoumdoum then; I will ask the people there to wipe clean the slate of our common past, filled with mistakes and a disregard for Christ's message; I will beseech them to take me in again, so we can start from scratch.'  That is what I said to myself a hundred times before making my decision.  You who are my children and my brothers, will you deny me this favor?"

In the audience, the elderly women, far from holding back their tears, were now sniffling shamelessly.  Those who kept bursting into laughter as they parodied the masquerade that had so delighted Soumazeu and Simsimabayane undoubtedly carried the day by their popular success, but certainly not by the force of their numbers.  One of them even provoked a storm of indignation by apostrophizing Brother Nicholas with an offensive question, the gist of which had never proved unpopular in the past:  "Brother Nicholas, is it true that a bunch of bananas costs a small fortune in your country, is it?  All in all, life is better here, no?"

At that moment, as he later admitted, Jo The

Juggler knew he was holding a losing hand; however, he didn't want to abandon the game completely, so he addressed Brother Nicholas in these words: "If we agree to take you in again, Brother Nicholas, do you promise to let Monadjo take complete charge of the boat from now on?"

"Believe an old man, I don't have any problem with that at all," Brother Nicholas replied without hesitation. "Let Monadjo from now on be captain of the boat; he has enough skill for that. I ought to know; I am the one who taught him."

Fortified with this promise and followed by the insurgent women, the two younger Rubenists left the scene, and the crowd dispersed.

As soon as the two Kola-Kolans found themselves alone at the infirmary, Jo The Juggler confided to Evariste, "since he absolutely wants to stay with us, well then, let him stay. In any case, it has already been decided, and there is nothing we can do about it. What good would it have done to fly in the face of that mob, seduced by the tremolos of a crafty old man. But as far as helping is concerned, you little scamp, he will have to help; I assure you of that. We will make a veritable slave of him; after all, it is his turn, and he is a builder. Where will we begin? With a hospital? I can imagine a beautiful one over there, on top of that knoll, you see? It will have an operating room and even a maternity ward. What do you say to that, you little scamp? That old hypocrite took great pains with a tyrant's dungeon; from now on, he will have to construct hospitals for the people.

"Even so, you little scamp, we will have to keep an eye on him; as a matter of fact, remember this: he will never stop spying on us, never stop lying in wait for us. At the least sign of relaxing our guard, wham, how quickly he will get rid of his Bible, as if it were a cumbersome burden."

"And we will pick it up with such asinine eagerness, I know; it is true—it has always happened that way. In the beginning, they wave their Bibles in the air, and we have the land. A hundred years later, we are the ones waving Bibles in the air, that is to say empty words, and as for them, they have the land, our land. It is true; that is the history of the American

Indians and of our brothers in South Africa; it is
perhaps our own history as well, in the process of
realizing itself. But even so, Jo, one miserable old
idiot all by himself! Do you really think he can lead
us back into slavery?"

"Ah so, you too, you scamp! You, even you are
letting yourself be caught in the snares of pity, just
like a backcountry booby. You too, are you going to
let yourself be corrupted by the putrid drivel of an
old charlatan? Have you then forgotten all the les-
sons you drew from their books and passed on to me so
often during our long march that I sometimes think I
have read as much as you? Am I to believe that instinct, my own pitiful instinct, shall prevail over
learning and knowledge? Haven't you yourself told me
a thousand times: 'Those people never have any
doubts, but as for us, we have doubts about everything
and above all about ourselves. That is their
strength;' don't you remember, you little scamp? Do
you think he has changed, simply because he is all
alone in our midst? Just the opposite, you scamp.

"So then, you too, you have reached the point of
doubting their maliciousness. Well, listen to me
carefully, you scamp; not that I intend to persuade
you with a long speech, I don't believe I have that
many arguments. Simply, from this day forward and as
long as Brother Nicholas remains among us, keep your
eyes open; watch carefully what happens every day.
However, don't forget to participate in the struggle
as well. But on this point, I have confidence in you,
because, despite your age, you are the bravest soldier
I have ever met, and Hurricane-Viet, such as I know
him, would be proud of you, second-lieutenant
Evariste."

"Your orders, Commander!"

That is how it all started, but the rest of us
did not know it until later, much later. For in spite
of appearances, this is really the beginning of our
story—a drama with a thousand turning points; a
woman's face now streaming with tears like a mourn-
fully chanting waterfall, now radiant with laughter,
like a sunlit sky; an echo reverbating one day with
gunfire and another with song; the fate of our people,
doomed to repeated falls, but always arousing them-

355

selves again and, in spite of everything, standing up
each time....

## EPILOGUE

After a lamentable divergence of opinion and even an apparently irreparable split, the paths of George Mor-Kinda and Mor-Zamba crossed unexpectedly one evening, as if by chance, at the home of Ngwane-Eligui the Elder, the aged mother of Abena, more commonly known throughout the Republic under his wartime pseudonym of Hurricane-Viet. It happened less than a month after Brother Nicholas' return.

Mor-Zamba was acting as if he were master of the house, and, after having seated the many guests and offered them something to drink, he was the one who first took the floor, expressing himself in solemn tones, as if he had expected who knows what peaceable outcome, perhaps even a reconciliation, to emerge from this meeting of old friends.

"Here is Ngwane-Eligui the Elder, the mother of Abena," he announced as he studiedly cleared his throat and addressed his two Rubenist comrades, a forced attempt at a smile on his face. "Yes, here is the mother of our leader, and many citizens of the Republic would envy us the privilege that has been vouchsafed us this evening of seeing this magnificent hero's mother in the flesh. Too preoccupied with recent events, you have until now scarcely had the leisure to make her acquaintance. Personally, ever since our presence in the city became common knowledge, I have come every day, so to speak, and conversed at length with her."

"You hardly deserve any credit for that," pointed out George Mor-Kinda, "seeing as it is your natural duty in your dual capacity as a son of this city, where the rest of us are merely guests, and even more as its present and future guide. As a matter of fact, have you ever been officially recognized? It is true; this endless hullaballou has sometimes caused us to lose sight of the essential."

"Of course we recognized him," the old woman, whose face was furrowed with wrinkles, declared rather hastily. "The difficulty did not lie with our recognition of him, but with his willingness to accept and forgive us. You see, so much time had passed! After such a long absence, and such an obvious break, how can two ends of a single existence be glued together again and brought back to life? On either side, are we not like the two stiff ends of a snake that has been cut in half?"

She had just placed a hurricane lamp on her right knee, and leaning quite close to the rounded glass, the heat from which was perhaps burning her cheek, she sceptically examined her son's photograph, given to her by Mor-Zamba; it was a photograph that showed him in three-quarter profile and allowed her to discern with great difficulty the image of a man with close-cropped hair, wearing a trench-coat replete with military epaulettes and displaying an ingenuous smile that etched a huge dimple on his one visible cheek; it was this dimple that fascinated her, transporting her back a good many years and recalling another huge dimple that an ingenuous smile had once etched on the two cheeks of a naked, nursing infant.

She went on: "Listen, even if he comes back some day, my son will find me no more than a shadow. But I know now that he will not come back, or at least that he will never again see me alive. Everything is better that way, isn't it? In his own family, those who knew him are now much less numerous than those who never saw him or who, if they saw him, are incapable of remembering him; for them, he will always be a man from somewhere else. It is like the second harvest of the year: the large, green stalks and the long, bulbous leaves are still there, but the corn is not the same. The countryside too appears to be exactly the same, and yet nothing is any longer what it was before.

358

"Of course we recognized Mor-Zamba, but as for him, did he truly recognize us? If you look closely, is there anything in common between the faces he saw long ago as a little wandering child and those that make up Ekoumdoum today—nearly all of them new and strange to him and filled with surprise when he appears? Even supposing they are still alive, those who were on familiar terms with him have changed so much they are likely to impress him as dreams, if not nightmares, rather than as fond memories.

"To the best of my ability to remember, he loved two women here; the first was a very young girl, whose blood was, it should be added, the same as his, although no one suspected it at the time. Thus, Providence itself must have inspired the father with that ferocious opposition, which we regarded as no more than a display of deep-seated malevolence, but which effectively protected these two children from the curse of incest, the worst of all. She is married now and living in a distant city, although the path between here and there has been forgotten in the meantime. Who among us can say with certainty if she is still of this world? The other woman, as it happened, died in childbirth shortly after Mor-Zamba was captured by the foreign soldiers.

"My poor Mor-Zamba, many people hated you and tormented you; others loved and supported you. Where are they all now? Why must we be shackled with the weight of so many dead souls? Engamba? He has not only disappeared; he has been completely forgotten. I have difficulty convincing myself that he ever really existed. As far as his wife is concerned, she is an old fool, more deaf than a pot; she hardly deserves to be counted among the living. And the son who was so formidable in those days and hurt you so badly—if you could once again see that bundle of rags, consumed with syphilis, how many tears of brotherly compassion you would shed for him, my dear child! Just think, your bitter enemy of former times can barely drag a few miserable fish from the furthest bank of the river these days.

"Yes, strictly speaking, my son told you the truth: when Abena returned to the city twenty years ago to say his goodbyes, Mor-Zamba's name was on

359

everyone's lips here. In fact, only a few days before, we had become privy to the astounding revelation of the close kinship, the shared blood, that linked the city of Ekoumdoum with the child we had scorned for no good reason, the child we had tormented and even betrayed by delivering him into the hands of the foreign soldiers who captured him. At that time then, we were dying to redeem ourselves, if possible, for all the monstrous evils which we had inflicted on him and which could unleash so many curses upon us. But what can you do--time passed, and the rank weeds of forgetfulness spread their thick carpet over the memory of the absent person; that is life, isn't it?"

"What our venerable mother has just said is certainly true, but it is only partly true," declared the spokesman for the young school-teachers who were present for the event. "Can you really posit, as a general rule, that absent people are always forgotten and that such is the law of life? We do not believe this to be entirely accurate. Let us take the case of Abena: we obviously forgot him for a while; we would be hard pressed to deny it. But you have to understand our situation. We were so young when he left. What is more, so many things, so many changes, so many innovations were introduced in the meantime. Just think: Father Van den Rietter, having already settled in, was joined by Brother Nicholas, that magician whose enchanted hands made school buildings appear here, a Chief's Palace there, and somewhere else a wondrous missionaries' residence, which became a matter of pride for all of us in Ekoumdoum, even though that might appear strange to you under the present circumstances. The construction of a large church was already underway when the crisis broke out, the crisis from which we have only just emerged. Will Brother Nicholas pursue his project to its completion? No one knows. As far as we were concerned, we looked very favorably upon such developments.

"In any case, all this was begging for our attention, intruding upon our dreams, and piquing our imagination. It is true: for a long time, our world was confined to the scene of these operations, which the genius of our fathers had never introduced to us. And even the growing prosperity of the Chief's family

360

delighted us, because we thought we saw ourselves mirrored in it, remaining unaware that our Chief was no more than a foreign tyrant imposed upon us by other foreigners. It is true, we had forgotten our Abena.

"But this lapse of memory was only temporary; after the recent events, we once again began to dream of our Abena, that hero whose blood is our blood; moreover, our young pupils never stop asking us about him. Well then, let us pose to you the same questions our young pupils address to us, all of us, every day. Your answers will certainly give us great pleasure ourselves, but above all they will enable us to satisfy the curiosity of our young pupils, who are always dying to know more about their illustrious older brother. So then, is it true that Abena will be coming back soon? Give us a clear answer on this point."

The two older Rubenists pondered the matter, encouraging each other endlessly with meaningful glances.

"You answer them," Mor-Zamba suddenly said to Jo The Juggler.

"No, it is up to you to reply," retorted the latter. "It is really your role. At a moment like this, no one would be capable of standing in for you."

"Well then," Mor-Zamba began after coughing several times. "Abena is certainly going to come back."

"But when?" his interlocutors insisted.

"When? I can not say with absolute certainty," replied Mor-Zamba. "The last time we (that is, George, who is here next to me, and I) encountered him was in the middle of a pitched battle in the Kola-Kola section of the capital. The gunfire was deafening; some men were falling; others were launching an assult. It was not possible for our discussion with him to last as long as we might have liked. Nevertheless, he assured us he would be returning soon, I mean as soon as his heavy military responsibilities would allow him the leisure to do so."

"He is certainly going to come," broke in Jo The Juggler, "and even quite soon; I can assure you of that. It is a matter of months, perhaps of weeks, providing that the way is prepared for him. And how is that to be done? By fighting. Commander Abena is a great military general, and his role is to liberate people, especially black people, from the oppression of tyrants—but by fighting and not otherwise. Mor-Zamba has come back here to rejoin his people and place himself at the head of their community. As for the rest of us, this young man Evariste and myself, how do you think our presence here would be justified, if we had not been sent to this city by Commander Abena himself as a militant avant-garde, charged with preparing the way for his triumphal return and his future battles. For that matter, let me tell you: each time there is a battle to be fought, wherever that battle may be taking place, you can always be assured of acting in accordance with this great hero's will by engaging in it without hesitation."

"Except perhaps with respect to his native city," corrected Mor-Zamba haltingly and not without stammering a bit. "We must all watch over the survival of Ekoumdoum and refrain from any imprudent action which might compromise it. This city is the cradle of Abena's birth, and I am personally convinced that he desires to find it intact on the day of his return, so he himself can decide, if need be, whether it would be better to sacrifice it on the altar of independence or make use of its enormous resources to sustain his generous-hearted struggle."

"But is he as strong as they say he is?" asked the young school-teachers.

"Commander Abena is very, very strong," Jo The Juggler replied proudly. "Don't hesitate to tell your young pupils this, and in complete confidence, as is appropriate when alluding to the force of such a man. His strength obviously resides in the weapons of his soldiers, but it resides as well and perhaps even more in his own generous heart and his eternally vigilant mind. Commander Abena loves the poor, the weak, the humble, the women, and the little children more than Jesus Christ himself did, and from a great distance his piercing gaze detects all threats hanging over their heads; from a great distance too he envisions all the moves by means of which he can demolish his adversaries, the oppressors of the humble, those over whom he will inevitably prevail in the end. And then he will be ruthless in the choice and execution of their punishment."

"For all of that," intervened Ngwane-Eligui the Elder timidly, "is it absolutely necessary to kill Zoabekwe? He is guilty of having committed serious mistakes, it is true, but more out of ignorance than malice, don't you think? Have you forgotten that Zoabekwe, like all the alleged children of the late chief, is an authentic child of our city and that the purest blood of Ekoumdoum flows in his veins?"

"Is that absolutely certain?" asked a young schoolteacher who until then had remained silent.

"If it is absolutely certain?" repeated Mor-Zamba in animated astonishment. "But there isn't the slightest doubt."

"And what if there isn't?" retorted Jo The Juggler just as animatedly. "Since when has blood of any kind exempted the guilty from paying the price for their crimes?"

"Quite true!" seconded the same schoolteacher. "Ezadzomo and Ezabiemeu also had our blood in their veins, and it was even more pure than that of just anyone. Nevertheless, they paid with their lives for an imaginary crime, they did."

"Terrible misfortunes have come crashing down upon Zoabekwe recently," Mor-Zamba broke in. "Why shouldn't they already be regarded as punishment enough?"

"One cannot decide such matters in advance," the usual spokesman for the schoolteachers asserted. "It is true that nothing can excuse so many abominable crimes, but it is also true that, within the memory of living Ekoumdoumians, no matter how old they are, we have never sentenced a man to death in our city. It has been customary to leave this barbarous practice to Whites and strangers. Are you not, like me, seized with terror at the very thought of taking on such a responsibility? Is not a cold sweat already running down your back?"

"When will Zoabekwe be tried?" asked Ngwane-Eligui the Elder imploringly.

"As soon as all the necessary conditions shall have been met," Jo The Juggler replied evasively.

"And in particular," specified Mor-Zamba, "when

the witnesses who could testify in his behalf shall have received guaranteed assurances they will be permitted to appear and even speak in public without exposing themselves to abuse."

"Well, well, this is something new!" exclaimed the two younger Rubenists in unison.

SELECTED BIBLIOGRAPHY

# Selected Bibliography

## Works by Beti:

*Ville cruelle.* 1954; rpt. Paris: Présence Africaine, 1971. (Published under the pseudonym Eza Boto)

*Le Pauvre Christ de Bomba.* 1956; rpt. Paris: Présence Africaine, 1971. Available in English as *The Poor Christ of Bomba.* Trans. Gerald Moore. London: Heinemann, 1971.

*Mission terminée.* Paris: Correa Buchet-Chastel, 1957. Available in English as *Mission to Kala.* Trans. Peter Green. 1958 (under the title *Mission Accomplished*); rpt. London: Heinemann, 1964 and New York: Collier, 1971.

*Le Roi miraculé.* Paris: Buchet-Chastel, 1958. Available in English as *King Lazarus: A Novel.* 1960; rpt. London: Heinemann, 1970 and New York: Collier, 1971.

*Main basse sur le Cameroun.* 1972; rev. Paris: Maspero, 1977.

*Perpétue et l'habitude du malheur.* Paris: Buchet-Chastel, 1974. Available in English as *Perpetua and the Habit of Unhappiness.* Trans. John Reed and Clive Wake. London: Heinemann, 1978.

*Remember Ruben.* Paris: Union Générale d'Editions (10/18), 1974. Available in English as *Remember Ruben.* Trans. Gerald Moore. London: Heinemann and Washington: Three Continents, 1980.

*La Ruine presque cocasse d'un polichinelle.* Paris: Editions des Peuples Noirs, 1979. Available in English as *Lament for an African Pol.* Trans. Richard Bjornson. Washington: Three Continents, 1985.

*Les deux mères de Guillaume Ismaël Dzewatama, futur cammioneur.* Paris: Buchet-Chastel, 1982.

*La Revanche de Guillaume Ismaël Dzewatama.* Paris: Buchet-Chastel, 1984.

In addition, Beti has written extensively for various journals, particularly *Peuples Noirs, Peuples Africains,* which he founded in 1978 and continues to edit. A complete listing of articles by and about Beti can be found in Richard Bjornson, "A Bibliography of Cameroonian Literature," (*Research in African Literatures,* forthcoming). Attention should also be drawn to Beti's earliest published work, the short story "Sans haine et sans amour," which appeared in *Présence Africaine (Les Etudiants noirs parlent),* 14 (1953): 213-220 and was written under the pseudonym Eza Boto.

## Works About Beti

Bestman, Martin. "Une Lecture de *Perpétue* de Mongo Beti." *Présence Francophone,* 24 (1982): 29-46.

_____. "Structure du récit et mécanique de l'action révolutionnaire dans *Remember Ruben.*" *Présence Francophone,* 23 (1981): 61-77.

Biakolo, Anthony. "Entretien avec Mongo Beti." *Peuples Noirs, Peuples Africains,* 10 (1979): 86-121.

Brench, A.C. "Two Pamphleteers from Cameroon: Ferdinand Oyono and Mongo Beti." In *The Novelist's Inheritance in French Africa.* London: Oxford University Press, 1967, pp. 47-74.

Brière, Eloise. "La Réception critique de l'oeuvre de Mongo Beti." *Oeuvres et Critique,* 3-4 (1979): 75-88.

_____. *"Remember Ruben:* Etude spatio-temporelle." *Présence Francophone,* 15 (1977): 31-46.

_____. "Résistance à l'acculturation dans l'oeuvre de Mongo Beti." *Revue Canadienne des Etudes Africaines/Canadian Review of African Studies,* 15 (1981): 181-99.

Britwum, Kwabena. "Irony and Paradox of Idealism in Mongo Beti's *Le Pauvre Christ de Bomba." Re: Arts and Letters,* 6, 2 (1972): 48-68.

Cartey, Wilfred. "Disillusionment and Breakup ... The Colonialist World." In *Whispers from a Continent: The Literature of Contemporary Black Africa.* New York: Random House, 1969, pp. 44-77.

Cassirer, Thomas. "The Dilemma of Leadership as Tragi-Comedy in the Novels of Mongo Beti." *L'Esprit Créateur,* 10 (1970): 223-233.

Chemain, Arlette. *"Ville cruelle:* Situation oedipienne, mère castatrice." *Présence Francophone,* 13 (1976): 21-48.

Deltelle, Danielle. "Un Message ambigü: *Perpétu* de Mongo Beti." *Ethnopsychologie: Littérature d'Afrique noire: Identité culturelle et relation critique,* 35, 2-3 (1980): 103-116.

Erickson, John D. "Mongo Beti: *Le Roi miraculé.*" In *Nommo: African Fiction South of the Sahara.* York, SC: French Literature Publications, 1979, pp. 165-186.

Flannigan, Arthur. "African Discourse and the Autobiographical Novel: Mongo Beti's *Mission terminée." French Review,* 55 (1982): 835-845.

Gakwandi, Shatto Arthur. "Beti's *Mission to Kala.*" In *The Novel and Contemporary Experience in Africa.* New York: Africana, 1977, pp. 37-42.

Garba, Adamo. "Et S'il n'en reste qu'un: Une Interview avec Mongo Beti." *Politique Aujourd'hui,* 2 (1976): 45-49.

Gérard, Albert. "Mongo Beti: Missionaire dans le roman africain." *Revue Générale Belge,* C4 (1964): 43-59.

Glinga, Werner. "Mongo Beti: *Remember Ruben.*" In *Der Unabhängigkeitskampf im afrikanischen Gegenwartsroman französischer Sprache.* Bonn: Bouvier, 1979, pp. 225-265.

Hesbois, Laure. *"Perpétue et l'habitude du malheur* ou Mongo Beti et la révolution avortée." *Présence Francophone,* 14 (1977): 57-72.

Hubbard, Louis J. "Women in Mongo Beti's *Perpétue." Annales de l'Université du Benin,* 4, 1 (1977): 63-73.

King, Adele. "Audience and Exile: Camara Laye and Mongo Beti." In *Artist and Audience: African Literature as a Shared Experience.* Eds. Richard

Priebe and Thomas Hale. Washington: Three Continents, 1979, pp. 141-148.

Kouame, Kouame. "Panorama socio-politique de *Perpétue.*" *Revue de Littérature et d'Esthétique Négro-Africaines,* 1 (1977): 101-118.

Lambert, Fernando. "L'Ironie et l'humor de Mongo Beti dans *Le Pauvre Christ de Bomba.*" *Etudes Littéraires,* 7 (1974): 381-394. Trans. and rev. as "Narrative Perspectives in Mongo Beti's *Le Pauvre Christ de Bomba.*" *Yale French Studies,* 53 (1976): 78-91.

_____. "Mongo Beti: La Dialectique du tragique et du comique." In *Littérature ultramarines de langue française: Genèse et jeunesse.* Eds. Thomas H. Geno and Roy Julow. Sherbrooke: Naaman, 1974, pp. 51-57.

Melone, Thomas. *Mongo Beti: L'Homme et le destin.* Paris: Présence Africaine, 1971.

*Mongo Beti: Ecrivain camerounais.* Eds. Roger Mercier, Monique Battestini, and Simon Battestini. Paris: Fernand Nathan, 1964.

Moore, Gerald. "Mongo Beti: The Voice of the Rebel." In *Seven African Writers.* London: Oxford University Press, 1962, pp. 73-91. Rev. as "Mongo Beti: From Satire to Epic." In *Twelve African Writers.* Bloomington: Indiana University Press, 1980, pp. 193-215.

Mouralis, Bernard. "Aspects de l'écriture dans *Perpétue et l'habitude du malheur* de Mongo Beti." In *Colloque sur Littérature et Esthétique Négro-Africaines.* Abidjan, Dakar: N.E.A., 1979, pp. 151-172. Rpt. in *Présence Francophone,* 17 (1978): 45-68.

_____. *Comprendre l'oeuvre de Mongo Beti.* Issy les Moulineaux: Classiques Africaines, 1981.

Nnolim, Charles. "The Journey Motif: Vehicle of Form, Structure, and Meaning in Mongo Beti's *Mission to Kala.*" *Journal of Black Studies,* 7 (1976): 181-194.

Noss, Philip. "The Cruel City." *Revue de Littérature Comparée,* 48 (1974): 462-474.

Oke, Olusola. "Une Lecture de *Perpétue et l'habitude du malheur* de Mongo Beti." *Peuples Noirs, Peuples Africains,* 29 (1982): 127-136.

Osofian, Femi. "Anubis Resurgent: Chaos and Political Vision in Recent Literature." *Le Français au Nigeria,* 10, 2 (1975): 13-23. Fr. trans. in *Peuples Noirs, Peuples Africains,* 14 (1980): 72-94.

Palmer, Eustace, "An Interpretation of Mongo Beti's *Mission to Kala.*" *African Literature Today,* 3 (1969): 27-43.

_____. "Mongo Beti." In *The Growth of the African Novel.* London: Heinemann, 1979, pp. 124-159.

_____. "Mongo Beti: *Mission to Kala.*" In *An Introduction to the African Novel.* New York: Africana, 1972, pp. 143-154.

_____. "Mongo Beti's *Mission to Kala:* The Revolt Against the Father." *Ba Shiru,* 9, 1-2 (1978): 4-16.

Ruhe, Ernst Peter. "Du Songe à la réalité ou de la réalité au songe: Die

369

jüngsten Romane Mongo Betis." *Romanistische Zeitschrift für Literaturgeschichte,* 1-2 (1982): 236-259.

Sherrington, Bob. "The Use of Mongo Beti." in *Francophone Studies.* Edited by Anne-Marie Nisbet. Kensington (Australia): New South Wales University Press, 1981, pp. 35-46.

Storzer, Gerald H. "Abstraction and Orphanhood in the Novels of Mongo Beti." *Présence Francophone,* 15 (1977): 93-112.

Smith, Robert P. "Mongo Beti: The Novelist Looks at Independence and the Status of Women." *CLA Journal,* 19 (1976): 301-311.

Smith-Bestman, Gisèle. "Signification des sujets dans *Mission terminée* et *Le Pauvre Christ de Bomba* de Mongo Beti." *Peuples Noirs, Peuples Africains,* 23 (1981): 109-119.

_____. "La colonisation et ses conséquences à travers *Mission terminée* et *Le Pauvre Christ de Bomba* de Mongo Beti." *L'Afrique Littéraire,* 65-66 (1983): 52-58.

Umezinwa, Wilberforce A. "Révolte et création littéraire dans l'oeuvre de Mongo Beti." *Présence Francophone,* 10 (1975): 35-48.